PK IS...

An objective of *The Public Relations Practitioner's Playbook for (all) Strategic Communicators* is to assist communication practitioners – no matter the discipline – in achieving *their* goals. To do that, dissect the author's "informal" definition of *public relations*:

Public relations is as simple as a thank-you note and as complicated as a four-color brochure.

It's as specific as writing a news release and as general as sensing community attitudes.

It's as inexpensive as a phone call to an editor or as costly as a full-page advertisement.

It's as direct as a conversation, text or email between two people and as broad as a radio or television program, or social media reaching thousands of listeners or millions of viewers.

It's as visual as a poster and as literal as a speech.

HERE, MY FRIENDS, IS THE BIG QUESTION:
What **IS** *public relations*?

It is a term often used – seldom defined!

In its broadest sense, ***public relations*** is "good work, publicly recognized."

Believe me, there are no secret formulas. ***Public relations*** is simply: the group itself saying –

- "This is who we are

- What we think about ourselves

- What we want to do – and

- Why we deserve your support."

M. Larry Litwin and Ralph Burgio © 1971; © 1999; © 2013

For information, updates and additions, visit:
www.larrylitwin.com

The Public Relations Practitioner's Playbook

for (all) Strategic Communicators

A Synergized* Approach
to Effective Two-Way Communication

*(The whole is greater than the sum of its parts.)

Fourth Edition

by M. Larry Litwin, APR, Fellow PRSA
Rowan (N.J.) University
Parsons (Iowa) College

AuthorHouse™ LLC
1663 Liberty Drive
Bloomington, IN 47403
www.authorhouse.com
Phone: 1-800-839-8640

Published by AuthorHouse   08/21/2013

ISBN: 978-1-4918-0454-4 (sc)
ISBN: 978-1-4918-0453-7 (hc)
ISBN: 978-1-4918-0452-0 (e)

Library of Congress Control Number: 2013913993

Dedication

Dedicated to my wife Nancy for her perseverance and patience as first reader and copy editor, our daughter Julie Beth and her husband Billy, our son Adam Seth and his wife Claire, and our grandchildren Alana Perri and Aidan M. Kramer, and Beatrix Grace Litwin. Their years of support, cooperation and love are the motivation that is *The Public Relations Practitioner's Playbook for (all) Strategic Communicators*.

The PR Playbook is also a tribute to the thousands of committed students who have passed through my classes on their way to successful careers in a communication profession.

In Memory

A special debt of gratitude goes to my late friend, classmate and business partner Ralph Edward Burgio. He was an incredibly talented communicator, scholar and gentleman. Without Ralph's guidance, patience, perfection and inspiration, *The Public Relations Practitioner's Playbook for (all) Strategic Communicators* would not have become a reality. His knowledge and influence are woven into every one of my lectures and throughout this book. My parents Jeanie and Eddie were the compass for everything I have accomplished. Mom always said, "Be the best you can be." To Mom, the word "can't" did not exist. Pop always said, "If you dream it and work hard, you can achieve it." No one worked harder. I offer the same advice to my students.

M. Larry Litwin, APR, Fellow PRSA

M. Larry Litwin, APR, Fellow PRSA, was born in South Philadelphia, raised in Camden and Pennsauken, New Jersey, lived in rural Iowa for three years, suburban North Jersey for two years and now resides in Berlin, N.J. after living in Cherry Hill, N.J. for 35 years.

Litwin is an established strategic adviser, teacher, mentor, role model and ethicist, and an award-winning public relations counselor and broadcast journalist, who has left a lasting impression on thousands of students and professionals.

He spent 42 years as an adjunct and full-time faculty member at Rowan (N.J.) University before retiring as associate professor to guest lecture at other universities in public relations, advertising, radio and television. His classroom is considered a "laboratory for practical knowledge" where he implements "edutainment" to motivate his students.

He is a graduate of Parsons (Iowa) College with a bachelor's degree in business where, in 2013, he was inducted as a member of its *Wall of Honor* joining 48 others. He received his master's in communication – educational public relations – from Glassboro (N.J.) State College. In 2002, he earned his APR (Accredited in Public Relations) from the Public Relations Society of America (PRSA). In 2007, Litwin was inducted into PRSA's *College of Fellows* – one of fewer than 445 members at the time.

During his 48 years in the communication profession, Litwin has worked as a public relations director for two school districts and as a radio and TV reporter, editor and anchor for ABC News in New York and KYW in Philadelphia. He was education reporter at KYW Newsradio for 10 years. He spent nearly two years in the U.S. Department of Labor as a deputy regional director of information and public affairs during Elizabeth Dole's tenure as labor secretary. He has also served as a strategic counselor, and public relations and advertising consultant.

Litwin was a governor's appointee to serve as chair of the New Jersey Open Public Records Act Privacy Study Commission, which recommended cutting edge legislation to assure that government records would be available to the public without exposing personal information – such as home addresses and telephone numbers – that should remain private and out of the public domain.

He has been secretary of the Philadelphia Sports Writers Association for nearly 45 years, chair of the board of trustees of the South Jersey Baseball Hall of Fame (SJBHoF) and a member of the Cherry Hill Public Library Board of Trustees. He served on the Cherry Hill Economic Development Council and as president of the Township's Alliance on Drug and Alcohol Abuse. He was a member of the South Jersey Scholar-Athlete Committee sponsored by the *Courier-Post* and *Coca-Cola*. In 2011, he was inducted into the SJBHoF.

Litwin has authored two books: *The ABCs of Strategic Communication – Thousands of terms, tips and techniques that define the professions* (AuthorHouse – 2014) and *The Public Relations Practitioner's Playbook for (all) Strategic Communicators – A Synergized Approach to Effective Two-Way Communication* (AuthorHouse – 2013). *The PR Playbook's* third edition was considered for the 2009 Pulitzer Prize. He is a contributor to several college textbooks and has written many articles for national magazines.

In 2012, Rowan University presented Litwin with its prestigious "Gary Hunter Excellence in Mentoring Award," its "Adviser of the Year Leadership Award for Exemplary Advising" (of a student organization), and named him to the Rowan University Faculty Wall of Fame and its Adviser Wall of Fame.

He is the 2006 recipient of the National School Public Relations Association's *Lifetime Professional Achievement Award* for "his excellence in the field of educational public relations, leadership and contributions to NJSPRA (New Jersey chapter) and PenSPRA (Pennsylvania chapter), dedication to NSPRA and the (public relations) profession, and advocacy for students and our nation's public schools." He has also been awarded the Sigma Delta Chi (Society of Professional Journalists) *Bronze Medallion for Distinguished Service in Journalism* and the first ever *Grand Award* presented by the International Radio Festival of New York.

In 2002, the Philadelphia chapter of PRSA honored Litwin with its *Anthony J. Fulginiti Award* for "Outstanding Contributions to Public Relations Education" – which recognizes a person who excels in education, either through their mentoring/teaching, their efforts to help shape the careers of future PR professionals or their contributions to PRSSA (student chapter). Philadelphia PRSA awarded Rowan University's PRSSA chapter its *Pepperpot* for "Excellence in Public Relations" in 2004 and 2006, the only non-professional organization or agency to ever be so honored. Litwin served as chapter adviser. In 2008, he received National PRSSA's "Outstanding Faculty Adviser" Award.

Larry and his wife Nancy have two children, Julie and Adam Seth. Julie is a second grade teacher in Atlanta. She and husband Billy Kramer have a daughter Alana and son Aidan.

Adam is assistant professor of management in The Johns Hopkins Carey Business School after earning his Ph.D. as a Fellow at Sloan School of Management, Massachusetts Institute of Technology (MIT). He and wife Claire Schwartz Litwin have a daughter Beatrix Grace.

Contents
Each chapter ends with PR Challenges – exercises designed to evoke the best strategic thinking of students and public relations professionals, as well.

Strategic Communication – A Brief History

Edward Bernays' Public Relations Functions
Ivy Ledbetter Lee's Principles
On The Importance of Truth – Warren Buffet
Public Relations 101
Advertising 101
Marketing 101
Grunig's *Four Models of Public Relations*
Corporate Public Relations
Arthur Page's *Seven Principles of Public Relations Management*
Government Public Relations – George Creel

**Anatomy of Strategic Communication or
The Whole is Greater than the Sum of its Parts – *Synergy***

Double (Triple) Bottom Line Theory
Fraser Seitel's "Real" Bottom Line of PR
Aladdin Factor
Knowing Your ABCs
Litwin's 9 P's of Marketing Communication
Public Relations is...
Business Leadership
MAC Triad Plus
Informization
Principles of Authentic Communication
Strategic Communicators
Business World Rules to Live By
Fingerprint
University of Wisconsin Strategic Communication Study
Business World Rules to Live By

TEC (A Total Effort to Communicate) –
Overview of a Successful Strategic Communication Program

Research Techniques Simplified – or – You Talk...We Listen

We asked. We listened. We acted!
Benchmark
Benchmark Study
Two-Way Communication Model
More Reasons to Conduct Research
Reasons *Not* to Conduct Research
MAC Triad Plus
Demographics
Psychographics
Geodemographics
Aladdin Factor – Be Strong
The Basics of Conducting a Survey
Seven Survey Methods
Types of Formal Sampling
Conducting Focus Panels
Key Research-Related Definitions
Research – Types of Probability Samples
Research – Types of Non-probability Samples
Research – Types of Informal Sampling
More Steps to Follow
There May Be Pitfalls
Research – Levels of Confidence
Resources – Publications
Resources – Websites
Research Terms Every Practitioner Should Know

Basic Strategic (Persuasive) Writing Techniques

Some Simple Rules
Rules Followed by the Best Writers
The 30-3-30 Principle
Helpful Hints for Broadcast Writing
Characteristics of an Effective Writer
Relate the image, do not sell it.
Active vs. Passive Writing
Verb Checklist

Contents

Chapter 6

Advanced Strategic (Persuasive) Writing Techniques

Chapter 7 229
Public Relations (Strategic) Planning and Budgeting

Contents

Legal Environment – Intellectual Property
Copyrightable Works
Copyright
Trademarks and Service Marks
Fair Use
New York Times v. Sullivan
SEC vs. Pig 'n Whistle Corp. Case (Conduit Theory)
Rely on Your Lawyer
First Amendment

Companion CD

Students, practitioners and instructors are encouraged to use the companion CD (available from **www.larrylitwin.com**). It contains every "PR Play" which can be projected for use in group sessions. The CD also contains a Public Relations (Strategic Communication) Plan plus audio and video PSAs (Public Service Announcements), student- and professionally-produced story-boards, electronic issue ads and commercials, a sample video news release and three PowerPoints® compatible with both *The Public Relations Practitioner's Playbook for (all) Strategic Communicators* and *The ABCs of Strategic Communication*.

Foreword

It seems a safe bet that the vast majority of college textbooks share the same destiny. Once their halcyon classroom years are over, it's an indeterminate stop at a dusty attic bookshelf and then the ignominy of a garage sale or a recycle bin. That's not much of an afterlife for all the sweat and anxiety that goes into crafting such books.

However, there is something about this particular book that not only makes such a dour fate unlikely but bodes well for it becoming a dog-eared addition to that small number of books aligned near your computer to be consulted again and in deciding how to deal effectively with some of the complex questions that arise daily in public as well as personal relations.

Essentially, this continuing, high-degree of usefulness separates this "Playbook" in general from other texts and handbooks – and specifically from others in the same field. Moreover, amid the tips and checklists that cut through the fog of indecision there is an underlying, time-honored philosophy that shines through: If you are going to become a strategic communication professional you first need to understand the importance of honesty and integrity in relations with clients and the public.

In this time when the morals and ethics of the public and private sectors of our society are under intense scrutiny, it would be hard to imagine any better advice. That makes *this* "Playbook" one for life as well as public relations and all of the strategic communication disciplines.

Ev Landers
Adjunct Professor
Temple (Pa.) University and Rowan (N.J.) University
Former Gannett Editor

Preface and Acknowledgments

Some years ago, a young graduate student contributed to a book for educational public relations specialists. It was a "how-to-do-it book, light on theory and without footnotes" that offered hundreds of tips and "ideas." Its title evolved into *School Communication Ideas that Work*.

Like that successful and widely used book, published in 1972, *The Public Relations Practitioner's Playbook for (all) Strategic Communicators* is how-to and hands-on. Edition three was considered for the 2009 Pulitzer Prize. The theory it contains is woven into thousands of proven techniques, tips, tactics, tools and strategies spread over more than 600 pages. Explanations, examples and anecdotes are in a language that should appeal to experienced practitioners, college students and organization volunteers who assist with public relations, publicity and other strategic communication disciplines. It won't do the work for the would-be publicity or PR practitioner or counselor, but it will make his or her job much easier.

Devotees of the *Public Relations Practitioner's Playbook* may have noticed, its title now includes *for (all) Strategic Communicators*. That's because the public relations profession has evolved into the more encompassing strategic communication, which includes not only public relations but public affairs, advertising, marketing, social media, graphic and web design and other areas of digital media convergence, strategic planning and campaigns.

"Strategic communication occurs in corporate, non-profit, governmental and agency settings," according to Elon (N.C.) University's website. "Organizations strategically communicate to audiences through publications and videos, crisis management through the news media, special events planning, building brand identity and product value, and communicating with stockholders (and stakeholders), clients or donors.

"Students are prepared to launch creative and meaningful careers in roles such as communication directors, writers, editors, videographers, designers and web editors."

In 2012, the Public Relations Society of America (PRSA) adopted a new definition for public relations: *"Public relations is a [two-way] strategic communication process [management function] that builds mutually beneficial relationships between organizations and their publics."* **(Bracketed items are not included in the PRSA definition, but are included in this Playbook because it is a more accurate description of the strategic communication counselor's role.)**

Thus the title change to better reflect where we are today and into the future as we, strategic advisers/counselors, are relied on more than ever as chief integrity officers, image and reputation protectors and, as strategic counselor James Lukaszewski notes, "the number one number two person" in many successful organizations.

The Public Relations Practitioner's Playbook for (all) Strategic Communicators – an anatomy of the strategic counseling professions – relies on my experience as a reporter, editor, public relations counselor, and strategic adviser and evaluator. It demonstrates that successful writers practice their craft with poise and eloquence. It is an extension of my classroom, which many students call, "Litwin's laboratory for practical knowledge." As former KYW Newsradio (Philadelphia) colleague Kim Glovas observes, "Larry's voice *is* the voice of this book."

Among those considered mentors – and contributors to this book – are Nick George, former managing editor at ABC Radio News, ABC sportscaster Howard Cosell, KYW Newsradio anchor Bill Bransome, print journalist extraordinaire Everett S. Landers and legendary broadcast journalist Edward R. Murrow. They spent countless hours helping me hone my skills and encouraging me to be an open, honest, thorough and valid (relevant) communicator. In addition to the tangible tools, they stressed such attributes as knowledge, loyalty, judgment, trust, credibility, ethics and integrity.

The Public Relations Practitioner's Playbook for (all) Strategic Communicators serves as a basic and supplemental text in introduction to public relations and graduate PR overview and strategic communication courses. It offers a refreshing, down-to-earth approach to which many students are just not accustomed. Rowan University students have been suggesting, for more than three decades, that my lectures be put into print (and digitized for tablets and smartphones) in one easily accessible volume. Many have been asking for a text that contains what they refer to as a "potpourri of proven strategic communication techniques." The companion CD-ROM contains, among its many tactics, three PowerPoints® that summarize the 17 chapters.

Dozens of students and graduates served as editors, focus panel members and advisers. While thousands of them inspired *The Public Relations Practitioner's Playbook for (all) Strategic Communicators*, a number deserve special mention for their hard-nosed editing and constructive criticism and recommendations: Linda Coonelly Alexander, Michael Baratta, Rosie Braude, Katie Hardesty, Corinthea Harris, Tara Bennett Lhulier, Mark Marmur, Nicole Galvin Materia, Amy Ovsiew and Rhyan Truett.

I am forever grateful to Katie and Linda, for serving as senior editors, to Stephanie Biddle, my production coordinator and webmaster, and to Adam Szyfman, CD producer. My wife Nancy deserves her own kudos (maybe even a medal) for her perseverance as first reader. Their contributions made *The PR Playbook* and CD-ROM a reality.

M. Larry Litwin, APR, Fellow PRSA
www.larrylitwin.com

CHAPTER 1

Strategic Communication – A Brief History

Loyalty, judgment, trust, ethics and integrity combine to make the public relations counselor/strategic adviser a valued member of any CEO's "cabinet" and a heavily relied on team player. For centuries, the chief communication officer (CCO – the strategic adviser) has been the conscience of an organization – *the* person most qualified to gauge and influence public opinion; to shape the truth through strategic messages. The CCO accepts that he or she lives by the basic philosophy – *The strategic counselor should be heard and not seen* – unless he or she is fronting a story as the spokesperson.

A firm or organization's CEO relies on the strategic counselor to be an alter ego. The person in that position must possess unwavering loyalty and trust. His or her judgment must be bulletproof. An example of that reliance would be "the fork in the road dilemma." If on a hike together, the CEO would look to the CCO to choose the safe and correct path. History shows, the CCO leads the way – no doubt making the strategic decision based on research.

Ethics and integrity go without saying. Strategic counselors live by these four words – open, honest, thorough and valid (relevant). As former General Electric® chairman and CEO Jack Welch says, "Honesty and integrity are the only way." Like others before him, Welch confides in strategic advisers who tell him what he *needs* to hear, not what he *wants* to hear.

But, as the saying goes, we are getting ahead of ourselves. Strategic communication has been with us for thousands of years. The Greeks had a word for it: semantikos – to signify, to mean. Semantikos means

PR Play 1-1
Bernays' Public Relations* Functions

- To interpret the client to the public, which means promoting the client
- To interpret the public to the client, which means operating the company in such a way as to gain the approval of the public
- To act as a public service
- To promote new ideas and progress
- To build a public conscience

Edward Bernays –
Crystallizing Public Opinion – 1923

* While Bernays, the father of public relations, was a strategist, he preferred public relations because it established a reciprocal understanding between an individual and a group – a true public relationship."

semantics, which can be defined as how to get people to believe something and then change, maintain or enhance their behavior. That is not a bad definition of strategic communication.

In 50 B.C., Julius Caesar wrote the first campaign biography, *Caesar's Gallic Wars*. He publicized his military exploits to convince (long term persuasion) the Roman people that he would make the best head of state. Candidates for political office continue to publicize themselves with campaign biographies and accounts of military exploits to this day.

In 394 A.D., Saint Augustine was a professor of rhetoric in Milan, the capital of the Western Roman Empire. He delivered regular eulogies to the emperor and was the closest thing to a minister of propaganda for the imperial court. Thus, Saint Augustine was one of the first people in charge of public relations/strategic communication. The modern equivalent would be the President's press secretary or communication director.

In 1776, Thomas Paine wrote "The Crisis," a pamphlet which convinced the soldiers of Washington's army to stay and fight at a time when so many were prepared to desert so they could escape the cold and hardships of a winter campaign. Paine was a master of political propaganda (a one-sided argument) whose writing could get people to believe something and act on it.

Benjamin Franklin made it a rule to forbear all contradiction to others, and all positive assertions of his own. He would say, "I conceive" or "I apprehend" or "I imagine" a thing to be so, or it appears to be so.

Franklin pioneered the rules for "personal relations" in an era before mass media had made possible a profession called "public relations."

In the middle of the 19th century appeared a man who was to become one of the leading publicists (one-way communication) of all time, P.T. Barnum. His accomplishments include the founding of the American Museum and the establishment of the Barnum and Bailey Circus. Barnum was a master of promotion who could fill his enterprises with customers by using what we today would call "sleazy methods" of publicity. For example, he announced that his museum would exhibit a 161-year-old woman who had been George Washington's nurse. He produced an elderly woman and a forged birth certificate to make his case.

William Seward, Lincoln's secretary of state in 1861, gained a large American audience through his understanding of media use. He told his friend Jefferson Davis (they were friends before the war): "I speak to the newspapers – they have a large audience and can repeat a thousand times what I want to impress on the public."

Seward might very well have been the first communicator to use what we now refer to as the *multi-step* or *three-step flow*. Once known as *two-step flow*, it is now called *multi-step flow* because of the influence of mass media. In *multi-step flow*, the message is created by the public relations or communication counselor/practitioner, given to the CEO or other spokesperson, who sends it to influential intermediary audiences – such as *Key Communicators* or *opinion leaders* (but not to the mass media) – who then carry the message to the general public. In the *Two-Step Flow Theory*, the message goes from the spokesperson (or CEO) to the mass media, skipping *Key Communicators* and delivering the message to the public. With the growth of the Internet and increased use of

> ### PR Play 1-2
>
> Ivy Ledbetter Lee professionalized public relations by following these principles:
> 1. Tell the truth
> 2. Provide accurate facts
> 3. Give the public relations director access to top management so that he/she can influence decisions

(mass/blast) emails, texting and Twitter®, strategic counselors now rely more than ever before on what has become known as the one-step (direct) flow. Thanks to electronic mail merge, these messages can be personalized into effective 1-to-1/mouse-to-mouse (personal) messages. Even back in the 1800s, strategic use of mass media was quick and might have been more credible than mass media is today (*The ABCs of Strategic Communication* – AuthorHouse).

Strategic communication became a profession in 1903 as Ivy Ledbetter Lee undertook to advise John D. Rockefeller on how to conduct his public relations. Rockefeller owned coal mines and the Pennsylvania Railroad. Miners were on strike and the railroad concealed the facts when its trains were involved with accidents.

Lee stressed relationship building long before it was fashionable by advising Rockefeller to visit the coal mines and talk to the miners. Rockefeller spent time listening to the complaints of the miners, improved their conditions, danced with their wives and became a hero to the miners.

After a railroad accident, Lee invited reporters to inspect the wreck and get the facts. The Pennsylvania Railroad then obtained its first favorable media coverage.

Lee professionalized public relations by following these principles:
1. Tell the truth
2. Provide accurate facts
3. Give the public relations director access to top management so that he/she can influence decisions

Lee defined public relations, saying: "Public relations means the actual relationship of the company to the people, and that relationship involves more than talk. The company must act by performing good deeds."

On The Importance of Truth:

Warren Buffett of Salomon Brothers: "If you lose money for the company, I will be understanding. If you lose one shred of the company's reputation, I will be ruthless."

Speaker of the House Sam Rayburn commenting on the integrity of Army Chief-of-Staff George Marshall: "When General Marshall comes to talk to us, we forget whether we are Democrats or Republicans. We just remember that we are in the presence of a man who is telling the truth."

PR Play 1-3
On The Importance of Truth:

"If you lose money for the company, I will be understanding. If you lose one shred of the company's reputation, I will be ruthless."

Warren Buffet – Berkshire Hathaway

Public relations and strategic communication took the next step toward professionalism in 1918 as Edward Bernays advised the president of the new country of Czechoslovakia to announce independence on a Monday, rather than on a Sunday to get maximum media coverage.

In 1923, Bernays published *Crystallizing Public Opinion*, in which he established several public relations principles. He said public relations had these functions:
• To interpret the client to the public, which means promoting the client
• To interpret the public to the client, which means operating the company in such a way as to gain the approval of the public

Bernays and Lee were stressing the idea that the corporation should accept social responsibility.

Bernays' ideas about social responsibility led to his refusal to accept unethical clients – clearly a strategic counselor's asset.

He created the concept that there are many publics – and each public needs to be appealed to. He advised strategic professionals to seek out group leaders and other key communicators (opinion leaders/influencers), who would be able to pass along ideas to other members of the public.

Bernays concepts include:
a. Public relations is a public service
b. Public relations should promote new ideas and progress
c. Public relations should build a public conscience

Bernays put his ideas into practice when he took on as clients Proctor and Gamble and the Columbian Rope Company.

Proctor and Gamble had produced a radio commercial, which was offensive to African-Americans. Bernays took these steps:
a. He changed the commercial.

---

b. He got the company to offer significant jobs to African-Americans.
c. He invited African-Americans to tour the plant.
d. He featured African-Americans in the company newsletter.

The Columbian Rope Company had an anti-union image. Bernays took these steps:

a. He produced a radio program featuring union and management panelists.
b. He persuaded the company to bargain with the union.
c. He offered tours of the plant.
d. He convinced the company to sponsor a vocational program.

> ### PR Play 1-4
> "I want strategic advisers who tell me what I *need* to hear, not what I *want* to hear. Honesty and integrity are the only way."
>
> Jack Welch – Former General Electric® Chairman and CEO

Edward Bernays may truly be called the father of public relations and Ivy Lee the first public relations or strategic communication counselor.

In more recent times, one leader who recognized the role strategic communication would play in his family and administration was Lyndon Baines Johnson.

Soon after President John F. Kennedy's assassination in Dallas and before being sworn in, Johnson summoned an obscure political strategist – the late Jack Valenti. Valenti is seen in the historic photo as Vice President Johnson is being sworn in (as President) aboard Air Force One. Valenti, later president of the Motion Picture Association of America, had no idea why he was brought in, but soon found out. President Johnson asked members of his staff to name a peer they considered loyal and trustworthy – a person with outstanding judgment, who practices with integrity and ethics.

Jack Valenti (lower left) after being named LBJ first special assistant.

According to Johnson, nearly everyone listed Valenti. So, it was Jack Valenti who became special assistant to the new president. It probably didn't hurt that Valenti, like Johnson, was a Texas native.

Valenti himself talked about his role as President Johnson's public relations counselor and chief strategic adviser. He said President Johnson, as with all great leaders, was a good listener and planner. But, Valenti says, Johnson depended on him for communication counseling – the same kinds of counseling and advice offered by Bernays and Lee. Valenti would tell the President what he *needed* to hear, not what he *wanted* to hear. That's why he had a seat at the (cabinet) table and that, according to Valenti, is why public relations and strategic communication must be an integral part of all integrated marketing communication – IMC. Valenti was President Johnson's "number ONE number TWO" person.

Whether it is strategic planning, researching audiences, evaluating the competition, crafting and delivering messages or developing crisis

(go to page 14)

PR Play 1-5
Public Relations 101
(Not paid – Uncontrolled)

- Management and *counseling* function
- Enables organizations to build and maintain *relationships*
- Thorough understanding of audience opinions, attitudes and values
- *Planned, deliberate* and *two-way*
- *Conscience* of organization
- Overseer of brand/*reputation*
- Provides *relationship* management

Public Relations and Strategic Communcation are leadership tools

PR Play 1-6
Advertising 101
(Paid – Controlled)

- Paid
- (Non) personal communication
- From identified sponsor
- Using (mass) media
- To persuade or influence
- Audience

PR Play 1-7
Marketing 101

Determine what people need (and want) and give it to them.

PR Play 1-8
Techniques to Succeed:
Grunig's *Four Models of Public Relations*

James Grunig and Todd Hunt developed four models of public relations. Each differs in the purpose and nature of communication.

Press Agentry/Publicity – One-way communication – uses persuasion and manipulation to influence audience to behave as the organization desires. (One way with propaganda as its purpose.)

Public Information – One-way communication – uses news releases and other one-way communication techniques to distribute organizational information. Public relations practitioner is often referred to as the "journalist in residence." (One way with dissemination of truthful information.)

Two-way asymmetrical – Two way communication – sometimes called "scientific persuasion" (short term rather than long term). Uses persuasion and manipulation to influence audience to behave as the organization desires – relies on a great deal of feedback from target audiences and publics. Used by an organization primarily interested in having its publics come around to its way of thinking rather than changing the organization, its policies or its views.

Two-way symmetrical – Two way communication – uses communication to negotiate with publics, resolve conflict, and promote mutual understanding and respect between the organization and its public(s). Research is used not only to gather information, but also to change the organization's behavior. Understanding, rather than persuasion, is the objective. (Every attempt is made for each side to understand the other's point of view. If your public agrees with you, then you must find a way to communicate with the public and motivate it to act.) Seems to be used more by non-profit organizations, government agencies and heavily regulated businesses (public utilities) rather than by competitive, profit-driven companies.

James Grunig and Todd Hunt – University of Maryland – 1984

PR Play 1-9

Corporate Public Relations/Strategic Coummunication

Arthur W. Page served as vice president of public relations for the American Telephone and Telegraph Company from 1927 to 1946. He is sometimes referred to as the "father of corporate public relations." Page was the first person in a public relations position to serve as an officer and member of the board of directors of a major public corporation.

According to the Arthur W. Page Society website, Page was responsible for the organization of public relations departments in each of the 21 Bell System companies and for assuring that they were headed by an officer in senior management. During the time he was an AT&T officer, it became the largest publicly held corporation in the world.

Both in belief and practice Page held that "all business in a democratic country begins with public permission and exists by public approval."

Throughout his life, Page devoted himself to his avocation as a counselor to private and public sector executives. He was on the boards of numerous corporations, charities, colleges and civic groups. He contributed his energy and inspiration to enterprises such as the Marshall Plan and Radio Free Europe. He was a special confidant to Henry L. Stimson, who served in the Cabinets of William Howard Taft, Herbert Hoover, Franklin D. Roosevelt and Harry S. Truman. Page is credited with writing, at Stimson's request, Truman's announcement of the dropping of the atomic bomb on Japan.

The principles of business conduct for which he became known have influenced thousands of American thought leaders during the past six decades. He, more than any other individual, laid the foundation for the field of corporate public relations.

As Fraser Seitel points out in his book *The Practice of Public Relations* (Prentice Hall), Page was a pacesetter, helping to manage AT&T's reputation as a prudent and proper corporate citizen. Page's "Five Principles of Successful Corporate Public Relations" (*Public Relations Quarterly* – Winter 1977) are as relevant today – for strategic communication – as they were in the 1930s:

cont.

PR Play 1-9 continued

1. To make sure management thoughtfully analyzes its overall relation to the public.
2. To create a system informing all employees about the firm's general policies and practices.
3. To create a system giving contact employees the knowledge needed to be reasonable and polite to the public. (Contact employees are those having direct contact dealings with the public.)
4. To create a system drawing employees' and the public's questions and criticisms back up through the organization to management (effective two-way communication through research).
5. To ensure frankness in telling the public about the company's actions.

Page explained how he implemented his philosophy through these seven additional "Principles of Public Relations Management":

*   *Tell the truth.* Let the public know what's happening and provide an accurate picture of the company's character, ideals and practices.
*   *Prove it with action.* Public perception of an organization is determined 90 percent by what it does and 10 percent by what it says.
*   *Listen to the customer.* To serve the company well, understand what the public wants and needs. Keep top decision makers and other employees informed about public reaction to company products, policies and practices.
*   *Manage for tomorrow.* Anticipate public reaction and eliminate practices that create difficulties. Generate good will.
*   *Conduct public relations as if the whole company depends on it.* Corporate relations is a management function. No corporate strategy should be implemented without considering its impact on the public. The public relations professional is a policymaker capable of handling a wide range of corporate communications activities.
*   *Realize a company's true character is expressed by its people.* The strongest opinions – good or bad – about a company are shaped by the words and deeds of its employees. As a result, every employee – active or retired – is involved with public relations. It is the responsibility of corporate communications to support each employee's capability and desire to be an honest, knowledgeable ambassador to customers, friends, shareowners and public officials.

cont.

PR Play 1-9 continued

- *Remain calm, patient and good-humored.* Lay the groundwork for public relations miracles with consistent and reasoned attention to information and contacts. This may be difficult with today's contentious 24-hour news cycles and endless number of watchdog organizations. But when a crisis arises, remember, cool heads communicate best.

PR Play 1-10
Arthur Page's Seven Principles of Public Relations Management

1. Tell the truth
2. Prove it with action
3. Listen to the customer
4. Manage for tomorrow
5. Conduct public relations as if the whole company depends on it
6. Realize a company's true character is expressed by its people
7. Remain calm, patient and good-humored

PR Play 1-11
Government Public Relations/Strategic Coummunication

No strategic communication history would be complete without a mention of journalist turned (one-way) communicator George Creel who headed the U.S. propaganda (one-sided message) effort during World War One.

According to www.firstworldwar.com, Creel's career began as a newspaper reporter in 1894 for the *Kansas City World*. Within five years he was publishing his own newspaper, the *Kansas City Independent*.

By the time the U.S. entered World War One in April 1917 Creel had begun to establish something of a reputation as an investigative journalist (or "muckraker" to some), having in the interim acted as editor for the *Rocky Mountain News* (1911).

Creel was a firm and outspoken supporter of Woodrow Wilson during the presidential campaigns of 1912 and 1916. Therefore, it was no

cont.

PR Play 1-11 continued

surprise that Creel would be Wilson's choice to head the Committee on Public Information (CPI) in 1917. Wilson's selection of Creel was controversial to Republican opponent Henry Cabot Lodge (Wilson's ongoing political nemesis) because of Creel's outspokenness.

While Creel acted to reduce the level of anti-German feeling in the country over the course of the following two years with unbiased news reporting, he nevertheless devoted his considerable energies to ensuring full public backing for the U.S. war effort. In fact, he mobilized public opinion in support of the war effort which stimulated the sale of war bonds through "Liberty Loan" publicity (one-way) drives.

To this end he extended the scope of his authority from Wilson to include all aspects of the U.S. media, including film, posters, music, paintings and cartoons (in some ways reminiscent of Charles Masterman's earlier efforts in Britain). Creel also arranged for the recruitment of 75,000 so-called "Four-Minute Men" – people who volunteered to speak for four minutes in public locations around the country in favor of the war effort.

Both of President Wilson's post-Armistice visits to Europe were overseen by Creel's department, with the result that Wilson was greeted with open adulation wherever he went. Creel's efforts also ensured a high degree of popularity in Europe for Wilson's 14 Points.

Domestically, however, Creel's irascible outspokenness ensured he found enemies among Wilson's conservative opponents, including Lodge. If anything, Creel's aggressive campaigning on behalf of Wilson for Wilson's 14 Points galvanized U.S. home opposition, and contributed to the ultimate rejection by Congress of the Treaty of Versailles.

Following the war, he published his memoirs, accurately entitled *How We Advertised America* in 1920, and went on to publish over a dozen more works.

He served with the San Francisco Regional Labor Board in 1933 and as chairman of the National Advisory Board of the Works Progress Administration two years later.

In 1934, Creel ran – unsuccessfully – for the Democratic Party's nomination for governor of California (author Upton Sinclair won the nomination). Creel devoted the rest of his life to writing.

PR Play 1-12

In June 1917, George Creel distributed the following "press" release detailing the protective role of U.S. naval destroyers in protecting Atlantic troop transport vessels.

Official Announcement by the U.S. Government Press Bureau Regarding Destroyers
by George Creel – June 1917

Accompanying the first U. S. Transport Fleet to France, German submarines attacked the transports in force. They were outfought by the American escorting destroyers, and at least one submarine was destroyed.

No American ship was hit, and not a life lost. The German submarines attacked twice. On both occasions the U-boats were beaten off with every appearance of loss. One boat was certainly sunk, and there is reason to believe that the accurate fire of our gunners sent others to the bottom.

For the purposes of convenience the expedition was divided into contingents. Each contingent was composed of troopships and a naval escort designed to keep off such German raiders as might be met with. An ocean rendezvous was arranged with the American destroyers now operating in European waters in order that the passage through the danger zone might be attended by every possible protection.

The first attack occurred at 10.30 p.m. on June 22. What gives it a peculiar and disturbing significance is that our ships were set upon at a point well on this side of the rendezvous, in a part of the Atlantic which might have been presumed free from submarines.

The attack was made in force, and although the night made it impossible to arrive at an exact count, it was clear that the U-boats had gathered for what they deemed would be a slaughter. The heavy gunfire of the American destroyers scattered the submarines. It is not known how many torpedoes were launched, but at least five were counted.

The second attack was launched a few days later against another contingent, the point of attack being beyond the rendezvous. Not

cont.

/‾‾\

PR Play 1-12 continued

only did the destroyers hold the U-boats at a safe distance, but their speed resulted in the sinking of at least one submarine. Grenades were used, firing a charge of explosives timed to go off at a certain distance under water.

In one instance the wreckage covered the surface of the sea after a shot at a periscope, and reports claim that the boat was sunk.

Protected by our high-seas convoy, destroyers and by French war vessels, the contingent proceeded and joined the others at the French port. The whole nation will rejoice that so great a peril was passed by the vanguard of the men who will fight our battles in France.

Source: Source Records of the Great War, Vol. V, ed. Charles F. Horne,
National Alumni 1923

_____/

(from page 7)

communication plans, as we proceed deeper into the 21st century, leaders have come to rely on strategic communication and their PR counselors. Their value is recognized because of their ability to step back and view the whole apple. They are staff members whom leaders turn to because of their deliberate, systematic, methodical, calculating and logistical approach.

If synergy (achieving objectives and goals) is key to an organization, its leader cannot hesitate to turn to the person who will help it achieve that desired outcome. That person could be the next Jack Valenti.

Portions provided by (N.J.) Rowan University Communication Institute

EXERCISES

PR Challenge 1-1
It is open for debate. Who is the true "father of public relations"? Is it Edward Bernays or Ivy Ledbetter Lee? Choose one and explain why.

PR Challenge 1-2
Former General Electric® Chairman and CEO Jack Welch says "bosses" should hire strategic advisers who tell them what they *need* to hear, not what they *want* to hear. What would you do if – after extensive research – your "boss" doesn't do what he *needs* to do, but rather what he or she *wants* to do?

CHAPTER 2

Anatomy of Strategic Communication or
The Whole is Greater than
the Sum of its Parts – *Synergy*

Relationships are the most powerful form of media. Building trust with clients, customers and other members of target audiences – stakeholders and potential stakeholders – takes patience because it can take time.

Every organization, large or small, profit or non-profit, must include *strategic communication* or – at the very least – *public relations* and should include *relationship (management) marketing* (see *The ABCs of Strategic Communication* – AuthorHouse) as both short- and long-term goals toward fulfilling its role as a good corporate citizen. Building these solid relationships requires a strong strategic communication program that employs effective two-way communication. At times, too many organizations want to grab their target audience by the arm to get them involved. But more subtle, yet ethical methods, should be the rule.

Workshop participants and students describe *The Public Relations Practitioner's Playbook for (all) Strategic Communicators* as "an anatomy of the profession and its many elements" (Chapter 17). It is both a handbook and textbook that takes a practical approach to the strategic communication professions – designed to maintain student interest over an entire semester, and serve as a refresher, containing the latest research results, for "time warriors" – busy professionals who want their information in the quickest, most succinct strategic form available.

This book is clearly aimed at our fastest growing populations – Generation X and the Millennial Generation (Generation Y). According to Yankelovich Partners, "The U.S. marketplace is undergoing a generational power shift. Gen Xers (born from 1965 to 1976) are driving the marketplace of the future." Gen Yers (born from 1977 to 1998), also known as echo boomers, millennials and Next Generation, are not far behind.

The Public Relations Practitioner's Playbook for (all) Strategic Communicators is a how-to book that delves directly into the DOs (and DON'Ts) of public relations. It illustrates successful methods rather than bogging down the reader in theories and formulae. This book provides road maps and blueprints (step-by-step approaches – designed "plays") for reaching destinations through various components of public relations. These are techniques used by the most respected practitioners. *The PR Playbook* should be a keeper for students long after they graduate – a reliable and credible source – because many of the techniques/tactics and tools mentioned have become recipes for the success of numerous projects. *The Public Relations Practitioner's Playbook for (all) Strategic Communicators* contains proven tips not found in other books.

Communicating effectively is communicating efficiently ("effectancy"). Public relations is no longer just publicity. To be effective, it must be a carefully planned two-way approach using as many appropriate vehicles and channels as possible. It is planned, deliberate, systematic, methodical, calculating and logistical – delivered in measured tones.

Thanks to digital technology, the way practitioners gather and dispense information has become (more) immediate. We don't necessarily have to know *how* to use that technology, but this book explains *why* we use it and how editors, news directors and the public expect to interact with us via the technology that has led to cross platforming – television, digital signage, smartphones, iPods®, iPads® and other tablets and devices featuring simple Internet access for podcasts, vidcasts, narrowcasting, blogs, tweets, texts and other forms of 1-to-1 or mouse-to-mouse (addressable advertising) communication, etc.

The exchange of information to the masses has become instant. This book helps pave the way for many of the changes through use of the Internet, video news releases and (live) video conferencing.

Double (Triple) Bottom Line:

The late Patrick Jackson of Jackson, Jackson & Wagner, said public relations has evolved from products (newsletters, brochures, etc.) to counseling, strategizing and training. Two-way communication is imperative.

Jackson created what is referred to as the "Double Bottom Line Theory," which has evolved into the "Triple Bottom Line Theory." He theorized:

First Bottom Line (Relationships):

- An organization's successful efforts to please its publics before and while doing business with them.
- Who knows what's in the public interest better than the public relations/strategic communication professional?
- Who knows if a public is satisfied with an organization's image, management and motive toward the public better than the public relations/strategic communication professional?
- Once this essential relationship is established, the company can do business with its publics.

Second Bottom Line (Revenue):

- The actual acceptance of the products or services by the public.
- The sale from the fruit of the relationship in the first bottom line leads to profits.

Who better to strategize the Double Bottom Line Theory – reputation leading to profits – than the public relations practitioner, relationship manager or chief communication officer? In fact, Bank of America® has an executive staff position – vice president for relationship marketing – responsible for achieving the first bottom line. Juniper Bank® and Staples® refer to their customer service personnel as relationship managers.

Some might argue that the "Double Bottom Line" has become the "Triple or Quadruple Bottom Line" – because the first step is no longer just building relationships, it is either:

- creating,
- maintaining, or
- enhancing

relationships. Once that is accomplished, organizations, profit or non-profit, are the beneficiaries through higher revenues which could and should translate, through proper management, into greater profits (through controlled spending) or contributions.

Third Bottom Line (Profit):

Revenue > Controlled Costs = Profit

(*Relationships* lead to *Revenue*. By *Controlling Costs*, organizations and companies should show a *Profit*.)

Fraser Seitel's "Real" Bottom Line of PR

Fraser Seitel is a former editor of the Public Relations Society of America's (PRSA) *Strategist* magazine and appears frequently on television as a public relations/strategic communication analyst. He says:
- Our fundamental role in PR is to defend and promote and enhance and sustain the reputation of our organizations.
- Our job in PR is to help ensure that that objective is achieved... through proper performance – effectively communicated.

Outstanding Features

The Public Relations Practitioner's Playbook for (all) Strategic Communicators takes a nonsense-free approach to the techniques used by such successful strategic counselors as Jackson. It accepts that students will be taught the theories behind those techniques during lectures and by doing research. But Generation X (born between 1965-1976), Millennial Generation (1977-1998) – so-called MTVers – and Generation Z (born after 1998 – also known as the Text or New Silent Generation) want to cut right to the chase.

Public relations is just one component of *integrated marketing communication* (*IMC*) becoming known simply as *marketing communication* (MC). A public relations or strategic communication program must achieve its goal of communicating clearly for *IMC* to be successful or *synergized*. If our goal is to communicate – "This is who we are; what we think about ourselves; what we want to do; and why we deserve your support" – it must be accomplished through a coordinated (unified and consistent) effort that is clear, calculated (measured tunes), concise, consistent, complete, specific, simple, open, honest, thorough and valid (relevant). This book uses established – but sometimes, forgotten – techniques to help achieve that goal.

Another important feature of *The Public Relations Practitioner's Playbook for (all) Strategic Communicators* is its references to research, planning, practicing the ABCs of strategic communication and examples practitioners have used. The overwhelming number of examples and techniques are those that have been consistently successful. However, this book does not shy away from techniques that did not achieve the expected results. There is nothing wrong with not "winning" every time so long as we know why we didn't win.

The *Aladdin Factor* (Jack Canfield and Mark Victor Hansen) plays a vital role in the practice of public relations – "anything is possible if you dare to ask." It's been said that asking questions is a sign of strength – not a sign of weakness.

Knowing Your ABCs

The ABCs of Strategic Communication is not only the title of a reference book containing nearly 8,000 terms, tips and techniques (AuthorHouse) and it is not only the key to a successful crisis communication plan (Chapter 14), it is also one of the key components that help place the strategic counselor at the board table in the CEO's cabinet room. What are the ABCs?

- A=Anticipate
- B=Be prepared
- C=Communicate clearly, calculatingly, concisely, consistently and completely

Anticipation is not predicting, but rather *being prepared* for whatever may happen. Even the best communicator can boast all he or she wants about having advance knowledge or a premonition but possessing that innate ability isn't the key. The key to a successful reaction is planning. President Dwight D. Eisenhower said it when he was a U.S. Army general: "The plan is nothing. Planning is everything." However, it must be kept in mind that a plan is just that – a plan. And, remember the findings of Sir Isaac Newton: "For every action, there is an equal and opposite reaction." In 1666, Newton found that forces came in pairs. However, in strategic communication, one action can generate dozens of reactions that could undermine the best laid plans.

Thus *Anticipating* in strategic communication should consider all possible reactions – not just those that might be opposite. Remember, as strategic advisers, PR counselors and other practitioners are heard and not seen, meaning, we write the strategic messages spoken by our "bosses" and others. Once those words pass their lips, it is nearly impossible to retrieve them, deny them or correct them.

Another concept, first mentioned by Rowan University Professor Anthony J. Fulginiti, APR, Fellow PRSA, is the *CBAs* of strategic communication. Simply put, strategists *conceive* with their head; *believe* in their heart; and *achieve* using their hands.

Both the *ABCs* and the *CBAs* are integral to the success of every communication effort, whether formal or not.

To better explain the concepts of *synergy*, the *ABCs* and *CBAs*, here are excerpts from an article (first published in 2002 and revised), written by the author, for *PRomo*, a Rowan (N.J.) University publication. Its concept holds true:

> This is the story of *synergy* – the newest "hot" term in the communication profession. Unlike some other words, terms and phrases, we hear *synergy* being used elsewhere.
>
> I feel proud when I hear it reported that the dedicated rescue efforts that were performed by the men and women at New York's Ground Zero (in the fall of 2001 following the worst tragedy in United States history) was *synergy* at work – everyone combining their best talents and efforts to get a job done; to reach a goal. The rescue teams demonstrated daily that, with the proper attitude and effective strategic planning, *synergy* would be achievable. Those rescue workers, like successful public relations specialists, realized no one is an expert in every area.
>
> And, there are numerous companies incorporating the word *synergy* into their branding campaigns. The Cincinnati Reds, for example, (until 2003) played their home baseball games on – make that in – Cinergy (a play on words) Field. So what if the power company, which spent millions in naming rights fees, misspelled one of my favorite words?
>
> Actually, when Cinergy Corporation was conceived from the combination of The Cincinnati Gas & Electric Company and PSI Energy, Inc., the largest electric utility in Indiana, its top management already recognized that to establish customer confidence and maintain its competitive edge, *synergy* had to be created, achieved – and maintained. Today, Cinergy is one of the leading diversified energy companies in the United States.
>
> So, when applied to communication, what is this word *synergy* all about?

In the most basic of explanations, *synergy* combines many of the ingredients of public relations, advertising, and other strategic communication disciplines (*the integrated marketing communication concept – IMC*) and blends them together so that the whole works better than the sum of its parts.

Sound simple? It is. Here is a list of those specialties included in the marketing mix:

- Advertising
- (Sales) Promotion*
- Public Relations*
- Direct (Response) Marketing
- Positive Association (Cause-Related Marketing)
- Sponsorship (Partnering) Marketing
- Positioning (Place)*
- Personal Selling* (Face-to-Face)
- Price* (Pricing strategies [Customary, psychological, price lining, prestige])
- Product* (itself)
- Packaging*
- Policy* (of the firm or company)
- Politics* (internal and external – the interaction of people – employees)
- *MindShare* (Brainstorming/Intellectual Property – using employee intellect as a resource)
- Brand Identity
- Interactive

* Litwin's 9 P's of Marketing

Ogilvy Public Relations Worldwide includes all of the above in its IMC package plus *Brand Identity* (a product or service's reputation), *MindShare* (staff members sharing information) and *Interactive* (communication flowing in all directions). Ogilvy refers to its approach as 360 Degree Branding®.

As we witnessed at Ground Zero, in addition to the research and planning needed for many projects, two other key elements are necessary to achieve our goal of *synergy* – teamwork and anticipation.

Teamwork – relying on fellow workers who might have more experience and expertise in a particular area. Anticipation –

(whether crafting a message or participating in some other major project) remembering Newton's Third Law, "For every action there is a reaction." (In strategic communication, it doesn't have to be equal and opposite – just anticipate the reaction[s]).

No one guarantees your campaign or project will achieve *synergy* every time, but if it isn't one of your goals, you will never know.

PR Play 2-1
PR is...

An objective of *The Public Relations Practitioner's Playbook for (all) Strategic Communicators* is to assist organizations in achieving their objectives and eventually their goals. To do that, dissect the author's "informal" defintion of public relations:

Public relations is as simple as a thank-you note and as complicated as a four-color brochure.

It's as specific as writing a news release and as general as sensing community attitudes.

It's as inexpensive as a phone call to an editor or as costly as a full-page advertisement.

It's as direct as a conversation, text or email between two people and as broad as a radio or television program, or social media reaching thousands of listeners or millions of viewers.

It's as visual as a poster and as literal as a speech.

HERE, MY FRIENDS, IS THE BIG QUESTION:
What **IS *public relations*?**
It is a term often used – seldom defined! In its broadest sense, ***public relations*** is "good work, publicly recognized." Believe me, there are no secret formulas. ***Public relations*** is simply: the group itself saying –
- "This is who we are
- What we think about ourselves
- What we want to do – and
- Why we deserve your support."

M. Larry Litwin and Ralph Burgio © 1971; © 1999; © 2013

This "definition" travels from the very simple and inexpensive to the more complex and very expensive – all the while keeping in mind the basic concepts of communication – a gesture or an oral or written message from one person (sender) to another (receiver). **PR is** (PR Play 2-1) includes techniques/tactics reminding us that effective communication is two way – radio talk (call-in) shows, phone calls to editors and opinion surveys. "The public talks…We listen!"

Business Leadership

Peter Giuliano, founder of Executive Communications Group of Englewood, New Jersey, says a critical aspect of business leadership is effective communication, and to be effective, one must know how to listen. It is an acquired skill. In fact, Roger Ailes, FOX News president, believes the best communicators listen 60 to 70 percent of the time and dispense information 30 to 40 percent of the time.

Giuliano offers these listening tips (whether it be oral or written feedback):
• Listen to what is being said as well as what is not being said, especially during times of stress.
• Examine problems, looking at them from all sides. Never play favorites and never jump to conclusions.
• Help others to turn mistakes into learning experiences. Don't chew people out for errors.
• When you need to make a tough call, take time to explain how you arrived at your decision and why you think it is best.

In addition to listening, another concept key to being an effective and successful communicator – outstanding writing skills. They are a prerequisite of an overwhelming number of organizations hiring employees who will be in contact with the public. *The Public Relations Practitioner's Playbook for (all) Strategic Communicators* offers two full chapters on public relations writing for print and electronic media. Other aspects of the book cover some of the basic elements of telling a compelling story:
• Have a set of ideas that represents the future and fits the market place. The story must be in context (one of the Seven C's of Communication [Chapter 15] – fitting the marketplace of ideas) and match the audience. Offering obsolete ideas will eventually be costly.

- Have a set of values that can be connected to deeply held values (without it, there is no survival).
- Possess a personal ability to tell the story.

PR is (PR Play 2-1) concludes with the ingredients of every good *mission statement* – the overreaching reason the organization came into existence. A *mission statement* should identify the organization, what it thinks about itself, its goals and why the organization needs support from its publics. Once accomplished, the first bottom line (relationships) has been achieved. The second bottom line (revenue/financial) will follow.

The Public Relations Practitioner's Playbook for (all) Strategic Communicators reminds communicators that two-way communication is much healthier than one-way communication or preaching. *The PR Practitioner's Playbook* has some other reminders based on these key words and phrases:

- Anticipation – For every action there will be reactions.
- Be prepared – Through research and planning no chief executive officer should ever experience surprise (thanks to his/her PR counselor/strategic adviser)
- Clarity/Understanding – Strategic messages are received by the target audience exactly how the sender intended the message to be received.
- Attitude – Does audience agree with the message? It is the predisposition to act – the inner feeling. Many argue, attitudes cannot be changed. *The PR Practitioner's Playbook* dispels *that* opinion.
- Opinion – Expression of the attitude.
- Message – Does the audience remember it?
- Behavior – Will the audience act on the message?
- Accountability – Responsibility for what we do (controlled autonomy).
- Cooperation – Is everyone involved?
- Availability – Can the public contact a company representative?
- GOST – Goal, objectives, strategies and tactics (in part, according to the Public Relations Society of America Accreditation Board – Sept. 14, 1992):
  1. Goal – The purpose of the plan (or project). The desired outcome of the plan of action. It must be attainable – realistic and reachable. A goal must be within the control of the goal setter.
  2. Objectives – Specific milestones that measure progress toward achievement of a goal; or single goals broken into subsets known as objectives. They are major aims in measurable terms. Objectives must:

a. Address the desired communication or behavioral outcome.

b. Designate the public or publics among whom the behavioral outcome is to be recognized.

c. Specify the expected level of attainment or accomplishment.

d. Identify the time frame in which those attainments or accomplishments are to occur.

3. Strategies – *What* must be done, *how* it will happen, to *whom* and a brief explanation *why*. (Influence the media to…). Strategies carry the message. They are the thoughtful, planned, general approval to the tactics ultimately undertaken. It is important to note that strategies do not indicate specific actions to be taken to achieve objectives. As with objectives, to achieve the goal, and tactics, to achieve the strategy, there can be multiple strategies to achieve an objective. Strategies are the thoughts behind achieving the objectives.

4. Tactics – Specific activities (tools) conducted to implement strategies of a public relations plan. Their purpose is to carry out the strategy (via news release, brochure, public service announcement, etc., which carry the message or strategy). Tactics/tools involve the use of specific personnel, time, cost and other organizational resources (time, agent, cost). Tactics achieve the objectives and, in turn, support the goals that have been set to carry out the mission or purpose of the organization.

(See more about public relations/strategic planning in Chapter 7.)

- MAC Triad (plus P and T) – **M**essage, **A**udience, **C**hannel (plus **P**urpose and **T**iming). Once the target *audience* is determined, a

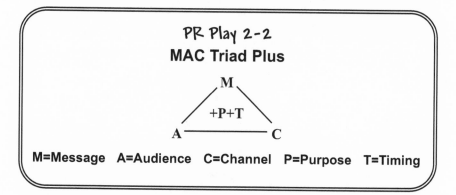

message is crafted and a delivery *channel* (media vehicle) chosen. The message's delivery must be at a time when the target audience is available and *listening* (more on *purpose* and *timing* are below). To be successful, all four (*message, audience, channel* and *timing*) must be correct and in sync. For example, the correct message delivered on the wrong channel is failure; the wrong message on the correct channel is a failure. When synergy is being achieved and goals are met it is called *informization*. (The message might not be received if the paradigm is broken.)

- Purpose – The very first question asked should be, What is the purpose of this project? Thus, it becomes a MAC Triad Plus with a "P" and "T" in the center.
- Timing – To assure a successful outcome using the MAC Triad Plus, proper timing is essential – especially when releasing the strategic message through the correct channel. Timing is also referred to as the "aperture."
- PR-PIE – Once referred to as the RACE acronym, more and more strategic communicators prefer these five steps of the public relations process:
  - Purpose [here's *that* word, again – see above]
  - Research [asking questions to discover and interpret facts]
  - Planning [GOST]
  - Implementation/Information [carrying out tactics, which equals communication]
  - Evaluation [judging and appraising results]

For those still using *RACE*, its four easy-to-remember steps in the effective communication process are:

- R=Research [determine target audiences]
- A=Action/Planning [craft messages]
- C=Communication/ Implementation (Information) [choose vehicles/deliver messages]
- E=Evaluation [judging and appraising results]

> **PR Play 2-3**
> **Informization**
>
> The act of disseminating information (message) to target audience through the proper channel at the correct time. It is the ideal use of the **MAC Triad Plus**.

In addition to PR-PIE or RACE, some also practice *ROPE* to assure all objectives are met:
- R=Research
- O=Organize
- P=Prepare
- E=Execute

Strategic communication *program* keep these reminders handy for reference. If some appear similar it is because of certain basic premises in public relations.

Projects, theories and products begin with a need or purpose. Research assists with identifying the audiences, messages and channels and also establishing baselines and benchmarks. Evaluation assists with determining success, through incremental corrections to measure message effectiveness.

> ## PR Play 2-4
> ## 10 Principles of Authentic Communication
>
> - Truth
> - Fundamentality
> - Comprehensiveness
> - Relevance
> - Clarity
> - Timeliness
> - Consistency
> - Accessibility
> - Responsiveness to feedback
> - Care
>
> Bojinka Bishop – Associate Professor – Ohio University (Athens, Ohio)

The successful public relations *program* brings people together through two-way communication, builds relationships that lead to the desired conclusion(s), triggers events through public participation, influences audiences, modifies behavior and motivates people to act (a "call to action"), and produces desired results.

Principles of Authentic Communication

Bojinka Bishop is associate professor at Ohio University (Athens, Ohio). She has developed these "10 Principles of Authentic Communication." They closely parallel PRSA's "Seven C's of Communication" (Chapter 15) – proving once again that repetition is the "mother" of all learning.
- **Truth** – being accurate and factually correct.
- **Fundamentality** – dealing with the core or essential issues and information.
- **Comprehensiveness** – telling the whole story, including the meanings and implications of the issue in question.

- **Relevance** – taking into account (what target public wants to hear and see) and making connections with the interests of the parties involved.
- **Clarity** – using language that is appropriate and understandable for those involved, explaining technical terms, organizing and illustrating the information logically and understandably (clear, calculated, concise, complete, consistent, specific and simplistic.)
- **Timeliness** – providing information when it is known, leaving sufficient time for response prior to decisions or actions.
- **Consistency** – not opposing or contradicting your own or your organization's other words or actions.

PR Play 2-5
Strategic Communicators

- Inform
- Persuade
- Get people to act
- Analyze conditions
- Assess policies
- Develop programs
- Make recommendations

PR Play 2-7
Fingerprint

Your strategic approach should contain your fingerprint – your personal brand.

CBS Sunday Morning

PR Play 2-8

A study by the University of Wisconsin suggests that these factors have a dramatic influence on strategic communication:
- The attitudes of top management
- Capabilities and personalities of public relations staff
- General organizational structure and policy
- Organization's tradition, goals and objectives
- Company product and market areas (in case of businesses)
- Company size and location
- Big government

University of Wisconsin

PR Play 2-6
Business World Rules to Live By:

- Plan
- Organize
- Staff
- Control
- Accountability

CBS Sunday Morning

- **Accessibility** – making information, relevant sources and opportunities for discussion easily available to all parties; assuring physical accessibility to meetings.
- **Responsiveness to feedback** – engaging in two-way communication, seeking others' views and concerns and allowing those concerns to influence the organization's actions.
- **Care** – showing respect, concern and compassion for the circumstances, attitudes, beliefs and feelings of other parties.

Ed Ziegler's (Rowan University – Marketing Director) educational approach (PR Play 2-11) relies on the *research* step in the *public relations process*. Once the *purpose* is determined, *research* becomes the justification for nearly every ensuing step in the journey that leads to the *desired outcome*. The *desired outcome* could be the *goal*, or a single or multiple *objective*(s) that lead to the goal.

> ## PR Play 2-9
> ## Objectives of Communicating
>
> 1. To convey information and share knowledge.
> 2. To increase understanding.
> 3. To gain acceptance and belief (to influence).
> 4. To provide action.

The two models most used in Ziegler's educational approach are the *AIDA* model and Herbert Lionberger's *Diffusion*

> ## PR Play 2-10
> ## Three Ingredients of Successful Strategic Communication
>
> 1. Good design makes a difference.
> 2. Defining your message is crucial.
> 3. Your voice must be heard.

Process. Both are discussion processes in which audiences adopt concepts, attitudes and behavior. Their intent, depending on which is chosen, is to initiate a connection in the mind of a prospective consumer – (AIDA) create **a**ttention, generate **i**nterest, develop **d**esire and initiate **a**ction or (AITEA/R – known as Lionberger's *Diffusion Process*) create **a**wareness, generate **i**nterest, encourage **t**rial, **e**valuation and **a**doption (or **r**ejection). Many times the adoption is verified by a purchase.

PR Play 2-11
Reaching the Desired Outcome – A Process

Education – Providing knowledge to targeted audiences (external or internal).

Knowledge – What publics (should) know about the organization, product, service or person sending the strategic message.

Attitude – Inner feelings – beliefs – a state of mind acquired through education and observation.

Behavior (opinion) – Expression of the attitude – what publics do or say after they receive strategic message(s).

Output – Is affected by *education, knowledge* and *behavior*.

Outcome – Determined by *output*. The firm or organization that achieves its desired *outcome* has been successful in educating and bringing about the desired behavioral changes – opinion.

Education > Knowledge > Attitude > Behavioral Change > Output=Desired Outcome (Synergy)

Ed Ziegler – Marketing Director – Rowan (N.J.) University

Says Lionberger: communication scholar and author of *Adoption of New Ideas and Practices*: "In the *awareness* stage the individual is exposed to the innovation but lacks complete information about it. At the *interest* or *information* stage the individual becomes interested in the new idea and seeks additional information about it. At the *evaluation* stage the individual mentally applies the innovation to his present and anticipated future situation, and then decides whether or not to try it. During the *trial* stage the individual makes full use of the innovation. At the *adoption* stage the individual decides to continue the full use of the innovation."

Everett Rogers, a pioneer in the use of the *Diffusion Process* and author of *Diffusion of Innovations*, asks, "Why is the *process* of any relevance to advertisers?" His response: "The purpose of marketing and advertising is to increase sales, which hopefully results in increased profits. It is through analyzing and understanding the adoption process that social scientists, marketers and advertisers are able to develop a fully integrated marketing and communication plan focused at a predetermined stage of the adoption process."

When considering adopting ideas, supporting a candidate or making a purchase, publics consider relative advantages, compatibility, complexity, trialability and observability. The Gallup Organization adds these additional factors that can influence *adoption*: complexity of idea; difference from accustomed patterns; competition with prevailing ideas; necessity of demonstration and proof; strength of vested interests; failure to meet a felt need; and frequency of reminders.

Another key communication model used to achieve synergy and help practitioners and strategic advisers change, maintain or enhance behavior is the Cracked Egg Public Opinion Persuasion Model (others include the MAC Triad Plus [page 25] and Shannon-Weaver Model [page 48]).

> **PR Play 2-12**
> **Factors that Affect the Adoption Process**
>
> • Relative advantage
> • Compatibility
> • Complexity
> • Trialability
> • Observability

The *Cracked Egg Model* is an eight-step process whose purpose is to shape or change public opinion:

1) Mass Sentiment – morals/values.

2) Incident/Issue(s) – interrupts morals.

3) Publics Pro/Con.

4) Debate – Strategic communicators (including advertisers) try to change peoples' attitudes to agree with theirs.

5) Time (opinions marinate) – very important or you do not have a true public opinion.

6) Public Opinion – the accumulated opinion of many individuals on an important topic in public debate affecting the lives of people. (You need all these elements or you do not have public opinion.)

7) Social Action – new law, or action, is taken against people. Society could be so traumatized that it goes overboard.

8) Mass Sentiment – Society develops a certain attitude/moral values due to the social action. Society becomes sensitized.

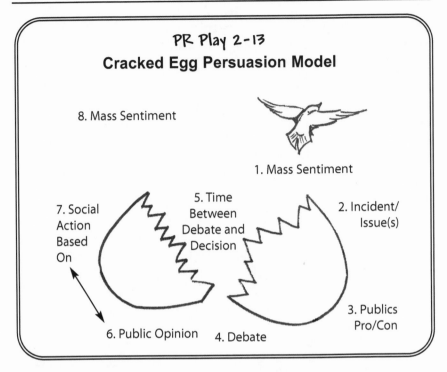

PR Play 2-13
Cracked Egg Persuasion Model

8. Mass Sentiment

1. Mass Sentiment

7. Social Action Based On

5. Time Between Debate and Decision

2. Incident/Issue(s)

6. Public Opinion   4. Debate

3. Publics Pro/Con

Attitudes – thus, opinions – *can* be changed

There may have been a time when it was not possible to change an attitude or the attitudes of many. But, thanks to mass media and technology, it's been proven: people's opinions can and do change once their attitude is altered. It is not easy – but it can be done.

Here are two vivid examples of attitudinal changes:

 George Wallace – in his 1963 inaugural speech after being sworn in as governor of Alabama – stated: "Today I have stood, where once Jefferson Davis stood, and took an oath to my people. Let us rise to the call of freedom-loving blood that is in us and send our answer to the tyranny that clanks its chains upon the South. In the name of the greatest people that have ever trod this earth, I draw the line in the dust and toss the gauntlet before the feet of tyranny . . . and I say . . . segregation today . . . segregation tomorrow . . . segregation forever."

During the American desegregation period, Wallace recanted those earlier opinions, which were altered by a change in attitude. In the late

1970s, Wallace became a born-again Christian, and around the same time apologized to black civil rights leaders for his earlier segregationist views, calling those views wrong. He said that while once he had sought power and glory, he realized he needed to seek love and forgiveness. It was because of this change in his worldview that Wallace realized the harm his earlier segregationist rhetoric and views had caused. His final term as governor (1983-

> ### PR Play 2-14
> ### Everett Rogers' Diffusion of Innovations (Adoption) Theory
>
> For any given product category, there are five categories of product/idea adopters among audiences:
> - **Innovators** – venturesome, educated, multiple information sources.
> - **Early adopters** – social leaders, popular, educated.
> - **Early majority** – deliberate, many informal social contacts.
> - **Late majority** – skeptical, traditional, lower socio-economic status.
> - **Laggards** – neighbors and friends are main info sources, fear of debt.

1987) saw a record number of black Alabamians appointed to government positions.

Another historical attitudinal change is that of President Lyndon Baines Johnson. Johnson has been credited with being one of the most important figures in the civil rights movement. His detractors believe he was merely an unprincipled politician who used the civil rights issue when he realized the worth of the "Black Vote."

As a Texas senator, Johnson's opposition to President Harry S. Truman's civil rights program disgusted Texas blacks. History shows he often used the "n" word when referring to African Americans. But, on the flip side, he sometimes stayed at black colleges and the African American community found him unusually helpful.

As the years passed, he claimed to be an idealist who dreamed of making America a "Great Society." It was Johnson who orchestrated the Civil Rights Acts of both 1957 and 1960 and put the presidential signature to the 1964 Civil Rights Act and the 1965 Voting Rights Act.

The Challenge – Changing Millions of Attitudes

Soon after entering the 21st century, changing attitudes and opinion became the battle cry of survival for the U.S. auto industry. According to CBS News (Jan. 13, 2007), Americans' attitudes toward General Motors®, Ford® and Chrysler® created a costly image crisis. A survey by the *Detroit News* found that 70 percent of buyers who avoided American cars said the main reason was concerns about quality and reliability.

David Champion, head of automobile testing for Consumer Reports®, said the stereotypes about Japanese and American cars were not far from the truth. His conclusion, at the time, was based on dozens of comparative performance tests. He found that American brands, for all of their improvements, did not measure up.

Jim Stone spent 40 years at Ford® and admitted that quality hasn't always been job No. 1 – once a Ford slogan. (Actually, it was "Quality Is Job One"® – but the slogan was dropped around 2000 after Ford® recalled 10s of thousands of cars and trucks.)

"When I first came in here and I started thinking on my own, I was actually told that I was not paid to *think*. I was paid to *do*," he said. "We got the feeling that: it's a part, you put it on; don't worry about it."

"Now," says Stone, "if the part doesn't fit, we stop the line, get it to fit and (most important) find out what the root cause is."

In contrast, Toyota® assembly line workers are instructed to look for problems and correct the mistakes.

Changing (American car manufacturing) plant procedures hasn't been easy, and changing customers' attitudes may be more difficult, according to Steve Spear. Spear is an MIT engineering lecturer who researched by working on a Toyota® assembly line.

He says perception is a hard thing to turn around. "If someone goes in and has an experience that doesn't disappoint, they won't tell anybody. If they have an experience which absolutely delights they tell one person. And if they have a disappointing experience they tell nine."

In 2002, GM® brought in Bob Lutz, a living legend in the auto industry, to help improve the look and quality of its vehicles. Lutz believes GM® has become as good as the other guys. But he admits that may not be good enough.

"At equal vehicles, most U.S. consumers today, especially on the (east and west) coasts, will say, 'OK, this Chevrolet® is as nice as my Camry® – as nice. Why (then should I) take the risk? I'll stay with the Camry," he said.

PR Play 2-15
Strategic Counselors can take a page from a championship coach's book on communication and leadership

Rick Pitino is the only coach in NCAA history to win national championships with two colleges – Louisville in 2013 and Kentucky in 1996. His Louisville title came on the day he was elected to the Basketball Hall of Fame. How does Pitino define a leader? He keeps it simple.

In his book, *Lead to Succeed*, he breaks down leadership into a 10-point game plan:
- Have a concrete vision – in other words, be clear about your vision for the group's future.
- Be your own messenger – direct communication is important not just on major issues, but on the day-to-day matters, as well.
- Build a team ego – it is the difference between mediocrity and being something special.
- Act with integrity – don't cut corners or bend rules; it will only undermine your effort.
- Act decisively – you won't always be right, but you must be willing to put your ideas and yourself on the line.
- Be adaptable – you must change, and so must those around you or everyone gets behind.
- Be consistent – have a strategy for when things go wrong to get through it quickly without panic.
- Maintain focus – this is a discipline, so you must train yourself at it, learning from the tough times.
- Live for the future, not in the past – short-term goals to manage the present, long-term goals for the future.
- Act selflessly – leaders are judged by the successes of the people they lead.

Courier-Post (Camden, N.J.) – April 2000

"Toyota may no longer be the best in the world in quality. Several domestic brands that score higher than Toyota® – doesn't matter. Toyota® has the reputation. They have good resale value."

So how does the American automotive industry change the attitudes of the American car-buying public – to get those people to consider GM®, Ford® or Chrysler® when the default choice is Toyota® or Honda®? "Because if we don't build it right, then you're not gonna (sic) buy it," Stone said. "And if you don't buy it, then we're out of a job."

Play 2-16
Leadership – What it takes

According to Rowan University Vice President Philip Tumminia, leaders possess three criteria:
• Title (given to him/her)
• Charisma/Connectivity (earned)
• Competence/Expertise (earned)

Les Hirsch, CEO of Touro Infirmary, New Orleans, says effective leaders require:
• Courage
• Tenacity
• Perseverance
• Mental Toughness
• (Willingness to accept) Responsibility

He says leaders cannot be afraid to make difficult decisions. They must be inspirational and create hope, optimism and enthusiasm for the future – and must never give up. And, says Hirsch, leaders believe that "failure is not an option."

It was President Jimmy Carter who said, "Leaders whose messages are not changing (or reinforcing) behavior are not true leaders."

PR Play 2-17

"If you call yourself a leader and nobody is following, you're just out getting some exercise."

Tavis Smiley – PBS Radio Host

Can American carmakers pull back in front in the race for quality? The stakes have never been higher. With Detroit losing billions of dollars in 2006 and laying off 70,000 employees, plant workers like Jim Stone now understand it's not just a matter of surpassing the Japanese – it's a matter of survival.

PR Play 2-18
Bill Russell's 11 Lessons on Leadership

1. Curiosity is a key to commitment and, specifically, to problem solving. Curiosity will always allow you to ask the right questions – Why? What if? How?
2. Everything you do begins with yourself, but for you to use ego to win you have to make it all about your team, Winning is a team sport and can only be accomplished through team ego.
3. Listening lets you hear what isn't being said as much as what is. Active listening helps you find a new language that helps others listen more effectively.
4. Toughness and tenderness are not opposites, but partners in effective leadership.
5. Invisibility is learning how to make opponents believe they can't beat you even when you are not there.
6. Craftsmanship is to you what quality is to your product or service. It involves making yourself the most complete colleague, leader or parent you can be.
7. Personal integrity is about setting standards and your choices, responsibilities and commitments.
8. Rebounding is changing the flow of the game from defense to offense. From reaction to action. It is about developing the highest level of resilience.
9. Imagination is the gateway to innovation. Innovation is the foundation of differentiation. Winning is the greatest form of differentiation.
10. Decision-making is for leaders. Decision-making is most effective when it is inclusionary – not exclusionary.
11. Everyone has an opportunity to win in life. Winning is hard work. Winning is a team sport. It is the culmination of attitude, aptitude and appetite.

Bill Russell – Basketball Hall of Fame – Inducted in 1974 –
Among 50 greatest players in NBA history

> ## PR Play 2-19
> ### Framework for Leadership
>
> The framework that comprises leadership is simple:
> - **Control**
>   a. Preparation
>   b. Follow-up
>   c. Proactive
> - **Consistency**
>   a. Organization
>   b. Repetition
> - **Campaign**
>   a. Planning/ "Premeditated"
>   b. Strategy/Timing
>   c. Measurable results

Lutz says the U.S. car industry has to do something more – much more – and create a buzz (media and public saying "good things" about American-made cars in an unsolicited manner).

"I like to say, we have to be more Catholic than the Pope." (That's quite a strategic message from Lutz.)

Former Lyndon Baines Johnson presidential adviser and past president of the Motion Picture Association of America Jack Valenti says great leaders have one thing in common – they are good listeners and excellent planners. They have come to learn the importance of communication counselors who serve as their strategic advisers.

Today's leaders must take this page from *The Public Relations Practitioner's Playbook for (all) Strategic Communicators* and constantly follow the advice of Dr. Philip Tumminia, Les Hirsch, Presidents Johnson and Carter, Jack Welch, and Jack Valenti.

While many "bosses" surround themselves with "advisers" who tell them what they want to hear, a main reason trusted strategic advisers have a seat at the board table in the cabinet room is – they don't hesitate to tell the "boss" what he/she needs to hear. And that is what the true leader wants to hear.

Many times, leadership boils down to all or most of the above plus a system of intelligent compromise, proper balance, teamwork, key focus points and common sense. Unfortunately, too often, common sense is the missing ingredient.

EXERCISES

PR Challenge 2-1

In your opinion, what are the five most important elements of this chapter? Come back to this question, once you have completed *The Playbook* and compare your response then to now.

PR Challenge 2-2

If you were asked to explain – in a few words – "The Triple Bottom Line Theory" and Pat Jackson's "Double Bottom Line Theory," what would you say?

PR Challenge 2-3

Which theory do you believe in: attitudes *cannot* be changed or that they *can* be changed? Why?

CHAPTER 3

TEC (A Total Effort To Communicate) – Overview of a Successful Strategic Communication Program

Whether it's called public relations, public information, community relations, public affairs, relationship (management) marketing, strategic advisement/counseling or another offshoot of communication, a successful program must be a two-way process.

An effective program seeks community attitudes and other public opinion while simultaneously disseminating information. To be effective, a program must reach everyone in its target audiences – not just a segment. In fact, strategic communicators now recognize that segmenting audiences is not enough. Audiences must be fragmented – demographically, psychographically and geodemographically – niched or narrowly defined and identified as an audience to be persuaded or convinced.

> **PR Play 3-1**
>
> Audience Segmentation/
> Fragmentation
> - Identify
> - Segment
> - Fragment
> - Profile
> - Rank

Known for years as *ISPR* – identify, segment, profile, rank – the accepted audience identification and ranking method has now become *IFPR* – identify, fragment, profile, rank (more later in this chapter).

Using the example of a school community relations program, audience fragmentation would identify, not just teachers, but rather math teachers or foreign language teachers; not just parents, but parents of band members, or football players or French club members; not just support staff, but rather bus drivers, or custodians or secretaries. It could and should include other community residents, students, support staff and business and professional people who work and/or live in the district. Each of these fragmented audiences might – and probably does – require a specific strategic message. An aggregate – all of the audiences as one – would suggest yet another strategic message, which would have to be broad enough to change or, at the very least, maintain behavior.

ISPR and *IFPR* are best explained this way:

Identify – Determine demographic, psychographic and/or geodemographic characteristics of individuals who may eventually be grouped based on similar needs and wants. Those niche audiences become target audiences when they become potential recipients of an organization's message. Audiences fall into four segments – internal, external, intermediary (message carriers) and special – which are then fragmented.

Segment – The division of a total market into groups, subgroups or sectors (demographically, psychographically and geodemographically) with relatively similar needs and wants. It's important that the proper message and channel be used to communicate to market segments at a time when the segments are available to receive the message. The purpose is to prioritize segments of the market to improve marketing profitability and to provide a means to choose the most appropriate communication media and messages for each target (fragment) audience. (See below.)

Fragment – A small, narrowly defined group with relatively similar needs and wants. Much like segments, but smaller and more defined. (Examples: Segment = Bald men; Fragment = Bald men with blue eyes who are left handed; or Segment = Women who are over six feet; Fragment = Women, at least six feet tall, who are natural blondes and left handed.)

Profile – Determining the importance of audiences after learning as much about them as possible. The four-step process – identifying, profiling, segmenting (fragmenting) and ranking audiences is best accomplished through *Demographics*, *Psychographics* and *Geodemographics*. Profiling is an important step, because it helps in determining where best to spend resources – both money and *MindShare*.

Rank – To arrange audience segment/fragments in order from most important to least important so that, in the case of limited resources, concentration and expenditures go to those fragments considered "key" to the outcome. When ranking, *need* to reach is a primary consideration.

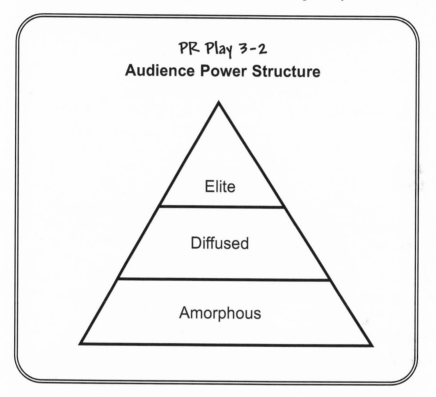

PR Play 3-2
Audience Power Structure

Elite

Diffused

Amorphous

Audience Power Models
- Elite Power Model – The high concentration is in the hands of a small, elite group that represents the industrial, commercial and financial interests in a community.
- Pluralistic or Diffused Model – It has several centers of power or power bases.
- Amorphous Model – Power is basically absent or latent. Many believe in the status quo or the way things are. The power structure has yet to form. Many times, new communities – condominium or other similar associations take time to evolve into power structures.

As mentioned many times throughout this book and by the best professionals – it is important to know your audience(s) so that the right message goes to the right audience using the proper channel at the proper time (informization). After all, you have to fish where the fishes are. That's the same mantra advertising professionals live by. Messages disseminated to the wrong audience are "wasted coverage."

Major Publics

Media Publics

Mass media

Local
  Print publications
    Newspapers
    Magazines
  TV stations
  Radio stations

National
  Print publications
  Broadcast networks
  Wire services

Specialized media

Local
  Trade, industry and association
    publications
  Organizational house and
    membership publications
  Ethnic publications
  Publications of special groups
  Specialized broadcast
    programs and stations

National
  General business publications
  National trade, industry and
    association publications
  National organizational house
    and membership publications
  National ethnic publications
  Publications of national special
    groups
  National specialized broadcast
    programs and networks

Member Publics

(Stakeholders – have a vested interest)

Organization employees
Headquarters management
Headquarters non-management
(staff)
Other headquarters personnel

Organization officers
Elected officers
Appointed officers
Legislative groups
Boards, committees

Organization members
Regular members
Members in special
categories—sustaining,
emeritus, student members
Honorary members or groups

Prospective organization members
State or local chapters
Organization employees
Organization officers
Organization members
Prospective organization
members

Related or other allied organizations
Business or corporate partners

Employee Publics

(Stakeholders – have a vested interest)

Management
Upper-level administrators
Mid-level administrators
Lower-level administrators

Non-management (staff)
Specialists
Clerical personnel
Secretarial personnel
Uniformed personnel
Equipment operators
Drivers
Security personnel
Other uniformed personnel
Union representatives
Other non-management
personnel

Community Publics

(Stakeholders – have a vested interest)

Community media
  Mass
  Specialized

Community leaders
  Public officials
  Educators
  Religious leaders
  Professionals
  Executives
  Bankers
  Union leaders
  Ethnic leaders
  Neighborhood leaders

Community organizations
  Civic
  Service
  Social
  Business
  Cultural
  Religious
  Youth
  Political
  Special interest
  Other

Investor Publics

(Stakeholders – have an invested interest)

Shareowners and potential
  shareowners (stockholders –
  have financial investment)
Security analysts and investment
  counselors
Financial press
  Major wire services
    Dow Jones & Co., Reuters
    Economic Service, AP, UPI
  Major business magazines
    BusinessWeek, Fortune, and
    the like - mass circulation
    and specialized
  Major newspapers
    The New York Times,
    The Wall Street Journal
  Statistical services
    Standard and Poor's Corp.,
    Moody's Investor Service,
    and the like
  Private wire services
    PR Newswire,
    Business Wire
  Securities and Exchange
    Commission (SEC) for
    publicly owned companies

Government Publics

Federal

Legislative branch
Representatives, staff, committee personnel
Senators, staff, committee personnel
Executive branch
President
White House staff, advisers, committees
Cabinet officers, departments, agencies, commissions

State

Legislative branch
Representatives, delegates, staff, committee personnel
Senators, staff, committee personnel
Executive branch
Governor
Governor's staff, advisers, committees
Cabinet officers, departments, agencies, commissions

County

County executive
Other county officials, commissions, departments

City

Mayor or city manager
City council
Other city officials, commissions, departments

Consumer Publics

(Stakeholders – have a vested interest)

Company employees
Customers
Professionals
Middle class
Working class
Minorities
Other
Activist consumer groups
Consumer publications
Consumer media, mass and specialized
Consumer leaders and organizations

Special Publics

Media consumed by this public
Mass
Print
Broadcast
Internet

Specialized within Special Publics

Leaders of this public
Public officials
Professional leaders
Ethnic leaders
Neighborhood leaders
Organizations composing this public
Civic
Political
Service
Business
Cultural
Religious
Youth
Other

PR Play 3-3
Stakeholders

Anyone with an interest (financial or otherwise) in a company or organization.

Jerry A. Hendrix – *Public Relations Cases* – © Wadsworth, Inc.

TEC – A Total Effort to Communicate

TEC's success, like that of most other (branded) strategic communication programs, is dependent on fully understanding audience fragmentation and knowing how to use it. By its very nature, *TEC* must be a year-round (365/24/7) communication program that pulls everything together. The comprehensive printed phase – hard copy or electronic/digital – (newsletters, brochures, annual report, special publications) is supplemented with face-to-face (WOM – word of mouth), other oral communication and electronic notification systems – either voice or texts. *TEC's* cost can be minimal or quite expensive. (Organizations may not have the money to implement all of it. But why not select the ingredients – ala carte – that could help the most?)

An effective two-way communication flow enables the Strategic Communicator to identify problems while they are still in the early stages – before they grow into crises. A sound feedback system will alert the organization or company that its community will accept one idea, but reject another, unless more explanation is forthcoming.

PR Play 3-4
Two-Way Communication Model

Sender>>>Message>>>Receiver

∧		V
∧	**Noise**	V
∧	**Noise**	V
∧	**Noise**	V
∧		V

<<<<<<<<< Feedback <<<<<<<<<

The sender-receiver model (page 48) is fashioned after the *Shannon-Weaver Communication Model* – developed by researchers Claude Shannon and Warren Weaver. They theorized that human communication comprises the same mechanistic components of Alexander Graham Bell's telephone system.
- Initiator (Sender/Encoder)
- Carrier (Message via a channel)
- Receiver (Decoder)
- Feedback (Is clarity being achieved? If not, why not? Is it the noise?)

If a message is not being received as intended it is the sender's fault. Communication is *shared comprehension* (two way) – seeking feedback (public opinion) and at the same time disseminating information. Every communication model must include the same essential elements as the *Shannon-Weaver Communication Model*.

How to Establish Effective Two-Way Communication
- Evaluate the current program – possibly conducting a public relations or communication audit (see *The ABCs of Strategic Communication* – AuthorHouse). What types of written communication are used on a regular basis? Does the organization communicate face-to-face (1-to-1) with its publics? How does it know what its community is thinking?
- Determine needs. To improve communication with staff, media or the public, create and design a website consistent with the organization's logo and other locking power devices used on such vehicles as standard letterhead(s), which help make the organization easily recognizable through its channels of communication. (Your organization is a brand. Such major brands as McDonald's® and Coca-Cola® have universally recognized logos.) The news media, especially, are deluged with releases of all kinds. If an organization establishes a professional-looking release and the highest degree of credibility, reporters and editors will learn to depend on your organization's releases for news – and even call, periodically, to tap the organization's intellectual property as a major resource.
- Prepare a method for feeling the public's pulse (Chapter 4). There are a number of relatively inexpensive "informal" methods. An email link on the organization's website encourages feedback, suggestions and other comments. An "open line" telephone with a direct line into the strategic communicator's office or even the CEO's office is also an excellent tactic. Another – which might seem antiquated to some, but is still effec-

tive with certain audience fragments – is the use of pre-addressed post-cards asking the public for ideas, questions and rumors. The website is quicker and easier for many, but not everyone has computer access or is computer savvy. It's important to remember that every person who writes, emails or calls must receive an immediate acknowledgement. Another inexpensive method for determining what a community is thinking is a Key Communicator Program – opinion leader/consumption pioneer/influentials (Chapter 15). This type of program involves respected community leaders who will tell an organization what is on their minds and probably the minds of their neighbors, customers and/or patients. These are people who can assist in changing the behavior (attitudes and opinions) of their neighbors and/or fellow employees.

More Suggestions For Improving A Company's Public Relations – Five Major Media

Sending the message: Make use of the five major media types available to the strategic communicator.

- **Print** – newspapers, magazines, newsletters, annual reports, etc.
- **Broadcast** – radio, TV.
- **Internet** – including Web 2.0 – social media (Chapter 10)
- **Face-to-face (1-to-1)** – the most effective because it is often the most believable and most credible. Third party endorsements are most persuasive (source credibility).
- **Special events** – focused happenings to attract attention (Chapter 15).

Which media should you choose? Rely on research and audience fragmentation. Keep in mind, you want to reach your target audience using an effective strategic message, the channel and media they rely on and trust at a time they are paying attention. It is called *informization* (Page 26).

Evaluating the message: Here are feedback suggestions:
- Obtain opinions from advisory committees and key communicators.
- Monitor social media and blogs.
- Listen to what is said at meetings of service and community groups.
- Listen to radio call-in shows and watch TV interview shows.
- Solicit comments on your organization/company website.
- Hold question and answer sessions at public meetings.
- Appeal to community resource programs.
- Have receptionists keep a list of common questions that callers might ask.

- Establish a speakers bureau.
- Include questionnaires in newsletters – electronic and print – sent to the public; clients; customers – and/or internal publics.
- Distribute "golden age cards" (special privilege – VIP – cards) to senior citizens who may want to use your organization's products or services.
- Make idea and question and answer cards available in stores, shops and professional offices.
- Hold focus panels.
- Create both comprehensive and/or "flash"(community) opinion surveys.

There May Be Pitfalls

Although *TEC* is a flexible program, there are times when many of the communication techniques seem to demand extra attention from the strategic communicator. For example, two or three rumors may break simultaneously, a number of emails may need replies, social media are buzzing, the "open line" telephone is unusually busy, the deadline for the community newsletter is near, and the CEO has asked the PR office (at the last minute) to prepare an after-dinner speech – for that night.

PR Play 3-5
Basic Planning Steps

1. Identify Issues (Determine purpose – Situation Analysis*)
2. Design Research Questions
3. Conduct Initial Research (Research Actions)
4. Select Goal – must be attainable – realistic and reachable
5. Write Backgrounder (Case) Statement [Chapters 5 and 6]
6. Identify and Rank Audiences
7. Craft Messages
8. Determine Channels
9. Determine Aperture (Best time to deliver messages)
10. Write Objectives
11. Craft Strategies (what, to whom, how and why)
12. Select Tactics (Vehicles/Tools)
13. Prepare Budget
14. Design Gantt Chart (Calendar Time Line) [Chapter 7]
15. Measure Your Work (Evaluate) – an assessment
16. Further Research (What changes would you make?)

*See Situation Analyses – PR Play 7-2

Be assured, community feedback is evidence that the advantages of a *TEC* program far outweigh the pitfalls. However, one thing is as imperative in public relations as it is in sports – to achieve success (which means reaching an attainable goal), one must follow through with a thorough game plan. Here are some steps to be followed (PR Plays 3-5 through 3-8):

The following *Public Relations Plays* can assist with many *TEC* approaches:

PR Play 3-6
Yale University's Six Persuasive Moments

1. Are you there? – available
2. Are you listening? – unconstrained
3. Do you remember me? – message/recall
4. Do you understand me? – audience/knows me
5. Do you agree with me? – attitude change
6. Will you act for me? – behavior

Yale University - 1998
Anthony Fulginiti, APR, Fellow PRSA – Rowan (N.J.) University

---

PR Play 3-7
Communicating With Older People

Communicating with older people often requires extra time and patience because of physical, psychological and social changes.

Some suggestions:
- Reduce background noises.
- Talk about familiar subjects.
- Keep your sentences short.
- Give the person a chance to reminisce.

PR Play 3-8
The Practitioner Should Strive To:

- Assure public relations-mindedness of organization officials.
- Obtain written definition of authority and responsibility (contained in organization or company policy).
- Gain confidence and cooperation of associates.
- Communicate with the entire organization (internal audiences) to assure principles and programs are known and understood.
- Provide service to other departments, staff and line (employees).
- Develop a desire and opportunities for mutual participation in the program.
- Promote a communication philosophy of candor (open, honest, thorough, valid [relevant]).

PR Play 3-9
Skills Possessed By
Successful Practitioners/Strategic Advisers

(See Chapter 17)

Writing
Editing
Research
Internet and Web 2.0
Media Relations
Advertising/Marketing
Counseling
Special Events
Public Speaking
Staff Training
Awareness of Current Events
Knowledge of Government Affairs (Lobbying)
Issues Management

PR Play 3-10
Concentrations Generally Associated with Strategic Communication
(Some according to PRSA*)

- **Advertising** – Paid, (non) personal communication from an identified sponsor using (mass) media to persuade or influence an audience.

- **Communication** – Transfer of information to establish social interaction.

- **Community relations** – An aspect of strategic communications having responsibility for building relationships with constituent publics such as schools, charities, clubs and activist interests of the neighborhoods or metropolitan areas where an organization operates. Dealing with and communicating with the citizens and groups within an organization's home region.

- **Counseling** – Professional strategic (public relations) advice and/or services, and evaluation.

- **Development** – An aspect of the communication profession that incorporates strategic communication to assist with fund raising for the expansion or improvement of an organization.

- **Financial (public) relations** – Sometimes referred to as investor relations. An aspect of strategic communication responsible for building relations with the investor public including: shareholders/stockholders; potential investors; financial analysts; the financial markets (stock exchanges); and the Securities and Exchange Commission.

- **Government (affairs) relations** – An aspect of relationship building between an organization and government at local, state and/or national levels especially involving the flow of information to and from legislative and regulatory bodies in an effort to influence public policy decisions compatible with the organization's interests (commonly called lobbying).

- **Industry relations** – Dealing and communicating with firms within the industry of which the organization is a part.

cont.

- **Issues management** – Systematic identification and action regarding public policies in their earliest stages, identifying these issues, measuring their development and planning and measuring organizational response.

- **Media relations** – Dealing with the communication media on a regular basis in seeking publicity for, or responding to media interest in, an individual, organization or event.

- **Member relations** – Dealing with internal and external communication aspects of member organizations.

- **Minority relations** – Mutually beneficial associations between social entities and the various minority publics in society especially African American, Hispanic, Asian and Native American groups at the local, regional or national levels.

- **Press agentry** – The promotion of an individual, product or service through the use of (free) publicity obtained from the (mass) media.

- **Promotion** – Methods and techniques designed to attract and retain listeners, viewers, readers, etc. to one of the (mass) media or to stimulate interest in a person, product, organization or cause.

- **Propaganda** – A one-sided message to influence or persuade a public. The use of ideas, information or opinion for the purpose of furthering or hindering a cause or promoting or denigrating an idea.

- **Public affairs** – The "daily link between the private sector and government," which interprets business to government, and government to business, within the context of a larger social responsibility to preserve the openness and integrity of the democratic process. The task involves issues management – especially those issues of concern to special interest activities in the shaping of public policies and legislation.

- **Publicity** – Dissemination of planned and executed messages through selected media, without payment to the media, to further the particular interest of an organization or person.

*Public Relations Society of America

PR Play 3-11
Public Communication

Public communication is at the heart of our economy, society and politics. Studios use it to promote their films. Politicians use it to get elected. Businesses use it to burnish their image. Advocates use it to promote social causes.

It is a field built on ideas and images, persuasion and information, strategies and tactics. No policy or product can succeed without a smart (strategic) message targeted to the right audience in creative and innovative ways. The ability to communicate this way – to communicate strategically – is what a Public Communication/Strategic Communication program is all about.

Keep in mind, however, superior *tactics* cannot overcome a *flawed* (business) *strategy*.

American University – School of Communication – Washington, D.C.
Ed Ziegler – Marketing Director – Rowan University – Glassboro, N.J.

Whether it is a strategic communication program fashioned after *TEC* or any other, the program and approach will contain its practitioner's *fingerprints*. It must be a program that is open, honest, thorough and valid (relevant) – a program that is well thought out with goals, objectives, strategies and tactics.

EXERCISES

PR Challenge 3-1
For years, audience segmentation was only four steps – identify, profile, segment and rank. A fifth, fragment, has been added. Why is it important to fragment audiences?

PR Challenge 3-2
What is difference between a *stakeholder* and a *stockholder*? There is one major characteristic that separates the two.

PR Challenge 3-3
How would you avoid falling into the "wasted coverage trap"?

CHAPTER 4
Research Techniques Simplified
Or
You Talk...We Listen

Conducting public opinion surveys and getting results that rival the professionals may be easier and less expensive than one would think. But it takes strategic planning. Effective strategic communication programs seek continuous feedback (public opinion) at the same time they are disseminating information – much like ongoing *push polling* (*The ABCs of Strategic Communication* – AuthorHouse).

The word *research* is derived from a French word meaning *travel through*. Whether primary (formal [you conduct]) or secondary (informal [previously conducted and available through such sources as the Internet]), *research* is the backbone of the strategic communication professions. It is universally accepted that research must be the very first step taken to assist in identifying target audiences, establishing baselines and benchmarks and tracking changes over time. (See *MAC Triad Plus* on page 61).

Succinctly, research is the *acquisition of information (AI)*. AI leads to "Knowledge Creation." *Research* is conducted to determine as much as possible about the likely behavior of an audience – *behavior testing*.

The method or technique chosen is driven by the survey's objectives and goal(s). *Research* is the journey. The results are the destination. What is done with the results dictates the survey's success. Often, too many surveys acquire information that is rich with data, but analysis poor. To be credible, the information or results must be made actionable.

> ## PR Play 4-1
> ## We asked. We listened. We acted!

The major entrepreneurial/business skill is knowing how to take an idea to market. *Research* generates the data that:

- Determines the *need* for the idea or product.
- Assists in crafting key message points.
- Determines the best channels or vehicles by which to deliver the message(s).

PR Play 4-2
Benchmark

- A standard for comparing similar items such as research findings, the creative elements of a campaign, advertising results, etc.
- A point of reference – baseline. (A person or organization that others aspire to match or exceed.)
- A standard for comparing products to determine competitors' costs and quality with one's own.

Communication is a two-way process. To be effective, a program must reach all of its important publics. However, different audiences may need different strategic messages.

Research in and of itself is done on a regular, albeit, informal basis. It is not restricted to the strategic communication professions. For example, if a young man is interested in the marital status of a woman, he might ask someone who knows the woman. That is *research*. If we want to know a particular restaurant's hours, we either call on the phone or check the Internet. That, too, is *research*. This chapter will examine the more formal approaches.

First, some justification: In the often-used PR-PIE acronym (Chapter 2 – Synergy), sequentially, a *Purpose (P)* must be determined and agreed on before any of the other steps should ever be taken. Once that is accomplished, the *Research (R)* must be conducted and analyzed before *Planning (P)* can begin. It is during the *Planning* stage that goals and objectives are established, strategies devised and tactics explored. The *I* stands for *Implementation*. That is the dissemination of the message. The *E* is for *Evaluation*. Each stage is important. But for many, the data analysis or *E* stage may be the most important because this is when the future of a project, campaign or product launch may be decided. In fact, an organization's future might hinge on research evaluation.

A number of devices or techniques are used to gain feedback from your publics. The most scientific, and usually most accurate, is the opinion survey. A sound feedback system will alert management that a community will accept one idea, but vehemently reject another – unless more explanation is forthcoming.

Guarantees in strategic communication can be dangerous, but not when it comes to scientific polling. It *is* guaranteed that surveys help us learn new aspects about the audiences being served – data that will help the practitioner do a better job of educating audiences or publics. A well-executed and analyzed survey helps us discover new methods to improve communication. It also helps build a better understanding of an organization's mission. Many successful practitioners have stated they enjoy their jobs more than ever – because with understanding, through opinion polls, comes the support they deserve.

However, it is important to remember that survey results are only a snapshot of time – meaning that if the same questions were asked of the same audience a day or two later the results could differ depending on new information gathered by those being questioned.

PR Play 4-3
Benchmark Study

A measurement of audience attitudes before and after a (strategic) public relations campaign. A starting point (baseline) so that behavioral change can be accurately measured.

Eileen Weisman – The W Group – Houston, Texas

Carol Eaton, Ph.D., is a communication research specialist with the Jefferson County Schools in Golden, Colo. She advocates research to improve communication with her district's publics – and to validate the work being done by the communication office.

Dr. Eaton uses research to:
• Replace hunches
• Identify root causes
• Improve decision making

- Inform her publics about progress
- Acquire a list of questions that may be circulating throughout her community

PR Play 4-4
Two-Way Communication Model

Sender>>>Message>>>Receiver

∧		V
∧	**Noise**	V
∧	**Noise**	V
∧	**Noise**	V
∧		V

<<<<<<<<< Feedback <<<<<<<<<

More Reasons to Conduct Research

- Source credibility – Well executed and analyzed surveys generate data that, when properly used, show company representatives who conducted and reported the results as honest, objective, knowledgeable and experienced (expert) on their subject and not just representative of a special interest.
- Decrease top management isolation – Too often, chief executives sit in their ivory towers and lose touch with their publics.
- Assist in the audience persuasion process – Determining attitudes (inner feelings) and opinions or behavior (expression of those attitudes) so that new messages can be crafted if attitudinal changes are needed.
- Identify Key Communicators (opinion leaders/influencers/consumption pioneers/leaders of people).
- Pretest messages.
- Uncover trouble spots.
- Generate news coverage through the dissemination of survey results.

Reasons *Not* To Conduct Research

Jackson, Jackson & Wagner (Exeter, N.H.), the public relations firm founded by the late Patrick Jackson, says an organization is wasting its time doing research if:

- The organization won't listen, respond or change.
- The audience is over-saturated.
- There is an unstable environment.

However, the stubborn practitioner still might try to take the research data and attempt to "move" the company or organization.

PR Play 4-5
MAC Triad Plus

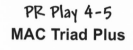

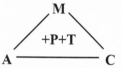

M=Message A=Audience C=Channel P=Purpose T=Timing

Because it has already been determined that a survey of some sort will be conducted, the *C* in the *MAC Triad* can be checked off. In this case, the *Channel* is the survey. The methodology (technique or research action) is still to be decided. That is where the *P* comes in. The strategic professional must ask, why? What is the *Purpose*? What do we want to learn from this exercise? The next step is targeting (identifying) the *Audience* or *Audiences*. It might be one or more of the many demographics. Timing is crucial to the execution of the plan. While all three coordinates of the *MAC Triad* must click, a successful outcome is dependent on the *timing*. Ask yourself, "What is the best time to engage the minds of my target audience to assure they see or hear the message?" Many practitioners refer to this as the aperture – or opening.

PR Play 4-6
Demographics

The vital statistics about the human population, its distribution and its characteristics (age, gender, income, education, etc.). Used for audience segmentation and fragmentation.

In many cases a survey's purpose will assist in crafting a future strategic message, the *M* in the *MAC Triad*, whether it is to persuade a public to adopt an idea or to purchase a product. However, it is not unusual to include a message in the introduction of the survey. For example, a local community trying to determine whether to enlarge a current library or build a new one could mention that choice in the survey's introduction. It helps communicate that the local government cares enough to ask its residents (used in push polling – see page 83).

PR Play 4-7
Psychographics

Psychological characteristics many times determined by standard-ized tests. Used for audience segmentation and fragmentation. Any attributes relating to personality, values, attitudes, interests or lifestyles. They are also called IAO variables (for Interests, Attitudes and Opinions). Combined with *demographics and geodemograph-ics, psychographics* play a key role in strategic planning.

PR Play 4-8
Geodemographics

A contraction of geography and demographics. A method of combining geographic and demographic variables. The demographics of individu-als or groups who reside in the same geographic area or region.

PR Play 4-9
Be Strong

"Asking questions is a sign of strength not weakness...so don't be afraid to ask questions."

Aladdin Factor

PR Play 4-10
How To Do It
The Basics of Conducting a Survey

1. Decide what you want to learn from the survey.
2. Ask why you want to learn this.
3. Ask yourself whether you could get this information without doing a survey.
4. Decide who your public or audience is going to be.
5. Determine the type of survey method (PR Play 4-11) you will use.
6. Establish confidence levels (PR Play 4-15) for your survey.
7. Determine the required resources – what, by when and who will perform the task.
8. Develop a timeline for your survey from start to finish – including pretesting.
9. Decide how the information will be analyzed and the results reported – keeping in mind that, if possible, a copy of the report or summary should be sent to those surveyed.
10. Report should be formatted to include:
    – title
    – table of contents
    – executive summary of findings
    – tabulation of data
    – comparative data
    – analysis of findings
    – recommendations
    – copy of questionnaire

Former Rowan University Communication Professor Donald R. Gallagher, strongly believed before the first question is put on paper and the first respondent is approached, a few preliminary questions must be asked:

1. **What is the purpose of the survey?** What is the problem? Is it the public's attitude toward some action your organization is taking? Its image? Its service or product? Don't try to cover too much in one survey. It might get too long and discourage many respondents.

2. **Is a public opinion poll the best way to get the needed information?** Be sure that some of the information you are seeking is not

already available from such other sources as the U.S. Census Bureau, county or local records.

3. **What are we going to do with the results?** Are you willing to implement the changes if the results are valid?

4. **What specific audiences will we question?** The entire universe (population) or a segment/fragment of the universe may be chosen depending on the purpose of the survey. Carefully examine the available demographics of the universe.

5. **How long should we take to conduct the survey?** If it takes too long, results will be outdated and of little value. A good guideline is to complete the interviewing within a period of 10 days or two weeks. Depending on the situation, the data may hold for just a few days or weeks and most certainly its life span will be no longer than 90 days.

6. **How much money do we have to conduct the survey?** With more money, you can survey a larger sample. This reduces the margin of error and gives you a broader view of the population surveyed.

7. **How will the data be analyzed, reported and applied?** Ask yourself whether you should use data processing such as *SPSS*® – originally, *Statistical Package for the Social Sciences* – a computer program used for statistical analysis and also the name of the company (SPSS Inc.) that sells it (among the most widely-used programs for statistical analysis in social science). A computer can be very helpful in tabulating the results. Hand tabulation will take a considerable amount of time. The results should be reported through a news conference, the Internet (website link), public meetings (internal and external), news releases and/or direct mail (see No. 12 below). As for applying the results, a "golden" rule to follow is: *We asked. We listened. We acted!*

8. **Should an outside agency conduct the survey?** It might be wise to hire an outside agency if you don't have the time or the trained people available to direct such a survey. The results might seem more credible to the public if an outside agency conducts the survey.

9. **When is the best time to conduct a survey?** In real estate, it is location, location, location. When it comes to feeling the pulse of a community, timing is everything. A time of crisis is not the best time. Look at the calendar and see what events might influence/interfere with a survey.

10. **How many people must be questioned to determine the thoughts of the entire population?** It is not necessarily the size of the sample, but rather how scientifically it was chosen. In an absolute scientific survey, everyone in a population has the same opportunity to be questioned as everyone else. Frank Newport of The Gallup Organization supports that premise. He says, "The method in which the sample is chosen is far more important than the sample size."

11. **What is the best method of gathering the information on a survey?** The seven most commonly used methods are the mail questionnaire, the drop-off/pick-up questionnaire, the personal interview, the telephone interview, the omnibus or piggyback survey, the Internet (Web and email) survey and focus panels. The personal interview is the best; the telephone method is the most functional; and the mail questionnaire is the worst. The jury is still out on the effectiveness of the Internet survey.

12. **When should the decision on publicizing results of a survey be made?** The date for publicizing a survey's results should be announced at the same session in which an organization or company is announcing that it is going to conduct a survey. By taking such a pro-active stance, the media, thus the public, will have confidence that no matter what the results reveal – positive or negative – they will be released. This will help gain on-going media support. It strengthens the organization's credibility.

PR Play 4-11
Seven Survey Methods

Personal Interview	Piggyback (Omnibus) Survey
Telephone Interview	Web and email Surveys (Internet)
Drop-off/Pick-up Questionnaire	[can be "snowballed"]
Mail Questionnaire	Focus Panels

Advantages and Limitations of Seven Survey Methods

Personal Interview

Advantages
- High percentage of return.
- Information apt to be more correct than the other methods.
- Additional information can be obtained.
- Respondent misunderstanding can be clarified.

Limitations
- Cost of transportation.
- Trained personnel required.
- Great amount of time needed.
- Cost of returned questionnaire is great.

Telephone Interview

Advantages
- Less expensive than personal interview.
- Short periods of time needed to complete survey.
- No cost for transportation.
- Minimal training of personnel.

Limitations
- Unlisted phones.
- Easy for respondent to hang up.
- Caller I.D.

Drop-off/Pick-up Questionnaire

Advantages
- High returns in short period of time.
- Respondent misunderstanding can be clarified.
- Minimal training of personnel.

Limitations
- Transportation costs.
- Need many volunteers or workers.

Mailed Questionnaire

Advantages
- Mailing costs are cheaper than transportation costs.

- May reach groups protected from solicitors and investigators.
- Respondent may be more candid.

Limitations
- The number of returns is usually low.
- Anyone at residence may fill it out.
- An irate citizen may collect many questionnaires from neighbors and answer all of them.
- The responses will not represent the thinking of total population.

Piggyback (Omnibus) Survey
(An alternative survey method – an organization "buys" a question or questions on another organization's survey. It is a money-saving technique. However, it must be determined that the piggyback/omnibus survey targets the same audiences you want to reach or this would be considered a major disadvantage.)

Advantages
- Less expensive.
- Makes use of a professional pollster's expertise.
- Can focus on a few questions while obtaining demographic data from administrator of larger survey.

Limitations
- Organization can obtain only a small snapshot of public opinion with one or two questions.
- Subject matter must be relevant to the general public.
- Must use the timelines of polling organization.
- Little or no control over question placement (unless predetermined).
- Must target the same audiences you are trying to reach.

Web and Email Surveys
Advantages
- Can be announced on banner ads or other websites or online networks.
- Email invitations to target audiences.
- Telephone individuals with an invitation to participate.
- Send post cards to invite participation.
- Can be "snowballed" – forwarded to each recipient's contacts (Snowball surveys may be random, but not scientific. This will increase audience, but results may not be reliable.)

Limitations

- Little control of exact characteristics of the respondents since a website is accessible to almost anyone with a computer and Internet access.
- Respondents with limited computer experience may become frustrated and either answer incorrectly or seek help from someone who may influence their responses.
- Could be a so-called "self-selected" or *volunteer* survey – you ask to be surveyed or go on Internet and answer questions from a pop-up window (similar to "intercept" survey [see *The ABCs of Strategic Communication* – AuthorHouse]).
- Many times, the results of these surveys are non-scientific.

Focus Panels

Advantages

- Good alternative to individual interviewing.
- Widely used in advertising, marketing and public relations to help identify attitudes and motivations of important publics.
- Used to form or pretest message themes and communication strategies before launching a full campaign.

Limitations

- Non-scientific (to conduct scientific focus panels is prohibitively expensive although it can be done).
- Informal rather than formal research technique.
- Develops qualitative (characteristic) information rather than hard data (quantitative).
- Results cannot be summarized by percentages or projected onto an entire population.

Types of Formal Sampling

Probability – Survey in which every member of the targeted audience has an equal chance (exactly the same odds) of being selected for questioning. (Also known as *Systematic* [*Scientific*] *Sampling* – a *Chance* Survey – more exact than *Random*.) Results reflect the opinions of the entire universe (total population) from which the sample is chosen because the sample is representative of the larger population being studied. The members of the sample are scientifically selected, that is, they are selected according to a system that gives everybody an equal chance of being asked to participate. Done correctly a sample should demonstrate what is already known about the total universe – age, gender, education, ethnicity, etc. If those factors match, it is an excellent indication that the sample is representative of the population being surveyed.

* Selection of sample is purely by *chance*.
* The size of the universe (total population) has no bearing on the size of the sample. *(go to page 76)*

PR Play 4-12
Conducting Focus Panels

Focus groups are a powerful means to evaluate services or test new ideas – but to conduct them without a thorough knowledge is a daunting task and probably will not generate the desired responses and other information.

According to Dr. Carter McNamara of Authenticity Consulting, LLC – Minneapolis, focus groups are interviews conducted in small groups – six to 10 people at the same time in the same group. One can get a great deal of information during a focus group/panel session.

Preparing for the Session

1. Identify the major objective (purpose) of the panel.
2. Carefully develop up to six questions (see below).
3. Plan your session (see below).
4. Call or email potential members to invite them to the meeting. Send a follow-up invitation with a proposed agenda, session time and list of questions the group will discuss. Plan to provide a copy of the report from the session to each member and let them know you will do this.
5. About three days before the session, call and/or email each member to remind them to attend.

Developing Questions

1. Develop five to six questions – Session should last one to one and a half hours – so that five or six questions can be discussed.
2. As with other surveys, determine what problem or need will be addressed by the information gathered during the session. For example, examine if a new product or service will work, or further understand how a program is failing, etc.

cont.

PR Play 4-12 continued

3. Focus groups are basically multiple interviews. Therefore, many of the guidelines for conducting focus groups are similar to the guidelines for conducting interviews.

Planning the Session

1. Scheduling – Plan focus panel to run from one to two hours, but an hour and a half is ideal. Lunch sessions have proven successful although you must tell participants that meetings could and probably will run longer than the normal lunch hour.
2. Setting and Refreshments – Hold sessions in a conference room, or other setting with adequate air flow and lighting. Configure chairs so that all members can see each other. Provide name tags for members. When providing lunch, keep it to a simple, easy-to-eat meal – and remember health conscious participants.
3. Ground Rules – It is critical that all members participate as much as possible, keeping the session moving along all the while generating useful information. Because the session is often a one-time occurrence, it is useful to have a few short ground rules that sustain participation and keep the focus. Dr. McNamara suggests the following three ground rules:
    • keep focused
    • maintain momentum
    • get closure on questions
4. Agenda – Consider this one from Dr. McNamara:
    • welcome
    • review of agenda
    • review of goal of the meeting
    • review of ground rules
    • introductions
    • questions and answers
    • wrap up
5. Membership – Focus groups are usually conducted with six to 10 members who have some similar characteristics – similar interests, similar age group, etc. Select members who are likely to actively participate and be reflective. A challenge is attempting to select members who don't know each other.

cont.

PR Play 4-12 continued

6. Have one or more co-facilitators take notes. Also, record the session with either an audio or video recorder. Don't count on the note takers (unless they are "court" stenographers) or your memory.

Conducting the Session

1. The major goal of panel facilitation is collecting useful information to meet the goal or objectives of the meeting.
2. Introduce yourself and the co-facilitator(s).
3. Explain the process and how the responses are being recorded manually and electronically.
4. Try to adhere to the agenda – (see "agenda" above).
5. Carefully craft each question before that question is addressed by the group. Allow the group a few minutes for each member to carefully record their answers. Then, facilitate discussion around the answers to each question, one at a time. Don't allow participants to talk over each other.
6. After each question is answered, carefully summarize what you heard (the note taker may do this).
7. Ensure even participation. If one or two people are dominating the session, then call on others. Consider using a round-table approach, including going in one direction around the table, giving each person one minute to answer the question. If the domination persists, note it to the group and ask for ideas about how the participation can be increased.
8. Closing the session – Tell members that they will receive a copy of the report generated from their answers, thank them for coming and adjourn the meeting.

Immediately After Session

1. Verify if the tape recorder, if used, worked throughout the session (and be sure to check it before beginning the session).
2. Check handwritten notes and add comments if necessary – clarify any hard to read notes and be sure to number the pages.
3. Write down any observations made during the session. For example, where did the session occur and when, what was the nature of participation in the group? Were there any surprises during the session?

PR Play 4-13
Key Research-Related Definitions
(Glossary at end of chapter)

- **Primary Research** – New research. Research you do yourself.
- **Secondary Research** – Information or data available through another's research (U.S. Census Bureau; Gallup, a newspaper, etc.).
- **Formal, scientific or quantitative research** – Rigorous use of the principles of scientific investigation such as the rules of empirical observation, random sampling in surveys, comparison of results against statistical standards and provision for replication of results.
- **Informal or non-scientific research** – Investigation without use of scientific method (usually undertaken as exploratory and/or preliminary to more rigorous methods).
- **Empirical Research** – Any activity that uses direct or indirect observation or experiment to gather information. Empirical data can be analyzed quantitatively and qualitatively.
- **Formative Research** – Usually not scientific. Formative research such as focus groups and mall intercept interviews with consumers are used to help test messages and materials designed to motivate target audiences. Formative research is a critical step in crafting research questions and usually occurs before a program is designed and implemented.
- **Identity** – What you are – how you want to be perceived.
- **Image** – How people perceive you.
- **Attitude** – Predisposition to act (inner feeling).
- **Opinion** – Expression of attitude (behavioral change).
- **Public Opinion** – Accumulation of individual opinions on an important matter in public debate affecting the lives of people.
- **Propaganda** – One-sided argument. The use of ideas, information or opinion for the purpose of furthering or hindering a cause or promoting or denigrating an idea.
- **Manipulation** – To control by skilled use; to influence shrewdly or deviously. To get into the one's mind.
- **Convince** – Change an attitude – for a longer period.
- **Persuade** – Change the audience's behavior or getting someone to do something – even for a short time.
- **Feature** – What comes with the package – characteristics.
- **Benefit** – How the audience perceives the feature.
- **Active Audience** – Interested.
- **Passive Audience** – Non-interested.

(from page 69)

- The results can be projected (reflection of opinions of universe or targeted audience) with a predetermined margin of error (the number of times, or likelihood, out of 100 that the results of the survey would fall within the same intervals. Plus or minus 3 means that three percentage points could be added or subtracted from the results. Example: Company A conducts a survey and determines that 68 percent of its customers are "Very Satisfied" overall. Generally speaking, if a similar survey were taken 100 times, 95 times out of 100 the results would show that anywhere from 65 percent to 71 percent of the customers are "Very Satisfied").

Types of Probability Samples:

- **Simple** – Sample resembles a lottery. Respondents are chosen from a "hat" or "box."
- **Stratified** – Sample is "tailored" to look like the target audience. If the survey's purpose is to determine the opinions of women 18 to 35, then only a scientific sampling of women 18 to 35 is drawn. It is also known as ***probability proportional to size*** because it puts the characteristics in the sample in the same proportion as they actually exist.
- **Systematic** – Sample uses lists and then draws every "nth" number on the list to put into the sample. **Formula**: Divide the sample size you want into the total number of names/numbers on the list. Between that number and the number one, choose a starting number by chance. That's your first respondent. Go every "nth" number from there (or allow a computer program or table of numbers to select respondents).
- **Area (cluster)** – Sample uses one of the other three methods to choose geographic sections of a community or subdivisions to get to a residential address on a street.

Non-probability – Each person in a universe (total population) is *not* given an equal chance of being included in the sample.
- Selection of sample is subjective and may not necessarily be by chance.
- Results cannot be projected to the universe (total population) with any known certainty.

Types of Non-probability Samples:

- **Purpose (Judgmental)** – Respondents are deliberately chosen by knowing the type of people they are or where they are located. (Example: Used in political polling of subjectively chosen polling places.)

- **Quota** – Selection of a group to be polled that matches the character-istics of the entire audience. (Example: Interviewers select respon-dents according to certain demographics such as age, gender, ethnic group, education, income, etc. If census data shows a universe [audi-ence being surveyed] has 57 percent women and 43 percent men, a quota sample would choose participants based on that data.)
- **Intercept** – Also known as *chunk*. Many times take place in shopping malls where interviewers stop passersby and ask for their cooperation.
- **Snowball sampling** – Also known as *chain sampling, chain-referral sampling, referral sampling* is a non-probability sampling technique where existing study subjects recruit future subjects from among their acquaintances usually by email or blast emails. Thus the sample group appears to grow like a rolling snowball. As the sample builds, enough data is gathered to be useful for research. As sample members are not selected scientifically, snowball samples are subject to biases. For example, people who have many friends are more likely to be recruited into the sample.

It is widely believed that it is impossible to make unbiased estimates from snowball samples, but a variation of *snowball sampling* called *respondent-driven sampling* has been shown to allow researchers to make limited unbiased estimates from snowball sam-ples under certain conditions. *Snowball sampling* and *respondent-driven sampling* also allow researchers to make estimates about the social network connecting the hidden population.

- **Volunteer** – Also known as *self-selected, convenience* or *casual survey*. Respondents volunteer themselves. The Internet, newspapers, radio and television stations, and magazines that encourage or allow listeners, viewers or readers to respond fall into this sampling technique.

Types of Informal Sampling

- **Newspaper and magazine articles** – Generally speaking, these could be news or feature stories. They could also be reports about other sci-entific research, which would make it secondary research for the read-er. Readers must be aware of agenda setting (see *The ABCs of Strategic Communication* – AuthorHouse).
- **Television and radio programs** – This would be similar to reading stories in newspapers and magazines.
- **Discussions with acquaintances** – An excellent method for gathering non-scientific data and general information on a topic.

PR Play 4-14
More Steps to Follow

1. List your needs (financial and personnel).
2. Get financial commitment to conduct the survey from start to finish.
3. Select the public that will be sampled and the actual names of people – if possible.
4. Design an easy-to-use format (research action) for the survey and compose the questions (research questions).
5. Refine your questions and adjust the format.
6. Train your interviewers (if you are conducting the survey in-house).
7. Adhere to guidelines to be certain that all steps of the survey project are completed on time.
8. Conduct the survey and prepare the responses for tabulation (Use *SPSS®* if possible).
9. Analyze the results.
10. Report your findings (with recommendations if requested).

- **Surfing the Internet** – A quick, easy and comfortable way to gather data whether scientific or not.
- **Observing public meetings** – Excellent method for feeling the non-scientific pulse of a universe.

There May Be Pitfalls

Conducting an opinion survey from start to finish sounds easier than it is. To achieve the kinds of results that you want takes many hours of hard work. And, no doubt, your superiors will want you to continue performing your other duties as well. You will have to be willing to work closely with other staff members of your company or organization and with staff members or outside vendors chosen to conduct the interviews. At times, you will probably ask yourself why you got involved in this kind of project in the first place.

But be assured, the feedback you have gathered from your audience or audiences should improve your total program – whether it be just public relations, marketing or total *integrated marketing communication*. The satisfaction of knowing this is what makes the advantages outweigh the pitfalls.

PR Play 4-15
Sample Size for Two Levels of Confidence
with Varying Degrees of Tolerance

Tolerance of Error In Percentages (+ or -)	95 Times in 100	99 Times in 100
0.5	38,400	66,000
0.7	19,592	33,673
1.0	9,600	16,500
1.5	4,267	7,333
2.0	2,400	4,125
2.5	1,536	2,640
3.0	1,005	1,833
3.5	784	1,347
4.0	600	1,031
4.5	474	815
5.0	384	660
6.0	267	458
7.0	196	337
8.0	150	288
9.0	119	204
10.0	96	165
15.0	45	74

Resources – Publications
• *A Hands-On Guide to School Program Evaluation*, Edward A. Brainard
• *Data Analysis for Comprehensive Schoolwide Improvement*, Victoria L. Bernhardt

- *How to Conduct Surveys: A Step-by-Step Guide,* Arlene Fink & Jacqueline Kosecoff
- *PACE: Polling Attitudes of Community on Education Manual,* Phi Delta Kappa International
- *School Climate: Measuring, Improving and Sustaining Healthy Environments Learning,* H.J. Freiberg (Ed.)

Resources – Websites

- Annenberg Institute for School Reform (www.annenberginstitute.org)
- Center for the Study of Testing, Evaluation and Education Policy (www.bc.edu/research/csteep)
- Gallup Organization (www.gallup.com)
- Harris Interactive (www.harrisinteractive.com)
- Monitoring the Future (www.monitoringthefuture.org)
- National Center for Educational Statistics (www.nces.ed.gov)
- Phi Delta Kappa (www.pdkintl.org)
- U.S. Department of Health and Human Services (www.os.dhhs.gov)
- Cracked Egg (Persuasion) Model (Chapter 2)

Research Terms Every Practitioner Should Know

active audience – Interested, already sold, but seeking more information.

anecdotal – Based on personal observation, case study reports or random investigations rather than systematic/chance scientific evaluation. Results are considered *anecdotal evidence.*

attitude – Predisposition to act (inner feeling).

banner – A question or demographic factor used as the basis for cross-tabulation.

before and after survey – Survey is taken of the target audience before communication is put into effect and repeated after the audience has been exposed to the communication. *Before* establishes the baseline.

benchmark survey – Same as before and after survey (above).

benefit – How the audience perceives the feature.

casual survey – Also known as *self-selected survey.* Respondents volunteer themselves. The Internet, newspapers, radio and television stations, and magazines that encourage or allow listeners, viewers or readers to respond fall into this sampling technique.

chance survey – A sample where each member of the population has an equal chance of being chosen. Also referred to as a scientific random sample; or simple random sample.

classification or demographic question – Survey question designed to generate data about the respondent such as age, education, income and gender.

closed-end or forced-choice question – Survey question in which only predetermined options are accepted as responses from respondents.

cluster sample – A form of probability (scientific or chance) sample where respondents are drawn from a random sample of mutually exclusive groups (usually geographic areas) within a total population – also called an area sample. Identifying these groups in advance could save costs.

communication audit – A complete analysis of an organization's communication – internal and external – designed to reveal how an organization wants to be perceived by designated publics, what it is doing to foster that perception and how it is, in fact, perceived.

confidence level-95 in 100 – In an infinite number of similarly designed and executed surveys, the percentage results would fall within a given margin of error in 95 percent of these surveys.

content analysis – Study of publications, print and electronic media reports, speeches and letters to measure, codify, analyze and/or evaluate the coverage of an organization, its people and its activities. In a strict sense, content analysis uses a rigorous, statistical methodology. In many cases it is less formally structured.

convince – Change an attitude for a longer period.

cross-tabulation – Statistical analysis of subset of data created from within the data. For example, how did all the men in the sample respond to the question?

database retrieval systems – Information compiled from print, broadcast and other sources stored in computer memories and made available on-line for random access and retrieval and subsequent print-outs.

demographics – The vital statistics about the human population, its distribution and its characteristics (age, gender, income, education, etc.). Used for audience segmentation and fragmentation.

depth interviews – One-on-one interviews with key respondents that are generally conducted using a prepared discussion guide rather than a questionnaire.

dichotomous question (simple) – Survey question that provides two contradictory response options. Choices can include yes or no, approve or disapprove, like and dislike.

empirical research – Any activity that uses direct or indirect observation or experiment to gather information. Empirical data can be analyzed quantitatively and qualitatively.

external factors – Elements of the problem situation that are found outside the organization (often addressed in the limitations section of a project).

feature – Prominent or distinctive characteristics of a product's use, construction or design. Also referred to as attributes.

focus group interviews – A qualitative public relations/marketing research technique where an independent trained moderator or facilitator interviews (leads discussion of) a small group of consumers (six to 10) from the target audience in an informal setting to get a reaction to an issue, new product, brand name, advertising or other communication efforts. Also referred to as a *Customer Panel*.

formal, scientific or quantitative research methods – Rigorous use of the principles of scientific investigation such as the rules of empirical observation, random sampling in surveys, comparison of results against statistical standards and provision for replication of results. Research that provides objective and systematic data gathered from scientifically representative samples (employs the scientific method).

formative research – Usually not scientific. Formative research such as focus groups and mall intercept interviews with consumers are used to help test messages and materials designed to motivate target audiences. Formative research is a critical step in crafting research questions and usually occurs before a program is designed and implemented.

geodemographics – A contraction of geography and demographics. A method of combining geographic and demographic variables. The demographics of individuals or groups who reside in the same geographic area or region.

identity – How an organization or firm wants to be perceived – what you are.

image – Much like reputation – how the public perceives an organization or firm. It is the opinion or concept of something that is held by the public and/or interpreted by the mass media.

impact evaluation – Determining to what extent a campaign informed, persuaded, influenced or changed public opinion and/or behavior in the desired direction.

informal methods – Exploratory research that is not gathered from scientifically representative samples. Includes personal contact, informants, community forums, advisory committees, field reports, and phone and mail analysis.

informal or non-scientific research – Investigation without use of the scientific method (usually undertaken as exploratory and/or preliminary to more rigorous methods).

intercept interview(s) – Random, but unscientific, consumer research method – often used at shopping malls and other areas (stadiums, college campuses, resorts) where large numbers of people congregate – where interviewers randomly stop passersby to ask questions and gather data. This method yields rich data on preferences, attitudes and needs – useful for screening a large number of concepts or issues quickly and at reasonable cost. *Intercept interviews* offer a quick, inexpensive method to pretest advertising campaign themes, headlines and value propositions.

intercept survey – Also known as *chunk survey*. Many times intercept surveys take place in shopping malls where interviewers stop passersby and ask for their cooperation.

internal factors – Perceptions and actions of key actors in the organization, structure and process of organizational units somehow related to the problem, and history of the organization's involvement.

judgmental or purposive sample – A sample based on the investigator's best judgment to determine what would be representative. Should be used only when the consequences of possible errors from bias would not be serious and when other sampling is impractical.

leading question – A question that is worded so as to lead a respondent to answer in a particular way. For example, "You don't like this competitive product, do you?"

Likert Scale – Response set that uses five options, generally verbs, responding to questions: *strongly agree/agree/neutral/disagree/strongly disagree* – measuring both quality and strength of responses.

mail survey – Research conducted by mailing questionnaires to the sample and tabulating the responses that are completed and mailed back.

manipulation – To control by skilled use. Getting into one's mind with persuasive, strategic messages. Sometimes considered shrewd or devious – but when messages are open, honest, through and valid, they are ethical.

margin of error – The range, plus or minus, within which results can be expected to vary with repeated random samplings, under exactly similar conditions. There is an inverse correlation between sample size and margin of error.

multiple choice question – Survey question that offers three or more alternatives. Often a three-point or five-point rating scale.

nth number of systematic sampling – A method of drawing a sample by dividing the sample size into the universe to obtain an interval to be used to select respondents. For example, if the universe were 1,000 and the sample size were 100 the interval would be 10. Consequently, every nth name from a directory could be the 9th, 19th, 29th, etc. A random method must be employed to select the starting point in the universe from which each nth name is to be drawn.

omnibus survey – Also called a piggyback survey or subscription study. A type of public relations or marketing research survey usually administered for one main organization, but may contain a question or questions from other firms or organizations for a fee. Some information, such as demographics and psychographics, may be shared. Organizations buy into other surveys either to save money or because they do not need a survey on their own. Omnibus surveys, like other polling, are commonly organized by a major professional marketing research company, where different cross sections of the community are interviewed by probability (scientific) sampling at regular intervals about attitudes and opinions toward issues, buying habits, product and brand preferences, etc. They are called Omnibus surveys because any marketer can join in for a fee to add questions.

open-ended question – Survey question that does not ask the respondent to select from given alternatives but instead allow answer in the respondent's own words. Answers are called verbatim.

opinion – Expression of attitude (behavioral change).

passive audience – Uninterested. Will usually rely on surrogates (stand-ins) to gather information.

personal interview – Face-to-face questioning of the respondent by the researcher. Once the most common surveying method.

persuade – Changing the audience's behavior or getting someone to do something – even for a short time.

population – The individuals whose opinions are sought in a survey. The population can be as broad as every adult in the United States or as focused as liberal Democrats who live in the Fifth Ward of Chicago and voted in the last election. The sample is drawn to reflect the population. Sometimes called the *universe*.

pretesting – A preliminary survey of a small sample to determine if the questionnaire is properly drawn.

primary research – New (original) research study. Research you do yourself.

problem statement – A brief summary of the problem written in present tense describing the situation and the general goal(s) of the program.

propaganda – One-sided argument. The use of ideas, information or opinion for the purpose of furthering or hindering a cause or promoting or denigrating an idea.

proportional sampling – A sampling method used to ensure that a survey contains representatives of each subset in the population being studied, according to the proportion of their representation in the universe. For example, if a certain population contains 53 percent women, a proportional sample would contain 53 percent women.

protocol – Sometimes referred to as research design. The controlling plan for a marketing research study where the methods and procedures for collecting and analyzing the information to be collected are specified. The plan of action follows a strict format to assure that objectives are met.

psychographics – Psychological characteristics many times determined by standardized tests. Used for audience segmentation and fragmentation. Any attributes relating to personality, values, attitudes, interests or lifestyles. They are also called IAO variables (for Interests, Attitudes and Opinions). Combined with *demographics* and *geodemographics*, *psychographics* play a key role in strategic planning.

public opinion – Accumulation of individual opinion on an important matter in public debate affecting the lives of people.

public relations audit – A research tool used specifically to describe, measure and assess an organization's public relations activities. Used to provide guidelines for future public relations programming. Can include public opinion surveys, content analysis, program evaluation and recommendations for the future.

push (survey) polling – Opinion surveys designed to provide information at the same time data is being gathered – communicates a message while asking a message. Information or leading questions could be manipulative and influence responses.

questionnaire – The introduction, explanation and questions posed – in person, on the phone or through the mail – by the researcher to the respondent.

random sample – A sample taken from any given population in which each person maintains an equal chance of being selected. This differs a bit from a scientific random sample in that a random sample may be taken from a predetermined audience such as students in a particular classroom or residents of a particular neighborhood. To be purely scientific, every member of the universe must have the exact same "chance" of being chosen as everyone else.

random-probability (scientific or chance) sample – A sample selected in such a manner that each element of the universe has an equal or known chance of being in the chosen sample.

readability tests – Tests designed to measure the grade level of reading skills a particular piece of writing demands from its audience.

readership (listenership or viewership) studies – Research conducted periodically to determine patterns of readership of print media and television.

reasonable certainty – Many times, referred to as *Reasonable Certainty* of "no harm." Something that appears clearly established or assured based on research and other investigation. Public relations counselors often rely on *Reasonable Certainty* before making recommendations.

reception analysis – Research that focuses on the way individuals draw conclusions or make meanings from strategic media messages. Reception analysis has some similarity with uses and gratifications research, but is much more likely to use an ethnographic approach involving in-depth interviews, participant observation, etc.

reference group – A group of people that a researcher uses as a guide for behavior in a certain situation. Also a group of people or an organization that an individual respects, identifies with or aspires to join. A group with which a person identifies in some way and whose opinions and experiences influence that person's behavior. For example, a basketball fan might buy a brand of athletic shoe worn by a favorite player.

reliability – The degree of accuracy with which data in a marketing research study has been collected. A reliable marketing research study should produce the same or similar results time after time.

representativeness – The degree to which a sample of an audience in a marketing research study represents the characteristics of the population as a whole.

research – A scientific systematic investigation to gather information about attitudes (predisposition to act or inner feelings) that form opinions (expression of the attitude) and establish facts. It is a search for knowledge. Research is conducted to improve the efficacy and/or effectancy of public relations and advertising. Seminal research is research never done before. Planned, carefully organized, sophisticated fact finding and listening to the opinions of others.

research design – Sometimes referred to as protocol. The controlling plan for a marketing research study where the methods and procedures for collecting and analyzing the information to be collected are specified.

research objectives – The purpose of a marketing research study. Many times, "purpose" becomes the first step in the Public Relations Process – even before research (research, planning, implementation, evaluation – known as PR-PIE when purpose is included).

researcher – The practitioner responsible for designing and carrying out the research project.

response bias – The inclination of respondents in a marketing research survey to give the answer they believe the interviewer wants to hear. Well-trained survey takers can recognize response bias and note it on the responses.

sample error – The degree to which the opinions of the sample may differ from the opinion of the entire population.

scientific random sample – A sample where each member of the population has an equal chance of being chosen. Also referred to as *Chance Survey* or *Simple Random Sample*. See *Random Sample*.

screening question – Questions designed to establish if the respondents have characteristics appropriate for the survey.

secondary research – The collection of marketing research data using previously published sources. Information or data available through another's research (U.S. Census Bureau; Gallup, a newspaper, etc.)

seminal research – Research never done before.

simple random (probability) sample – A method of selecting a subgroup from a population in which each member of the population has an equal chance of being selected. For example, drawing names from a hat.

situation analysis – The process of gathering and evaluating information on internal and external environments to assess a firm's current strengths, weaknesses, opportunities and threats (SWOT), and to guide its goals and objectives. It sets the table for public relations planners by detailing necessary information gathered through scientific and non-scientific research – identifying target audiences and determining the strategic direction the organization should take. Some public relations practitioners define situation analysis as a one-paragraph statement of the situation and refinement of problem definition based on research. A second paragraph identifies potential difficulties and related problems to be considered.

snowball sampling – A non-probability – nonscientific – method (especially on the Web) that relies on referrals from initial subjects to generate additional responses.

SPSS® – Statistical Package for the Social Sciences – released in its first version in the 1960s – is among the most widely used programs for statistical analysis in social science. It is also used by market researchers, health researchers, survey companies, government, education researchers and others.

stratified sampling – A form of probability sample where respondents are chosen from a random sample of homogeneous (similar) sub-groups (according to a common characteristic) where the total population has been divided. Creating a sample by sorting respondents into groups that have a common characteristic – demographics and psychographics – distinguishing them from other groups. Characteristics could include age, income, use of a product, business size or type of business.

structured research – Surveys that use a questionnaire as the basic tool.

survey research – A method of systematically probing public opinion and soliciting feedback.

systematic sample – In research, a sample drawn strictly according to a pre-determined formula – for example, every eighth, or 14th, or 24th, etc. name is chosen. This is a random approach. Computer software is now available to select scientific (chance) and other random samples.

tabulation – Organization of research data in tabular form (display of several items or records in rows and columns) showing responses to all questions – with correlations and cross references.

telephone survey – Research conducted by calling respondents by telephone and administering a survey instrument.

tracking (study) poll – A type of research study that (ideally) follows the same group of subjects – or a universe with similar demographics and psychographics – over an extended period (regular intervals) of time.

universe – In marketing research, the total group that a researcher wishes to study and measure. Also, all people who are prospects for a specific product or service. See *population*.

validity – In marketing research, obtaining the right and truthful information for the purposes of the study – the soundness and effectiveness of the survey instrument. Is the instrument measuring what it is supposed to measure? Is the sample being measured representative of the entire universe it is supposed to be reflecting?

EXERCISES

PR Challenge 4-1

Your CEO asks you to describe the difference between a random survey and a random scientific or chance survey. In 100 words or less, what would you say? Keep in mind cost, reliability and desired result.

PR Challenge 4-2

What are the advantages and disadvantages of employing intercept surveys?

PR Challenge 4-3

Are there any advantages to using omnibus surveys? How would you "sell" that concept to your CEO?

PR Challenge 4-4

Under what circumstances would you recommend *"snowball polling"* and why?

PR Challenge 4-5

If you want your focus panel to be a scientific study, how would you choose the participants?

CHAPTER 5
Basic Strategic (Persuasive) Writing Techniques

Our best communicators write and speak to be understood – to *ex*press, not to *im*press. Former presidents Ronald Reagan, John F. Kennedy and Franklin Delano Roosevelt adhered (whether subliminally or intentionally) to the adage: "simple; relevant; repetitious."

It was Kennedy who, on January 20, 1961, in his inaugural address, used the phrase, "Ask not what your country can do for you, ask what you can do for your country." And, Roosevelt, responding to the Japanese attack on Pearl Harbor, stated, "Today is a day that will live in infamy."

Reagan was the first president to incorporate the "transfer effect" – known as gallery tributes – into his speeches. For such important presentations as the State of the Union, he would invite "ordinary" citizens to sit in the gallery and cite them for one good deed or another. His purpose was to get the rest of us to relate to those people and their accomplishments in the most direct and simple terms.

To be a good writer takes practice. To become an excellent writer takes experience. Earning the reputation of being an excellent strategic (persuasive) writer takes both. Writing is *effective* only when the message transmitted has evoked the intended response from the receiver. The strategic communicator can strengthen his or her position by becoming the organization's writing resource – helping colleagues understand the value of writing copy that gets read and achieves its objectives.

Some Simple Rules
Rule number one: Always have at hand a dictionary and an *Associated Press Stylebook*.

Rule number two: Use them.

There are other valuable books, as well: *The New York Times Manual of Style and Usage, U.S. News & World Report Stylebook for Writers and Editors, The Elements of Style* by Strunk and White, and *The ABCs of Strategic Communication* (compiled and written by this book's author). Keeping these books at your side or in your backpack or briefcase will demonstrate that you carry a well-equipped strategic writers' "toolbox."

While some might argue that strategic writers must embellish to persuade, look no further than the daily newspaper (traditional or online) to prove them wrong. A goal should be learning to make molehills from mountains rather than mountains out of molehills. Strategic writers are not creative writers. Strategic writers are not novelists. That doesn't preclude using dynamic, action verbs – words – that (in editors' terms) make a story move. Avoid the use of so-called "weasel" words. Think altitude and your copy will *move* and achieve its objective of changing behavior.

Strategic writers must be persuasive in crafting and delivering an organization's key message points (KMPs). The excellent ones are adept in preparing news releases (both print and electronic), media advisories, fact sheets, backgrounders, feature articles, photo captions, public service announcements, letters to the editor, op-ed pieces, pitch letters, position papers, speeches, copy for newsletters, brochures, annual reports, issue ads and obituaries. Preparing scripts for visual presentations could also be a responsibility.

All copy must be written in simple spoken English. There is no need to use a polysyllabic word that might not be quickly understood when a one-syllable word will do.

Writing for the electronic media – particularly broadcast media – is a bit different. After mastering the art of journalistic writing for print, it is easy to adapt to writing for broadcast. True strategic professionals include *The Associated Press Broadcast Stylebook* in their "toolbox."

No matter the media, strategic writers should follow NFL Films® founder Ed Sabol's communication credo:

• Tell me a fact and I'll learn.

• Tell me a truth and I'll believe.

• But tell me a story and it will live in my heart forever.

PR Play 5-1
Rules Followed By The Best Writers

Those who use effective communication techniques will stress these *20 Rules for Good Writing* from the Writers Digest School:

1. Prefer the plain word to the fancy.
2. Prefer the familiar word to the unfamiliar.
3. Prefer the Saxon (more simple) word to the Roman (Latin derivation).
4. Prefer nouns and verbs to adjectives and adverbs.
5. Prefer picture nouns and action verbs.
6. Never use a long word when a short one will do as well.
7. Master the simple declarative sentence.
8. Prefer the simple sentence to the complicated.
9. Vary your sentence length.
10. Put the words you want to emphasize at the beginning or end of your sentence.
11. Use the active voice.
12. Put statements in a positive form.
13. Use short paragraphs.
14. Cut needless words, sentences and paragraphs.
15. Use plain, conversational language. Write like you talk.
16. Avoid imitation. Write in your natural style.
17. Write clearly.
18. Avoid gobbledygook and jargon.
19. Write to be understood, not to impress.
20. Revise and rewrite. Improvement is always possible.

Observers believe Sabol's advice is the success behind NFL Films®. The bottom line: outstanding strategic writers fully understand and pay attention to writing's fundamentals – persuasive and otherwise.

The 30-3-30 Principle

Copy should be prepared using the 30-3-30 principle. Is your copy aimed at the 30-second reader, the three-minute reader or the 30-minute reader? To be effective, write for all three audiences.

In simple terms, the 30-second reader relies on headlines or "blurbs" (pull quotes) to get their information. The three-minute reader is looking for the five W's (who, what, when, where and why) right off the top or

PR Play 5-2
*Helpful Hints for Broadcast Writing**

1. Write simple spoken English.
2. Never use a long word when a short one will do.
3. Try to keep one thought to a sentence.
4. Vary sentence length.
5. Use verbs. Do not drop verbs. Listeners need verbs.
6. Use picture nouns and action verbs.
7. Use the active voice.
8. Try to use the present or the present perfect tense.
9. Avoid using "today." Try to give *your* news story or release the most up-to-date peg you can.
10. Do **NOT** use synonyms – avoid synonyms. Synonyms can confuse the listener.
11. Do **NOT** use pronouns. Repeat proper names.
12. Avoid direct quotes – paraphrase (it's safer).
13. Always find a way of repeating location. Repeating the location toward the bottom of the story (or throughout video news release) is important to the listener or viewer.
14. Keep adjectives to a minimum. Adjectives tend to clutter speech and obscure the main line of the story.
15. Don't use appositions. (A construction in which a noun or noun phrase is placed with another as an explanatory equivalent – example: Litwin, the public relations specialist, was born in Philadelphia.) Please **DO NOT** use appositions. Most appositions are not natural to speech. Appositions often confuse the listener because he/she cannot see the necessary punctuation.
16. Use simple sentences. This would usually mean not starting a sentence with a prepositional phrase or a participle phrase.
17. Attribution. Almost always comes at the beginning of sentence...**NOT** at the end. (Example: Use – Company spokesperson Daniel O'Neill pointed out that this year's contributions will be the biggest ever. **Don't use** – "This year's contribution will be the biggest ever," said Daniel O'Neill, company spokesperson.
18. Place yourself in a story or two. If you are writing the newscast (or release) for air in Philadelphia and the story is about a college in Philadelphia, say...*Here in* Philadelphia.
19. When you write a broadcast release or a news story this way it must follow that it be delivered naturally – but with authority – and if delivered naturally, it means proper names may not always be emphasized – often the verb is emphasized – *natural* inflection.

*Portions adapted from "Writing - here at ABC"

in the lead paragraph. The 30-minute reader, a rarer breed today, will continue and read the so-called "back" (or remainder) of the story. Accomplish all three in your writing and it will be successful.

USA Today and *CBS Broadcasting's* all news radio stations are successful because they recognize their audiences are busy and may lack the attention span needed to read or listen to "reams" of material about the message they are trying to communicate. While their writing may be directed at those first two audiences, *USA Today*, especially, takes the 30-minute reader into consideration with its centerpiece (center package) stories in each section.

Characteristics of an Effective Message

A goal of effective strategic writing is persuading target audiences to take the action we planned – bring about an intended behavioral change. Even though one of our objectives might be influencing outcomes, our writing must be open, honest, thorough and valid (relevant). Our messages must be clear, concise, understandable, interesting, complete and relevant to our target audiences.

Clarity is defined as the message being received and interpreted by the target audience exactly as it was intended to be received. That is a real challenge even for the best writer.

To assure your copy evokes the intended response, make it lean, mean, punchy and stimulating – aimed at grabbing the reader. Effective strategic copy is methodical, calculated, compelling, engaging, pithy, appealing and dynamic. The best persuasive writers can do it *all*.

Be certain your writing:
- "Relates" the image, doesn't "sell" it
- Appeals to the target audience
- Answers: who, what, where, when, why and how
- Contains news
- Eliminates jargon
- Emphasizes key points
- Presents necessary background information (doesn't assume anything)
- Contains complete information (for the 30-minute reader)
- Takes a friendly and positive approach
- Contains current information (not outdated)
- Can fulfill a request if one is being made
- Makes smooth transitions (a constant flow of ideas)

- Contains quotes (but must be accurate and attributed)
- Adheres to the adage of "better writing through self-editing" (think, write and rewrite)
- An effective message is:
  - timely
  - mistake free (no misspellings, uses proper punctuation, *The Associated Press Stylebook and Briefing on Media Law* style)
  - composed of short sentences and paragraphs to improve comprehension (Vary sentence length, about 17 words on the average, but maximize at 30 words.)
  - important (has significance and impact)
  - factual
  - sincere and authentic
  - consistent
  - appropriate (socially acceptable)
  - persuasive
  - carefully organized with a logical sequence
  - specific and concrete (not too general and abstract)
  - concise and to the point (avoid redundancy and irrelevancy, but a bit of repetition can't hurt especially for electronic media)
  - interesting and commands attention
  - objective and responsible (possesses credibility)
  - lively in style
  - readable (use the Gunning Fog Index or Flesch-Kincaid Formula available in Microsoft Word under tools)
- An effective message uses:

PR Play 5-3
Strategic writers "relate" the image, not "sell" it.

  - simple, easily understood language (clarity in writing – clear, calculating (measured tones), concise, complete, consistent, specific, simplistic – is vital) that is grammatically correct
  - words that evoke emotion
  - familiar, easily understood words
  - words with purpose
  - words that have clear meaning (avoids confusion and is not ambiguous)

Frank Grazian, former news editor at the *Asbury Park (N.J.) Press* and professor emeritus at Rowan (N.J.) University, teaches that vigorous writing demands active forceful verbs. He says they supply momentum that carries the thought in a sentence from beginning to end.

"Weak, colorless and passive verbs drain a sentence of its strength and motion. They function as parasites that feed upon the lifeblood of a thought and render it impotent."

According to Professor Grazian, to improve your writing, check your verbs first. Deleting verbs that slow down the pace of a sentence and substituting them with verbs that bring sentences to life can improve any piece of writing.

He suggests checking the verb force against five criteria:
1. Cut out unnecessary verbs.
   * *My father was a man who liked to read.* Simply put, it should read: *My father liked to read.*
2. Avoid passive voice – use active voice.
   * The fence *was jumped* by the horse. [passive]
   * The horse *jumped* the fence. [active]
   * The book *was written* by the author. [passive]
   * The author *wrote* the book. [active]
   * The wagon *was pulled* by the horse. [passive]
   * The horse *pulled* the wagon. [active]
3. Avoid linking verbs.
   * Rather than *Linda is a teacher at Cherry Hill High School* write *Linda teaches at Cherry Hill High School.*
   * Rather than *Nancy has two rare cookbooks* write *Nancy owns two rare cookbooks.*

The rewritten versions employ active verbs that add life to the original sentences.

4. Eliminate needless adverbs.
   * Adverbs modify or restrict the meanings of verbs. Adverbs tend to reduce the energy of verbs and slow down the entire sentence.
     – Rather than *A writer's sentence should move smoothly* write *A writer's sentences should flow.*
     – Rather than *The tennis players rested momentarily* write *The tennis players paused.*

PR Play 5-4
Grazian's Verb Checklist

Circle every verb in your piece of writing. Then do the following things in the order listed:

1. Cut out unnecessary verbs:
   - Decide which are the main and secondary verbs in each sentence.
   - Watch for main verbs disguised as secondary verbs.
   - Look especially for verbs preceded by one of the following words:
     - that
     - who
     - which
     - it (followed by is or was)
     - there (followed by is, are or were)
   - Eliminate as many secondary verbs as possible.
2. Avoid the passive voice:
   - Strive to keep 80 per cent of your verbs in the active voice.
3. Avoid linking verbs:
   - Look for all forms of the verbs *to be* and *to have* and for verbs such as *seem*, *look* and *get*.
   - Permit no more than 30 percent of your verbs to be linking verbs.
4. Eliminate needless adverbs:
   - Look for words ending in *ly* that appear near your verbs.
   - Check for adverbs that are superfluous and eliminate them.
   - Eliminate as many other adverbs as possible by searching for verbs that can stand alone.
5. Use dynamic verbs:
   - Recheck each active verb to make certain it is the most dynamic verb you can employ.
   - Find a synonym that conveys the meaning with greater vigor.
   - Watch for weak verbs followed by nouns that should be changed to a verb.

PR Play 5-5

"Write your first draft from your heart. Write your second draft from the head...then polish it."

David Trottier – "The Screenwriting Center"

PR Play 5-6
Grazian's Noun Checklist

1. Eliminate nouns with complex endings.
   - Look for nouns that end in *tion, tive, ability, ment, able, ness, ance.*
   - Change them to verbs, phrases or clauses.
2. Change general nouns into specific nouns.
   - Never use a noun referring to an entire group when you should use one pertaining to a member of that group.
   - Talk about *he* or *she* rather than *them.*
3. Change non-visual nouns into visual nouns.
   - Get rid of those abstract nouns and replace them with nouns that your reader can picture.
4. Look for nouns that can be changed into verb forms.
5. Eliminate weak adjectives.
   - Look for words preceding nouns.
   - Replace vague adjectives with precise adjectives.
   - Eliminate other adjectives by finding nouns that can stand alone.
6. Eliminate needless adverbs modifying adjectives.
   - Seek out the main offenders: very, quite, rather.
   - Eliminate them by using nouns that can stand alone.

    – Rather than *Alana soaked the sponge thoroughly* write *Alana saturated the sponge.*

- There are times when adverbs are not necessary. For example, the adverb *closely* in the sentence "Aidan clung *closely* to his mother" overworks the verb "clung" which means adhered closely.

5. Use dynamic verbs, not the first one that comes to mind.
   - Rather than *walk* try *trudge, step, stride* or *march.*
   - Rather than *use* try *employ, apply, wield* or *handle.*

PR Play 5-7

Publications and Other "Products" Commonly Produced By Strategic Communicators

- news releases (both print and electronic)
- media advisories (media alerts; news and photo memo; invitation to cover)
- fact sheets
- histories
- backgrounders
- feature articles
- photo captions
- public service announcements (PSAs)
- letters to the editor
- op-eds
- pitch letters
- position papers
- counseling papers
- newsletter copy (newsletters)
- brochures
- annual reports
- issue ads
- obituaries
- visual presentations
- speeches (Chapter 13)

Crafting News Releases

Like all copy produced by the strategic writing specialist, news releases should be well written and error free. News releases are the backbone of a media kit. They must be mechanically sound, logically organized and credible. And they must also adhere to the accepted format. A well written news release is not unlike an "executive summary." With minor variations, follow these suggestions for **news releases for the print media**:

- Use company or organization letterhead (8½ x 11) – even if the release is being sent electronically. Your letterhead is *your* brand. If emailing, send the release both as an inline attachment (within the body of the email) and as a regular attachment (Word document), which could be downloaded.
- Include the name, phone numbers and email of a contact person.

- Put the date sent (March 10, 2014) with the release date below it (for example, For Release: Thursday, March 20, 2014 or it might read For Release: Upon Receipt).
- Assign a number to it for easy reference (Release No. 2014-36).
- Headline. (There is no consensus on whether editors like headlines suggested by the release writer – some do, some don't.)
- Use a slug (one-, two- or three-word summary of story for quick identification by editors and reporters).
- Datelines are optional (see *Associated Press Stylebook*).
- Restrict copy to no more than two pages (typed or word processed), double-spaced (about 250 words per page). For traditional newspapers, 250 words equals approximately six column inches. In broadcast, 150 words equals about 60 seconds of air time. Some strategic writers single space their releases. They would contain about 500 words or approximately 12 column inches of editorial copy. Whichever format is adapted, maintain consistency.
- Most times, use the "inverted pyramid" style. (According to Ken Blake, Ph.D. of Middle Tennessee State University, "To understand what the 'inverted pyramid' means, picture an upside-down triangle – one with the narrow tip pointing downward and the broad base on top. The broad base represents the most newsworthy information in the news story, and the narrow tip represents the least newsworthy information in the news story. When you write a story in inverted pyramid format, you put the most newsworthy information at the beginning of the story and the least newsworthy information at the end.") Journalists and strategic writers are moving away from using the "inverted pyramid."
- Do not split paragraphs at the bottom of a page or carry an incomplete sentence to another page.
- Do not hyphenate words at the end of a typed line (most computer programs will take care of this for you).
- If the story contains more than one page, print **MORE** at the bottom of each *non*final page (just below the completed paragraph).
- At the top of each succeeding page (remember, try to complete your story in two pages), type the slug on the far left followed by the phrase *page 1 of 2* (*page 2 of 2*, etc.), *add 1* or *page 2*. If you happen to go to a third page, it would read *the slug/page 3 of 3 or add 2,* or *page 3*. (Many editors prefer *page 1 of 3* format.)
- At the end of the release, type **30**, ### (use three hash marks) or **end**.

PR Play 5-8
Preparing Your News Release

What's unique? What makes your event stand out? This is the hook that will catch an editor's eye. Keep the reader in mind: What does he/she need to know? Then use that theme in the narrative.

Put it in writing: Typed or typeset, please, double-space. Email is preferred. Always use your organization's letterhead. Write the release so it's clear in the first paragraph what's happening. Give information about the five W's and one H – who, what, where, when, why and how – by the third paragraph. Try not to exceed one page. Use upper-and lower-case letters. Explain all acronyms.

Detail, detail, detail: Provide backup materials. For a speaker, provide a resume. Give directions to the event. Don't forget rain-date information. Double-check all facts in your release – spellings of names and places, dates, times, numbers, etc.

Think like an editor or reader: Always include a contact person's name, day, evening and cell phone numbers and email address. Also give a phone number at the event. A phone ringing in a closed office does no one any good. This information is critically important for evening, weekend or holiday events.

Get the reader involved: Is the contact phone number for the editor the same one for readers who want more information? If not, please provide it. Also helpful: an appropriate Web page and email address. Consider who will get the calls – will the contact person expect them? Get permission before giving home or cell phone numbers.

Listing Events

How to submit: The *Courier-Post* searchable Events Finder Calendar, available through www.cpsj.com, provides a direct route to our online and print calendars. Look for the calendar icon on the right side of the website and click on "Submit Event." Fill out the form and your listing will be posted as soon as the next day. If you want your listing to get into print, submit it two weeks in advance.

cont.

PR Play 5-8 continued
Submitting Photos

How to take the image: Facial photos have the best chance of being published. Group photos, check-passing and hand-shaking images are less likely to be used. Be sure to accurately identify people in the photos – double-check the spelling. To take the image, fill the lens by just shooting the head and shoulders of the subject. Avoid having something above someone. The object will look like it's coming out of the subject's head.

Email it: In the email's subject field, give a brief description about the image, such as the event's title. Include all caption information, including a call-back number and name.

Technical details: Images should be at least 200 dpi (dots per square inch) resolution and compressed in a .JPEG file.

Avoid These Pitfalls

- Don't expect your release to be printed as submitted. We will edit for grammar, punctuation, spelling, libel, style and brevity.

- We get many requests to cover events. We are more likely to cover an event if we receive notice well in advance and the notice indicates the significance of the event to our readers.

- Don't be upset if we can't cover your event. We have compiled a list of readers' top interests that helps us prioritize. We particularly look for events that reflect diversity and that connect to readers' lives. Please let us know about your next event.

- Don't forget to keep a copy of the release for your records.

After Publication

If an error is published, immediately notify the appropriate editor.

Courier-Post – Camden, N.J.

- Print only on one side. (News people don't usually look on the back of a sheet of paper. If your release is being sent electronically, this is not an issue.)
- Do not staple multiple-page releases (if mailed or hand delivered).
- Releases must be readable and legible (no script or italics fonts) – Times Roman, Univers and Arial are good fonts for news releases.
- Releases should be snail (regular) mailed, emailed (in Word), faxed (nearly extinct) or delivered in some other manner one week prior to the event. This gives the editor ample time to plan. (The same holds true for a *Media Advisory* or an *Invitation To Cover*.)
- Check with each newspaper, radio and TV station in your market to determine how each prefers to receive releases, media advisories, etc. (regular mail, email with attachment or as part of a regular email).

A practitioner who has ample time to write releases for the *electronic* media (see Broadcast News Writing later in *this* chapter) as well as *print* should follow the above mechanics for *broadcast writing*, plus:
- Try to keep it to one page. Radio and TV stations will carry the story as a short (a 15- to 30-second story read by the anchor) unless they choose to send a reporter or do a phone interview. (75 words equal 30 seconds.)

PR Play 5-9
Common News Release Errors

- Improper formatting
- Failure to *slug* the release
- Putting *boilerplate* information in first paragraph rather than last graph (Always put *boilerplate* in last graph above the 30 or ### (three hash marks). Below the "end" mark would make it an *"Editor's Note."* [see page 105])
- Spelling errors
- Grammatical errors
- Punctuation errors
- Sentence construction errors – incomplete sentences or run-on sentences
- Too wordy – boil writing down to the least common denominator
- Lack of attribution
- Lack of a local "hook"
- Incomplete contact information
- Not being available when the media needs verification

PR Play 5-10

Typical Format for a General News Release with Explanations

Today's Date: Sept. 3, 2013
Release No. 2013-36

Contact: M. Larry Litwin, APR, Fellow PRSA
856-555-1212 (Office)
856-555-1414 (Home)
856-555-1515 (Cell)
larry@larrylitwin.com
www.larrylitwin.com
Release Date: At once

Rules for Formatting News Release

(SAMPLE NEWS RELEASE/page 1 of 3)

GLASSBORO, N.J. – This is an example of what news editors look for when they receive professionally crafted news releases. They should be typed and printed on 8½ x 11 paper (or sent as email inline attachments and/or email attachments). Never print releases on both sides of the paper. They should be sent to the appropriate reporter, editor or news director via regular mail, fax or email, depending on the recipient's preference. If the recipient is facing a deadline, choose email or hand deliver to expedite the process. Many in the media suggest a follow-up call to assure your release has gotten to its destination. Do not pressure the reporter or editor. Ask simply, "Do you have any questions about the news release I sent to you?"

SLUG: A one-, two- or three-word label used to identify a story for easy reference. The "slug" is also used for releases that go beyond one page. It should be included on the top of page 2, etc. at the upper left (slug/page 2 of 2, add 1 or page 2). The slug on this release is: SAMPLE NEWS RELEASE/page 1 of 3 and may be in parentheses.

DATELINE: The point of origin of a news story. It may contain the date the release was written/sent rather than on top above **Release No. (N** may be upper or lower case) A **DATELINE** is directly under the slug.

CONTACT IDENTIFICATION: The name, address and phone number of the source (organization sending release) should appear at the upper left. The release should also include the name, phone numbers and email of the contact person for more information. If company letterhead is used, contact information can be adjusted accordingly.

cont.

- MORE -

PR Play 5-10 continued

(SAMPLE NEWS RELEASE/page 2 of 3)

RELEASE DATE: The earliest date a release may be used. Most releases should be for at once or immediate. If not immediate, stipulate *Hold for release* or *Embargoed until Day*, *Date* and *Time*.

MARGINS: Use wider than normal margins. Most releases are double-spaced. However, the federal government single-spaces its releases, but double spaces between paragraphs. Double space between *Release Date* and the suggested *Headline*.

HEADLINES: While many editors and news directors prefer no suggested headline, a headline such as the one above, helps provide a brief description of a release's contents. It is longer than the slug.

LENGTH: Try to keep news releases to one page, about 250 words. Use the "better writing through self-editing" principle. If your release goes onto a second page, never carry a paragraph from the bottom of one page to another. Under the last paragraph on a page, type the word **MORE** to indicate the release continues on the next page. On the top of page 2 type: Slug/page 2 of 2, add 1 or page 2 (see above).

STYLE: The easiest and most popular lead for a news release is the summary lead (who, what, when, where, why or event, date, time, place). To assure your copy evokes the intended response, make it lean, mean, punchy and stimulating – aimed at grabbing the reader. Most newspapers prefer releases be written in *Associated Press Style*.

DOUBLE CHECK: Never trust your computer's spell check. Make sure your spelling and grammar are 100 percent correct. Proofread every original three times – once for content, once for spelling and once for grammar, syntax and punctuation. If your copy needs approval, get it signed or initialed. Quotes should be cleared with your sources.

END MARK: A code, such as "30" or ### (three hash marks) or end – used to signify the end of a release (so the editor or reporter doesn't look for another page.)

- MORE -

cont.

PR Play 5-10 continued

(SAMPLE NEWS RELEASE/page 3 of 3)

BOILERPLATE: A short piece of text, usually no more than a single short paragraph, describing a company, person, product, service or event. It is standard wording about an organization that usually appears near the end of organization- or company-issued news releases and always above the End Mark (30 or hashmarks). Anything below the End Mark is not considered part of the release. Here is a sample boilerplate:

The Atlantic City Convention & Visitors Authority serves as the destination's principal marketing arm, stimulating economic growth through convention, business and leisure tourism development. The Authority oversees the management of the Atlantic City Convention Center and Boardwalk Hall on behalf of its parent agency, the New Jersey Sports and Exposition Authority.

###

(EDITOR'S NOTE: Almost always goes below *End Mark* (30 or three hash marks). Contains extra information to guide an editor or a brief message. For example, this book's author would include in an editor's note to its readers: "Be sensitive to deadlines, know the definition of news, make certain your release has a strong lead and a 'hook,' is timely, relevant to readers and is factually correct. Be available for that all important fact-checking [verification] phone call.")

PR Play 5-11
Inverted Pyramid Style

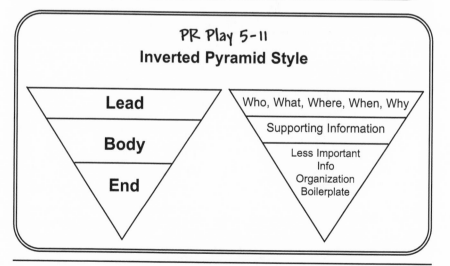

Lead	Who, What, Where, When, Why
Body	Supporting Information / Less Important Info
End	Organization / Boilerplate

PR Play 5-12
Sample Print Release

Burwyn **b** **Associates**

P.O. Box 692, Cherry Hill, NJ 08003/609-555-1212/www.larrylitwin.com

Sept. 9, 2013
Release no. 36

For information call: Larry Litwin at 515-555-5555
larry@burwyn.com
Release: Upon Receipt

FAIRFIELD UNIVERSITY HOSTS FIRST BLOOD DRIVE

(FIRST BLOOD DRIVE)

FAIRFIELD---Fairfield University is sponsoring its first-ever Green Cross blood drive on Monday, Sept. 23 from 9 a.m. to 6 p.m. in Roberts Gymnasium on the campus.

"Our town is in desperate need of several types of blood, not only because of the current shortage, but on a regular basis," states Millard G. Roberts, university president. "It is our obligation to get involved with the Green Cross and with local residents in sponsoring such events as a blood drive."

Donors must be 18-years-old to give blood. However, 16 and 17-year-olds may donate only if they have a letter signed by their parent. As an incentive to reach its 50-pint goal, donuts and beverages will be served. The University is giving donors a gym bag carrying the logos of the Green Cross, Fairfield University and a local sports shop. McDonald's will give each donor a coupon good for one Happy Meal. And, each will get two free tickets to watch Fairfield's Class A Falcons play baseball.

Anyone with questions or wanting more information may call the University's information office at 515-555-5555 or visit www.fairfieldu.edu.

###

Communications Specialists

PR Play 5-13
Sample Radio/TV Release

Communications Specialists

Burwyn
b
Associates

P.O. Box 692, Cherry Hill, NJ 08003/609-555-1212/www.larrylitwin.com

Sept. 9, 2013
Release no. 36

For information call: Larry Litwin at 515-555-5555
larry@burwyn.com
Release: Upon Receipt

FAIRFIELD UNIVERSITY HOSTS FIRST BLOOD DRIVE

(FIRST BLOOD DRIVE)

FAIRFIELD---Fairfield University is sponsoring its first-ever Green Cross blood drive on Monday, Sept. 23rd from 9 a.m. to 6 p.m. in Roberts Gymnasium on the campus.

University president, Millard G. Roberts says the town is in desperate need of several types of blood, not only because of the current shortage, but also on a regular basis. He states it is everyone's obligation to get involved with the Green Cross and with local residents in sponsoring such events as a blood drive.

Donors must be 18-years-old to give blood. However, 16 and 17-year-olds may donate if they have a letter signed by their parent. As an incentive to reach its 50-pint goal, donuts and beverages will be served. The University is giving donors a gym bag carrying the logos of the Green Cross, Fairfield University and a local sports shop. McDonald's will give each donor a coupon good for one Happy Meal. Donors will also be given two free tickets to watch Fairfield's Class A Falcons play baseball.

Anyone with questions or wanting more information may call the University's information office at 515-555-5555 or visit www.fairfieldu.edu.

###

PR Play 5-14
Social Media Release Template

SOCIAL MEDIA NEWS RELEASE TEMPLATE, VERSION 1.5

http://www.company.com/socialmedianewsroom/todaysnews

| CONTACT INFORMATION: | Client Contact Phone #/Skype Email Blog Website | Spokesperson Phone #/Skype Email Blog | Agency Contact Phone #/Skype Email |

NEWS RELEASE HEADLINE
Subhead

CORE NEWS FACTS
- Bullet-points or narrative

LINK & RSS FEED TO PURPOSE-BUILT DEL.ICIO.US PAGE
The del.icio.us page offers hyperlinks (and annotation in "Notes" field) to relevant content sources, providing context and on-going updates.

PRE-APPROVED QUOTES FROM CORPORATE EXECUTIVES, ANALYSTS, CUSTOMERS AND/OR PARTNERS
Recommendation: up to 2 quotes per contact. Be prepared to offer additional quotes to content publishers who desire exclusive info.

"3 LINKS THAT MATTER" (OPTIONAL)
Provide more info without overwhelming the reader. Links should highlight relevant data that add context to the news (e.g., blog posts, white papers). A URL "snipping" service like TinyURL is recommended.

BOILERPLATE STATEMENTS

RSS Feed to Corporate News Releases

OPML Feed to Corporate Blogs

"SHARE THIS"
Universal bookmark widget

"SPHERE IT"
Context related web search

TECHNORATI TAGS

MODERATED COMMENTS
Offer RSS and email update options

Type your comment here...

TRACKBACKS/ BLOGS THAT LINK TO THIS NEWS

SHIFT communications

PHOTO
e.g., product picture, executive headshot, etc.

MP3 FILE OR PODCAST LINK
e.g., sound bytes by various stakeholders

GRAPHIC
e.g., product schematics; market size graphs, logos

VIDEO
e.g., CEO's view of the news, brief product demo

PR Play 5-15
News Release Checklist

1. Is the lead direct and to the point? Does it contain the most important and most interesting aspects of the story?
2. Has the local angle been emphasized?
3. Have who, what, when, where and why been answered in the first few paragraphs?
4. Are sentences short and concise? Paragraphs short? Words common and concrete?
5. Has editorial comment been placed in quotation marks and attributed to the appropriate person?
6. Are quotations natural? That is, do they sound as though they could have been spoken?
7. Has newspaper style (AP or other) been followed faithfully throughout the release?
8. Are spelling, grammar, syntax and punctuation correct?
9. Have all statements of fact been double-checked for accuracy (fact checked and back checked)?
10. Has the release been properly prepared, typed and double-spaced?
11. Is inverted pyramid being used?
12. Have you thoroughly researched your subject? Do you understand its complexities and the precise meanings of the words and terms you are using?
13. Does your writing stay within the range of your knowledge?
14. Have you told readers only as much as they need to know to understand the point?
15. Have you used plain English as much as possible and avoided jargon?
16. Have you substituted common words for technical terms without losing meaning?
17. Are all technical terms which could not be avoided fully explained?
18. Has the proper format been used? That is:
    - Are contact names, phone numbers, fax numbers, email address, etc. for further information included?
    - Is the release dated? Is release time indicated? (Release number if used)
    - Headline
    - Slug (on page one and all other pages)
    - Dateline
    - No hyphenated words at end of typed line
    - No paragraphs carried from the bottom of one page to another
    - (MORE) on the bottom of page before a jump
    - Slug on top left of pages two, three, etc.
    - - 30 -, ### or end after the final paragraph to signify the end of the release
    - If mailed in hard copy, do not staple multi-page releases

    # # #

- Do not use quotes. Paraphrase, instead.
- When paraphrasing, place the attribution before the phrase. (After winning the British Open, Tiger Woods said it was the greatest day of his life. In print, it would be written *"It was the greatest day of my life," Tiger Woods said, after winning the British Open*).
- Type in upper and lower case (14 or 16 point type). The days of typing in all CAPS for electronic media are gone.

Crafting Media Advisories

Media Advisories are sometimes referred to as *Media Alerts*, *News and Photo Memos* or *Invitations To Cover* (I-2-C). The recommendation is that the *Media Alert* be written first. It establishes the five W's and – with the addition of a few quotes and narrative writing – transitions into the *news release*.

With minor variations, follow these suggestions for preparing *Media Advisories*, *Media Alerts*, *News and Photo Memos*, and *I-2-Cs* (for the most part, they are synonymous) that will persuade the media to bring their cameras and cover *your* event:

- Use company or organization letterhead (8½ x 11).
- Include the name, phone numbers and email of a contact person.
- Put the date sent (Sept. 1, 2013).
- Use either of the following formats:
  - Event
  - Date
  - Time
  - Place
  - Details (One paragraph summary, singled spaced. If a release has been written, refer to it either by slug or i.d. number if one has been assigned.)
  - Directions

  or

  - What
  - Who
  - When
  - Where
  - Details
  - Directions

PR Play 5-16

Contact: Nicole Galvin, Director of Communication
Phone: 555-555-1212
Fax: 555-555-1414
Cell: 555-555-1616
Email: galvin@njtown.net
or visit www.chplnj.org

MEDIA ALERT

FOR IMMEDIATE RELEASE: December 1, 2013

**Gov. Rebecca L. Timms to Lead Groundbreaking Ceremony
For New, State-Of-The-Art
Cherry Hill Public Library**

WHAT: Gov. Rebecca L. Timms will lead state, county and
                 local officials in groundbreaking ceremony for the
                 new Cherry Hill Public Library (CHPL).

                 Other dignitaries include:

                 • New Jersey Secretary of State Gloria Thomas
                 • New Jersey Community Affairs
                   Commissioner Susan Bass Levin
                 • Cherry Hill Mayor Linda Alexander
                 • Dr. Stephen C. Barbell, president of the
                   Cherry Hill Library Board of Trustees
                 • State legislators, Camden County freeholders,
                   Township council members and representatives
                   from community organizations

WHEN: Monday, Dec. 16, 2013
                 11:30 a.m.

WHERE: Next to current Cherry Hill Public Library
                 1100 Kings Highway North

                           ###

PR Play 5-17
Media Kit Contents

- Cover memo (list of media kit's contents)
- List of participants
- List of partnering or cooperating organizations
- Media Advisory/Media Alert/News and Photo Memo/Invitation to Cover (There is little difference. Choose one heading and stick with it for all of your media kits and media announcements.)
- News Releases
- Straight (hard stories)
- Features (soft stories)
- Biographies of speakers and key personnel
- Fact Sheets
- Backgrounder
  - Historical
  - Statistical
- Pictures and other graphics and visuals (suggested captions)

- Public Service Announcements (on CD or flash drive [USB])
- Position Paper(s)
- Op-Ed piece(s)
- Letter(s) to the Editor
- Texts of speeches
- Quote sheet
- Testimonials
- Fillers (newsy notes)
- Clip sheets (news clips)
- Logo repros or slicks – include on Flash (USB) drive, CD or DVD
- Collateral materials – Brochures/Publications
  - Annual reports
  - Magazines
  - Newsletters
  - Videos (DVD/Flash [USB] drive)
  - Free samples (if ethical)
  - Entire media kit should be duplicated on Flash (USB) drive, CD or DVD

With the advent of the Internet and other technology, the debate over media kits and their effectiveness has grown louder. Don't allow the cons to be a deterrent. Prepare a media kit for the Web just as you would for hard copy (Chapter 5). Those reporters interested in this resource would be encouraged to take advantage of it by downloading it from the website's "Newsroom." For those who attend the news conference, the media kit should contain a version on disk or Flash (USB) drive – known as electronic press kit (EPK) – as well as hard copies of such major components as news releases and fact sheets. For those organizations that really want to impress, think about distributing the kit on a low capacity, inexpensive "flash drive" that plugs into a computer's USB port.

PR Play 5-18
Before Crafting a Media Kit

1. Define the purpose for the media kit.
2. Identify the publics you need to reach.
3. Identify the media reaching those publics.
4. Determine which media will receive the kits.
5. Consider how each item in the media kit relates to the purpose of the kit.
6. Consider how the news media recipients will use each item in the kit.
7. For every item included in the kit, ask these questions:
   a. How do you expect the audience of each news medium to use the information (anticipation)?
   b. How does what you are providing each news medium convey that expectation to the medium's audience?
   c. What do you expect audiences of these media to do as a result of receiving this information? How do you measure that? (This question is significantly different from asking if the news media used the media kit or how much of it was used and when. That can be measured. It is the audience's response that you need to know to determine if the kit's contents were effective. This evaluation is part of a communication audit.)

Public Relations Writing: Form and Style –
Doug Newsom and Jim Haynes
M. Larry Litwin, APR, Fellow PRSA – Rowan (N.J.) University

Other Vehicles

Writers who have mastered the release and *Associated Press Stylebook* can write for anyone. PR Play 5-17 is a list of items reporters might find in the typical *media* kit.

Cover memos serve as a table of contents, but without page numbers. It lists the media kit's components in order. The *media kit* could also include news conference participants and an event's partnering organizations.

A copy of the *media alert* should be included near the front of the *media kit*. Why? Because many times the *event* is assigned to a reporter (or camera crew) who might be hearing about it for the first time.

Biographies are briefs about key personnel or news conference participants. They comprise a few short paragraphs about a person's career
and professional achievements – generally one or two pages:

- Create and distribute a "biographical data form" and conduct interviews to collect biographical information.
- Include information on current job duties, (present and past) work
experience, education and professional credentials, community and
charitable involvements, notable awards and honors. Personal information (family, home address, etc.) is usually *NOT* included.
- As you would in crafting a news release, use plain, simple language
but make it interesting. Lead with an interesting, distinctive or unusual point about the person's job or experience.

Fact sheets are a brief overview of a subject – generally one page.

Use headings much like *media alerts* with the headings running verti-
cally down the left side of the page with brief content to their right.
Headings could include:
- Company name
- Brief history (nut graph similar to a boilerplate)
- Location
- Principals/company officers
- Mission
- Products or services
- Clients
- Experience or brief history
- Contact information

Fact sheets could also be prepared in a "who, what, when, where, why"
format using headings, short phrases, key statistics, etc. (not written in
complete sentences).

Backgrounders (PR Play 5-19) are targeted at the media – the intermediary audience. They are a detailed history of an *event* (or impact of an
issue – although *issues* are better explained in a *position paper*) in a factual manner, rather than the company or organization's history. That
would be a separate document – *History* (pages 115 and 117).

An **oral (presentation) backgrounder** is an informal news briefing – many
times off the record – in which an organization official explains to reporters
the background of an action or policy soon to be announced (Chapter 9).

A written *backgrounder* includes developments in a factual manner – generally one to three pages in length, but absolutely no more than five pages. Journalists need the information as complete, yet written as succinctly, as possible. Use the following as a guideline to writing your *backgrounders*:

1. Outline main points of the backgrounder before writing.
2. What is its purpose?
3. How did it evolve?
4. Are there issues (advocacy) – positive or negative – which inspired the event?
5. Write in third person; use a hard-hitting, factual style; avoid use of opinions (they would be on quote sheet).
6. General information could include: audiences and their reactions; market effects; motivation for behavior; "environmental" influences; revenues expended; public opinion of event or similar events.

Before crafting the written *backgrounder*:

- Conduct thorough research to understand – and better explain – the evolution of the event.
- Outline main points of the backgrounder before writing.
- Begin with a sentence or two that identifies the issue/subject being explored, followed by an historical overview that traces the development of the issue/subject.
- Conclude with a sentence or two on the current significance and status of the issue.

In PR Play 5-19, the American Farm Bureau Federation covers the above information using its own format – which it consistently follows for all of its backgrounders.

A *history* is the evolution of a company or organization including key dates, key personnel and accomplishments (PR Play 5-20).

Features should be distributed the same as general news releases. Because *features* go to the media with no guarantee of usage, it might be a good idea to pitch them in advance. They can be time consuming to research and write.

Some *features* take extensive research. They might be about people, places or events. They should contain ample quotes that make the story more compelling by helping relate the topic to the audience.

PR Play 5-19
Example of Backgrounder from the American Farm Bureau Federation

MINIMUM WAGE

Issue: Should Congress raise the minimum wage?

Background: Prior to 1996, available evidence indicated that minimum wage increases caused unemployment among certain types of workers, particularly entry-level workers and teenagers who are not offered employment in favor of extending hours for existing workers and automating where possible. There has also been some indication that minimum wage increases lead to ripple wage inflation in higher wage brackets.

Legislative History: In 1996, Congress raised the federal minimum wage by 44 percent to $5.15 per hour. This was a 90-cent increase over a brief two-year period. In 1998, some in Congress proposed an additional increase to $6.15, just six months after the last increase was fully phased-in. In January 1999, the President called on Congress to raise the minimum wage to $6.15 in his State of the Union address. Several bills were introduced in the 106th Congress to increase the minimum wage. A number of amendments had been proposed on unrelated Senate legislation to increase the minimum wage to $6.25, in two 50-cent increments over a two-year period. Proposals to increase the minimum wage by a similar amount also figured prominently in House debates at the end of 1999 on tax relief legislation.

In October 1999 the House of Representatives passed legislation to increase the federal minimum wage by $1.00 over a two-year period. The Senate followed suit in March 2000 by passing a $1.00 three-year increase. The differences between these proposals remain unresolved. No final action was taken on these proposals.

Legislation has been introduced in the 107th Congress to raise the federal minimum wage to $6.15 per hour over three years, and to raise the minimum wage to $6.25 over two years. The proposal to raise the minimum wage to $6.15 per hour will be offered by Republicans and tied to various small-business tax breaks. Congress may consider these competing bills in the fall of 2001.

AFBF Policy: AFBF Policy specifically opposes increases in the minimum wage and any indexation of the minimum wage to inflation.

Action: AFBF will oppose any legislation to increase the minimum wage.

January 2002*

*(While this Backgrounder may be from 2002, it remains an excellent example – fewer than 350 words.)

PR Play 5-20
Example of a History

From Normal to Extraordinary:
A History of Rowan University

Rowan University has evolved from its humble beginning in 1923 as a normal school, with a mission to train teachers for South Jersey classrooms, to a comprehensive university with a strong regional reputation. In the early 1900s, many New Jersey teachers lacked proper training because of a shortage of schools in the state that provided training. To counter the trend, the state decided to build a two-year training school for teachers, known then as a normal school, in Southern New Jersey. The town of Glassboro was an early favorite because of its excellent rail system, harmonious blend of industry and agriculture, natural beauty and location in the heart of South Jersey. Several towns in South Jersey competed to be the site of the new normal school because of the economic benefit and prestige such an institution would bring. In 1917, to sway the decision in their favor, 107 residents of Glassboro raised more than $7,000 to purchase 25 acres, which they offered to the state for free if they selected Glassboro as the site.

The land tract included the Whitney mansion and carriage house. Before the purchase, the entire property belonged to the Whitney family, prominent owners of the Whitney Glass Works during the 1800s. This show of support, along with the site's natural beauty, convinced the selection committee that Glassboro was the perfect location.

In September 1923, Glassboro Normal School opened with 236 young women arriving by train to convene in the school's first building, now called Bunce Hall. Dr. Jerohn Savitz, the University's first president, expanded the curriculum as the training of teachers became more sophisticated. Despite the rigors of the depression, the program was expanded to four years in 1934, and in 1937 the school changed its name to New Jersey State Teachers College at Glassboro.

The College gained a national reputation as a leader in the field of reading education and physical therapy when it opened a clinic for children with reading disabilities in 1935, and added physical therapy for the handicapped in 1944. The College was one of the first in the country to recognize these needs and was in the forefront of the special education movement.

Rowan's second president, Dr. Edgar Bunce, created a junior college program in 1946 to serve World War II veterans taking advantage of the GI Bill.

cont.

PR Play 5-20 continued

In the 1950s, Dr. Thomas Robinson, the University's third president, expanded the curriculum, increased enrollment and added several buildings to the campus. In 1958, the school's name was changed to Glassboro State College to better reflect its mission.

The University received worldwide attention when it hosted a historic summit conference between President Lyndon Johnson and Soviet Premier Aleksei Kosygin. The conference was held in Hollybush, the former Whitney Mansion. The University was chosen because of its strategic location midway between Washington, D.C. and New York. The meetings between the two leaders June 23-25, 1967, led to a thaw in the Cold War and eased world tensions.

The University's fourth president, Dr. Mark Chamberlain, guided the College through its next phase of growth as enrollment doubled and the College became a multi-purpose institution. As new majors and a Business Administration Division were added, the four divisions grew into schools and a board of trustees was formed. With a 1978 Division III National Championship in baseball – the first of 11 national championships – the athletic program established itself as one of the premier athletic programs in the country.

The fifth president, Dr. Herman James, assumed the leadership of the College in 1984. Under his direction Rowan expanded by establishing the first doctorate program among the state's public institutions and adding the colleges of engineering and communication.

Dr. James was also responsible for the construction of a new $16.8 million library, an $8.6 million student recreation center, and the $30 million engineering school facility.

In July 1992, industrialist Henry Rowan and his wife, Betty, donated $100 million to the institution, then the largest gift ever given to a public college or university in the history of higher education. Later that year, the school changed its name to Rowan College of New Jersey. The College achieved university status in 1997 and changed its name to Rowan University.

Dr. Donald J. Farish was appointed the sixth president in July 1998. Under his leadership, the University implemented an aggressive improvement plan that addressed academic and student support initiatives as well as campus construction and renovation projects.

Major construction projects included the University townhouses; Science Hall; Education Hall; and the Samuel H. Jones Innovation Center, the first building of the South Jersey Technology Park at Rowan University.

During his tenure, the University also entered into a public-private partnership that led to the construction of Rowan Boulevard, a $300 million, mixed-use redevelopment project that links the campus with Glassboro's historic downtown. The corridor is home to more than 1,300 students and a Barnes & Noble collegiate superstore.

cont.

PR Play 5-20 continued

During this period, Cooper Medical School of Rowan University — the first new medical school in New Jersey in more than 30 years and the first-ever M.D.-granting four-year program in South Jersey — was developed in partnership with Cooper Health System.

The Board of Trustees named Dr. Ali Houshmand Rowan's seventh president president in June 2012.

Dr. Houshmand joined Rowan University as provost and senior vice president for Academic Affairs in September 2006. Early on, he established the College of Professional and Continuing Education (now the College of Graduate and Continuing Education), oversaw the restructuring of the summer school and graduate school and established the Office of Institutional Effectiveness and Planning.

The medical school welcomed its first class in summer 2012 into a new $139 million, six-story building near Cooper University Hospital in Camden.

Today, Rowan University includes Colleges of Business, Communication & Creative Arts, Education, Engineering, Humanities & Social Sciences, Performing Arts, and Science & Mathematics. Rowan also includes School of Biomedical Sciences, College of Graduate & Continuing Education and School of Medicine.

Rowan has attracted the attention of national organizations that evaluate colleges and universities. *U.S. News & World Report* ranks Rowan University in the "Top Tier" of Northern Regional Universities. Kaplan included the University in "The Unofficial, Biased Insider's Guide to the 320 Most Interesting Colleges." Also, Kiplinger's named Rowan University one of the "100 Best Buys in Public Colleges and Universities" and the Princeton Review included Rowan in the latest edition of "The Best Northeastern Colleges."

Rowan's approximate 15,000 students can select from among 80 undergraduate majors, 55 master's degree programs and a doctoral program in educational leadership. The University is one of only 56 institutions in the country with accredited programs in business, education, engineering and medicine.

From the modest normal school begun almost 90 years ago, Rowan University has become an extraordinary comprehensive institution that has improved the quality of life for the citizens of New Jersey and the surrounding states.

Features are usually prepared for newspapers and magazines, but don't hesitate to distribute them to radio and TV stations. They could encourage live or taped coverage.

Photo captions are the brief text under pictures – an explanation of what is in the picture. They use short, but full, descriptive copy to accompany a picture or illustration. *Captions* usually answer the five W's, but the key word is *brief*. Stand alone pictures *need photo captions*.

PR Play 5-21
Sample Letter to the Editor (Via *Courier-Post* website)

M. Larry Litwin, APR, Fellow PRSA
17 Pine Valley Road
Berlin, NJ 08009-9492
856-555-1212
larry@larrylitwin.com
www.larrylitwin.com

March 10, 2013

To the editor:

By its very nature, *public relations* is a term often used – seldom defined. In its broadest sense, *public relations* is "good work, publicly recognized." Public relations counselors realize it is much more than that. However, too many times, "good work" does go unrecognized.

Not in this instance. In the midst of catastrophe, John Firth, president of the company that owns the two Cherry Hill restaurants (Chili's and Porterhouse Steaks & Seafood) destroyed by fire early last Sunday morning proved employee worth – and he and Quality Dining, Inc. of Indiana should be publicly recognized.

Minutes after being awakened by the alarm company, Firth was on a plane heading to the site. By early afternoon he and his management team were well into their crisis plan.

By 10 p.m., less than 16 hours after the first alarm was struck, every one of the employees at the two restaurants that burned down had been placed in jobs at other area Chili's with no interruption in work and no interruption in pay.

Firth and Quality Dining should be the cover story for every entrepreneurial magazine. His actions are those of a true leader and Quality Dining is the benchmark for businesses – big and small. It is apparent, they live by the credo, "By putting your employees first, you are putting your customers first."

Sincerely,

M. Larry Litwin
M. Larry Litwin, APR, Fellow PRSA
Associate Professor – Public Relations/Advertising
Rowan University

PR Play 5-22
Sample Letter to the Editor

WHITE HOUSE
Washington, DC 20201

September 1, 2013

Editor
New York Post
1215 Park Avenue
New York, NY 10019

Dear Editor:

The White House is disappointed with your front-page story about President Clinton's chief political adviser, Dick Morris.

While Mr. Morris may have committed an indiscretion (and that has yet to be proven), he has assured us that in no way has he compromised the President, White House or most importantly, his country, which he is extremely proud of and proud to serve.

As of this writing, the accusations against Mr. Morris are only that, accusations. A woman, who by her own admission, is less than honorable, has made the alleged charges.

While we agree it is *The New York Post's* job to report the news, we believe it should be done in an objective and straightforward manner. We don't believe your paper took that high road on this story.

The White House staff, President Clinton and nearly all Americans believe in *first amendment* rights. However, *freedom of speech* (when it comes to straight news coverage) should not include innuendo and subtle editorializing.

As you know, President Clinton has already addressed the so-called "Dick Morris affair." If you would like to discuss this letter or the issue further, please contact me, or any member of my staff. We all stand ready to cooperate.

Sincerely,

Seth Adams

Seth Adams
Director
White House Communications Office

PR Play 5-23
Demand Attention in Your Cover Letter

These tips for your cover letter come from: www.allbusiness.com:
- Make yourself stand out. Get the competitive edge by writing a cover letter that focuses on your unique and exceptional qualities.
- Target the right person. Sending your letter to the proper person can make all the difference.
- Stay simple. Keep your cover letter brief. Never send a letter more than one page in length. Half a page is ideal. Be sure to use clear, professional language while steering away from buzz-words, acronyms, jargon or anything overly personal.
- Make it shine. The overall visual impression of your cover letter can be just as important as what is written in it.
- Be an attention getter. Don't waste your first paragraph by writing a dull introduction. It needs the same type of "hook" or lead one would use in writing a news release or feature.
- Cover letters (all business letters) must adhere to standard business letter format. Prospective employers will notice if the proper format is not used.

A *cutline* is much more brief. An example would be a few words under a "head shot" identifying the person by name and title. A *cutline* is sometimes called a *nameline* or an *underline*. Many times, *cutlines* accompany stories.

Public service announcements (PSAs) deal with public welfare issues and radio and TV stations usually run them free of charge (Chapter 10).

Letters to the editor can be a valuable public relations tool. They can be used to promote an issue, counter an editorial or take a stand. Because newspapers receive so many letters, a 250-word maximum can help get yours printed.

Pitch letters are appeals or pleas to an audience or a prospect. PR practitioners must employ their best persuasive skills to get the expected result. (See more on page 128.)

Job application cover letters are among the most important *pitch letters* written.

Among *media kit* components discussed in Chapter 6 are *position papers*, *op-eds* and *annual reports*.

Position papers are detailed statements on a question or questions at issue. They, too, must be supported by persuasive arguments (Chapter 6).

Speeches – either entire speech or a gist could be included in a *media kit*. (Chapter 11).

Newsletter copy is a combination of many aspects of strategic writing. It is suggested that once a style is developed it be strictly adhered to. *Newsletters* become "logo" pieces for firms and organizations. Consistency in both their physical layout (appearance) and writing style help it become instantly recognized. News and feature stories should be written in *Associated Press Style*.

Brochure copy can be and usually is less objective. Its purpose is to promote or persuade an audience to purchase a product or support a cause, program, issue or organization (Chapter 12). Again, it should be written in *Associated Press Style*.

Annual reports (Chapter 6) are financial reports required by the Securities and Exchange Commission for publicly held corporations. Many privately held companies and medical, charitable and educational institutions also print annual reports.

Although no rules call for the narrative in an *annual report* to be written in *Associated Press Style*, for consistency, it should be.

Issue ads (also called *advocacy ads*) are similar to *public service announcements* except that, because they are taking a stand, it may be more difficult to get "free" space in traditional newspapers or magazines. Many times, *non*-profits that take a strong stand may have to solicit corporate funding to get their message printed (unless they can afford to buy the space themselves). These are ads that attempt to persuade about an issue. Some visible examples are *pro life*; *pro choice*; *pro war* and *antiwar*.

Business memos are an integral part of every professional's life. Knowing the proper format helps organize the information and achieve the memo's purpose.

Purdue University's Online Writing Lab offers these "troubleshooting" tips: The heading segment follows this general format:
TO: (readers' names and job titles)
FROM: (your name and job title)

DATE: (complete and current date)
SUBJECT: (what the memo is about, highlighted in some way)

- Make sure you address the reader by his or her correct name and job title. You might call the company president "Amy" on the golf course or in an informal note, but "Amy Anderson, President" would be more appropriate for a formal memo.
- Be specific and concise in your subject line. For example, "Frustrations" as a subject line could mean anything from a production problem to a personal frustration. Instead use something like, "Providing laptops would eliminate students' frustrations."

Crafting the Pitch Letter

Whether you are pitching an *op-ed*, an event or requesting another organization's partnership or sponsorship, your pitch letter could be the so-called "deal breaker." It is the first thing that an editor or other decision maker sees and it could make or break your chances of getting your event covered, *op-ed* (Chapter 6) published or a major corporate sponsorship established. Make a good first impression! Here are some helpful tips:

- **Make it look professional:** This is representing you, remember?
- **Establish credibility:** Who are you? If you are pitching an *op-ed,* tell the editor exactly why you are qualified to write this *op-ed* or why it is that the organization you represent is qualified.
- **Keep it succinct:** Editors, news directors and CEOs are busy people. Include only the relevant information. If you are pitching an event, be certain to send a *media alert* to the same editor.
- **Explain why the issue or event is important:** Why would the readers of this newspaper or television viewers care about this issue? Why should the editor print it? Why should a major corporation support you and your event? In the most diplomatic terms, convince the editor or news director that he or she is missing something big if your *op-ed* doesn't go to print or your event doesn't get coverage – or a CEO that his or her company needs you as much as you need its financial support.
- **Find the right contact person:** Go straight to the source. Use the listings on a website to make sure your pitch goes to the decision maker and not to a gatekeeper.
- **Include contact information:** Include your address, phone number and email address.
- **Sign your letter:** Especially if you are sending hard copy.

PR Play 5-24
Sample Cover Letter No. 1

Nicole Galvin
4175 Edgewood Park
Glassboro, NJ 08028
732-555-5555
nikgalvin252525@rowan.com

June 24, 2013

Mrs. Kathy Rozanski
R. Grace Bagg Alumni Center
201 Mullica Hill Road
Glassboro, New Jersey 08028

Dear Kathy:

If your offer still stands, I would greatly appreciate the opportunity to be a candidate for the 2013-2014 Graduate Assistantship.

As you know, I have been a dependable student-worker and intern for the Alumni Association during my entire career at Rowan University. Today, I would like to further my education as well as my job.

It would be an advantage to hire me for the position because I already possess the skills that another candidate would have to learn. Some of my skills include knowing the alumni database (Millennium), taking phone registrations, using the mail-merge option in Microsoft Word, composing alumni booklets and assisting in the execution of young alumni events. Additionally, I have worked at several on-campus happenings such as Homecoming, Sports Hall of Fame, Comedy Night and class reunions.

After working in this office for four years, I feel like I am part of a family. Secretary Janice Brown once told me, "You are one of my favorite students. I treat you as if you were my own." It would be an honor to continue as a member of that very special family for one more year.

Thank you again for considering me. I can be reached at 732-555-5555 and nikgalvin252525@rowan.com.

I look forward to hearing from you soon!

Very truly yours,

Nicole Galvin

Nicole Galvin

Encl: Resume

cont.

PR Play 5-24 continued
Sample Cover Letter No. 2

Katie Guzperson
724 Elm Street
Fairfield, Iowa 52556
guzperson@iowatown.com

January 7, 2013

Ms. Stephanie Spagnola, Editor
ELLE Magazine
1926 Broadway
New York, NY 10019

Dear Ms. Spagnola:

I've been described as "mature beyond my years, articulate, loyal, possessing a passion for the profession, an outstanding writer, a skilled organizer and strategic thinker." I am Katie Guzperson and I want to bring those attributes to Elle magazine.

For as long as I can remember, I have wanted to live in New York City and work for a fashion magazine. I grew up in Maryland, went to college in Missouri and then New Jersey and currently live in a wonderful Midwestern town. Over the years, I have never lost sight of my big dreams in the big city.

I want very much to meet with you to talk about the vacant editorial assistant position in your beauty department and convince you I possess the qualities and experience necessary to fill the position.

For the past year and a half I have been working in the Mayor's Office in Ottumwa, Iowa. The fast-paced environment, volume of tasks and variety of work is routine. Daily challenges have forced me to strengthen my skills as a writer, organizer and strategic thinker. I live in a deadline-driven environment.

Please contact me at 515-555-1212 or guzperson@iowatown.com so that I can personally discuss my skills and share my enthusiasm with you. I look forward to hearing from you.

Sincerely,

Katie Guzperson

Katie Guzperson

Encls: Resume

PR Play 5-25
Sample Business Memo

MEMO

DATE: June 3, 2013

TO: Julie Kramer, Vice Chair
Michael Gross, Secretary
Members –
     Seth Adams
     Beatrix Grace
     Aidan Marshall
     Alana Perris

FROM: M. Larry Litwin, APR, Fellow PRSA, Chairperson

SUBJECT: N.J. Privacy Study Commission – N.J. Data Practices Report

I have attached the draft report from the New Jersey Data Practices Subcommittee.

Please read this report before the Commission's next meeting on Friday, June 21, 2013 at 10 a.m. With your approval, I will present the report to the entire Commission at that time. Our goal is to discuss it at length at the July meeting and adopt it no later than August 30, 2013.

If you have any questions or suggested revisions, please send them to me so that I can gather and disseminate them to all of you prior to the June 21 meeting.

If I do not receive any questions or suggested revisions before the meeting, I will assume we are all in agreement and we can distribute it in its current form.

Thank you.

Larry

PR Play 5-26
Sample Business and Pitch Letter

**CHERRY HILL
PUBLIC LIBRARY**
THE HEART OF TOWN

**1100 Kings Highway North
Cherry Hill, NJ 08034-1911
856-555-1212
www.chplnj.org**

November 11, 2013

Ms. Amy Ovsiew
Chief Operating Officer
Overwood Memorial Health Care System
900 Rancocas Road
Getwell, NJ 08099

Dear Ms. Ovsiew:

Since the new Cherry Hill Public Library opened, it is evident that more and more people are discovering the value of their local library and truly taking advantage of all we have to offer in our new 72,000 square foot state-of-the-art resource center. In just the first 10 months alone, we have added 16,000 new card holders of all ages.

We recognize that with this increased demand comes greater responsibility. Libraries today are more than just books and in Cherry Hill, it is our mission to meet the informational, educational and cultural needs and interests of our patrons – residents, visitors and members from other municipalities, and the men and women who might live elsewhere, but work in our town. The Cherry Hill Public Library has truly become a regional gathering place – thanks in no small part to meeting and function rooms, and other common areas.

cont.

PR Play 5-26 continued

In addition to having the latest library resources, such as books, reference materials and technology, we also provide quality programs – author series, computer classes, children's events, art exhibits, and workshops and lectures on a range of topics from home organization to vital health information – all from the area's leading sources.

Overwood Memorial Health Care System is a well-respected major resource in the region. The Cherry Hill Public Library is quickly moving in that direction. We would like to invite you to join us in a unique partnership opportunity. Our new facility is a community destination point with more than 50,000 visitors making use of our facilities each month. This partnership would be an investment for Overwood Memorial Health Care System that would reap major benefits from the exposure to the Cherry Hill regional audience.

Please review the enclosed options. Attaching your corporate name and reputation to our events accompanied by a beautifully engraved and strategically placed name plate in the library would demonstrate another major Overwood commitment to the residents of Camden and Burlington Counties.

I will call you in a few days so we can get together to talk about this in person. Better yet, if your schedule permits, I would be proud to take you on a tour so that you could see, firsthand, what all the buzz is about in and around Cherry Hill. The Cherry Hill Public Library has indeed become the talk of the town.

Sincerely,

Stephen C. Barbell

Dr. Stephen C. Barbell
President – CHPL Board of Trustees
Encls.

Eliminate Unnecessary Words

Thomas Jefferson asks, "Why use several words when one will do?"
Rowan University Professor Anthony Fulginiti, APR, Fellow PRSA,
helps solve the problem by answering the question of "redundancies":
"Are you repeating your idea by using unnecessary additional words?"
He says, "That wastes time and reduces effect." Professor Fulginiti
offers this solution:

- Think carefully about the words you use. Do you need to use all of
  them?
- Avoid these redundancies:
  - revert *back* (can you revert forward?)
  - 9:45 p.m. *at night* (is there a p.m. in the morning, too?)
  - bitter *tasting* (bitter *is* a taste)
  - connect *together* (can you connect apart?) *Exception: Cleave
    together* and *cleave apart*)
  - *really* and *truly* on time
  - *has the capability of* (use *can*)
  - *somewhere in the neighborhood of* (use *about*)
  - *in the event that* (if)
  - past *history* (history *is* past)

At the end of this chapter are two skills exercises. Try your hand at
them and share your results with a colleague or other friend. Remember,
as a public relations practitioner, you are your firm or organization's
writing resource. One of your responsibilities is helping others understand the importance of writing effective copy – copy that gets read so
your goals are reached.

Feel free to send your edited skills tests to the author (larry@larrylitwin.com).
One more editing round might just be "chicken soup for the soul" – and
give you an edge.

Gunning Fog Index

The Gunning Fog Index, developed by Robert Gunning in *The Technique
of Clear Writing,* and other readability indexes are important because
every public relations practitioner should possess the same mindset –
being an outstanding writer. That is the number one prerequisite of
employers in and out of the profession. And, the ease of reading is key.
The best writers – whether in public relations or other genres – realize if
readers have to work to understand the message, they will stop reading.

PR Play 5-27
Write to *Express* Not *Impress*

Professor Grazian warns, "Using words to impress rather than communicate can prevent a goal from being reached." He offers the following alternatives:

Why Use This?	When This Will Do
In the near future	Soon
Utilization	Use
In order to	To
For a period of three months	For three months
For the purpose of	To
Factual information	Facts
At the present time	Now
Basic fundamentals	Basics
In the vicinity of	Near
Approximately	About
On the part of	By
Many in number	Many
A majority of	Most
Consensus of opinion	Consensus
Bring to an end	End
Ask the question	Ask
Take a negative position	Oppose
For the purpose of	For
By means of	By; with
Due to the fact that	Because
For the simple reason	Because
Excessive verbiage	Verbiage
With the result that	So
With the exception of	Except
Subsequent to	After
Prior to the start of	Before
At this point in time	Now
In the event that	If
On a few occasions	Occasionally

Practice the "Effort-Benefit Ratio" – when you make people work, they stop reading. Communicate with clarity – clearly, calculatingly (measured tones), concisely, consistently and completely (specifically and simply).

Gunning Fog is the easiest to use, most popular and considered most effective readability index. Here is how it works (PR Play 5-43):

Steps in Applying Gunning
1. Select a sample.
2. Count 100 words (continue counting until you finish a sentence).
3. Determine the average number of words per sentence.
4. Divide the number of sentences into the number of words. (Remember, an average sentence should not exceed 17 words.)
5. Determine the percentage of hard words.
   a. Count all words containing three or more syllables. Do *not* count:
      • proper nouns
      • verbs made into three syllables such as excited, persuasive or devoted
      • words of three or more syllables that are combinations of easy words such as butterfly, lawmaker, bumblebee.
6. Add the two factors (Steps 4 and 5) and multiply by 0.4

The result is the minimum grade level at which the writing is easily read.

Writing for Broadcast

To broadcast journalism majors and in newsrooms across the country, they were known simply as Bliss and Patterson – quintessential writers for broadcast news professionals. Their basic work rules (*Writing News for Broadcast* – Columbia University Press – 1994) for broadcast journalism carry over to strategic writing for radio and television – the importance of which is too often overlooked in public relations training.

Edward Bliss Jr. joined the faculty of The American University after 25 years with CBS News where he served as a writer-producer for the legendary Edward R. Murrow. John M. Patterson, also a CBS News veteran, was on the faculty of the Graduate School of Journalism at Columbia University.

Bliss and Patterson note that not every newsroom – whether print or broadcast – prepares copy the same way. However, just as in print, broadcast news writing has basic rules – as basic as *The Associated Press Stylebook* or as basic as turning on the water. Here is a summary adapted from Bliss, Patterson and ABC Radio News' Nick George.

Format

Double space. When writing for radio, use the full page, allowing about an inch for margins. In television, use the right half (or two-thirds) of page for news copy. The left side of the page is for video information and direction. Strategic writers who write for broadcast should be more concerned with radio rather than TV. Pieces that make it to TV will be copied and pasted or retyped by a show's writer.

If the broadcaster does a voice-over (V/0), that is shown, too. There is also room on the left side of the page for the director to note cues and timings.

Type all news copy in upper and lower case just as you would for print releases. However, you might want to think about typing broadcast releases in 14 or 16 point fonts and using a serif font like Times Roman or Courier.

There are at least two reasons why broadcast copy usually is typed in upper and lower case. One is that video information frequently is typed in capital (upper case) letters to set it apart from what the broadcaster reads. It *looks* different, so the chance of mix-up is reduced. (Anything that reduces the likelihood of a mix-up in television operations is welcomed.) The other argument for upper and lower case in news copy is that it enables the broadcaster to recognize proper names and the beginning and ending of sentences more readily.

Use paragraphs. When you start your story, *indent*. Number the pages of broadcast releases the same as you would number print releases. If it is a three page release, the header should contain the slug and Page 1 of 3; slug/Page 2 of 3, etc.

As in print, if more than one page is required, make the sentence at the bottom of the first page a *complete sentence* and, in fact, make it a *complete paragraph*. A new paragraph would start at the top of the next page.

If it takes *only* another line to complete a story, and you have come to the bottom of the page, don't start another page for just that one line. Type it in a slightly reduced font size to make it fit.

Edit

As in printed releases, all copy should be edited, re-edited and edited one more time.

Clarity and simplicity of language are as important in broadcast writing as they are in print and maybe more so. Not only must a reporter or anchor deliver the message as intended, he/she must be able to read it on the air with ease.

Punctuation

Do not over punctuate. With rare exception, the only punctuation marks you need in writing for broadcast are the period, comma, question mark, em dash (pause) and ellipse (pause). (Note that no comma appears in the preceding sentence between *em dash* and *ellipse. The Associated Press Stylebook* dictates the (serial) comma before *and* in a series generally is omitted.)

Forget the semicolon. In fact, only in rare instances do strategic writers use the semicolon in print releases.

Place commas after phrases like, "In Philadelphia," "Here in this country," "At the national conference," etc. when used at the start of a sentence.

Never hyphenate at the end of a typed line, whether writing for broadcast or print.

Regardless of what the dictionary says, hyphenate words like *semi-annual, bi-annual, non-fiction, anti-pollution, co-operation* (but do not split a hyphenated word at the end of a typed line). By ignoring the dictionary in such cases, you are helping the broadcaster read what you have written. The only excuse for punctuation in your release is the help it gives the broadcaster in reading, so the listener – your target audience – can better understand what he or she hears.

Two hyphens or an em dash indicate pauses. Three periods (...) are used in much the same way as the em dash. Adopt whichever you prefer, but be consistent. Keep in mind that three periods (ellipse) used for print releases have a different purpose. In print, they signify that part of a quote has been omitted.

On the subject of quotes in broadcast copy, care must be taken not to distort what is being said. Repeat: Be careful in editing what a person says even if you, as the strategic/public relations writer, are crafting the quote. Make certain that the newsmaker knows what he/she is saying.

Whether broadcast or print, stick to the general, accepted rules for punctuation.

Abbreviations

Most abbreviations are to be avoided. As a general rule, words used in broadcast copy should look the way they are read.

Names of states are written out in full: *Arizona*, not *Ariz*; *New York*, not *N.Y.*; Pennsylvania, not Pa. The same goes for counties and countries. One exception is *U-S*, though *U-S* is less used than *United States* in general conversation and has a stilted sound when used repeatedly in a news broadcast.

Names of the months and days of the week are written out in full: *January*, not *Jan.; Friday*, not *Fri.*

Military titles are written out. Never abbreviate such ranks as *Pvt., Capt., Gen.* and *Adm. Pfc.* may be regarded as an exception. This is because *Pfc.* frequently is read *P-F-C* as well as *Private First Class*.

Avoid such abbreviations as *Adj. Gen., Dist. Atty.* and *Asst. Dir.*

The abbreviations *Dr., Mr., Mrs.* are fine. *Prof.* for *professor* or *Supt.* for *superintendent* should not be used.

The abbreviations A.M. and P.M. are permissible (note: in print they would be lower case, a.m. and p.m.). Other time abbreviations like *E.S.T.* and *E.D.T.* are not. They should be spelled out, *Eastern Standard Time, Eastern Daylight Time.*

Generally, abbreviations like *U-N, I-R-S* and *P-R-S-A* should be with hyphens to ease the reading as separate initials.

A good rule of thumb is to punctuate when each initial is read separately. It is *not* necessary to use the hyphen in abbreviations like *NASA, PRaction, OPEC* or *OPRA* and other acronyms which are read as one word.

Generally, a first reference of an organization should be the entire name of an organization – *Public Relations Student Society of America (P-R-S-S-A)*. Succeeding references, as in print releases, would be the initials *P-R-S-S-A*. In broadcast writing, words within parentheses are not read. They are for clarification, only. Initials of commonly known organizations usually do not need clarification: *F-B-I, I-R-*S, *Y-M-C-A*.

Numbers

Write out numbers *one* through *nine*. Use figures for 10 through 999. After 999, write out *thousand, million, billion,* etc., For example write:

- 9-thousand 54, instead of 9,054
- 7-million, 6-thousand, instead of 7,006,000
- 12-billion, 700-million, instead of 12,700,000,000

The reason for this is whereas the eye can readily take in, and the mind almost instantaneously translate, a three-digit number such as 714, the mind finds it more difficult to translate a number like 8,670,000. You, the writer, translate for the broadcaster when you write out the number as 8-million, 670-thousand.

Round off large numbers. For example, if the allocation for a building project is $45,520,000, you can say the allocation is *forty-five and a half million dollars*. You could say the allocation amounts to *just more than 45 million dollars*.

Most stylebooks say *one thousand, one million,* etc. are preferable to *a thousand, a million,* etc. The reasoning is, to a listener, *a thousand* may sound like *eight thousand*.

Sometimes distances – inches, feet and yards – can be roughly translated to make a smaller figure. Thus, 36 inches can be translated into three feet, or one yard, and 5,000 feet into nearly one mile.

Fractions always are written out: *one-half, three-fourths,* etc. Fractions can be used to simplify – again by translating. "One-third of the money will go for housing" is better broadcast copy than "Thirty percent of the money will go for housing." And it is easier to say, "Gas prices have almost doubled," than to say, "Gas prices have risen 95 percent."

The fewer numbers thrown at listeners (or viewers) the better. While acceptable for print copy – and even expected – numbers can clog broadcast copy. Listeners cannot read the numbers and will probably have trouble remembering why they are being used, unless they are of significant importance to a story. For example, "Rowan University has announced a *one billion dollar* expansion of its main campus that will include new athletic facilities, a second recreation center, student townhouses, a hotel-conference center and the largest outdoor shopping mall in Southern New Jersey."

Dates

In writing the day of the month, add the *st, nd, rd* or *th* which the broadcaster would add to the date if you did not. For example, make it *June 24th*, not *June 24* (as in print-release writing), but *March fifth*, not *March 5* or *March 5th*.

Symbols

Do not use them. Symbols such as $, &, % and # are detested by most broadcasters who would rather not see them. Instead, use *dollar, and, percent,* and *number.* Also don't use such abbreviations as *No.* as in *No. 005.* Write it *Number 005.* (Some broadcasters would favor Number Zero, Zero, Five or Double Oh 5 just as they would favor N-C Double A.)

Active Voice

Active voice in broadcast is viewed as it is in print. Whenever possible, use verbs in the active voice. This is one of the basic principles in writing news. "He piloted the plane" is a much stronger statement than "The plane was piloted by him." Passive voice is weak.

Write Right

26 Tips to Improve Your Writing, Dramatically.

Roger A. Shapiro

Illustrations by Ray Petty

Cover Design by Nikki E. Hladky

Knowing how to write for broadcast could be a real plus and could put one practitioner a notch ahead of another. But, whether writing for print or broadcast, the key, according to Roger Shapiro, president of Mitchell Rose – A Communications Consultancy (Ewing, N.J.), is to write, right. In fact, Shapiro authored a book with that title, *Write Right.*

"Writing right," says Shapiro, "improves marketing communication, creates sales and profits, grows your business, motivates people and accelerates your career.

"Great writers can move mountains – convince others to change opinions. Great writers string together words to produce results."

Shapiro offers 26 tips in *Write Right* compiled from years of experience. They are a constant reminder that persuasive writing is hard work – "a tough job."

Here are some of Shapiro's suggestions:
- Think in terms of a product or service's benefits and value
- How will your message be perceived?
- Ask yourself the question, "What do you want the reader to do after taking the time to read your release, your ad, your brochure, your website or any other marketing tool you created?"
- Pre-write. It includes the first step in the public relations process – research. It is imperative that writers understand the assignment, ask questions, review content, evaluate obstacles, and clarify opportunities and objectives.
- Consider the following:
  - Who is your reader (target audience)?
  - What is the audience's demographic profile (consider psychographics and geodemographics, too!)?
  - Why would a reader not love this product/service/idea?
  - What are the benefits?
  - Who cares about your business?
  - What do you want the reader to do?
  - Why are you writing this PR or marketing "piece"?
  - How should the reader take the action you want taken?
  - What are the negatives?
  - What is the downside of taking this action?
  - What vocabulary will your reader not understand?
  - What vocabulary will your reader expect to see to feel your empathy?
  - What problems does the reader face?
  - How does this product/service/idea compare to others?
  - When should the reader act?
  - How should the reader respond?
  - What difference will this product/service/idea make in the reader's mind?
  - What else should I (the writer) know before tackling the assignment?
- Use words that motivate, sell, promote – words that are alive, more direct and more attention grabbing.
- Think visually – use words that paint pictures.
- Results mechanisms could include a phone number, website, business reply card (bounce back card), keeping in mind, the more response options you offer, the greater your response ratio will be.

- Proofreading tips:
  - Read backwards
  - Use someone else
  - Cross read – have someone read late inserts or changes, numbers and other facts to you – to reconfirm corrections and statistics are accurate.
  - Use spell check only as a back up.
  - Recheck phone numbers, addresses, websites and email addresses. (Always call the number and access the website.)
  - Proofread one more time before "sending" the document.

Shapiro reminds us that "every word matters. Great copy is written, rewritten, edited and rewritten again. Your words have milliseconds to make an impression. Your effort is to grab attention immediately – and to keep that attention as the reader continually chooses to continue or quit.

"Using the right word, for the right audience, for the right reason is a critical decision."

PR Play 5-28
Importance of Proper Punctuation
Please punctuate the following line...

"A woman without her man is nothing"

Option one: A woman without her man, is nothing.

Option two: A woman, without her, man is nothing.

PR Play 5-29
Your Goal: Achieve the 6 C's
(Assessing your writing)

- Clarity: Say what you mean, mean what you say
- Correct: Avoid errors to avoid confusion
- Connection: Engage your reader
- Compelling: Motivate an action
- Conviction: Live the branding
- Consistency: Stay on message – always

Roger Shapiro – Mitchell Rose, A Communications Consultancy – Ewing, N.J.

PR Play 5-30

Below are some overworked longer words. Next to each is a shorter or simpler word or phrase that often serves as a good substitute, compliments of Prof. Grazian.

Why Use This?	When This Will Do	Why Use This?	When This Will Do
Accumulate	Gather	Facilitate	Make Easy
Acquaint	Tell	Initial	First
Additional	Added	Initiate	Begin
Aggregate	Total	Locality	Place
Ameliorate	Improve	Maintenance	Upkeep
Anticipate	Foresee	Materialize	Appear
Apparent	Clear	Modification	Change
Assistance	Aid	Objective	Aim
Cognizance	Knowledge	Obligate	Bind
Commence	Begin	Obligation	Debt
Commitment	Promise	Occasion	Cause
Compensation	Pay	Optimum	Best
Construct	Build	Participate	Take Part
Contribute	Give	Proceed	Go
Demonstrate	Show	Purchase	Buy
Encounter	Meet	Subsequent	Next, Later
Endeavor	Try	Sufficient	Enough
Equivalent	Equal	Terminated	Ended
Expedite	Hasten	Transmit	Send
Explicit	Plain	Utilization	Use
		Voluminous	Bulky

Associated Press Style (Print) Guidelines – Summarized at Rowan (N.J.) University

No public relations writer or reporter should ever be without the *Associated Press Stylebook and Briefing on Media Law*. It numbers nearly 500 pages. Some years ago, Rowan University highlighted the book for its students. That summary, first compiled by Jack Gillespie, professor emeritus, follows. (Complete copies of *The Associated Press Stylebook* can be purchased from most bookstores and online).

The style items that follow deal with the problems most often found in news stories. In fact, they account for 99 percent of all style errors. If you learn to follow these print and Web guidelines, you'll produce clean copy, free of unnecessary mistakes.

PR Play 5-31
Nine Parts of Speech

Parts of speech are the basic types of words in the English language. Being able to recognize and identify them will help you better understand English grammar, use the correct word and be a better public relations writer. As Roger Shapiro stresses, using the right word in the right form is key in communicating your message. Think of a person named Ina V Cappa. It might just help you remember the nine parts of speech.

Interjection – Interjections are words used to express emotional states (wow!; amazing!; unbelievable!).

Noun – A noun is a word used to name something: a person/animal, a place, a thing, or an idea (pencil, car, building).

Adjective – An adjective modifies (describes) a noun or pronoun (handsome, amazing, powerful).

Verb – Verbs generally express action or a state of being (bolster, craft, publish).

Conjunction – Joins together words and phrases (and, but, because).

Adverb – An adverb is a word that modifies an action verb, an adjective or another adverb (quickly, slowly, very).

Pronoun – A pronoun is a word that replaces a noun. They eliminate the need for repetition (he, she, it, we, they).

Preposition – Prepositions are words that, like conjunctions, connect a noun or pronoun to another word in a sentence (under, over, into, out, on, at).

Article – An article is used to introduce a noun (the, a, an).

PR Play 5-32
Writing Leads

Five major types of leads:

1. **Straight news lead (summary lead – who, what, when, where)** Rowan University's Public Relations Student Society of America holds its annual Organ Donor Awareness Day on Thursday, April 10 from 10 a.m. to 3 p.m. at the Mark M. Chamberlain Student Center.

2. **Modified straight news lead (stressing a major theme)** A Philadelphia orthopedic surgeon, a leader in bi-lateral hip surgery, has been named president of the American Medical Association.

3. **Informal lead (designed to pique interest)** Hundreds of free flash drives (32 GB) are being distributed this Thursday at Rowan University's Chamberlain Student Center. (Story is about Organ Donor Day. Flash drives open to a full screen ad stressing the importance of organ donation.)

4. **Feature lead (often used in magazine articles or human interest newspaper "soft" stories)** On Thursday, she boards a plane for Florida, but she hasn't packed even one bathing suit. (Story about a student who is heading to spring training to meet up with her father who has mapped out a week of watching baseball. It's father-daughter bonding.)

5. **Multi-paragraph lead (used when a number of facts want to be covered before getting into the body of a story).** May be used in either a hard story or feature. [Jim Salisbury of *The Philadelphia Inquirer* wrote the following on March 14, 2007]

They came from all over Florida, from as far away as California and as close as down the street. They came on chartered jets and commercial flights, in buses and cars.

They came with memories and funny stories. They came with tears in their eyes and voids in their hearts.

The list of attendees included team owners and executives, a Hall of Famer, MVPs, World Series heroes, players, coaches, managers, umpires, scouts, groundskeepers, clubhouse attendants and assorted other baseball folks. Some were longtime teammates. Some were longtime rivals.

cont.

PR Play 5-32 continued

Yesterday, they were all just friends of John Vukovich, the good-guy baseball man and Phillies' giant who died of brain cancer at age 59 last week.

More on leads

Summary Lead – Easiest to write. It is the five W's.
- Be Concise
- Be Specific
- Use Strong, Active Verbs
- Emphasize the Story
- Stress the Unusual
- Localize and Update Your Lead
- Be Objective
- Attribute Opinions
- Strive for Simplicity
- Begin With News
- Emphasize the News

Other Types of Leads and Suggestions

Quotation Leads
Question Leads
Suspenseful Leads
Descriptive Leads
Shocking Leads – with a twist
Ironic Leads
Direct-Address Leads
Other Unusual Leads
Avoid "Agenda" Leads
Avoid "Label" Leads
Avoid Lists
Avoid stating the obvious
Avoid the negative
Avoid exaggeration
Avoid misleading readers

cont.

PR Play 5-32 continued
Writing Leads – Checklist

1. Be specific rather than vague and abstract.
2. Avoid stating the obvious or the negative.
3. Emphasize your story's most unusual or unexpected developments.
4. Emphasize your story's most interesting and important developments.
5. Emphasize your story's magnitude and its impact on its participants and readers.
6. Use complete sentences, the proper tense and all the necessary articles – "a," "an" and "the."
7. Be concise. If it exceeds three typed lines, examine a lead critically to determine whether it is wordy or repetitious or contains some unnecessary details. If so, rewrite it.
8. Avoid writing a label lead that reports your story's topic but not what was said or done about it.
9. Begin your lead with the news – the main point of the story – not the attribution or the time and place your story occurred.
10, Use a relatively simple sentence structure and avoid beginning the lead with a long phrase or clause.
11. Use strong, active and descriptive verbs rather than passive ones.
12. Avoid using in your lead unfamiliar names and names requiring lengthy identification that could be reported in a later paragraph.
13. Attribute any quotation or statement of opinion appearing in the lead.
14. Localize the lead and emphasize the latest developments, preferably what happened today or yesterday.
15. Eliminate statements of opinion, including one-word labels such as "interesting" and "alert."
16. Remember your readers. Write a lead that is clear, concise and interesting and that emphasizes the details most likely to affect and interest your readers.
17. Read the lead aloud to be certain that it is clear, concise and easy to understand.

Fred Fedler – *Reporting for the Media*

PR Play 5-33
Sample Media Kit

Rosie's Noodle Bar

322 Walnut St. ◆ Philadelphia, PA 19106
215.706.1986 ◆ Fax 215.706.2006

Contact: Rosie Braude, Director of Public Relations
Email: rosieb@hotmail.com

Cell: (732) 706-8606
Fax: (732) 706-8608

Oct. 24, 2013

MEMO

Enclosed are a number of items to help persuade your coverage of Rosie's Noodle Bar's grand opening:

- Media Alert
- News Release
- Public Service Announcement (PSA) for radio
- Photographs of Rosie's Noodle Bar to illustrate photo opportunities
- Letter to the Editor
- Fillers
- Biographies of the owners and head chef
- Quotable Quotes for immediate media use
- Appendix of Sources
- CD-ROM

DATE:	Friday, Nov. 8, 2013
TIME:	8 p.m.

PR Play 5-34
Sample Media Kit

Rosie's Noodle Bar

322 Walnut St. ♦ Philadelphia, PA 19106
215.706.1986 ♦ Fax 215.706.2006

Contact: Rosie Braude, Director of Public Relations
Email: rosieb@hotmail.com

Cell: (732) 706-8606
Fax: (732) 706-8608

Sent: Oct. 24, 2013

FOR IMMEDIATE RELEASE

MEDIA ALERT

EVENT: The grand opening of Rosie Braude and Cindy Lewandowski's premier restaurant, Rosie's Noodle Bar.

DATE:	Friday, Nov. 8, 2013
TIME:	8 p.m.

PLACE: 322 Walnut St., Philadelphia, PA 19106
(Please see directions, attached)

Details: Entertainment moguls Rosie Braude and Cindy Lewandowski will finally open the doors to their long awaited restaurant, Rosie's Noodle Bar. This $3.2 million project has taken nearly eight months to complete, but will easily become the most popular restaurant in Philadelphia. With three floors and a rooftop terrace, the modern design perfectly complements the Rosie's Noodle Bar menu. Renowned chef Frederico Antonioni supervises the 90 foot long pasta bar where customers choose between 22 different pastas, 12 sauces and 18 additional food choices. Guests include celebrities Taylor Swift and Bill Murray, "Project Runway's" Tim Gunn, author Candace Bushnell, Philadelphia Phillies' Ryan Howard, TV chef Rachael Ray, director Steven Spielberg, and longtime friends, restaurant owner Steven Starr, celebrity Patrick Dempsey, *The Philadelphia Inquirer* food critic Craig LaBan and singer Kanye West.

###

PR Play 5-35
Sample Media Kit

Rosie's Noodle Bar

322 Walnut St. ◆ Philadelphia, PA 19106
215.706.1986 ◆ Fax 215.706.2006

Contact: Rosie Braude, Director of Public Relations
Email: rosieb@hotmail.com

Cell: (732) 706-8606
Fax: (732) 706-8608

Sent: Oct. 24, 2013
Release no. 1

FOR IMMEDIATE RELEASE

GRAND OPENING OF ROSIE'S NOODLE BAR

(ROSIE'S NOODLE BAR)
PHILADELPHIA, PA—Public relations executive Rosie Braude teams with director Cindy Lewandowski for the grand opening of their first restaurant, Rosie's Noodle Bar. Located at 322 Walnut St. in Center City, the unveiling will take place on Friday, Nov. 8 at 8 p.m.

"After eight months of preparation, I cannot wait to open the doors of Rosie's Noodle Bar," Braude says. "This dream has been a longtime coming for Cindy and me. I'm so glad it has finally turned into a reality."

The $3.2 million project consists of three floors and a rooftop terrace for an outside dining experience. As indicated by its name, the menu is dominated by 22 different types of pastas. Customers create their own meals by adding one of 12 different sauces and any of the 18 additional sides to their choice of pasta. The selections are all laid out on a 90 foot long pasta bar.

"We really emphasize creativity here," Lewandowski says. "We want you to make Rosie's Noodle Bar your own."

While customers can craft their own dishes, award-winning Chef Frederico Antonioni provides a list of 13 house specialties.

"Some people need a little direction when they are offered so many choices," Antonioni says. "My house specialties combine exotic ingredients to create delicious, mouth-watering meals."

Guests for the grand opening include Philadelphia natives Bob Saget and Will Smith, the Food Network's Rachael Ray, *The Philadelphia Inquirer* food critic Craig LaBan, author Candace Bushnell and many more.

For more information call Rosie Braude at (732) 706-8606 or e-mail rosieb@hotmail.com.

###

PR Play 5-36
Sample Media Kit

 Rosie's Noodle Bar

322 Walnut St. ◆ Philadelphia, PA 19106
215.706.1986 ◆ Fax 215.706.2006
www.rosiesnoodlebar.com

Contact: Rosie Braude, Director of Public Relations
Email: rosieb@hotmail.com

Cell: (732) 706-8606
Fax: (732) 706-8608

Oct. 24, 2013

FACT SHEET

Company Name: Rosie's Noodle Bar

Location: 322 Walnut Street, Philadelphia PA 19106

Principals: Rosie Braude (pronounced Bro-dee) and Cindy Lewandowski

Product: Gourmet restaurant – specializing in pastas, sauces and gravies

Founded: 2006

Mission: Rosie's Noodle Bar offers its clients fine dining in a relaxed
                     atmosphere designed to satisfy the most discriminating palate. House
                     specialties combine exotic ingredients to create delicious, mouth-
                     watering meals guaranteed to encourage a return visit.

Other Information: Restaurant is laid out over three floors and a rooftop terrace for an
                     outside dining experience. The menu is dominated by 22 types of
                     pastas. Customers create their own meals by adding one of 12
                     different sauces and any of the 18 additional sides to their choice
                     of pasta. The selections are all laid out on a 90 foot long pasta bar.

PR Play 5-37
Sample Media Kit

Rosie's Noodle Bar

322 Walnut St. ◆ Philadelphia, PA 19106
215.706.1986 ◆ Fax 215.706.2006
www.rosiesnoodlebar.com

Public Service Announcement – PSA

Rosie's Noodle Bar Grand Opening

322 Walnut St.

Philadelphia, PA

Start Date: Oct. 31, 2013

End Date: Nov. 8, 2013

Contact: Rosie Braude

Phone: (215) 706-1986

Email: rosieb@hotmail.com

30 seconds, 81 words

Recorded cassette and CD enclosed

Also available for download at

www.rosiesnoodlebar.com

What's cooking in Philadelphia?

Noodles! Noodles! Noodles!

 Friday, November 10th marks the grand opening of Rosie's Noodle Bar...322 Walnut Street in Olde City. Proceeds from opening day go to breast cancer research. Never have you had so many choices. Mix and match 22 different pastas, 12 sauces and 18 additional food choices. For more information on how you can help eradicate breast cancer and enjoy the best pasta in the Delaware Valley...call 215-706-1986. That's 215-706-1986 for Rosie's Noodle Bar in Philadelphia.

PR Play 5-38
Sample Media Kit

Rosie's Noodle Bar

322 Walnut St. ◆ Philadelphia, PA 19106
215.706.1986 ◆ Fax 215.706.2006

www.rosiesnoodlebar.com

Contact: Rosie Braude, Director of Public Relations
Email: rosieb@hotmail.com

Cell: (732) 706-8606
Fax: (732) 706-8608

BIOS

Rosie Braude, Co-owner
After graduating with a master's degree in public relations from Rowan University, Rosie Braude joined Profile PR in Philadelphia, specializing in restaurant public relations. She quickly climbed the agency ladder and soon became the executive vice-president of public relations, overseeing the launch of restaurant mogul Stephen Starr's four new restaurants. After five years of experience there, Braude left Profile PR and opened her own public relations agency specializing in restaurant and consumer products public relations and special event planning. She currently lives in New Jersey with her husband and two children.

Cindy Lewandowski, Co-owner
Specializing in film, editing and TV production, Cindy Lewandowski has taken the Philadelphia media industry by storm. Lewandowski began at Philadelphia 6ABC as assistant director to the morning news. Within the year, she was promoted to director and became the most sought-after director in Philadelphia. Two years later, Lewandowski moved to Los Angeles, where she directed episodes of "Grey's Anatomy," "Heroes" and "House." After a few years, Lewandowski left the TV industry for a change of pace in the restaurant business. She moved back to Philadelphia and resides with her husband and three cats in Center City.

Frederico Antonioni, Head Chef
Born and raised in Sicily, Italy, Frederico Antonioni worked in the kitchen of his parents' restaurant for 10 years before opening his own café. After three years of success and numerous awards, Antonioni moved to California and became the top chef at Los Angeles's most famous Italian restaurant, Trattoria Tre Venezie. There, he won three Pizza and Pasta Italian Food Awards (PAPA), received the Best of Italian Food 2005 award and earned a Five Star Diamond Award Entrée for his four cheese spinach cannelloni wrapped in bacon. Antonioni has produced two segments specializing in pasta dishes on the Food Network.

PR Play 5-39
Sample Media Kit

Rosie's Noodle Bar

322 Walnut St. ♦ Philadelphia, PA 19106
215.706.1986 ♦ Fax 215.706.2006

Contact: Rosie Braude, Director of Public Relations
Email: rosieb@hotmail.com

Cell: (732) 706-8606
Fax: (732) 706-8608

LETTER TO THE EDITOR

October 24, 2013

Readers Editor
The Inquirer
Box 41705
Philadelphia, PA 19101

Dear Editor:

A recent article in the Food section of *The Philadelphia Inquirer* describes Philadelphia as a "city overrun by New York City wannabe restaurants with overly exotic menus, obnoxious décor and outrageous prices. The last thing this city needs is another hangout built to attract celebrities and the upper echelon of Philadelphia society."

What an incorrect analysis. Restaurants and native cuisine enrich the culture of Philadelphia. Innovation and modernism are in. They are the trend. People are attracted to the new and exciting.

Ask Stephen Starr. How can you condemn the 20 insanely successful restaurants he has built around Philadelphia? They bring in revenue and attract tourists. His restaurants add to the Philadelphia brand.

Philadelphia is not trying to be like New York City. It has no need to try and be like New York City. Philadelphia is the "City of Brotherly Love" and home to the Liberty Bell, Benjamin Franklin and the Philadelphia Phillies. This city does not follow in anyone's shadow—it blazes its own path.

Sincerely,

Rosie Braude

Rosie Braude
Co-owner and Director of Public Relations
Rosie's Noodle Bar

PR Play 5-40
Sample Media Kit

Rosie's Noodle Bar

322 Walnut St. ◆ Philadelphia, PA 19106
215.706.1986 ◆ Fax 215.706.2006
www.rosiesnoodlebar.com

Contact: Rosie Braude, Director of Public Relations
Email: rosieb@hotmail.com

Cell: (732) 706-8606
Fax: (732) 706-8608

FOR IMMEDIATE RELEASE

QUOTES

Rosie Braude, Co-owner

"Philadelphia is full of restaurants serving the most outrageous concoctions in the most fashionably decorated buildings. That is what Philadelphia is all about. We want to bring that to you, but on your own terms. Create your own crazy, adventurous meal or stick with the traditional favorite. We aim to please."

Cindy Lewandowski, Co-owner

"The purpose of Rosie's Noodle Bar is to add to the culture of Philadelphia. This is the 'City of Brotherly Love'– the city of Ben Franklin, the Liberty Bell and the Eagles. This is the city of Rosie's Noodle Bar. Our restaurant will uphold the traditions and reputation that make Philadelphia such a strong city. That is our promise to you."

Frederico Antonioni, Head Chef

"In all of my years as a professional chef, I've never witnessed such a unique dining experience. I feel so privileged to be a part of this ground breaking restaurant idea."

"Rosie's Noodle Bar offers Philadelphia an unlimited amount of choices in a comfortable, modern setting. Go up to the rooftop and enjoy farfalle with scallops, asparagus and chopped garlic gloves in a deep red wine sauce. Don't like scallops? Choose lamb instead. Don't like the rooftop? Sit in a booth next to the pasta bar and watch the chefs prepare the meals you create. That's the beauty of Rosie's Noodle Bar. It's all about you."

PR Play 5-41
Sample Media Kit

Rosie's Noodle Bar

322 Walnut St. ✦ Philadelphia, PA 19106
215.706.1986 ✦ Fax 215.706.2006
www.rosiesnoodlebar.com

Contact: Rosie Braude, Director of Public Relations
Email: rosieb@hotmail.com

Cell: (732) 706-8606
Fax: (732) 706-8608

PHOTOGRAPHS

Rosie's Noodle Bar – exterior

Rosie's Noodle Bar – interior

Floors one and two

The noodle bar

Rosie's Noodle Bar – interior

Downstairs seating

The bar

###

PR Play 5-42
Sample Media Kit

Rosie's Noodle Bar

322 Walnut St. ◆ Philadelphia, PA 19106
215.706.1986 ◆ Fax 215.706.2006
www.rosiesnoodlebar.com

Contact: Rosie Braude, Director of Public Relations
Email: rosieb@hotmail.com

Cell: (732) 706-8606
Fax: (732) 706-8608

FOR IMMEDIATE RELEASE

FILLERS

PRE-TESTING THE NOODLES AT ROSIE'S NOODLE BAR

Rosie's Noodle Bar, opening on Nov. 10, invited local food critics and food connoisseurs to a pre-opening taste test last night. The Philadelphia Inquirer's restaurant critic, Craig LaBan and longtime Philadelphia food and restaurant critic Maria Gallagher were among the 10 guests asked to sample award-winning Chef Frederico Antonioni's 13 house specialties.

"One word – fresh," LaBan said. "The combination of high quality, nice presentation, enjoyable atmosphere and innovative ideas is just what Philadelphia needs. Rosie's Noodle Bar will definitely be the hit of the holiday season."

Located at 322 Walnut St., Rosie's Noodle Bar features a 90 foot long pasta bar where customers choose between 22 different pastas, 12 sauces and 18 additional food choices.

COUNTING CARBS: FINDING THE RIGHT MEAL WHILE EATING OUT

You've finally convinced yourself to stay on that "No Carb" diet. No bread. No pasta. No potatoes. You will lose weight this time.

That is until your boss invites you out to dinner with a client.

Eating out on a diet is so hard. Temptation is too easy. Your boss always orders one of those deep fried appetizers and you don't want to look like you don't appreciate his kindness. You eat some and ultimately destroy your diet. One exception leads to many and you become a carb-guzzling machine.

How can you avoid this? Some restaurants offer entrees designed for carb conscious customers. But what do you do at the restaurants based on carbs, like IHOP or Panera Bread? New Philadelphia restaurant, Rosie's Noodle Bar has created tasty alternatives to its unfriendly carb menu.

Along with its 22 different pastas, 12 sauces and 18 additional food choices, Rosie's Noodle Bar offers tofu pasta—soybeans and other ingredients shaped like pasta—or bean sprouts. These two alternative "pastas" can be mixed with the various sauces and add-ins along the pasta bar.

Just because you have to go out to dinner, doesn't mean you need to break your diet. Many restaurants want to help you, not hurt you. Stand strong. Even in the most diet unfriendly restaurants, there is a meal for you.

###

PR Play 5-43
Gunning Fog Index
Writing Sample*

In general, construction of pictograms follows the general procedure used in constructing bar charts. But two special rules should be followed. First, all of the picture units used must be of equal size. The comparisons must be made wholly on the basis of the number of illustrations used and never by varying the areas of the individual pictures used. The reason for this rule is obvious. The human eye is grossly inadequate in comparing areas of geometric designs.

Second, the pictures or symbols used must appropriately depict the quantity to be illustrated. A comparison of the navies of the world, for example, might make use of miniature ship drawings. Cotton production might be shown by bales of cotton. Obviously, the drawings used must be immediately interpreted by the reader.

COMPUTATION
129 words in 10 sentences = average sentence length is 13

26 hard words out of 129 = 20%

13.0 (Average sentence length) plus
20.0 (Percentage of hard words)
33.0 (Total)
Multiply by X 0.4

Grade level of readership = 13.2

* Use entire 129 word sample

Academic Degrees

The preferred form is bachelor's degree, master's degree and doctorate, all lowercase and with an apostrophe for the first two. Use B.A., M.A. and Ph.D. only when the need to identify many individuals by degree on first reference would make the preferred form cumbersome. Use the abbreviations only after a full name, never after just a last name.

When used after a name, the abbreviation is set off with commas: George Youknowwho, Ph.D., spoke at the dedication ceremony.

Do not use two titles with a name as in: Dr. George Youknowwho, Ph.D., spoke at the dedication ceremony.

Acronyms

Put an acronym or initials in parentheses after the full name of an organization or regulation. For example: Aluminum Company of America (ALCOA) or New Jersey Interscholastic Athletic Association (NJSIAA) or Open Public Records Act (OPRA). You can use the acronym or initials in subsequent references once they have been established. You can use some well-known acronyms, such as FBI, IRS, CIA and YMCA, in all references.

Addresses

Use the abbreviations Ave., Blvd. and St. only with numbered addresses: 1400 Massachusetts Ave., but Massachusetts Avenue. Spell out alley, circle, drive, road, terrace, court in all address forms. Spell out and capitalize First through Ninth when used as street names. Use figures and suitable endings for 10th and above. Some publications do abbreviate words like terrace, road and drive, and some even lowercase all letters of the abbreviation, but most follow the above guidelines. Learn the styles of the publications you deal with.

Book and other titles

Capitalize the principal words, including prepositions and conjunctions of four or more letters, and put quotation marks around book, movie, opera, play, poem, song, television program, lecture, speech and works of art titles. Do not underline titles.

Follow the same capitalization rules but do *not* put quotes around the Bible.

Use italics for catalogs of reference material, almanacs, directories, dictionaries, encyclopedias, gazettes, handbooks, magazines and newspapers.

Cents

Always use an Arabic number and the word cents with penny amounts: 1 cent, 2 cents, 25 cents, 43 cents.

Compound adjectives

Hyphenate all compound adjectives (modifiers) except when the first word ends in ly. For example: odd-numbered years, up-to-date material, newly discovered manuscript, early blooming rose. Also, 5-year-old boy (note Arabic number). He is a 5-year-old, (but a boy 5 years old is also correct because it is not a modifer).

Dates and days

Do not use st, nd, rd or th with dates (except when writing for broadcast). Use figures alone. Do not use *on* before dates. It's an excess word. The committee will meet May 8, not *on* May 8.

Do *not* abbreviate days of the week except in tabular (column) format. Don't use *on* with days. They met Thursday, not *on* Thursday.

Dimensions

Use figures and spell out inches, feet, yards, etc. to indicate depth, height, length and width. Hyphenate adjectival forms before nouns. Some examples: He is 5 feet 10 inches tall. She is a 5-foot-4-inch dynamo. The team signed a 7-footer. The tool shed is 20 feet long, 10 feet wide and 8 feet high. The room is 9 feet by 12 feet. She bought a 9-by-12 rug for the room.

Dollars

Use the dollar sign and Arabic numbers. Examples: $15, $24, $2, $463. Do *not* use a decimal and two zeroes with even-numbered amounts such as those in the examples. But *do* use the decimal with amounts such as $15.25, $4.95 and $365.85.

For large dollar amounts, use a dollar sign, Arabic number and the appropriate word: $2 million, $15 billion. For amounts like $2,543,000, $3,100,000 and $15,637,000,000, the correct form is $2.5 million, $3.1 million and $15.6 billion.

Hours

Do not use a colon and two zeroes with an even-numbered hour. For example: 2 a.m., not 2:00 a.m.; 9 p.m., not 9:00 p.m. But use the colon with 8:15 a.m., 6:45 p.m., etc.

Internet

Style for technology and the World Wide Web continues to evolve. But whether writing for print or broadcast always use upper case for Internet, Web and website (lower case *s* for site) and lower case for email.

Months

When you use a date with them, abbreviate all months that can be abbreviated. For example: Dec.15, Jan. 3, Oct. 4. When the month stands alone or is used with the year only, do not abbreviate. Examples: December, December 2009. (Note: No comma between December and 2009.)

Numbers

Use Arabic numbers for acts of a play, addresses, ages, aircraft names, betting odds, TV channels, chapters, congressional or other political districts, course numbers, court decisions, dates, decimals, distances, earthquake magnitudes, election results, formulas, fractions, handicaps, heights, highway designations, latitude, longitude, miles, model numbers, monetary units, with No., page numbers, percents, political divisions, proportions, ratios, recipes, room numbers, route numbers, scene numbers, scores, serial numbers, sizes, spacecraft designations, speeds, phone numbers, temperatures and years.

For amendments to the United States Constitution, spell out and capitalize First through Ninth, as in the Fifth Amendment. Use figures and the appropriate ending for 10th and above, as in the 21st Amendment. Always capitalize amendment when you use it with a number.

For centuries, spell out and use lowercase for first through ninth. All others use an Arabic number with the appropriate ending, such as 10th and 20th. The word century is always lowercase unless it is part of a proper name, as in 20th Century Fox.

For court names, use Arabic numbers with endings and capitalize the name of the court: 5th Circuit Court.

For decades, use Arabic numbers and add s with *no apostrophe*. Examples: 1920s, 1890s.

For fleet designations, use Arabic numbers with appropriate endings: 6th Fleet.

For uses not covered above, spell out whole numbers below 10, use figures for 10 and above: two cars, 36 trucks, six buses, 475 bicycles.

Generally, spell out large numbers like two million and three billion.

People Titles
Put long titles after names and in lowercase, except for the words that are usually capitalized. For example: Carlton Quackenbush, Yale University vice president for planning, will speak here tonight.

Short titles used in front of names usually take capitals if the title is official. For example: President George Goodman, Vice President Harry Throckmorton. The exception: *occupational* titles, as in attorney George Flowers and editor Paul Petunia.

Do not use Mr. in any reference except in an obituary. (Note: *The New York Times* and a few others are exceptions to this rule.) Some publications continue to use Mrs., Miss and Ms. (only *after* the first reference) in all stories. Some use them in all stories except sports stories. The trend now leans toward not using them at all, just as with male subjects. Whatever you do, make sure you're consistent throughout the story.

Abbreviate the following titles before full names: Dr., Gov., Lt. Gov., Rep., the Rev. and Sen. Do *not* continue to use the title beyond the first reference. For example, the first reference might be Sen. Claude Claghorn, but in subsequent references, use only Claghorn. The first reference might be Dr. Michael Malapractiss, but in subsequent references, use only Malapractiss.

Spell out all titles except Dr. and Mrs. when you use them in a direct quote. Examples: He said, "Dr. Paul Sampson saved my life." "Mrs. Helen Murphy will get the award," the chief said. "Senator George Capp introduced the bill," Flagstaff said. "I trust Reverend Harry Tyson," the woman said.

Punctuation

Do not use a (serial) comma before the last item in a simple series: They picked Claude, Carmichael and Luther.

The period and the comma always go inside the quotation marks. (There are no exceptions.) The rule holds for full quotes, partial quotes and even for quotes used for emphasis. "No one can break this rule and expect to pass the course," the professor said. He would not make an exception for the young man in the front row other students call "Scoop."

The question mark and the exclamation point go inside when they apply to the quoted matter only and outside when they apply to the whole sentence. Some examples:

- Who wrote "Gone With the Wind"?
- He asked, "How long will it take?"
- Did you hear him say, "I won't go"?
- "Never!" she shouted.
- I hated reading "Silas Marner"!
- "Well, I like that!" she exclaimed.

According to *The AP Stylebook*, the semicolon goes inside when it applies to the quoted matter only and outside when it applies to the whole sentence. Most other stylebooks insist it *always* goes outside. Common practice these days seems to show it on the inside more than the outside. So take your choice, but be consistent. (In strategic writing, use semicolons sparingly except in a series.)

Seasons

Lowercase spring, summer, fall and winter and all derivations, such as springtime. Capitalize only when part of a formal name, as in Winter Olympics.

States

Abbreviate all states when they are used with a town or city except for Alaska, Hawaii, Idaho, Iowa, Maine, Ohio, Texas and Utah. For example: Alexandria, Va., but Bangor, Maine.

Do not abbreviate states when they stand alone. For example: He was a Nebraska resident. (See *AP Stylebook* for proper abbreviations. *AP Style* does not use postal zip code abbreviations.)

Suspensive Hyphenation

Use suspensive hyphenation to cut down on the number of words in a sentence. Some examples:

We designed the program for 3- and 4-year-old children.

He received a 10- to 20-year sentence after he was convicted of armed robbery.

(For more on punctuation, see *The Associated Press Guide to Puctuation* by Rene J. Cappon. It is available for under $10 at www.apbookstore.com.)

EXERCISES

Test Your Editing Skills

PR Challenge 5-1

Newspaper (Associated Press Style) Test

Those who edit or write company or organization news releases and/or publish newsletters (hardcopy or online) often use some kind of style manual for consistency. The most used style manual is *The Associated Press Stylebook.*

Here is a quiz based on *Associated Press style.* See how many items you can get correct. Circle the correct answer.

1. The preferred spelling is:
    (A) goodbye (B) goodby.

2. Which punctuation is preferred?
   (A) Joseph Smith, Jr. (B) Joseph Smith Jr.

3. The preferred style for time is
   (A) 8 P.M. (B) 8 p.m. (C) 8:00 P.M. (D) 8:00 p.m.

4. Formal speech titles should be:
   (A) surrounded with quotation marks (B) underlined.

5. To form the possessive of a plural noun ending in "s"
   (A) Add only an apostrophe (B) Add an apostrophe and an "s."

6. Which form is preferred for titles following a Name?
   (A) Claire Schwartz, vice president (B) Claire Schwartz, Vice
   President

7. The preferred Associated Press spelling in most instances is:
   (A) under way (B) underway?

8. On occasion, it is necessary to split an infinitive to convey the meaning.
   (A) True (B) False.

9. Which word is preferred in all plural uses?
   (A) persons (B) people

10. The period and comma always fall within the quotation marks.
    (A) True (B) False.

11. Which is correct style:
    (A) February 14 was the target date (B) Feb. 14 was the target date?

12. Which is correct?
    (A) "This blood drive is a matter of survival", said Millard G.
    Roberts, Parsons College president.
    (B) "This blood drive is a matter of survival," said Millard G.
    Roberts, Parsons College president.

13. Which is the correct version for print?
    (A) He proposed a 300 million dollar budget.
    (B) He proposed a $300 million budget.
    (C) He proposed a $300,000,000 budget.

14. Which is correct?
    (A) Alana has a seven-year-old brother.
    (B) Alana has a 7-year-old brother.

15. Which is correct?
    (A) Coach Litwin lives at 17 Pine Valley Avenue
    (B) Coach Litwin lives at 17 Pine Valley Ave.
    (C) Coach Litwin lives at Seventeen Pine Valley Avenue
    (D) Coach Litwin lives at Seventeen Pine Valley Ave.

PR Challenge 5-2

Eliminate unnecessary words from the following sentences by editing or rewriting.

1. Don't use a nail that has any rust at all on it.

2. He lived in the city of Philadelphia in the state of Pennsylvania.

3. It happened sometime during the month of May in the year 2009.

4. He was employed in the services of the Hardesty Cable Co. for a 35-year period of time.

5. President Obama put in his appearance at the hour of noon.

6. Throughout the whole course of the entire play, Miss Coonelly wore a blue colored dress made out of silk material.

7. It is an actual fact that the government of this city ended up by expending monetary funds totaling the sum of $500,000 in the year that just passed.

8. We discovered when we ate our evening meal that everything tasted delicious while we dined.

9. The unforeseen accident took place all of a sudden at the corner of Elm Street and Finley Street when the two vehicles crashed into each other.

10. The editor of the newspaper, *The Daily Record*, condensed the story in his summary to fewer words by reducing its 500-word length to only about half of its former number of words in the original version.

PR Challenge 5-3

Eliminate unnecessary words from the following sentences by editing or rewriting.

1. She was wearing a dress that was made of silk and that had been borrowed from a friend of hers.

2. This story here will have to be typed all over again.

3. As soon as commencement time comes in June, 652 graduating seniors will receive their degrees from their alma mater.

4. History, which is considered as one of the social science subjects, is not a requirement for graduation.

5. Chi Psi is going to present a prize to the team that is the winning one. Pi Sigma is going to present one also to the team that comes in first.

6. They prefer to eat their food without any seasoning having been put on it.

7. Sam Scoggins is the type of an individual who is completely lacking of any vestige of ambition.

8. This is a contest that is open only exclusively to bald-headed men.

9. We all thought that Adam had moved to California. But he soon returned back home.

10. During the Smithville trial, it became the norm, rather than the exception, for Judge Thomas Fairfield to call for a sidebar conference or a temporary recess.

PR Challenge 5-4

Craft a *media alert* for an event of your choice. Be certain to include every one of the five W's whether or not you use that format or the event, date, time, place, details, etc. format. Be certain to follow the format and include contact information.

PR Challenge 5-5

Craft a *general news release* for the above *media alert*. Be certain the *news release* format is followed and include compelling quotes that help to engage the reader.

CHAPTER 6
Advanced Strategic (Persuasive) Writing Techniques

Chapter 6 is purposely sandwiched between "Basic Strategic Writing" (Chapter 5) and "Public Relations (Strategic) Planning and Budgeting" (Chapter 7) because it moves students and professionals to the next level. It covers tactics, tactics and more tactics – the elements, components, tools and products (vehicles) strategic communicators place on the channels our target publics rely on to receive the messages we deliver. Keep in mind that outstanding writing is the number one skill prospective employers – across the board – want in the people they hire.

This chapter covers:

[ ] Crafting the Situation Analysis

[ ] Behavioral Analysis Checklist

[ ] Crafting Key Message Points (KMPs)

[ ] Crafting Objective Copy

[ ] Crafting Strategy Copy

[ ] Crafting Tactic Copy

[ ] Crafting a Mission Statement

[ ] Crafting a Vision Statement

[ ] Guidelines for Making a Case Presentation

[ ] Crafting a Brief Case Statement

[ ] Crafting an Expanded Case Statement

[ ] Crafting a Case Solution

[ ] Crafting a Counseling Paper

[ ] Crafting a Three-Minute Drill

[ ] Crafting a Position Paper

[ ] Crafting an Op-Ed

[ ] Crafting an Obituary

[ ] Crafting a Briefing Book

[ ] Crafting an Annual Report

[ ] Crafting a Proposal

Crafting the Situation Analysis

A *Situation Analysis* (*SA*) is the process of gathering and evaluating information on internal and external environments to assess a firm's current strengths, weaknesses, opportunities and threats, and to guide the firm's goals and objectives. It sets the table for strategic planners by detailing necessary information gathered through scientific and non-scientific research – identifying target audiences and determining the strategic direction the organization should take. Some strategic communicators define an *SA* as a one-paragraph statement of the situation and refinement of the problem definition based on research. A second paragraph identifies potential difficulties and related problems to be considered.

While Chapter 7 offers three distinct approaches to writing an actual Situation Analysis, the *research* phase – the first step in the public relations planning process – is below. This suggested template – and others adapted from Rowan University public relations – strategic communication "handouts" – concentrates on the *research* structure *for* the *SA*:

1. Literature and database search
2. Real state analysis (where organization is, currently)
3. Ideal state analysis (where organization wants to be in the future)
   - Goals
   - Audience assessment
     - audience segmentation
     - audience behavioral analysis
     - audience force field analysis (conflict analysis)

- Communication strategy
- Time frame
- Budget

To write the *real state analysis,* interview your organization's upper management team to gain their insights about their own and similar organizations. Then, interview experts or authorities about the issue. Finally, interview potential targets of the proposed plan or campaign.

To write the *ideal state analysis,* indicate the goals of the organization (from management) and complete an audience assessment. These three steps comprise an audience assessment:

1. Segment (fragment) audiences by types (opinion leaders, social role models, end users, etc.).
2. Analyze audience behavior (use the behavioral analysis checklist on next page). Also, look at factors influencing your target's behavior-information level, motivation, availability, access and cost.
3. Complete an audience Force Field or Conflict Analysis (Chapter 15) using different criteria. Write about your observations. Some observations may sound like directions for the plan/campaign.

Write about your basic communication strategy (Unique Persuasive Proposition [*UPP*]), central theme, basic messages and possible channels); conclude with a realistic time frame and budget analysis based on the organization's resources and job to be done.

Use this inventory as a checklist and possible outline for your situation analysis:

- **Global objectives** – Obtain from management.
- **History of the client or organization** – Use real/ideal state analyses.
- **Link between challenge and communication** – Determine if problem can be solved by communication.
- **Audience segmentation/fragmentation** – Include types of targets, intermediaries, internals.
- **Factors controlling audience behavior** – Use the behavioral checklist.
- **Messages and appropriateness** – Use Force Field/Conflict Analysis.
- **Competition** – Identify from industry and non-industry factors.
- **Positioning** – Relate to niche marketing – your company's theme and where it fits in relative to competition.
- **Channel and media selection** – Use the *MAC Triad Plus.*

- **Timing** – Determine best times to deliver strategic messages to target audience.
- **Budget** – Create a workable budget. A budget can only be useful if it is workable and realistic. If your goals aren't attainable and practical, then you're less likely to follow the budget.

The *Situation Analysis* guides the plan. It says, "This is what we found and these items should work."

Behavioral Analysis Checklist

- Which groups should be segmented/fragmented because of their prior involvement in the issue? (Beliefs and disbeliefs – perception of a problem and a campaign solution for it)
- What aspects of the problem will be central when discussed in messages that arouse the target segment?
- Are there differences arising from language sending (encoding) and receiving (decoding)? (Remember cognitive attributes must be decoded – literacy, jargon, etc.)
- Will targeted segments know how to do what you want them to when they are persuaded?
  - cognitive plans (thoughts or perceptions)
  - procedural plans (problem solving strategy)
  - activity plans
  - test criteria plans
- Without an intention (plan), behavior might not develop.
- What rewards and means do the targets want? Messages about existing needs and products are more relevant than messages about new desires and products.
- Messages must contain reasons to arouse the target.
- Does the target not believe it is responsible for the behavior suggested by the campaign? If the audience feels it can't cope, it will refuse to act.
- Does the target display useable values? (Terminal values – *comfortable life* vs. instrumental values – *ambitious*).
- What part does emotion play in the target's perception of the problem? Fear appeals with solutions work better than fear appeals alone.
- Which (mass) media channels are best? (Authoritative, trustworthy, etc.)
- What role does the One-Step, Two-Step or Three-Step Flow play? (For community development, health communication, social services et al.) [See *The ABCs of Strategic Communication* – AuthorHouse]

PR Play 6-1
Crafting Key Message Points (KMPs)

- **Messages should account for constraints in the audience.**
  - How people process information *clutter*
  - The need to arouse people to pay attention
    (*A-I-D-A* [Chapter 2])
  - The need for the audience to remember the messages
    (*USP* [unique selling proposition]; **cue** [arousal] words)

- **Messages should employ continuity devices that help relate all messages in a campaign.**
  - Slogans
  - Symbols
  - Personalities (endorsements)
  - Audio
  - Visualizations (layout size, color, complex images, incongruity [car on a lake], affective images [children, pets])

- **Messages should recognize language and cultural differences. Always pretest.**
  - Adapt the message to the target audience.
  - Use the "seven plus or minus two" theory.
    - Remember – people can retain between five and nine (seven) message points – e.g., telephone number.

- **Establish a copy platform to carry the copy message points.**
  (*The ABCs of Strategic Communication* – AuthorHouse)

Message Delivery
- Cost effectiveness
- Message frequency
- Media mix
- Media scheduling
- (Mass) media

Adapted from Rowan (N.J.) University Case Studies in Public Relations and Public Relations Planning "handouts"

- What about group theory? Does the target look for cues from role or referent groups?
- Should resistor groups be treated as targets because they perceive themselves as defenders against your proposition? (Crisis management)
- Can your audience learn or adopt your proposition in the time you've allowed for the campaign? Does the client have realistic expectations?
- Does the potential campaign have enabling factors that will convince the target to overcome obstacles to perform the behavior? (Lowering car financing rates during a recession)

Objective Copy

PR Play 6-2
Whys and Hows of Objective Copy

"What" **STATEMENT**
Define terms, describe real state, reveal research.

"Why" **JUSTIFICATION**
Ideal state, bridge real and ideal states – public relations theories, psychology of audiences.
Avoid focusing only on channel justification.

"How/Know" **BEHAVIOR**
Target audiences only, not client.

"How/Do" **TECHNIQUE**
Strategy copy only (not tactics), messages from real state, persuasion theory.

"Gain" **BENEFITS**
Tied to **BEHAVIOR** – point for point, corollary benefits.

"Proof" **EVALUATION**
Tied to **STATEMENT** – specific techniques.

Adapted from Rowan (N.J.) University Case Studies in
Public Relations and Public Relations Planning "handouts"

Crafting Objective Copy

* Should state a behavioral outcome
"Students shall know that AIDS cannot be transmitted by social contact."
Better: "Students shall *correctly state* AIDS cannot be transmitted by social contact – touching, sharing drinking glasses or utensils." (Inherent messages.)
Campaign objectives might specify outcomes such as "knowing," "believing," "sensing," "being aware of," "holding an attitude or an opinion."
Better campaign objectives are stated through behaviors such as "telling," "stating," "demonstrating," "selecting," "buying."

* Should state a deadline
"By July 31, 50 percent of high school students shall have attended the 'Evening with the Stars' show at the planetarium."

* Should specify performance
...by essential elements
"Students shall be able to identify five of the 20 constellations portrayed in the planetarium show."
...by a percentage of the whole
"At the end of the evening, 25 percent of the students shall be able to recite the order of the planets and their distance from the sun."
...against baseline data
"The number of students who can differentiate comets, meteorites and planetesimals shall rise by 30 percent over the previous semester's number."

Objective Copy Guidelines – Specifics

* State the campaign's outcomes specifically.
* Specify the exact knowledge, attitude or behavior desired. State or imply specific bits of knowledge, specific aspects of attitude or specific behavior tasks to be achieved.

Use only third person references to client, counselor and material. Write the following sections:

Statement

First, express to client or manager *what* needs to be done as evidenced from research. Speak to *need*. Specify that as part of the goal, the objective must be reached if you're to accomplish the goal. (Based on the research, client is told what he/she *needs* to hear, not what he/she necessarily *wants* to hear.)

Justification

Next, justify the objective according to any reasonable criteria: *audience* – the most common method; *counseling* – as a change in the organization's identity; *communication* – that will affect audiences; *cost* – as the established budget will bear.

Behavior

Then, write about the measurable change specified in the objective. Write about information, attitude or behavior change in audiences. You can cite behavior retention, behavior modification or behavior elimination. State the baseline measurement and the percentage of movement from it (if appropriate).

Technique

Now, write about the *strategic approaches* you'll use to reach the objective. Merely state them. Save the full explanation for strategy copy. Remember, strategies are partly objective (what) and partly tactic (how). Make certain you write about both aspects. Then suggest the *tactics* you'll use to implement your strategies. Again, merely state them, don't elaborate.

Clients or managers must understand this connection:

audience → message → strategy → tactic → effect.

Each *tactic* will receive sufficient explanation in the *strategy/tactic* copy.

Benefit

Write strong benefit or payoff copy. This section does most of the persuading that your plan is on target. Key the benefits, *item for item*, to the purposes you expressed in the justification. Picture it objectively, but graphically. Allude to future and multiple uses. Convey the idea that clients or mangers need the benefits.

Proof

Illustrate which evaluation method will be used to prove how the objective will be achieved. Describe the techniques you'll use. Remember, you'll need to prove that the work can and will be done.

Example of an objective:

"To increase KYW Newsradio's listenership (behavioral outcome) among 18-34-year-olds (public) by 15 percent (level of accomplishment or change) within the next six months of this year (time frame)."

Adapted from Rowan (N.J.) University Case Studies in
Public Relations and Public Relations Planning "handouts"

Planning Strategies and Tactics
Strategies

Strategies are *approaches* to do the work of the *objectives*. View strategies as intermediate steps between an objective and the specific tactics that will do the actual work.

Example:

Goal: "Become No. 1 radio station in Philadelphia market."

Objective: "To increase KYW Newsradio's listenership (behavioral outcome) among 18-34-year-old (public) by 15 percent (level) within the next six months of this year (time frame)."

Strategy: "Alter programming to make it more appealing to a younger listening audience."

Tactic: "Interview target audience (18-34-year-olds) to learn listener preferences both on radio and Web 2.0 (Internet)."

Note how the strategy uses prior research that identifies a listener void or disenfranchisement because of programming that could be deemed "old fashioned." This "old-fashioned" programming constrains 18-34-year-olds from fully enjoying 24/7 news programming.

Planners reason that they cannot improve listnership until they remove the audience constraint. The strategy removes it.

Untutored planners might have skipped this strategic step and gone straight to a *tactic*. It might have looked like this:

"Buy advertising aimed at 18-34-year-olds focusing on program benefits."

These untutored planners might honestly think they're improving efforts to attract listeners because it sounds like they are ("ad").

Strategies work when planners accomplish these tasks:
• Logically look at objectives as effects and strategies as causes.
  Example: Increased listenership (effect) happens if 18-34-year-olds are

part of decision making (cause). Effective planners are logical thinkers.

- Divide the objectives into manageable parts – focusing on audiences or major jobs to be done as multiple causes.
- Change an audience – usually an attitude but it could be knowledge or behavior. Notice how the change becomes the necessary cause.
- Prepare an audience or public for a tactic. Tactics activate the cause – put it into play (action = time + cost + agent).

Tactics
Planners make strategies work by matching the audience in the *strategy*, the message to be sent and the right channel to do the job. In the example, the *tactic*...

"Interview 18-34-year-olds for their preferences about news stories, features and delivery of the news."

...identifies the audience (group leaders), message (we're interested in your opinion) and channel (interviews).

If the *strategy* specifies something other than an audience, messages and channels still work because of implied audiences. However, in the end, for messages to be received by a targeted audience, all elements of the *MAC Triad Plus* must be accomplished.

Example:
Strategy: "Position KYW Newsradio as a market (and national) leader in all news (24/7) radio."

Implied audiences: media, other industry leaders, competitors, other age groups. Messages: leadership, accuracy. Channels: mass media, Internet, industry advertising, viral marketing and public relations.

Crafting Strategy/Tactic Copy
Generally use first person reference. It will signal creative ownership of the elements.

Statement
- Begin with a *definition of the strategy*.
- Then, list the *tactics* you will employ to implement the strategy.
- Offer a suggested *list of activities* that will make this happen. Make a detailed list. Your manager or client should see how much is involved. Remember: Envision (picture) the process as much as you define it.

Examples:

"Listeners' wants and needs will be met through (KYW Newsradio conducting) opinion surveys among various audiences to gather specific programming ideas." (**Strategy**)

"KYW Newsradio will conduct a series of focus panels of 18-34-year-olds to gather specific programming ideas." (**Tactic**)

"KYW Newsradio will survey fragments of its listening audience – primarily 18-34-year-olds – to determine programming preferences." (**Tactic**)

(List of specific activities follows...)

"KYW Newsradio will conduct a number of special events aimed at attracting 18-34-year-olds to tell them what we offer and to better understand what they want in all news programming." (**Strategy – behavioral change**)

"We will host event at 'National Constitution Center' to engage 18-34-year-olds in one-on-one interviews to determine programming likes and dislikes." (**Tactic – more specific**)

"We will host event at 'Alana's Hangout' – a popular nightspot for 18-34-year-olds to engage them in one-on-one interviews to determine programming likes and dislikes." (**Tactic – more specific**)

Justification

Justify your strategy/tactics in terms of the appropriate connection between:

purpose → audience → message → channel → timing → cost

(*MAC Triad Plus*)

Remember to specify the difference between the general media (print, face-to-face, broadcast, Internet, special events – generally used in the strategy statements) and the specific versions of those media called channels – news releases, brochures, position papers, etc. – generally used in tactics statements). *Example:* If you select a broadcast medium (TV or FM radio station to promote KYW Newsradio, an AM station) you might also select news releases as the best print channel).

Benefits

State the product of the strategy/tactics or the outcome (effect) to the target audience. Specify the expected outcome in terms of predicted knowledge, new awareness or change in behavior. Think comprehensively about this.

Proof

State specifically how you will evaluate the success of your strategy. Do this for both *quality* and *process evaluation* – how well was the communication tool made and delivered. And how well did it work.

There are *five* elements we can measure in public relations. When preparing this summary for a boss or client, write it as a one-page summary, if possible. Make certain to include:

- Agent: (1) Who will carry out the strategy? (2) Do you have the resources to do it?
- Cost: (3) How much will it cost? (4) Is it under budget?
- Time: (5) How long will it take to make and deliver the strategy and when will it happen?

Crafting a Mission Statement

A clear and succinct reason the organization came into existence – its purpose. It answers the question: "Why we are here to serve you – why are we in business? (This is who we are; what we think about ourselves; what we want to do; and why we deserve your support.) The corporate mission statement, with a broad focus and a customer orientation, provides management with a sense of purpose. A brief statement defines "What business are we in." It should have a broad focus and a customer orientation.

Writing a Mission Statement

One of the hardest "products" for strategic counselors to write is the *mission statement. Mission statements* can tell a lot about your business, so it's important to take time, look at some mission statement examples, and put effort into writing a good one.

What is a Mission Statement?

You should think of a *mission statement* as a cross between a slogan and an executive summary.

PR Play 6-3

Add punch to your strategies
with these *action verbs* and other *key words*

abstract	began	cooperate	enrich
accelerate	bolster	coordinate	establish
accomplish	boost	counsel	evaluate
account	broaden	craft	examine
achieve	budget	create	exchange
act	build	critique	execute
activate	buy	dance	expand
adapt	calculate	define	expedite
add	capture	delegate	experience
administer	catalogue	demonstrate	explore
advance	categorize	describe	extend
advertise	challenge	design	facilitate
advise	change	determine	familiarize
aid	choreograph	develop	fluency
align	clarify	devise	focus
allocate	classify	diagram	follow
amuse	coach	discover	forecast
analyze	collaborate	direct	formulate
answer	communicate	discern	found
anticipate	compare	display	furnish
appoint	compile	distribute	generate
approach	complete	draw	gentrify
approve	compose	earn	govern
arbitrate	comprehend	educate	handle
arrange	compute	eliminate	help
assemble	conceive	employ	hire
assess	condense	enable	identify
assist	conduct	encourage	implement
assume	construct	engineer	improve
attain	consult	enhance	increase
augment	contract	enlarge	infer
awaken	control	enlist	influence
award	convince	entertain	inform

cont.

PR Play 6-3 cont.

initiate	observe	record	structure
innovate	organize	recruit	style
inquire	orient	redefine	substitute
inspect	originate	redesign	suggest
install	oversee	reduce	summarize
institute	participate	refer	supervise
instruct	perform	regulate	support
integrate	persuade	reinforce	survey
interpret	plan	renew	strategize
interrogate	prepare	reorganize	synthesize
interview	present	render	systematize
introduce	preside	represent	teach
intuit	probe	request	tend
invent	problem solve	require	trade
inventory	process	research	train
investigate	produce	resolve	transform
judge	proficiency	respond	translate
launch	profit	responsible	troubleshoot
layout	program	restructure	tutor
learn	progress	revamp	understand
lecture	project	review	unify
liaison	promote	revise	unite
link	propose	rewrite	update
list	prove	select	upgrade
maintain	provide	schedule	use
manage	publicize	screen	utilize
manipulate	purchase	seek	valuate
market	qualify	select	vend
mediate	quantify	set up	verbalize
merge	question	sing	verify
model	raise	sketch	volunteer
modify	read	solve	write
monitor	received	stimulate	work
motivate	recommend	streamline	
negotiate	reconstruct	strengthen	

PR Play 6-4
Mission Statement Example –
Thomas Jefferson University Hospital

Thomas Jefferson University Hospital is dedicated to improving the health of the communities we serve. We are committed to:

- Setting the standard for excellence in the delivery of patient care, patient safety and the quality of the healthcare experience.
- Providing exemplary clinical settings for educating the healthcare professionals who will form the collaborative healthcare delivery team of tomorrow.
- Leading in the introduction of innovative methodologies for health-care delivery and quality improvement.

We accomplish our mission in partnership with Thomas Jefferson University and as a member of the Jefferson Health System.

PR Play 6-5
Vision Statement Example –
Thomas Jefferson University Hospital

- To be a national leader for excellence and innovation in the delivery of healthcare and patient safety, continually improving the quality of services and the patient care experience.
- To be the model of service in our focused clinical service lines and in related patient-oriented research and clinical trials.
- To provide exemplary clinical settings that support the education of future healthcare practitioners, both as individuals and as members of the collaborative healthcare delivery team.
- To be an "employer of choice," providing a highly rewarding environment for our employees.

Just as slogans and executive summaries can be used in many ways so, too, can a mission statement. An effective *mission statement* should be able to tell your company story and ideals in less than 30 seconds.

PR Play 6-6

Encompassing Mission Statement –
The Rothman Institute

The Rothman Institute delivers world class orthopaedic care through exceptional service, compassionate physicians and staff members, quality patient care, advanced technology and science, as well as unsurpassed patient and staff education – the results of which universally exceed our patients' expectations.

Our Company
Rothman Institute Orthopaedics will lead the healthcare industry through the provision of unsurpassed service and quality care, and the continuous development and education of our physicians and employees.

Our Patients
Our patients are the most important aspect of our healthcare practice. We will provide our patients with unparalleled service, respectful, high-quality care and education in a safe and comfortable environment that promotes the enhancement of mobility and the quality of life.

Our Community
Our commitment to the communities we serve is the foundation of our civic responsibilities. We will provide employment opportunities, charitable services and contributions, supporting the local economy. Through our responsible citizenship and community engagement efforts, we will make the community a better place to live.

Our Physicians
Our strength lies in the knowledge, innovation, expertise and exacting standards of our physicians. We will bring the same passion for excellence that makes us the preferred provider of care for employers, referring physicians and athletic teams to our daily operations and interactions with our highly trained specialists.

Our Employees
Our employees are the heart and soul of our company and their contributions are essential to accomplishing our mission. We will invest in each employee through the provision of optimal working environment, encouragement of self-expression and professional development, cultivation of self-esteem, and promotion of positive relationships.

"Exceptional Care, Exceptionally Caring"

PR Play 6-7
Mission Statement Example – Ben & Jerry's®

Ben & Jerry's® takes a unique approach to a mission statement. The corporation posts three mission statements, side by side – one for each of its approaches/commitments – product, economic and social.

Our Mission Statement
Ben & Jerry's® is founded on and dedicated to a sustainable corporate concept of linked prosperity.

Our mission consists of 3 interrelated parts:

Product Mission	Economic Mission	Social Mission
To make, distribute & sell the finest quality all natural ice cream & euphoric concoctions with a continued commitment to incorporating wholesome, natural ingredients and promoting business practices that respect the Earth and the Environment.	To operate the Company on a sustainable financial basis of profitable growth, increasing value for our stakeholders & expanding opportunities for development and career growth for our employees.	To operate the company in a way that actively recognizes the central role that business plays in society by initiating innovative ways to improve the quality of life locally, nationally & internationally.

Central To The Mission Of Ben & Jerry's®
is the belief that all three parts must thrive equally in a manner that commands deep respect for individuals in and outside the company and supports the communities of which they are a part.

How should I write a Mission Statement?

Here are some basic guidelines in writing a *mission statement:*

- A mission statement should say who your company is, what you do, what you stand for and why you do it.
- An effective *mission statement* is best developed with input from all the members of an organization.

- The best *mission statements* tend to be three to four sentences long.
- Avoid saying how great you are, what great quality and what great service you provide.
- Examine other *mission statements*, but make certain your statement is you and not some other company, firm or organization. That is why you should not copy a statement.
- Make sure you actually believe in your *mission statement*. If you don't, it's a lie, and your customers or clients will soon realize it.

Crafting a Vision Statement

Susan Ward of Cypress Technologies defines a *vision statement* as a picture of your company in the future, but so much more. Your vision statement is your inspiration, the framework for all your strategic planning.

A vision statement may apply to an entire company or to a single division of that company. Whether for all or part of an organization, the vision statement answers the question, "Where do we want to go?"

What you are doing when creating a vision statement is articulating your dreams and hopes for your business. It reminds you of what you are trying to build.

While a vision statement doesn't tell you how you're going to get there, it does set the direction for your business planning.

Guidelines for Making a Case Presentation

Making a *Case Presentation* precedes other case products – to help explain where you are headed. The *Case Presentation* is taking the research and other hard work committed to paper and explaining it using the most up-to-date technology. A case study is a retrospective – an evaluation of a communication challenge and how it was handled by an individual or organization. The study is methodical, includes research and usually a strategic plan.

Evaluators, preparing as if they were presenting to a client, work with a group or team. Teams use individual members' skills to their best advantage. Members are encouraged to look within themselves to their own talent and motivation. Each member should consider the art as well as the science of presenting information in a clear, logical way. Skillfully persuade others to see things as you do. Be gracious with your audience – even those who disagree with you.

Follow the basic outline presented here, but improvise, create and add your own stylistic touches – your fingerprint.

- Begin with an overview of the case. Do not repeat it word for word, but give enough information for others to follow.
- List the *issues* involved in the case. Use visuals to help your audience follow you. Issues are *statements of fact* about a situation (what people think about something). Generally, they include an audience, a topic and a tone. Example: *"Residents (audience) are concerned (tone) that exposure to certain gases (topic) may be a hazard to their health."* Caution: Issues may contain both causes and symptoms. It is important to understand, and in some cases, explain the differences.
- List the *research* done in the case or that you would do.
- List the *audiences*. Identify, segment, fragment, profile and rank them. Make certain to cover internal and external audiences. Do not forget intermediary audiences.
- List *objectives*. These are outcomes you (or your case characters) expect to accomplish. These are not activities. They focus on the "what" to be done. Generally, they will have an audience, a purpose (information, attitude, behavior) and a measurable term in them – along with what you wish to accomplish.
- List *strategic approaches*. These are the communication or counseling techniques you (or your case characters) plan to use to change behavior to accomplish your objectives. They focus on the "how" and "why" of getting the job done. Generally, they are versions of print, broadcast, Internet, face-to-face, special event or research activity. Use good, strong action verbs to demonstrate how you will achieve your accomplishments. Strategies are the thoughts behind each objective.
- List *tactics* (*strategic actions*). These are specific versions of the strategic approaches. Example: A *strategic approach* might be *"Conduct* an aggressive print campaign..."* A *tactic* (*strategic action*) might be *"Produce* and *disseminate* inline newsletter to 50,000 email recipients through a blast email."
- List results or outcomes. Specify how measurement should or did take place.
- Discuss what you would have done differently. Entertain questions.
- Make certain you use visuals, handouts and other aids that will help you do the job. Keep all sight lines clear between the audience, the speaker and the visuals. Visuals must be professional.

- Don't overrun one another as you speak. Assign "areas" to each person so you handle questions in an orderly manner. Set up the room professionally – speaker standing, others seated and supporting the speaker. Use tables, lecterns, flip charts, Smartboards®, PowerPoints®, etc. Remember, others may be using a presentation room immediately prior to you. Or, you may not be able to get in as early as you wish. Be prepared to move quickly.
- Be prepared → be confident → be professional.

Crafting a Brief Case Statement

A *brief case statement* is actually an issue or impact statement (*The ABCs of Strategic Communication* – AuthorHouse) – a single declarative sentence. Once that has been approved, it is usually expanded into a "white paper," an expanded case statement (see below).

Before writing the *brief case statement*:
- Conduct thorough research to understand subject completely.
- Consider the impact of an issue in a factual manner.
- Outline main points to be included before writing.
- Consider the current significance and status of issue.
- Write in third person; use a hard-hitting, factual style; avoid use of opinions (they would be on quote sheet).

Brief Case Statement – Example
Victims' families face financial crisis due to slow decision-making and payment of relief donations from a charity consortium formed to organize funds in the aftermath of 9/11.

Crafting an Expanded Case Statement

After getting approval on the case statement (the single declarative sentence), the expanded statement, the "white paper," is lengthened to include background, history, issues and audiences. The issue statement, case statement and case solution combine to support findings and eventual position if one is required.

Part One - *Statement*
Begin with an *impact statement* – the single sentence that states what the organization faces in the case – the problem or challenge. For example, "Johnson & Johnson faces a drop in sales and a loss of customer confidence because of the recent deaths from cyanide-laced Tylenol."

Part Two - *Background*

Continue with a *description* (historical, chronological, cause and effect, etc.) of events or facts contributing to the problem. Include the following elements (if available):

- Characters or organizations in the case
- Intentional or accidental communications
- Audiences and their reactions
- Market effects
- Motivation for behavior
- "Environmental" influences
- Revenues expended
- Public opinion affected

Part Three - *Issues*

List and prioritize the *issues* which the organization faces. Include the following:

- Issues affecting internal audiences
- Issues affecting external audiences
- Issues affecting intervening audiences
- Issues affecting the "communication environment"

Part Four - *Audiences*

List potential *target audiences* and desired *effects* on them through a communication plan. Remember *education, knowledge, attitudes and behavior* (PR Play 2-11) are the four effects PR deals with. List management *imperatives* – what management wants to happen. List the controllable and uncontrollable *variables* the communicator must deal with. Do not list solutions to the problem (they come later).

Adapted from Rowan (N.J.) University Case Studies in
Public Relations and Public Relations Planning "handouts"

Expanded Case Statement – Example

Case Statement

Victims' families face financial crisis due to slow decision-making and payment of relief donations from a charity consortium formed to organize funds in the aftermath of 9/11.

Background

On September 11, 2001, terrorists launched attacks on the World Trade Center in New York City, the Pentagon in Washington, D.C. and a jet passenger plane in Pennsylvania. The attack on America caused more than 6,000 deaths. More than 15,000 children lost one or more parents.

This has caused financial crisis for many families. Main income providers died. Families are in upheaval, with the financial burden to be shouldered by a widowed spouse and in some cases, small children.

Charities quickly set up relief funds for these victims. A consortium of approximately 125 charities was created to organize donations for distribution to the families. Collections have reached over $1 billion, but three months later, the families have yet to see any funds.

Audiences
Victims' families - (internal)
Charity consortium - (internal)
Media - (intermediary)
American Public - (intermediary/external)

Issues
- Victims' families face financial distress due to the consortium's inability to send timely relief.
- Long-term relief measures have not been taken for continued support to the victims' families.

Solutions
To determine immediate relief needs, the 9/11 Victims' Association will send out 6,026 applications to assess those needs on a case-by-case basis. The application will consist of the following questions:
- Did the loss of a loved one leave you as sole financial provider for your household?
- What are your primary financial concerns at this time?
- Are these needs an emergency? For example, are you at risk of losing your home in the next 90 days?
- In dollars, how much would you estimate as your total emergency debt?

After applications are sent by the association, the victims have 15 business days to return their forms, along with proof of any claims (i.e., bills and other paperwork). The 9/11 Victims' Association will review the claim, establish emergency need, and forward the paperwork to the charity consortium. A maximum of $50,000 will be granted for each claim. After receipt of the paperwork, the charity consortium has 15 business days to issue a check to the families.

To speed up long-term distribution of the funds, the 9/11 Victims' Association will form a committee with spokespeople from the association and the charity consortium to establish the following:

- Long-term payment plans and timelines for individual cases.
- Total entitlements for each individual case (need based or standard).
- Accountability for all funds donated by the public.
- Any additional issues regarding funds as they arise.

The committee has six months to finalize all decisions for long-term support. All decisions made, and any additional pertinent information, will be posted on a website maintained by the 9/11 Victims' Association. A toll-free number will be established for both long- and short-term inquires. A national media campaign will be implemented to publicize both the website and hotline. This will be accomplished through news conferences open to all media. Paid advertisements will be placed in newspapers and on radio and television in areas near disaster locations for greatest impact. Blast emails and other proactive tactics will be delivered via the Internet.

Crafting a Case Solution

Part One - *Statement*

Begin with the *impact/issue statement* (Some refer to the *impact statement* alone as the *case statement*) – the single sentence that states the problem or challenge facing an organization. For example, state "The U.S. Army faces a serious challenge in attracting recruits because of the fear of being deployed to fight in Iraq, Iran or Afghanistan."

Part Two - *Issues*

List the *issues* facing the organization which result from the *case statement* analysis. Make certain to *prioritize* the issues. Remember, issues are *statements of fact* about a situation (what people think about something). Issues may be challenges, problems, audience research, employee reactions, media cooperation or the lack of it, etc. They may be negative and/or positive.

Part Three - *Audiences/Approaches*

List the *target audiences* in priority order and the desired effect the organization would like to have on each. Then, sketch a *broad approach* to solve the problem.

Make certain the approach includes the following items:
- Research activity
- Message content (by *audience*)
- Channel selection (by *audience*)
- Evaluation (by *issue*)

State the approach in general terms. (Full strategic communication plans go further and list everything in detail.) For example, state "The U.S. Army needs to attract able-bodied men and women willing to defend their country and do whatever is necessary to achieve peace in the Mideast. A viral marketing campaign would be an excellent approach because it uses third-party endorsers and source credibility for personal persuasion..."

Part Four - *Resources*
List the resources available to the organization. Include people, financial assets, time, networking connections, barters with other organizations, etc.

Part Five - *Benefits*
List the *specific benefits* the organization will enjoy from the approaches selected. The list should take the *organization's viewpoint.* For example, say, "The U.S. Army will see a significant increase in the number of men and women interested in enlisting in the U.S. Army or one of the other armed services because of the opportunities they offer.

Portions provided by Professor Anthony J. Fulginiti, APR, Fellow PRSA – Rowan (N.J.) University

Case Solution – Example No.1
I. Statement
The American Red Cross faces a serious loss of blood supplies because donors fear the possibility of contracting AIDS when they donate.

II. Issues related to this problem
- Research reveals that past donors are less anxious than new donors about this false consequence because of their experience with the Red Cross.
- New donors report being more influenced by word-of-mouth and rumor than by official Red Cross communication efforts. The Red Cross can reach this group only through mass media.

- Exit surveys of donors reveal that the donor population is only "somewhat concerned" about the issue (Likert scale response set). The studies also show that 85 percent of this group asks about the possibility of contracting any disease when they donate. The group also reveals that respondents comfortably proceed with donations following verbal reassurance by Red Cross personnel at the donation sites.
- Media reports, especially by ABC-TV news, have raised the level of fear. The network covered an ABC "study" in which respondents raised the question. The report did not contain official comment by the Red Cross.
- Hospitals are seeing a rapid "spike" upward in requests by patients to donate their own blood prior to their procedures. Apparently, these patients report no fear because the needles used are used on them alone.

III. Audiences/Approaches
A. Audiences involved in this case
- Past donors: The Red Cross needs to reassure these faithful donors that nothing has changed in the process of collecting blood. They were safe before. They remain safe. This group can be used as endorsing intermediary channels.
- New donors: Need to hear from past donors that their fears are unfounded. A description of the donation process will affirm that a needle is used once and never again. This group would be more acceptable of a graphic display of the process rather than mere words.
- The media: All media are intermediaries with the general public. All should receive blood donation campaign literature, visuals and footage of the donation process. ABC should be enticed into doing a follow-up story from the Red Cross' point of view.
- Potential hospital patients can be useful in the donation campaign, especially if they seek family and friends to donate to the hospital prior to their procedures, The Red Cross must signal that the Red Cross donation process is identical to the hospital collection process.

B. PR Approaches
- *Research:* Conduct national telephone surveys, intercept studies at collection centers, and focus group studies of message/channel effectiveness.

- The Red Cross should begin an intensive eight-week donation campaign focusing on the confidence past donors have about the process. The use of past donors will not only retain past donors, but also gain new ones.
- The campaign will use television, radio and transit advertising to reach the widest possible audience. The Red Cross will approach ABC-TV with an offer to allow video taping at donation sites and will provide the network with professionals (source credibility/third party validation) involved in the process for comment.
- Collectors at donation sites will become secondary believable messengers (source credibility). Collectors will state they would not hesitate to collect blood from family or friends, or donate themselves.
- *Special event*: Blood Donor Day – promoting safe blood donation. Coordinated by Red Cross national PR staff and Fleischman-Hillard/New York, the campaign will be available to local Red Cross chapters to replicate in their localities. Event will use medical and social professionals who deal with AIDS to calm fears.
- *Evaluation:* The Red Cross will see a reduction in the fear factor involved in blood donation through survey studies, cooperation of national media in the campaign and successful citation of believable message bearers by potential donors.

IV. Available resources
- $3 million campaign budget
- Excellent media relationships with all campaign outlets, including ABC-TV
- 100 past donors willing to become part of the advertising and PR campaign
- 200 collectors willing to participate in the campaign and endorse the collection process
- Three national AIDS groups willing to participate and volunteer their professionals
- Five regional PRSSA chapters willing to conduct "safe donor" campaigns

V. Benefits

- The Red Cross will see a significant decrease in the fear factor, evidenced by a national scientific telephone study.
- The Red Cross will see a 10 percent increase in donations in the two months during the campaign and the three months following the end of the campaign.
- The Red Cross will improve its media relations, especially as a source for future media stories, such as the growing number and type of patients in hospital emergency rooms needing blood; catastrophes and disasters requiring the confidence of afflicted people in the safety of resources rushed to them – particularly blood supplies.

Case Solution – Example No. 2

(Disclaimer – Researched and written prior to opening of new ball park)

I. Statement

The Philadelphia Phillies' fans are uninterested in attending Phillies games and Phillies' management feels that the new stadium will eliminate all of their problems.

II. Issues

1. The fans are uninterested in attending the Phillies home games.
2. The Phillies franchise feels the new stadium will change the public's negative perception of the team.
3. Employees demonstrate negative attitudes toward fans from the minute they arrive at the parking lots.

III. Audiences/Approaches

A. Audiences

Management – We want management to realize that they need to start repairing the organization's problems now and not wait until a new Stadium opens.

Coaches – We want coaches to get the whole ball club to do more newsworthy activities off the ball field.

Players – We need players to get more into the spotlight on and off the ball field.

Employees – We need employees to have better customer relations toward the fans and feel more appreciated within the organization.

Support staff supervisors – We need support staff supervisors to better appreciate their parking lot attendants, ticket sellers and takers, ushers and concession personnel.

Sports Media – For the organization to be able to compete within the Greater Philadelphia market, the sports media need to cover more Phillies' events, on and off the ball field.

PR Play 6-8
Crafting a Counseling Paper

All public relations counselors and strategic advisers should be able to craft (through research) and write a counseling paper. Follow these directions and format and your paper should serve your superior and client well.

DIRECTION
- Conduct original research on the issue, problem or challenge presented. The research could come from newspapers, the Internet, broadcast news reports, professional publications, or actual public relations practice.
- A *counseling paper* should be about 1,000 words (four typed pages, double spaced, 12 point type).

FORMAT
Section I – Background
  Section I names the organizations or individuals involved and identifies the problem or challenge.
  Example: An Internet company (Collegepapers.biz) specializes in writing term papers for students. The company has been criticized for offering an unethical service and has even been in court to defend against lawsuits.

Section II – Issues
  Section II specifies the issues involved. Make certain to include all appropriate audiences. (See *Section III*)
  For instance: Collegepapers.biz stock is dropping, public opinion has turned against it, and customers and advertisers fear it will go out of business.

cont.

PR Play 6-8 continued

Section III – Criteria

Section III lays out the criteria necessary for an effective plan – what you want your recommendation to accomplish. It specifies the necessary features, benefits and acceptable risk of any decision (plan). It must specify the target audiences best served by the plan – boss, client, consumers, mass public opinion, specific public opinion, media, etc.

For instance: Public relations must come up with a decision (plan) that: establishes *Collegepapers.biz* as only a research company in the minds of academics and the law; advertises it as a handy source of researched papers for students and other customers to use as they see fit; keeps advertisers interested; avoids bankruptcy; and keeps stockholders happy.

Section IV – Analysis of Options

Section IV presents and analyzes each option – at least three – a public relations counselor could recommend to a superior or client. Each option must contain pro and con effects (use *Force Field or Conflict Analysis* to support your counsel) of each option for superior or client.

For instance: Collegepapers.biz can sell the company; conduct a media ad (guerilla advertising) and news release blitz; offer a recognizable and legal disclaimer; persuade academics to join in the research, thereby weakening the attack and "sanitizing" the activity. Think in terms of pros and cons (Force Field/Conflict Analysis – Chapter 15).

Section V – Recommendation

Section V specifies the recommended option that best serves the client. It also argues for its adoption through a recounting of the accruing benefits and/or avoidance of unacceptable effects.

For instance: Sell *Collegepapers.biz;* position it with a new image as a "research use only" product; and persuade publics *Collegepapers.biz* is doing nothing different than students would do in getting the ideas of *Collegepapers.biz* writers themselves, although in a more labor intensive and time wasting way.

Adapted from Rowan (N.J.) University
Public Relations "handouts"

Fans – We want to them to attend the games and feel appreciated by the ball club.

B. Research activity

Our research has shown that fans are not attending the ball games for a few reasons: they do not feel comfortable within the ball park because the employees are rude to them because the employees do not feel appreciated by the ball club. The fans, also, do not feel appreciated by the ball club. The management feels that a new stadium will eliminate all negative feelings toward the ball club. Many coaches and players are self-centered and need to start concentrating on what they can do to "fix" the ball club's problems. The sports media are not covering Phillies' external events because they do not know when activities are scheduled and because the Phillies are not in their good graces.

C. Message content

Management – Create a family atmosphere now.

Coaches – Get yourselves and the players more involved in the Greater Philadelphia community.

Players – Get more involved and *everybody* wins.

Employees – You are an integral part of the organization.

Sports Media – We are doing great things, come and see them.

Fans – Come be part of the Phillies' family.

D. Channel selection

Management – Counseling session.

Coaches – Counseling session.

Players – Counseling session.

Employees – Customer training/relationship marketing model (Hire outside consultant).

Sports Media – Increase the public relations information they receive.

Fans – Reach them through television, radio, print, billboards, special events and other cross-platforming tactics – Web 2.0, blast emails, etc.

E. Evaluation
Issue 1
- Issue – The fans are uninterested in attending the Phillies games.
- Solution or Behavior Change – The fans will feel that the Phillies are a family and will therefore want to go to the games.

Issue 2
- Issue – The Phillies' franchise feels the new stadium will change the public's negative perception of the team.
- Solution or Behavior Change – Management will start fixing the Phillies now and will create a family atmosphere.

Issue 3
- Issue – Employees demonstrate negative attitudes toward fans.
- Solution or Behavior Change – The employees will feel appreciated by the ball club and will be nicer to the fans.

Issue 4
- Issue – Local sports media fail to cover Phillies events.
- Solution or Behavior Change – The local sports media will feel better about the Phillies, learn about more of their off-the-field activities and therefore increase coverage.

IV. Resources
- A strong Philadelphia Community
- 18 radio and television sponsors
- Numerous Philadelphia-based charities and other non-profits
- Ample time to prepare before new ball park opens
- The new ball park

V. Benefits
- Philadelphia Phillies will see an increase in attendance, news coverage and marketability.
- Management, coaches, players, employees, sports media and fans will feel a newfound sense of pride in the Phillies.

Portions written by Jillian Tota – Rowan (N.J.) University Graduate

Counseling Paper – Example
I. Background
The major roadway Route 322 runs through the middle of Rowan University's campus. It is a high-volume road that has existed at its current location long before the University was established. As Rowan's campus and population continue to grow, consideration must be given to

whether or not Route 322 poses more danger to pedestrians than convenience to travelers. The ideal time to plan for any alterations is now – during (the new) Downtown Glassboro's construction – while the community is already adjusting to changes in Rowan's campus layout and configuration. Route 322 on the Rowan campus is known locally as Mullica Hill Road.

II. Issues

1. Con Issues
   - Students, faculty and employees at Rowan University frequently cross Route 322 on foot to access both sides of campus. This is becoming increasingly dangerous as the population grows in terms of pedestrians and drivers.
   - Route 322 motorists must be especially aware of pedestrians as they travel the roadway through campus. However, many are often distracted by various factors. Cell phones, MP3 players, other vehicles or simply not focusing on driving affect a driver's awareness and actions.
   - Any changes to Route 322 may affect local Glassboro residents as well as commuters and other motorists who pass through the town on a regular basis.
   - A major project on Rowan's campus may affect the tuition students and their parents pay and Rowan's future enrollment (student population) as tuition is a top consideration in the college decision process.
   - A major construction project would be funded by taxpayers. Currently, approving a tax increase with the state of the economy will be difficult as many people value saving their money and tightening their budgets.

2. Neutral Issues
   - Local businesses may be affected if the roadway is redirected and customer traffic decreases or increases in the area.
   - Route 322 is the most efficient route for many of its drivers at its current location. A change in its course will inconvenience some by making their travel time longer but aide others by making their travel time shorter depending on the direction taken.

PR Play 6-9
Position Paper – Simple Approach
Stating *Your* Position

1. **Problem** – State the problem – starting with a brief background and historical information on the issue.
2. **Effects/Issues** – Include information on opposing viewpoints to help paint a complete picture of the issue.
3. **Position** – State the organization's position clearly. Use objective evidence, expert testimony and valid statistics to support that position and to contradict the position of the opposition.
4. **Benefits** – Allude to features that support your position. Those features produce benefits to audiences. Don't hesitate to offer alternative solutions relating to the problem or issue.

---

3. Pro Issue
   - The current economy is demonstrating a high number of layoffs in many industries. A project to change Route 322 would provide employment to construction workers for several months.

III. Criteria
The solution to this problem must: maintain the access provided by Route 322 from one side of Rowan University to the other with minimum inconvenience, provide a safe environment for Rowan University's pedestrian population and affect the least number of publics with any needed changes.

IV. Options Analysis
Option 1
Route 322 could be redirected around the Rowan University campus. This would guide drivers in a new course to avoid the interaction with pedestrians the road currently causes as it divides the campus.

- Cons: drivers would be forced to add minutes to their travel time if surrounding roads are turned into the alternate route, surrounding roads that currently have little or no traffic in quiet areas would cause inconvenience by the increased traffic, signs would need to be changed to direct Route 322's (bypass) redirection and the actual road would still be in the same place giving the same access to drivers even if Route 322 is rerouted – unless through traffic is prohibited.

▪ Pros: little construction would be necessary because surrounding roads would be used and it would require a relatively low budget.

Option 2
Close Route 322 to vehicle traffic and construct a new roadway around the campus allowing the same travel time and direct path through Glassboro.

▪ Cons: it would require an expensive budget (affecting taxpayers), extensive planning and temporary detours (affecting local residents) while the construction takes place.

▪ Pros: the guaranteed safety of the pedestrians on Rowan's main road and the number of jobs that would be generated for construction workers.

Option 3
Build elevated pedestrian walkways over Route 322 and insert speed bumps along Route 322.

▪ Cons: temporary detours during construction and funding to be paid by taxpayers.

▪ Pros: construction for this project would take less time than the other projects, necessary budgets would be less than the other proposals, safety would be guaranteed for pedestrians using the walkways, Route 322 would not need to be redirected, drivers would be forced to reduce their speed and drivers would have fewer distractions.

Option 4
Erect road signs (yield to pedestrians, slow speed warnings), insert speed bumps and make no changes to Route 322 or the painted-on (marked) crosswalks.

▪ Cons: all the current dangers of the roadway would still exist.

▪ Pros: it would require a very low budget, speed bumps would slow down vehicles and there would be no new inconveniences to Route 322 travelers.

V. Recommendation
Option 3 is the recommended solution. It has the least number of negative effects of all the options and has the most positive results. It also meets all the necessary criteria for an effective plan. This option would create a

minor number of inconveniences compared to the other options and would ensure the safety of the Rowan community. Pedestrians would have a safe walkway to access both sides of campus. With the speed bumps inserted along Route 322, vehicles would be forced to slow down. The other proposals would bring unnecessary challenges and fail to address all the issues. Constructing elevated pedestrian walkways over Route 322 – with speed bumps along the roadway itself – is the best plan.

Written by Rachel S. Sachs – Rowan (N.J.) University Graduate

Crafting a Position Paper

A *position paper* presents an arguable opinion about an issue. Its goal defines and presents an organization's stand on an issue of public interest in a persuasive and fact-based manner. Its purpose is to convince the audience that your opinion or that of your superior or client is valid and worth paying attention to. Ideas (approaches) that you are considering must be carefully examined, ensuring you have developed your argument and organized the paper. It is very important to ensure that all sides of the problem (the issues) are addressed and presented in a manner that is easy for your audience(s) to understand. Your job is to take one side of the argument and persuade your audience that you have well-founded knowledge of the topic being presented. It is important to support your argument with researched evidence to ensure the validity and credibility of your claims, as well as to address counterclaims to show that you are well informed about both sides.

A *position paper* can be several pages long. There are a number of approaches available to successful strategic advisers when an organization decides to accept the challenge of taking a position on a problem or issue facing society. Below are suggestions of how to do it, followed by examples.

Stating *Your* Position
More Detailed Approach

Issue Criteria
To take a side on a subject (Step 3 – PR Play 6-9), you should first establish the arguability of the topic. Ask yourself the following questions to ensure that you will be able to present a strong argument:

PR Play 6-10
3-Minute Drill

The *Three-minute Drill* is an abbreviated version of the *counseling paper*. It was conceived by public relations strategic adviser James Lukaszewski, ABC, APR, Fellow PRSA, CCEP. In essence, it is a simpler written approach that carries out the counseling "tactic." In Jim's words, "It helps solidify why respected public relations strategic counselors are the number one, Number Two (person in the organization) – *the* trusted adviser." Keep in mind that each 150 words equals one minute. Think in terms of: Issues, Questions, Situation:

1. **Situation Description**
   Explanation – Introduction (60 words)
   Briefly describe the nature of the issue, problem or situation that requires decision, action or study. "This is the subject and here is what we know."
2. **Analysis (60 words)**
   A description of what the situation means, what its implications are, and how it threatens or presents an opportunity to the organization. "Here is why it matters."
3. **Goal (60 words)**
   A clear, concise statement of the task to be accomplished (sometimes the reason or purpose for accomplishing it), the target to be reached and when. "Our destination."
4. **Options (150 words)**
   Provide at least three response options to address the situation as presented and analyzed:
   1. Do nothing
   2. Do something
   3. Do something more
5. **Recommendation (60 words)**
   Make a specific choice among the options you presented. Be ready with a recommendation and supporting information every time because the boss is going to ask you for one.
6. **Justification**
   Unintended consequences (60 words)
   Briefly describe the reactions or circumstances that could arise resulting from options you suggested, including that of doing nothing. Identify the solution option with the fewest negative intended or unintended consequences.

James Lukaszewski, ABC, APR, Fellow PRSA, CCEP – www.e911.com (created in 1998)

cont.

PR Play 6-10 cont.
3-Minute Drill – Example

(Rutgers-Rowan Merger)
June 5, 2012

Situation

New Jersey's public higher education has struggled for years – South Jersey the particular concern. Govs. McGreevy and Corzine's previous attempts to restructure the state's higher education failed to garner adequate support. Gov. Christie is adamant change will occur under his administration – mandating restructure by July 1. Rutgers must present Christie a potential plan concerning Rutgers-Camden and Rowan Universities' futures. **(60 words)**

Analysis

Rowan University needs assistance. The university is $517 million in debt. Its bond rating stands to benefit from some type of partnership with Rutgers. Rutgers – including all three locations – is in good financial standing. Research shows students and alumni feel strong allegiance to the internationally-recognized Rutgers brand. Identical surveys completed by Rowan students and alumni reveal mediocre pride. **(60 words)**

Goal

The goal, when considering the plan of action Rutgers will support, is to choose the plan most beneficial to Rutgers' stakeholders. Selecting the plan that best benefits the university, its students, faculty and staff – in New Brunswick, Camden and Newark – is the university's top priority. Rutgers is arming itself with a plan – before one out of its control is chosen. **(60 words)**

Options

Rutgers has three potential options for Christie:

1. Leave the universities as they are. Rutgers-Camden would continue as Rutgers' South Jersey satellite campus. Rowan would remain as is.

2. Rutgers-Camden and Rowan enter a joint venture. The schools combine names, academic programs and resources, but continue to keep separate campuses. Rowan's Glassboro campus would host the Communication, Education, Engineering, and Fine and

cont.

PR Play 6-10 cont.

Performing Arts Schools. Rutgers-Camden's campus would host the Business, Law and Nursing schools. The Arts and Sciences School at each university would divide. Rowan would host the Liberal Arts School while Rutgers-Camden would host the Sciences School. These campuses would host each school's upper level courses. General education courses would be hosted at each campus.

3. Rutgers-Camden absorbs Rowan entirely, becoming Rutgers-South Jersey. As in the second scenario, the two campuses would host different programs, but have general education requirements available in both locations. **(150 words)**

Recommendation
Following recommendation two, Rutgers-Camden and Rowan enter a joint venture: Rutgers-Rowan. Each school preserves its identity. If Rowan loses its name, it could offend its benefactor, Henry Rowan. Alumni loyal to the Rowan name could halt donations as done previously, when Glassboro State became Rowan in 1992. By keeping Rowan's name, both schools benefit from the Rowan name. **(60 words)**

Justification – Unintended Consequences
Christie may sign an executive order, overriding option one.

Option two preserves Rowan's identity, alleviates its financial pressure and achieves research university status.

Two and three's program separation keeps majors at the school where they've acquired reputation. Offering general education courses at both campuses gives the option of completing one's degree at one campus or taking advantage of both locations. **(60 words)**

Rhyan Truett – Rowan (N.J.) University Graduate

- Is it a real and relevant issue, with genuine controversy and uncertainty?
- Can you distinctly identify more than one position?
- Are you personally interested in advocating one of these positions?
- Can the issue be managed?

Analyzing an Issue and Developing an Argument

Once the charge is made to develop a *position paper*, research must be done on the subject matter. While you may already have an opinion on the topic and an idea about which side of the argument your organization should take, you need to ensure that your position is well supported. Listing the pros and cons of the topic will help you examine your ability to support your counterclaims, as well as a listing of supporting evidence for both sides. Supporting evidence includes:

- **Factual Knowledge** – Verifiable information agreed on by almost everyone.
- **Statistical Inferences** – Interpretation and examples of an accumulation of facts.
- **Informed Opinion** – Opinion developed through research and/or expertise.
- **Personal Testimony** – Personal experience related by a knowledgeable party (source credibility).

Once you have made your pro and con lists (*Force Field* or *Conflict Analysis*), compare the information side by side. After considering your audience, as well as your own viewpoint, choose the position you will take.

In considering the audience, ask yourself the following questions:
- Who is your audience?
- What do they believe?
- Where do they stand on the issue?
- How are their interests involved?
- What evidence is likely to be effective with them?

Organization

Your introduction should start with a brief background and historical information on the issue, much like the *simple approach*. After effects and issues are listed, take a position, eliminating any question in the audience's mind as to where your organization or client stands.

A Suggested Outline (Checklist) for a *Position Paper*:
I. Introduction

___ A. Introduce the problem.

___ B. Provide background on the topic.

___ C. Include a brief sentence on your view of the problem, issue or challenge.

II. Issues/Arguments – Pros and Cons

___ A. Summarize the issues, claim and counterclaims.

___ B. Provide supporting information for issues, claim and counterclaims.

___ C. Refute those issues not in agreement with yours.

___ D. Give evidence (strong support) for your argument.

III. Your Argument

___ A. Assert point No.1 of your argument.

___ 1. Give your opinion.

___ 2. Provide support (benefits).

___ B. Assert point No. 2 of your argument.

___ 1. Give your opinion.

___ 2. Provide support (benefits).

___ C. Assert point No. 3 of your argument.

___ 1. Give your opinion.

___ 2. Provide support (benefits).

IV. Conclusion

___ A. Restate your argument.

___ B. Provide a plan of action (Public relations plan if requested).

Portions from: University of Hawaii – West O`ahu's and Rowan (N.J.) University
Case Studies in Public Relations and Public Relations Planning "handouts"

Position Paper Example

Problem: The Deptford Mall and Collegetown strip center have attracted large numbers of residents, visitors and college students from the business area of downtown Glassboro. Since the 1960s, the Glassboro economy and the downtown area have plummeted, leading to a deterioration of its downtown shopping district.

In an effort to revitalize the town, borough officials proposed a plan and are asking for support.

This plan includes:
• Improving the local economy by attracting big businesses including Barnes & Noble, Applebee's, Olive Garden and many more.
• Providing businesses with the most technically advanced broadband services available in the county.
• Building a new road connecting the Rowan University campus to the downtown business area.
• Installing a brick paved pedestrian walkway including decorative street lamps, trash receptacles and trees with tree grates.
• Coordinating non-profit organizations to establish an arts district along the main fairway of the downtown.

The Borough of Glassboro has partnered with the JGSC Group and master developer Jingoli & Son. The town council has requested the aid of Rowan University and other local businesses in the revitalization of downtown Glassboro.

Issues: Although the revitalization project for downtown Glassboro will increase local revenue and improve the town's image, this idea has drawbacks, especially for Rowan University.

By allotting more money externally, Rowan University will not be able to expand its campus as quickly. There are many areas of the University that still need improvement. Buildings need repair, computers need upgrading and student housing needs to be increased. Rowan University must fix the problems inside its network before helping outside.

The creation of a new road linking the Rowan University campus and the downtown area will increase traffic and activity. A highway already travels through the middle of campus. With the attraction of new restaurants and stores, more cars and trucks will be driving through. This can be a danger to Rowan students and pedestrians.

On a local level, the introduction of big companies will put mom-and-pop shops out of business. These are local diners and stores that have survived the hard times and truly represent Glassboro.

Position: Rowan University will aid in the downtown Glassboro revitalization project. This is an opportunity to improve the town and indirectly improve the University.

Based on the 2006 research report by Braude et al., high school juniors and seniors rated the importance of local entertainment (restaurants, stores, hangouts) when choosing a college, giving a mean score of 6.8 on a scale of 1-9, 1 being unimportant and 9 being important. Currently, Rowan University does not have much to offer within walking distance. Students need to drive to Deptford to find a mall, Starbucks and chain restaurants, and most freshmen do not have cars on campus. Developing downtown Glassboro will increase local activity and increase Rowan University's appeal to prospective and current students.

One of Rowan University's greatest obstacles at the moment is providing enough housing for its student body. Developing downtown Glassboro will also create housing opportunities for Rowan. More housing will equal a satisfied student body and the chance to enroll more students, therefore increasing revenue.

With the increase of more companies and corporations, students who must work while in school can find jobs closer to campus. This proximity can also promote partnerships and internships for Rowan University students.

Benefits: Rowan University can attract more students by developing Glassboro into a true college town. The revitalization of Glassboro will create local resources for students as well as improve the town's economy.

Rowan University's plan of action consists of:
- Donating a $1 million grant to be dispersed over 10 years
- Researching the opinions and wants of residents and students
- Creating a pedestrian-friendly road from Whitney Avenue and Route 322 to College Avenue named Rowan Boulevard
- Building a townhouse complex between Main Street and Rowan Boulevard to house students

Rosie Braude – Rowan (N.J.) University PRSSA Past President

Crafting an Op-Ed

A newspaper or magazine editorial expresses the opinion of the editor or publisher. An *op-ed* (traditionally printed on page opposite the editorial page), on the other hand, is a signed opinion piece written by the reader of a newspaper, magazine or other source, on a topic relevant to the publication's audience. *Op-eds* (PR Play 6-11) express personal or organization opinions, positions or view points.

An *op-ed's* objective might be to use a public forum to reach the general community or to express an opinion about a documented need or problem.

PR Play 6-11
Op-ed Example

Courier-Post
www.courierpostonline.com • Sunday, December 3, 2000
Cauldron of chaos clouded the election

(Op-ed/*A Perspective* – shown as it was submitted)
(695 words)
By M. Larry Litwin

(The writer, a former KYW Newsradio reporter/anchor, is now an associate professor of communication at Rowan University, Glassboro N.J. He lives in Cherry Hill N.J. and can be contacted at litwin@rowan.edu.)

For political junkies the past few weeks have been our Olympics and World Series. But none of us ever expected our "Super Bowl" to go into an indeterminable overtime. As many of my colleagues have stated, "It just doesn't get any better than this."

cont.

PR Play 6-11 continued

(Litwin Op-Ed/Page 2 of 3)

While news of the Florida election voter count changes — if not by the minute, certainly by the hour (and hopefully it will be determined by the time this piece is printed) — we must put into perspective how this entire embarrassing mess began. First, let it be said, I do not believe either of the candidates is trying to steal the election. Each believes he is the rightful winner and should be the next President of the United States.

Let us review some early events of Election Night 2000. As a former member of the media, it pains me to admit that the major faux pas was a matter of dollars and cents — in retrospect, cents that don't make very much sense.

In their infinite wisdom, the major television networks and The Associated Press decided to pool their resources and form an entity known as *Voter News Service (VNS)*. (A cost-saving move that failed miserably.) It was the responsibility of VNS to provide the media with raw voting data from exit polls. In the past, the respective competing news services conducted their own exit polls (at a considerable cost).

Network officials explained that their plan was to use teams of experts to analyze the VNS data, and then plug it into complicated formulas to determine election winners — sometimes as soon as the polls closed. Because the margin between the two candidates in Florida was so small the models failed. And because all of the major news services were using the same data, their models were predicting similar results. In the days of competition, maybe, just maybe, one of the news services would have revealed a different result forcing its competitors to do some rethinking.

That being said, let us not place all the blame on the news services, the small margin or the hanging or pregnant (dimpled) chads. The real culprit is those 19,100 ballots in West Palm Beach — the butterfly ballots with double punches that seniors apparently had problems with. (Incidentally, at least one college-educated 27-year old voter complained about the difficulty of lining up the ballot with the holder so that she could punch the chad next to her favorite candidates.)

We haven't heard much about those double-punched ballots because (and rightfully so) they have been disqualified. Reflect back to Election Night. Between 7:49 and 8 p.m., NBC, MSNBC, CBS, CNN, FOX and ABC declared Gore the winner in Florida. That's when this entire frenzy really began.

Those projections were based on the same VNS data — data gathered during exit polls. Thousands of West Palm voters told the pollsters that

cont.

PR Play 6-11 continued

(Litwin Op-Ed/Page 3 of 3)

they had voted for Gore/Lieberman. They told them because that was their intent or their will. Apparently, it was also their mistaken belief.

Give this some thought: what if the seniors and others in Palm Beach County, who double-punched their ballots voting for both Patrick Buchanan and Al Gore had actually voted only for one or the other?

Those ballots would not have been disqualified and the exit polls and VNS would more than likely have been accurate. Thus, the Gore-Lieberman ticket would have won in Florida with at least a 10,000-vote plurality (assuming, conservatively, that Gore would have received at least half the votes) giving the Democrats the state's 25 electoral votes and the Presidency.

Whoops! Not so fast. There's the very real possibility that George W. Bush and the Republicans would have instigated their own litigation and maybe not just in Florida. They may have asked for recounts in Iowa, New Mexico, Oregon and elsewhere.

Where does this leave us? It presents a challenge that few other Presidents-elect have had to face. Our next President will truly have to unite this nation by first unifying a closely divided Congress. But Presidents and this country have faced some pretty difficult challenges in the past. Our track record and history show that we have a penchant for meeting those challenges.

###

Much like *position papers*, *op-eds* should be written forcefully and effectively – because, after all, they are attempting to affect *behavior* – change, enhance or maintain it. A well-written opinion piece with a fresh viewpoint has a good chance of getting published. A good *op-ed* can transform the political balance of power.

Op-ed articles reach broad audiences that include the most influential people in your community. Although a newspaper may completely oppose your view, many editors want to present both sides.

Generally, *op-eds*:
- Are lengthier editorial pieces which offer informed and animated opinions from the perspective of a recognized authority.
- Begin with an interesting and clear statement of the issue.
- Include specific examples and use appropriate third party support to add validity to arguments.

PR Play 6-12
Newspapers recognize a person's death in several ways:

Standard six-point-type (agate type) death notices – Ordered by the family, usually through the funeral home making arrangements, and paid for in the same way as classified advertising (PR Play 6-16).

Obituaries – Relatively brief news (feature) articles (written by reporter or prepared by public relations practitioners and supplied to the media) about the deaths of private citizens, published in the obituary section (*obituary* is often shortened to *obit*) of a newspaper at the editor's discretion. (See page 222.) They usually include quotes (PR Play 6-17).

Celebrity obituaries – Longer stories giving full biographies of famous people or community members of note. They almost always include quotes.

Obit editorials – Opinion articles passing judgment on the value and worth of the lives of prominent individuals (PR Play 6-18).

News articles – Articles about a person's death if it is caused by a major public event such as a traffic accident or an airplane crash.

PR Play 6-13
A Typical Obituary Formula:
(See page 222)

A reading of obituaries in the *Boston Globe* suggests that the newspaper uses the following formula – a fairly typical one (whether traditional newspaper or online):
- Lead (name, age, address by municipality, occupational title or identifying description, fact of death, when, where, sometimes why)
- Information about where the deceased was born and reared
- Education history
- Employment history
- Military service
- Honors
- Memberships
- Hobbies
- Survivors
- Funeral arrangements

PR Play 6-14
Some Obituary Leads

Here are some common ways of writing obituary leads:

J. James Blanchard, 67, of Fairfield, former English Department chair at Parsons College, died Tuesday in Jefferson County Hospital after a short illness.

Harry S. Johnson, 75, of Cherry Hill, a man of many talents and much knowledge, died of heart failure April 28 at Philadelphia General Hospital.

Edward Litwin, 88, who operated a corner grocery store in Camden for 50 years, died of cancer Thursday at Samaritan Hospice in Mount Holly.

Eddie Litwin, 88, of Coconut Creek, Fla., formerly of Cherry Hill, died of cancer Thursday at Samaritan Hospice at Virtua Hospital in Mount Holly.

Tim Russert, NBC News' Washington bureau chief and moderator of "Meet the Press," died Friday after suffering a heart attack at the bureau. He was 58.

Russert was recording voiceovers for Sunday's "Meet the Press" broadcast when he collapsed. He was rushed to Sibley Memorial Hospital in Washington, where resuscitation efforts were unsuccessful. (Russert's is a two paragraph lead.)

- Offer a conclusion that summarizes the main point and leaves a strong impression.

Duke University's Terry Sanford Institute of Public Policy suggests these guidelines for crafting an *op-ed*:

Questions to ask
- Consider your audience: Who are they? Are they readers of a small-town newspaper, a technical journal, a national newspaper, an independent activist press, etc.?
- What do they already know about the issue, and what do you need to tell them?
- Why is your issue important?
- Is your topic interesting?

PR Play 6-15
Language for Obituaries

1. Don't replace the simple *died* with silly euphemisms such as *went to the great beyond, bought the farm* or *cashed in his chips.*
2. Most editors feel that death, when it comes, always takes the same amount of time; it is only the cause of death that is fast or slow. Therefore, don't use the phrase *sudden death* or say someone died *suddenly.* Often, the phrase you want is *died unexpectedly.*
3. When giving place of birth, don't say someone was a *former native.* Native indicates place of birth. If someone were born in Fairfield, Iowa and died in San Francisco, he or she is still a native of Fairfield.
4. A Roman Catholic Mass is celebrated; don't say held. Be sure to capitalize Mass.
5. Don't omit *the* before Rev. Check *The Associated Press Stylebook and Briefing on Media Law* for proper terminology for other members of the clergy.
6. Don't misspell *cemetery* as *cematary.*

- Can you manage the material within the specifications set by the newspaper?
- Does your topic assert something specific and propose a plan of action?
- Do you have enough material to support your opinion?
- What action would you like your readers (or officials) to take? (A "call to action.")
- Why should readers trust your opinion? That is, why should they find your particular perspective, expertise or experience worth thinking about?

Actions to take
- Have an opinion: take a stand (express it)!
- Make your point early on. The very first sentence should give readers a sense of what your topic will be. How will that sentence grab your readers' attention (much the same as a news release or news article lead)? How will the first paragraph make readers stay with you to the end?
- Be respectful of counterarguments. Acknowledge – but do not libel – opposing viewpoints.
- Pick up an actual newspaper and read the *op-ed* pages.

PR Play 6-16
Death Notice – Example [Paid for by Family]

LITWIN, EDWARD (EDDIE)

On December 28, 2006 of Coconut Creek, Fla. formerly of Cherry Hill. For 65 years, loving, wonderful and devoted husband of the late Jean (nee Cohen) Litwin. Cherished father of Janice and Steve Barbell, Larry and Nancy Litwin and Eileen and Lenny Weisman. Adored No. 1 Poppy of grandchildren Bryen and Melissa Barbell, Lisa (Barbell) and Peter Levasseur, Julie (Litwin) and Billy Kramer, Adam Litwin, Josh Weisman and Alison Weisman; and great-grand-children Elliana and Joshua Barbell, Sarah and Ethan Levasseur, and Alana and Aidan Kramer. Brother of Sylvia Weinbrom and Mitzi Harris, and brother-in-law of Philip (Sandy) and Marvin (Charlotte) Cohen. For nearly 50 years, Eddie and his brother Philip owned and operated Litwin Bros. Food Market in North Camden. Eddie was a member of South Jersey Hebrew Association, Bloomfield Park (Pennsauken) Volunteer Fire Company and Deborah.
Relatives and friends are invited Friday beginning 2 p.m. to:

PLATT MEMORIAL
CHAPELS, Inc.
2001 Berlin Road
Cherry Hill, NJ 08003

where funeral services will begin promptly at 2:30 p.m. Interment will follow at Crescent Memorial Park, Pennsauken, N.J. The family will return to the home of Janice and Steve Barbell and respectfully request contributions in his memory be made to Deborah Hospital Foundation, 200 Trenton Road, Browns Mills, NJ 08015 or Samaritan Hospice, 5 Eves Drive, Suite 300, Marlton, NJ 08053.

How to get your op-ed published
Culled from advice offered by numerous experts*

* Duke University, Thoreau (Oregon) Institute, A National Call TO Action, National Association of Children's Hospitals, and Professors Denis Mercier and M. Larry Litwin, APR, Fellow PRSA – Rowan (N.J.) University

• Determine which newspapers in your community publish *op-eds*. Read them to better learn what *that* newspaper expects in an *op-ed*.

PR Play 6-17
Obituary – Examples

Version No. 1 – *The Philadelphia Inquirer*

Edward Litwin | Grocer, 88

Edward Litwin, 88, who operated a corner grocery store in Camden for 50 years, died of cancer Thursday at Samaritan Hospice in Mount Holly.

Mr. Litwin, who grew up in Camden, dropped out of school at 9, after his mother died, to help support his family. He sold produce from a pushcart, his son, Larry, said, and by 15 was operating his own store at Eighth and Elm Streets with help from relatives.

Mr. Litwin also started a wholesale business. On a delivery to a South Philadelphia grocery, he met the owners' daughter, Jean Cohen. They married in 1940.

During World War II, he worked at the Penn-Jersey Shipbuilding Co. while continuing to run the Elm Street store. After the war, his brother Philip joined him at the store, which was renamed Litwin Bros.

The men supported churches, schools and organizations in Camden, Larry Litwin said, and were so respected in the community that the grocery was undamaged in the race riots in the late 1960s. He said,

"Word on the street was, 'Don't touch Litwins' store.' "

The business did come under assault on July 1, 1974, when a robber fired shots into the store. A child was killed and several people were wounded, including Mr. Litwin, who was shot five times. He recovered and continued to operate Litwin Bros. until 1985, when he retired to Coconut Creek, Fla.

Mr. Litwin was a member of the South Jersey Hebrew Association and the Bloomfield Park Volunteer Fire Company in Pennsauken.

He was an expert in the craft of paper tole and donated his work to raise funds for Deborah Heart and Lung Center in Browns Mills.

In addition to his son, he is survived by daughters Janice Barbell and Eileen Weisman; two sisters; six grandchildren; and six great-grandchildren. His wife died in 2004.

The funeral was yesterday at Platt Memorial Chapel in Cherry Hill. Burial was in Crescent Memorial Park in Pennsauken.

cont.

PR Play 6-17 continued

Version No. 2 – *Courier-Post*

Camden grocer Edward Litwin dies

By BILL DUHART
Courier-Post Staff

MOUNT HOLLY N.J. – Dec. 29, 2006 – Edward Litwin, 88, of Coconut Creek, Fla., formerly of Cherry Hill, died of cancer Thursday at Samaritan Hospice at Virtua Hospital in Mount Holly.

Litwin, the founder and owner of a Camden grocery store at Eighth and Elm Streets that is still operating and still bears his name, made headlines 32 years ago after being shot five times during a holdup at his store.

The July 1, 1974 robbery left four others wounded, including a 3-year-old girl, and claimed the life of a 13-year-old boy. One of the bullets hit Litwin in the throat and one remained lodged in his back near his spine for the remainder of his life, a family member said. He never spoke above a whisper after that.

But that didn't stop him from continuing to operate the market with his brother and partner, Philip, for 11 years after the stickup.

When his family pleaded with him not to go back, Edward explained, "That's what I know. That's what I do," said his son, Larry Litwin, 61, of Winslow. "The store was an institution in North Camden. My father never let anyone go hungry if they didn't have money. His line was "pay me when you have it.' "

Litwin opened the store in 1935 when he was 17 years old. He sold it in 1984, but continued to operate it until 1985, his son said.

The store was one of the few that cashed checks for shoppers. The robbers who shot him got away with about $10,000, which was on hand to cash checks, police reports at the time said. All of the bandits were eventually caught.

In addition to his son Larry, Litwin is survived by two sisters, Sylvia Weinbrom of York, Pa., and Mitzi Harris of Evesham; daughters Janice Barbell of Winslow and Eileen Weisman of Houston; six grandchildren, including former Cherry Hill Councilman Bryen Barbell; and six great-grandchildren.

He was also the father-in-law of former Cherry Hill Councilman and library board president Stephen Barbell.

Funeral services will be at 3 p.m. today at Platt Memorial Chapel, 2001 Berlin Road. Interment will follow at Crescent Memorial Park, Pennsauken.

PR Play 6-18

Obituary Editorial – Example

Tim Russert, 1950-2008
No agenda, just facts

The sad, unexpected death of veteran broadcast journalist Tim Russert was tragic. But in the eulogies of the esteemed NBC news-man, who died Friday of a heart attack at age 58, there is a lesson that would benefit all Americans if applied. Russert, as host of the long-running Meet the Press interview program as well as a familiar inquisitor for televised debates, was always the epitome of objectivity.

In an era where entire network news operations are accused of bias, Russert never played favorites. His sharp questions were meant to educate the public, not to skewer a particular candidate or any other newsmaker at the receiving end of his very direct inquiries.

Russert's excitement was contagious whenever he was called upon to explain what could be expected next in an election or with any other subject he felt was important to millions of TV viewers. But that's what happens when truth is revealed.

Russert's style provides a model for other journalists at a time when many are seen as having an agenda other than presenting the facts. As the nation continues its quest to select a new president, journal-ists like Russert, whose objectivity was unquestioned, are an asset.

The Philadelphia Inquirer – June 17, 2008

- Check the newspaper's guidelines for their rules regarding *op-eds*. Some papers will only print your *op-ed* if it has not been sent to another paper. Some limit the number of words. Find out your paper's limit and write your article within five or 10 words of that length. Check the guidelines before writing your *op-ed* so that you don't waste your time. Become familiar with the word length, style, format, messages and anything else that is distinctive. Incorporate these elements into your *op-ed*.
- If you plan to verbally "pitch" your *op-ed,* prepare and rehearse a 15-second statement of its contents and purpose to better convey – in the shortest time – your idea (to the contact person).

- Send your *op-ed* to the largest news-paper first, unless you are targeting a specific geodemographic. If it is rejected, try another, then another. Do not be discouraged if it takes a number of contacts to score a "hit."
- **Bonus**: Once your *op-ed* is published (printed or online), copy it with the newspaper's banner (flag) and date. Send it to *key communicators* and other *influentials*. The printed word carries incredible power.

> **PR Play 6-19**
> ## Contents of
> ## A Complete Obituary
> - Basic facts
> - Character portrait
> - Quotes
> - Warts and wrinkles
> - Historical notes

- When deciding on your topic, narrow your scope to something that pertains to the readership of that paper.
- Make your argument accessible to a general audience – although appealing to a particular audience segment or niche (fragment) is still acceptable if they are among a publication's readers.
- Make your point early on and make sure it is clear. The first sentence should reveal exactly what you intend to write about.
- Don't just attack other groups – make your own point about an issue.
- Bring in a local connection to a national issue if possible. That's what editors and readers want.
- Demonstrate the standing (credibility) that you have regarding the issue. Readers will be persuaded (and maybe even convinced) of your dedication and conviction if you show them where you are coming from.
- Avoid writing about tired subjects – timeliness is of the essence. Try to "peg" it to a recent event.
- Know something about the publication you are sending your "piece" to and the type of "pieces" they print.
- Do not use profane language or commit libel.

Some other suggestions:

- Brevity of paragraphs – *op-ed* paragraphs should be two or three sentences long. Sentences should be short enough that each paragraph contains no more than 50 words.
- Brevity of words – never use a three-syllable word where a one-syllable word will do.
- Use jargon only if it is brief and the meaning is absolutely clear.

```
PR Play 6-20

Briefing Book Components
(See page 222)
```

1. A brief history of your organization, firm or school district.
2. As many demographics as possible including the community.
3. General staff make-up.
4. Names of key staff members, awards won, etc.
5. Names and years of famous graduates or employees (of school district or college).
6. Is there anyone of note living in community?
7. Have there been any controversies of late?
8. What kinds of questions might be asked during any Q&A, with staff or media (students or parents if site of visit is a school)?
9. List possible surprises, because there should be absolutely no surprises. Every possible scenario must be anticipated.
10. Include copies of brochures, other publications and collateral materials, and pictures of key personnel.
11. Include pronunciations for unusual names.

- Avoid acronyms: Better to repeatedly spell out terms such as "environmental impact statement" than to lose the reader in a jungle of EISs, DCAs, EPAs, EEOCs and STDs.
- Minimize the use of numbers: Don't say, "Planners expected 75,000 riders per day, but actual ridership was only 37,500 per day." Many readers won't immediately grasp the difference. Say instead, "ridership was half of what was expected."

These are basic rules for individual paragraphs. Here is one way to write the *op-ed* as a whole:
1. Ask, what is the message you want to get across? Are you opposing a plan, objecting to rail transit, or proposing to reform an agency?
2. List all your arguments in no particular order. Will the plan lead to congestion? How much will the rail transit line cost individual taxpayers? Is the agency keeping secrets from the public?
3. Pick three, four or five arguments that will most appeal to your readers. For example, most readers have jobs, so arguments about jobs are less persuasive than issues about congestion, local taxes or politics.

PR Play 6-21

Sample Briefing Book Table of Contents

Briefing Book for the President
A Visit To Gibbsboro, New Jersey
Camden County
10 a.m. Monday, Nov. 25, 2013

CONTENTS

Section Divider Tab

A. **LOGISTICS**
   - Itinerary
   - Road Maps and Directions: From Philadelphia International Airport to Gibbsboro
B. **DEMOGRAPHICS**
C. **LIST OF KEY BOROUGH OFFICIALS**
   - Include Photos
D. **CONTROVERSIAL ISSUES**
   - Potential Questions
E. **GIBBSBORO ELEMENTARY SCHOOL**
   - General Information
   - 2012 No Child Left Behind Report
   - N.J. Department of Education School Report Card (2011-2012)
   - Board of Education Members
F. **HISTORY AND BACKGROUND OF GIBBSBORO**
   - Relevant News Article
   - Historic Photos
G. **FAMOUS FACES**
H. **FAMOUS PLACES**
I. **PUBLICATIONS AND RELEVANT NEWS ARTICLES**

Diane Johns – Rowan (N.J.) University Graduate Student

PR Play 6-22

Basic Components of An Effective Annual Report
(See page 223)

- Chairman of the Board Letter
- Sales and Marketing
- 10-Year Summary of Financial Figures
- Management Discussion and Analysis
- CPA Opinion Letter
- Financial Statements
- Subsidiaries, Brands and Addresses
- List of Directors and Officers
- Stock Price Trend

---

4. Include your name, title, phone number and email on the typed *op-ed*. Type the *op-ed* double-spaced on an 8 ½ x 11 sheet of paper (or the equivalent electronically). Include your name and contact information as a header on each page and a slug (key word or phrase) prior to the page number (ROAD RAGE/Page 1 of 3). This is to assist the editor in the event the pages become separated from one another.

5. Write your first draft. Connect your theme to your "peg" in the first paragraph, followed by one to three paragraphs for each supporting reason, with the most important reasons first. One or two paragraphs should conclude by reinforcing your theme.

6. Read your draft and ask: What is the most powerful paragraph here? Is it the closing paragraph? Does a paragraph about one of the four or five arguments point out a particularly absurd part of the plan? Whichever one it is, rewrite the *op-ed* with the most powerful, most exciting paragraph first to grab the reader's attention – remembering to connect it with your "peg."

7. Use bullets. If you make several short points, rewrite them as bullets. Bullets draw the reader's attention and keep the article readable.

8. Liven up your writing by writing in active voice rather than passive voice and by eliminating bureaucratese and personalizing your arguments. Don't say, "It has been decided that . . . ." when you can say "The council decided . . . ." Don't say, "the plan will cost $10 billion" when you can say "The plan will cost $10,000 per local resident."

---

9. Do a word count. If you are over your limit, delete the last (and therefore least important) of the four or five arguments. Then find places where you are just plain wordy. A good editor can cut a first draft in half without losing any meaning, but you have to edit yourself (or find a friend who will do it) because the newspaper won't bother.
10. Check your spelling on the computer and have someone else read it for grammar, punctuation and syntax.

PR Play 6-23

More Annual Report Tips

The Annual Report Library (San Francisco) offers these tips to help create an effective annual report:

- Tell a story.
- Keep it simple.
- Make it readable.

Some other points to keep in mind when planning an annual report:

- The budget.
- Desired involvement of COB/CEO/CFO (Chairman of the Board/Chief Executive Officer/Chief Financial Officer).
- The production team. (Committee or one person? Who calls the shots?)
- Experience of graphic designers/photographers/writers.
- What to include? (The major purpose of report.)
- How "innovative" should the report be? (Die cut layout, inserts, response cards).
- Paper, binding, size, print run.
- Online version (with an easy link from Web home page).
- Theme for report.
- Know what to avoid and what needs additional explanation.
- Competitors and competition – how much to include.
- Corporate responsibility – how much to include?
- Testimonials from outsiders are especially effective when accompanied by photo.
- Test final "galley" copy for readability, interest and comprehension.
- Look at other reports and critique them.

---

11. Send the *op-ed* to the publication. Be sure to research whether a newspaper or magazine prefers email or hard copy. It should already be in the publication's guidelines. And, don't get upset if they cut a sentence or paragraph. Just be glad they printed it.

Crafting an Obituary

Learning to prepare obituary copy is important for the PR practitioner. Many times, when a key staff member passes, the media will call. Obituaries are reports on people who die – a description of someone's life and notice of death. (See PR Plays 6-12 to 6-19.)

The "obit" should announce the person's death, describe life's highlights, mention family and summarize funeral arrangements. It may seem "cold," but many organizations (and news outlets) prepare obituaries while people are still alive. In newsroom talk, they keep them in the "can" and update them periodically.

Crafting a Briefing Book

Briefing books are compiled by a public relations staff in anticipation of a visit to your organization or facility by a VIP – a local or federal official – or media members.

The typical *briefing book* (PR Plays 6-20 and 6-21) contains summaries; fact sheets; news releases; short biographies with pictures of key people in the organization; brief descriptions of an organization, company or other entity; a brief history of the organization; as many demographics as possible including surrounding community; staff make-up; names of key staff members, awards won, etc.; anyone of note living in community or associated with organization; controversies or issues that should be known; possible questions that might be asked during any Q&A with staff or media; and a list of possible surprises (because there should be absolutely no surprises – every possible scenario must be anticipated) particularly if the expected visit is from a mayor, governor or president of the United States.

Be sure to include copies of brochures and other collateral materials, and pronunciations for unusual names.

Crafting an Annual Report

Although no rules specify the narrative in *annual reports* to be written in *Associated Press Style*, for consistency, they should be. Here are some other suggestions:

Producing Annual Reports

[See example at http://www.reportgallery.com]

- Begin a year in advance.
- Work closely with CFO (chief financial officer).
- An annual report includes, but does not have to be limited to, the following sections:
  - Table of contents
  - Mission statement
  - Letter from chairman
  - Management discussion and analysis
  - Sales and marketing update
  - Subsidiaries, brands and addresses
  - Auditor's report
  - CPA opinion letter
  - Financial statements including a 10-year summary of financial figures
  - Narrative of past year's operations
  - List of Directors and Officers (with pictures)
  - Stock prices (with recent history)
  - Photos and charts

SMUCKER'S® Annual Report (62 pages) contains:

SMUCKER'S® Table of Contents:

PR Play 6-24

Some Steps in Crafting a Proposal

1. A good proposal begins with a clear idea of the goals and objectives of the project.
2. Gather background information.
3. Identify audiences.
4. Consider partnerships.
5. Organize a good and compatible working team. Distribute duties and develop a firm schedule (Gantt Chart) of activities needed to prepare the proposal in time to meet the proposal deadline.
6. Start writing in a clear, concise, systematic format.
7. A good proposal is always readable, well-organized, grammatically correct and understandable.
8. Be explicit in your narrative about how the program will make an improvement.
9. Include budget information.
10. Include endorsements and/or testimonials.

PR Play 6-25

Outline Example for Grant Proposal
(Refer to Internet for Proposal Examples)

Grant Proposal by: Organization and Contact

TO: Foundation or Benefactor

Submitted on: Insert date

Executive Summary
- Requesting Organization's Background and History
- Description of Programs
- Description of Audiences Served
- Description of this Project (include examples)
- Budget
- Key staff members
- Project Evaluation

PR Play 6-26

Sample Grant Proposal Letter

August 13, 2013

Mrs. Linda Alexander
Program Officer
Corporate Foundation Giving
500 Benefactor Parkway
Rowan City, CA 94001

Dear Mrs. Alexander:

Rowan University's Public Relations Student Society of America (PRSSA) respectfully submits its proposal to the Corporate Foundation Giving for $100,000 to support PRSSA's electronic public relations education program for inner city youth.

PRSSA has embarked on a number of similar programs, but this is our most ambitious to date. Our plans call for offering a variety of programs that serve financially-challenged high school students in the Greater Philadelphia region. We fully expect this program to become the cornerstone of our community service projects with a strategy to take state-of-the-art technology directly to the students.

To achieve our goal, we partnered with a number of other student organizations here at Rowan – the Ad Club, Marketing Club and WGLS-FM. We look forward to any advice you might have that will lead us toward a successful project. Thank you for considering our request. Please call Nicole Galvin, our outreach director, if you have questions or need additional information.

Sincerely,

Aidan Kramer

Aidan Kramer
President

It is recommended the annual report's cover contain the following information:

Annual Report for Year ____

The ____ th **Report**

June 30, 20?? (end of fiscal year)

Name of Firm

Crafting a Proposal

The corporation for Public Broadcasting, National Science Foundation and other non-profits rely heavily on grants. To acquire grants takes persuasive proposals. Non-profits agree that a good proposal stems from a good concept. The best proposals are those to which the reviewers respond, "Of course, I wish I had thought of that!" (See PR Plays 6-24 and 6-25.)

The most important component is to pitch a project that benefits your audience. It must answer the question, "What's in it for me?"

That said: a proposal must be written in sufficient detail to allow decision makers to understand:
• what the project expects to accomplish
• if the proposing group (or yourself) has the necessary expertise to achieve the goal and objectives
• the potential of the project
• the impact and cost effectiveness
• the evaluation process

EXERCISES

PR Challenge 6-1

Research and write a position paper on the following topic:

Immigration

Review the risks and benefits of various positions on immigration reform. Your recommendations to your boss, Senator Thomas Mindless, I-Texas, could carry considerable weight in certain political circles. Give special attention to problems along the border with Mexico. Consider:

1. Whether the U.S. should continue building a border wall.
2. What to do with the 11 million illegal immigrants already in the country. Should they get work permits? Should they be permitted to apply for citizenship?
3. Should the U.S. open the border and let everyone in who wants to live here?
4. What positions on these issues present the least political risks? Compare risks vs. benefits. Include advice as to how Sen. Mindless could present his positions to the media.

PR Challenge 6-2

Research and write an *op-ed* for your local newspaper (both print and online). Select a topic of interest to you. It should run about 500 words with the intent of mustering community support for your topic or issue.

CHAPTER 7

Public Relations (Strategic) Planning and Budgeting

Effective two-way communication is the lifeblood of most successful organizations – profit and non-profit, public and private. All organizational activities are related to communication. Information about an organization affects the public's perception of it – its image. (Does your organization's image match its identity – how it wants to be perceived?)

Successful communicators have a common goal: to influence the receivers' (targeted publics) attitudes or behaviors. To achieve that goal, we must:
• Convey information and share knowledge
• Increase understanding
• Gain acceptance
• Provide action

No matter how accomplished we might think we are as communicators, it takes thorough planning *and* money to accomplish our public relations and other strategic goals. If we are going to spend money – ours or our client's – then an integral component of our plan is the allocation of funds. In addition to crafting a plan, this chapter covers budget development – strongly based on the tactics within the Strategic Communication Plan.

Much like the debate over the proverbial chicken and egg theory, strategic communicators and other executives must decide which should come first – the plan or the budget. More on public relations (strategic communication) budgeting later. Many, if not most, times, a budget evolves from the plan's tactics.

The Public Relations (Strategic) Plan

Back in the 1980s, the publication *communication briefings*® published a "bonus item" titled "How to Prepare a Public Relations Plan." While some aspects have changed over time, the framework remains the same.

Rowan University Professor Anthony J. Fulginiti, APR, Fellow PRSA, noted that like other planning efforts, the strategic plan begins with research and ends with research. Early research determines the *MAC Triad Plus* – messages, audiences, channels and timing of communication. Later research evaluates the plan's effectiveness.

In between, the plan should specify "what's" to be done, "why" and "how" it should be done. Proper planning is strategic and tactical. It includes events, media relations, policy changes and other possible tactics – depending on the plan's strategies and objectives. Thoughtful and careful execution is critical to synergy and success. However, superior *tactics* cannot overcome a flawed (business) *strategy*.

PR Play 7-1
Basic Planning Steps

1. Identify Issues (Determine purpose – Situation Analysis*)
2. Design Research Questions
3. Conduct Initial Research (Research Actions)
4. Select Goal – must be attainable – realistic and reachable
5. Write Backgrounder (Case) Statement [Chapters 5 and 6]
6. Identify and Rank Audiences
7. Craft Messages
8. Determine Channels
9. Determine Aperture (Best time to deliver messages)
10. Write Objectives
11. Craft Strategies (what, to whom, how)
12. Select Tactics (Vehicles/Tools)
13. Prepare Budget
14. Design Gantt Chart (Calendar Time Line) [Chapter 7]
15. Measure Your Work (Evaluate) – an assessment
16. Further Research (What changes would you make?)

*See Situation Analyses following PR Play 7-2

PR Play 7-2
Public Relations Planning GOST – Plus Mission

Generally, a public relations plan or strategic campaign will have only one *goal* – many times based on an organization's purpose or mission. That *goal* (realistic and reachable/attainable) may have several *objectives* associated with it. Each *objective* could have a number of *strategies*, although experts believe the *strategies* (messages) should be limited so that audiences remember them. However, the number of *tactics* that can be developed for a given strategy is almost infinite [certainly, there are many ways to deliver the message(s)].

Mission or Purpose – A clear and succinct reason the organization came into existence – its purpose. It answers the question: "Why we are here to serve you – why we are in business? (This is who we are; what we think about ourselves; what we want to do; and why we deserve your support.) The corporate mission statement, with a broad focus and a customer orientation, provides management with a sense of purpose. A brief statement defines "What business are we in." It should have a broad focus and a customer orientation. Example:

Mission Statement – Cherry Hill Public Library

The Cherry Hill Public Library (CHPL) is dedicated to providing a variety of library materials and services, access to innovative technologies, and a wide range of programs to meet the informational, educational and cultural interests of the community. CHPL recognizes its value and responsibility to society as an educational, social and cultural resource – committed to upholding the public's access to information.

Adopted April 26, 2006

Goal – The desired outcome of the plan (or project). The primary result an organization is attempting to achieve through its public relations efforts. Where the organization wants to be sometime in the future. Usually a more specific expression of a mission or purpose. Often related to one specific aspect of the mission or purpose. Is commonly described as the outcome of a plan of action. (Example – The Cherry Hill Public Library (CHPL) will become known as "The Heart of Town.")

cont.

PR Play 7-2 continued

Objective – Single goals broken into subsets known as objectives. They are specific milestones that measure progress toward the achievement of a goal. Objectives must:

1) address the desired result in terms of behavioral change; 2) designate the target public(s); 3) specify the expected level of accomplishment; 4) identify the time frame in which the accomplishments are to occur. Objectives are major aims in measurable terms. It is that measurement that helps determine – in the evaluation stage – the success of the overall strategic plan. (Example – **1.0*** Within the next year, increase the number of family memberships at the CHPL by 25 percent.)

Strategy – A general, well thought out plan of action. What must be done, to whom, how it will happen, and why you want it to happen. It is a broad plan of action an organization uses to achieve one or more of its objectives. (Example – **1.1** Demonstrate that the CHPL is committed to achieving and maintaining excellence in providing public library services to the community – meeting the needs of residents, businesses, organizations and their employees and members.) Strategies carry a strategic message or messages – even if implied or subliminal – to targeted audiences. They are the thoughts behind an objective.

Tactic – Specific activity, tool or task conducted to carry out and achieve strategy. (Example – **1.1.1** Produce and distribute e-newsletter Book Bytes using school district distribution list to reach younger families and make available in hard copy for those who would rather not receive it electronically. The same distribution offer would be given to all other organizations in the municipality.)

A key to public relations (strategic) planning is remembering that tactics help achieve a specific strategy, which helps achieve a specific objective. When successfully combined, synergy has been achieved because the goal has been reached.

(*To view a complete, award-winning plan, "Philadelphia Phillies – A Crisis Communication Plan Commissioned by *Courier-Post*" go to www.larrylitwin.com and click on Student Resources, Classroom handouts, No. 49. Plans use a decimal system for easy reference. The plan received the 2006 Pepperpot Award from the Philadelphia chapter of the Public Relations Society of America for Crisis Communication and the Frank X. Long Achievement Award for "excellence in writing and creativity.")

Situation Analyses

Professor Fulginiti teaches his students to conduct a thorough *situation analysis (SA)* prior to developing comprehensive strategic communication plans aimed at achieving specific goals. He says, "The situation analysis is a 'case statement' about the project. It sets the table for planners by detailing necessary information." The *SA* is the tool or template, used to gather and evaluate internal and external environments, which leads to the eventual strategic plan. Professor Fulginiti's *SA* is a 10-step process.

PRSA, on the other hand, recommends using an eight-step *SA* approach. Laurie J. Wilson, APR, Fellow PRSA, in *Strategic Program Planning for Effective Public Relations Campaigns* (4th ed., 2004) uses 15 steps.

Fulginiti Process

1. **Global ambition (Goal)**
   a. Suggest potential objectives of the plan.
   b. Write these potential objectives as *ideal outcomes*.
2. **History of the client or organization (Real State)**
   a. Interview client (review strategies/tactics).
   b. Interview potential target and other publics.
   c. Interview experts.
   d. Review literature.
   e. Check experience of similar organizations.
   f. Write and rank all issues.
3. **Positioning (Ideal State or position when plan is accomplished)**
   a. Write ideal "market" position resulting from plan.
   b. Write and rank ideal issues as polar opposites of real issues.
4. **Audience segments/fragments/profiles/ranks (Ideal State Analysis)**
   a. Rationale for target public segments/fragments/profiles/ranks.
   b. Behavioral analysis (information, attitudes, motivation, access, cost).
5. **Messages (Ideal State Analysis)**
   a. Force field (conflict) analysis (change vs. resistance variables).
   b. Other indicators.
6. **Channel and media selection (Ideal State Analysis)**
   a. Communication strategies, publics/channels must match to assure message delivery.
   b. UPP (Unique Persuasive Proposition), benefits, themes.

7. **Competition (Real State)**
   a. Check real marketplace competition and noise in the communication channel.
8. **Budget (Ideal State)**
   a. Suggested and projected – not actual.
9. **Timing**
   a. Suggested and projected – not actual.
10. **Final issues (Real vs. Ideal State)**
    a. Rewrite issue list that will lead to objectives and achievement of the ideal state.
    b. Share with client/boss – do issues and *SA* resonate (validate each other)?

PRSA Eight Step SA

1. **Research** – Situational analysis, internal communications audit, survey data of target audiences.
2. **Statement of goals** – To enhance the reputation and recognition of the company or organization with its publics.
3. **Objectives (short/long-term)** – Addressing desired result in terms of opinion change or behavioral outcome for each public within a specified time frame and level of outcome.
4. **Outline strategies** – Well thought out plan of action. It contains the message(s) to help influence behavioral change(s).
5. **Tools/activities** – Tactics or specific activities (actions) to implement each strategy for each targeted audience or public.
6. **Timetable** – Specific time frames for activities (see Gantt Charts – PR Play 7-3).
7. **Budget** – Specific dollars connected to specific activity (tactic) cost.
8. **Evaluation** – Relate to objective being evaluated for each public and identify method and source of data.

Wilson's *Public Relations Strategic Program Planning Matrix*

While both the Fulginiti and PRSA situation analyses are widely used, so, too, is Wilson's. Her 15-steps are an excellent road map leading to the development of a public relations (strategic) plan.

1. **Background** – A combination of primary and secondary research providing background information on the industry and client, the

product or program, market situation and current trends in opinion and attitude.

2. **Situation Analysis** – A one-paragraph statement of the current situation and refinement of problem definition based on research; a second paragraph identifies potential difficulties and related problems to be considered.

3. **Central core of difficulty** – A one-sentence statement of the heart of the problem and potential harm to client if not resolved.

4. **Preliminary identification of publics and resources** – The first part identifies and profiles all potential publics that may be affected by the problem or need to be motivated to aid in its solution; the second part identifies intervening publics and other resources (tangible and intangible) that can be drawn on for the campaign.

5. **Campaign goal(s)** – The end to be achieved is to resolve the central core of difficulty.

6. **Objectives** – Specific, measurable, attainable and time-bound results that will facilitate achievement of the campaign goal(s).

7. **Key publics** – Audiences necessary to achieve the campaign objective and goal(s); identify self-interests to aid in the development of messages that will motivate them; assess current relationships with each public and identify the strategic cooperative community to assist in identifying influentials.

8. **Message design** – Identifies the primary and secondary messages for each key public, taking care to incorporate each public's interest.

9. **Strategies** – Identifies specific strategies for each public designed to reach that public with its specially designed messages.

10. **Tactics** – Specific media tools or methods to support each strategy for each specific public; each strategy will need to be supported with a number of tactics designed to convey the message to that public through the channel designated by the strategy.

11. **Calendar** – A time-task matrix such as a Gantt Chart to integrate implementation of the strategic plan; the calendar should be organized by public and strategy, scheduling each tactic.

12. **Budget** – Organized by public and strategy, the budget should project the cost of each tactic in very specific terms; it also should indicate where cost will be offset by donation or sponsorship.

13. **Communication confirmation** – The communication confirmation table converts the plan devised for each public into short words in tabular form; the strategies and tactics for each public are reviewed to

ensure they are appropriate to send the messages; the message should be confirmed in accordance with the public's self-interests; the table provides verification of the analytical process to assure the plan will reach the publics with the appropriate messages to motivate them to action such that the campaign goal(s) is accomplished.

Key Public	Self-interests	Influentials/KCs	Strategy	Tactics/Tools	Message
1.					
2.					
3.					

14. **Evaluation criteria** – Identifies specific criteria to measure success based on the campaign goals and objectives.
15. **Evaluation tools** – Specific evaluation tools appropriate to measure each of the evaluation criteria including those in the calendar and budget.

No matter which *Situation Analysis* model is chosen, it will express all the important factors of the *MAC Triad Plus*. Once accomplished, the *SA* becomes a public relations (strategic) plan.

Planning Charts

Successful public relations practitioners and advertising executives live by the rule "plan backwards." Several charts are available to strategic planners whose lives are built around meeting deadlines.

While *Gantt* (PR Play 7-3) is the most popular of the planning charts, some practitioners use *PERT*, a project management charting tool used to schedule, organize and coordinate tasks within a project. *PERT* stands for *Program Evaluation Review Technique*, a methodology developed by the U.S. Navy in the 1950s to manage the Polaris submarine missile program.

A similar methodology used by some is the *Critical Path Method* (CPM), also developed in the 1950s for project management in the private sector.

Charts may be adjusted frequently to reflect the actual status of project tasks and tactics. Establish impingement points – those that must be "hit" on a particular date (usually horizontal across the top of chart with tactics vertically down the left side – although, for ease of reading, may be duplicated down the right side.) Gantt Chart software is readily available. Gantt Charts can be designed from Microsoft Office Excel®.

Flowcharts may be added to this category. They are commonly used in business presentations to help audiences better visualize a plan's contents and the process. Gantt Charts are the preferred planning tool because of their ease in following progress and deadline dates.

Gantt Chart

A Gantt Chart is a horizontal bar chart developed as a production control tool in 1917 by Henry L. Gantt, an American engineer and social scientist. Frequently used in project management, a Gantt Chart provides a graphical illustration of a schedule that helps to plan, coordinate and track specific tasks in a project. Gantt Charts may be simple versions created on graph paper or more complex automated versions created using project management applications such as Microsoft Project or Excel.

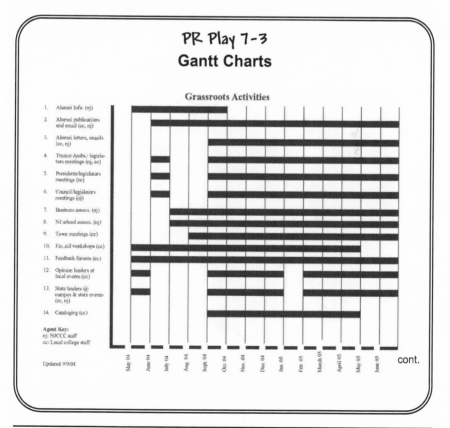

cont.

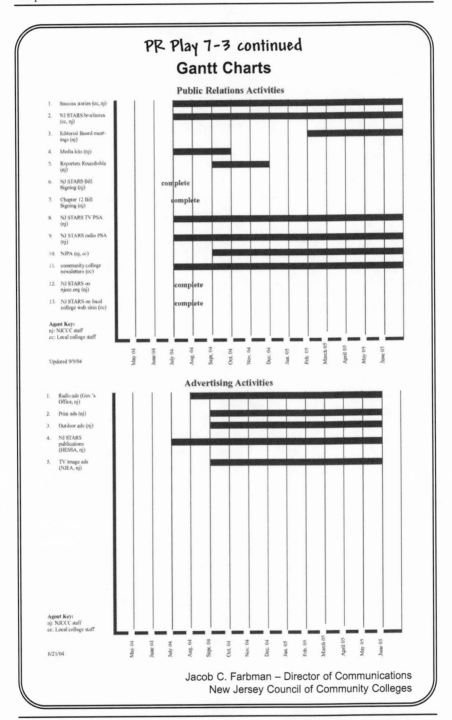

PR Play 7-3 continued
Gantt Charts

Public Relations Activities

1. Success stories (cc, nj)
2. NJ STARS brochures (cc, nj)
3. Editorial Board meetings (nj)
4. Media kits (nj)
5. Reporters Roundtable (nj)
6. NJ STARS Bill Signing (nj) — complete
7. Chapter 12 Bill Signing (nj) — complete
8. NJ STARS TV PSA (nj)
9. NJ STARS radio PSA (nj)
10. NJPA (nj, cc)
11. community college newsletters (cc)
12. NJ STARS on njccc.org (nj) — complete
13. NJ STARS on local college web sites (cc) — complete

Agent Key:
nj: NJCCC staff
cc: Local college staff

Updated 9/9/04

May 04, June 04, July 04, Aug. 04, Sept. 04, Oct. 04, Nov. 04, Dec. 04, Jan. 05, Feb. 05, March 05, April 05, May 05, June 05

Advertising Activities

1. Radio ads (Gov.'s Office, nj)
2. Print ads (nj)
3. Outdoor ads (nj)
4. NJ STARS publications (HESSA, nj)
5. TV image ads (NJEA, nj)

Agent Key:
nj: NJCCC staff
cc: Local college staff

6/21/04

May 04, June 04, July 04, Aug. 04, Sept. 04, Oct. 04, Nov. 04, Dec. 04, Jan. 05, Feb. 05, March 05, April 05, May 05, June 05

Jacob C. Farbman – Director of Communications
New Jersey Council of Community Colleges

A Gantt Chart is constructed with a horizontal axis representing the total time span of the project, broken down into increments (for example, days, weeks or months) and a vertical axis representing the tasks that make up the project (for example, if the project is outfitting your computer with new software, the major tasks involved might be: conduct research, choose software, install software). Horizontal bars of varying lengths represent the sequences, timing and time span for each task.

Using the same example, you would put "conduct research" at the top of the vertical axis and draw a bar on the graph that represents the amount of time you expect to spend on the research, and then enter the other tasks below the first one and representative bars at the points in time when you expect to undertake them. The bar spans may overlap, as, for example, you may conduct research and choose software during the same time span. As the project progresses, secondary bars, arrowheads, or darkened bars may be added to indicate completed tasks, or the portions of tasks that have been completed. A vertical line is used to represent the report date.

Gantt Charts give a clear illustration of project status, but one problem with them is that they don't indicate task dependencies – you cannot tell how one task falling behind schedule affects other tasks.

PR Play 7-4

Thorough Planning + Proper Execution=Positive Results

Wayne Stewart – Johnson & Johnson®

PR Play 7-5

Collaborate > Create > Succeed

Cargill® Foods – Minneapolis

PR Play 7-6
A Planning Rule

Generally, a public relations (strategic) plan or campaign will have only one goal – many times based on an organization's purpose or mission. That goal may have several objectives associated with it. Each objective could have a number of strategies, although experts believe the strategies (messages) should be limited so that audiences remember them. However, the number of tactics that can be developed for a given strategy is almost infinite [certainly, there are many ways to deliver the message(s)].

PR Play 7-7

Set goals that are SMART: specific, measurable, attainable, realistic and tangible, and also include a time frame.

Hallie Crawford – Career Coach and Trainer – Atlanta

Public Relations/Strategic Communication Budgeting

CNNMoney.com says budgets are a necessary evil. They are the only practical way to get a grip on your spending so you can make sure your money or your department's money is being used the way you want it to be used.

Creating a budget generally requires three steps:
• Identify how you spend money now.
• Evaluate your current spending and set goals that take into account your financial objectives.
• Track your spending to make sure it stays within those guidelines.

Budget allocations to make and maintain the effective program are relative to the organization's size, commitment and goals. But one thing is certain – budgeting is an art. And in some organizations, because of a lack of total management support, the strategic communicator must be creative in developing his or her budget.

Only recently has the budgeting process been included in public relations – and other strategic communication – training programs. None of us are budgeting specialists unless we've taken finance courses or attended workshops. We should rely on such experts as our business manager or controller for advice and guidance. It is usually the "business/money person" who establishes the guidelines we use to operate our public relations department.

As Cutlip, Center and Broom write in *Effective Public Relations*, "Budgeting is rarely a one-person job. Each is called on to estimate and itemize *variable costs* that will be incurred to implement the public relations plan during the next budget year. *Variable costs* are those associated with activities such as printing, rent for special events facilities, speakers' fees, website management, photographers, advertising, travel and entertainment.

"The department head, or someone designated, adds the estimated *variable costs* to the unit's *fixed costs,* including such expenses as salaries and benefits, overhead for office space, phone, service, equipment leases, supplies, subscriptions and service contracts."

It is important to develop a good working relationship with the "money person" in your firm or organization. Ultimately, he or she will make the adjustments necessary to make your public relations budget fit into the overall budget of the organization.

Too often, budgets are put aside after they are approved and therefore *NOT* used as management tools. Budgets, when properly researched, crafted and adhered to, are in fact the backbone of every department and organization.

A first step in budgeting – remember, a budget is only part of an overall plan – is to create expense function categories (tactics). No matter the size of the budget – minimal or extensive – it is a valuable chart (prediction) of what might be required to accomplish the PR office's objectives, strategies and tactics.

When budgets are used in conjunction with other elements of program planning, they provide guidance for:
• Scheduling staff resources
• Contracting for services
• Tracking project costs
• Establishing accountability

PR Play 7-8

Three Helpful Budgeting Guidelines

1. Know the cost of what you propose to buy.
2. Communicate the budget in terms of what it costs to achieve specific results.
3. Use the power of your computer to manage the program.

Cutlip offers three guidelines that may be helpful:

1. *Know the cost of what you propose to buy.* If you plan to do a special mailing, find out the exact costs of photography and artwork, printing and folding, mailing lists, labeling and sorting, delivery, postage and everything needed to complete the job. Don't guess, because you will have to live within the budget that gets approved and deliver what was promised.
2. *Communicate the budget in terms of what it costs to achieve specific results.* The actual details of variable and fixed costs used to develop the budget should be of interest to management or to a client. Managers who must approve the budget typically want to know how much it will cost to achieve goals and objectives. They look to you (the PR specialist) to manage the process in a cost-effective fashion.
3. *Use the power of your computer to manage the program.* Develop a master spreadsheet (Excel®) as well as spreadsheets for individual projects ("personal" templates). By tracking each project and linking each to a master spreadsheet, you can estimate cash-flow requirements in advance and monitor expenses against cost estimates.

Remember, a budget is a working document that should be monitored often. It is your best estimate of the allocations needed to meet goals and objectives for a fiscal year. Many department heads review their current operating budget weekly if not daily.

Budget Approaches

Upper management should establish *budgeting approaches* used by its particular organization. There are two primary approaches to establish a public relations or advertising budget:

TOP DOWN (vertical) BUDGETING – Budget allocation comes from a superior. In many cases, the top management team develops the numbers and the respective departments are given the allocations. **Management sets the total figure. The strategic counselor then allocates it among various activities.** (This is more of a macro-budgeting approach.)

BUILD-UP BUDGETING – Sometimes referred to as a "grass roots budget." Based on the previous year's budget. New programs and activities, as well as PPI (producer price index), must be factored in. Many times, this is a wish list. As with other methods, all line items must be justified. Previous budget history within the department should also be considered. **Estimate how much each activity will cost and then add them up.** (This is more of a micro-budgeting approach.)

PR Play 7-9

An important point to remember or understand about budgeting is that it reflects the emphasis that the organization has decided to give to your department.

Within these two approaches are a number of specific procedures or methods – some more formal than others.

ZERO-BASED BUDGETING – Assumes no present cost approved. Every item and cost must be justified as it enters the plan (total justification needed). Activities are evaluated yearly from a zero base. It's probably a good idea to use *zero-base budgeting* every few years to eliminate unnecessary programs and expenses.

TASK-OBJECTIVE BUDGETING – A method that builds a budget by asking what it will cost to achieve the stated objectives through implementation of tactics. Quite simply, it includes fixed costs plus costs of tactics and tools contained in the *public relations (strategic) plan(s).*

HISTORICAL BUDGETING – A relatively simplistic version of budgeting. It's based on previous budgets (several years). A budget may simply be based on last year's budget with a percentage increase for inflation or *some other marketplace factor.*

COMPETITIVE BUDGETING – Used when factoring in your competition. If you must increase your activities to develop more aggressive campaigns in your respective market, then you must employ the *competitive method*. You may want to analyze the competition to justify your requests. You will also want to coordinate with **Research and Development** to gather support data on your customers, the competition and their resources. Many times, when using this method, allocations are predicated or dependent on market share.

PERCENT OF SALES BUDGETING – A technique for computing the budget level that is based on the relationship between cost of PR or advertising and total sales. To help justify increases, it is important, if not imperative, to show that if your organization projects a 10 percent increase in sales, then your PR or advertising budget might be worthy of a 10 percent increase.

FLEXIBLE BUDGETING (FLEXIBLE BUDGET) – Not necessarily an accepted method by most finance people. However, some organizations do allow use of this method. Example: As time passes, the department head may decide to increase or decrease projected budget line items to accomplish the best possible job of managing the strategic function in light of the current events. However, some organizations are allowing (projected) bottom lines in budgets (based on some of the above techniques) to be adjusted during the fiscal year. Those (projected) budgets are evaluated periodically and adjusted according to a number of criteria set forth by upper management. It should be noted that public (government) agencies may not unilaterally alter a budget once it is approved.

COMBINATION OF METHODS – Just as it says, the process of combining various budgeting techniques to adopt your final workable budget.

PR Play 7-10
Budgeting Rules of Thumb

Strategic counselors must:
1. Have realistic budgets.
2. Use them to direct staff efforts.
3. Review them frequently with clients and top management.
4. Be able to link costs to performance (tactics) and outcomes.

It has already been established that the administrative or organizational budget is composed of program budgets – components of the overall firm or organization's budget. The public relations department, for example, is one of those programs. Therefore, the public relations budget is a percentage of the overall institution's budget.

One suggestion, especially if you are dealing with a new program, is to build the program first and then determine how much money must be allocated. Some considerations:

- It could be a fixed percentage.
- It could be "project appropriate."
- It could be based on the estimated cost of the projects planned for the year.
- Does the PR office operate with an administrator in charge?
- The PR administrator must do a careful analysis of the program for the year and estimate how much the firm must provide.

Some organizations believe in the ***Bill-Back Method***: As work is done for various departments by the public relations department, it is billed-back – much like an in-house agency. Costs are transferred to the public relations budget from the department receiving services from PR.

There is no magic formula to budgeting. And, no matter which budgeting approach or combination of approaches is used, the public relations/strategic planning steps in PR Play 7-1 (first listed in Chapter 3) must be must be followed.

A Reminder

Budgets are financial plans or blueprints that must be regularly monitored. Budgets illustrate allocations for various programs and line items (fixed costs, tactics, tools, etc.) over a period of time.

Plans are road maps that take organizations or clients to a destination.

Strategic counselors who tie their program budgets to their *PR (strategic) plans* experience a high degree of success in meeting their goal and objectives.

Whether or not the PR practitioner is proficient with numbers, constructing a realistic budget – and living within it – offers a new appreciation of the economic realties of the environment in which you are practicing. As called for, budgets and plans should be adjusted – never losing sight of the objectives and goal.

PR Play 7-11
Primary Approaches to Budgeting

1. Top Down Budgeting
2. Build-up Budgeting

Within these two primary approaches/methods

- Zero-Based
- Task-Objective
- Historical
- Competitive
- Percent of Sales
- Flexible
- Combination

PR Play 7-12

Line item or running budgets use this – or a similar – format. Line items are inserted as needed for a complete budget. Whether the budget is for an entire organization, department or project, "running" (line) budgets are recommended. They keep track of revenue sources, projected expenditures and eventually, actual expenses. Thanks to Excel® you could develop columns for the previous year, the full current year and the full next year, showing projected and actual expenditures (historical budget) – for comparison purposes. (See PR Play 7-13)

Line Item	January	February	March	April	May	June	July
Revenues							
Total Revenues							
Expenses							
Total Expenses							
Total Revenues							
Net Profit/Loss							

PR Play 7-13
Burwyn Arts Center – Program Line Item Budget

Fiscal Year 2010

PUBLIC RELATIONS BUDGET PROPOSAL – BURWYN ARTS CENTER

	FY 08 Actual	FY 09 Requested	FY 09 Actual	FY 09 Spent	FY 09 Surplus	FY 10 Request	% Inc./Dec.	FY 10 Actual
Personnel								
Salaries	$63,500	$67,945	$66,675	$66,675	0	$70,008	5%+	$69,678
Hourly Wages	22,756	3,000	2,300	2,785	15	3,000	7%+	3,000
Health Insurance	7,245	7,900	7,897	7,897	0	8,766	11%+	8,500
Dental Insurance	624	668	650	659	-9	714	7%+	715
Workman's Comp.	5,715	6,000	5,950	5,977	-27	6,263	5%+	6,150
Temporary Services	2,000	2,500	2,000	1,994	6	2,500	25%+	2,000
Employee Morale	200	250	200	195	5	250	6%+	225
	$82,040	$98,263	$86,172	$86,182	-10	$91,501		$90,268
Operations								
Office Supplies	$5,625	$6,000	$5,750	$5,673	77	$6,000	4%+	$5,850
Computer Supplies	1,265	1,500	1,400	1,945	55	1,600	14%+	1,500
Postage	16,720	18,000	17,500	18,233	-733	22,000	22%+	21,000
Telephone/Fax	5,400	5,750	5,600	5,542	58	6,048	8%+	5,850
Overnight Delivery	1,000	1,200	1,000	998	2	1,200	20%+	1,100
Clipping Services	2,000	2,000	2,000	1,838	162	2,100	5%+	2,100
Photography	3,500	3,750	3,600	3,430	170	3,800	5%+	3,700
Equipment Maintenance	600	600	600	461	139	600	0%+	600
Special Events	3,000	2,500	2,000	1,876	124	2,000	16%+	2,000
	$39,110	$41,300	$39,450	$39,396	54	$45,848		$43,700
Advertising								
Print Design	2,000	2,500	2,250	2,100	150	2,500	10%+	2,250
Print Placement	22,000	25,000	24,000	23,238	762	25,000	4%+	25,000
Radio Production	3,000	3,000	3,000	3,150	-150	3,500	17%+	3,350
Radio Placement	24,000	27,500	25,000	24,654	346	27,500	10%+	26,000
Outdoor Production	-0-	-0-	1,800	1,875	-75	-0-	NA	-0-
Outdoor Rental	7,200	7,200	5,400	5,500	-100	-0-	NA	-0-
	$51,000	$67,500	$61,450	$60,517	$933	$58,500		$56,600
Publications								
Design	$4,300	$4,750	$4,500	$4,325	$175	$5,000	10%+	$4,800
Typesetting	3,800	4,200	4,000	4,135	-135	4,500	13%+	4,000
Mechanical Prep	2,400	2,600	2,500	2,490	10	2,750	10%+	2,500
Printing	24,000	26,000	25,000	25,345	-345	28,000	12%+	26,500
Distribution	1,500	1,600	1,500	1,425	75	2,000	25%+	1,600
Miscellany								
Consultants' Fees	$4,500	$5,000	$4,750	$4,675	$75	$5,000	5%+	$4,800
Professional Development	750	1,000	800	785	15	1,000	20%+	900
Travel	1,250	1,500	1,400	1,356	44	1,750	25%+	1,400
Entertainment	500	500	500	482	18	500	0%+	500
Memberships, Dues	1,200	1,400	1,400	1,350	50	1,450	4%+	1,450
	$8,200	$9,400	$8,850	$8,648	$202	$9,700		9,050
Totals	$216,350	$246,013	$233,422	$232,463	$959	$248,049	7%+	$239,018

Mark Fields – Rowan (N.J.) University Graduate Student

Public Relations (Strategic Communication) Budgeting Key Terms

all-we-can-afford method – A simple method of determining a budget (for public relations, advertising, etc.) where the amount allocated is the amount that can be afforded; also called the What-We-Can Afford Method, the Affordable Method and the Arbitrary Method.

PR Play 7-14
How Agencies Are Paid

Agencies bill clients through commissions, hourly rates, project fees or a combination of all three. Below is an explanation of all three:

Commission – A form of compensation to an agency for designing and placing advertisements. Historically, this was calculated as 15 percent of the amount spent to purchase space or time in the various media used for the advertising. In recent years, the commission has, in many cases, become negotiable and may even be based on some measure of the campaign's success.

Fee – A payment made by a client to a public relations or advertising agency in lieu of, or in addition to, the agency's commission for such projects as a display ad design, commercial or public service announcement script, newsletter, research project, etc. Also referred to as a *Project Fee* or *Flat Fee*.

Hourly Rate – Compensation paid to a public relations or advertising agency based on the amount of time – plus materials (out of pocket expenses known as OOP) – spent providing its services.

Bona fide agencies will usually recommend which of the compensation methods – or combination of the three – is best for a prospective client.

bill-back method – As work is done for various departments by the public relations department, it is billed-back – much like an in-house agency. Costs are transferred to the public relations budget from the department receiving services from PR.

budget determination (public relations or advertising) – Decisions pertaining to the amount to be allocated to public relations (advertising) expenditure in a given period; common approaches to budget determination include arbitrary allocation, percent of sales, competitive parity, objective and task, and budgeting models.

competitive necessity – As strategic counselor, you determine budget allocations or the budget itself of a competing organization and attempt to match it. How is this accomplished? It may not be as difficult as it sounds. "Corporate espionage" (not necessarily illegal, but it *is* unethical) may be used. But in many cases, all you have to do is ask.
(See *The ABCs of Strategic Communication* – AuthorHouse)

PR Play 7-15
Typical Public Relations Agency Fee Schedule – Burwyn Associates

FEES AND EXPENSES
Burwyn Associates' fees are based on hours worked, plus expenses (materials) – for the services provided. A portion of Burwyn's fees is payable in advance each month. We refer to this payment as our "retainer." (For ongoing programs, the retainer is equivalent to one-12th of the estimated annual budget). Fees for the month in excess of the retainer amount, and expenses, will be billed at the end of the month. If the retainer exceeds the total of fees and expenses, the excess is credited. Any retainer balance remaining at the end of our engagement will be refunded.

Hourly Rates

	Ongoing Programs*	Projects**	Crisis & Special Situations***
President, EVP, COO	$275	$325	$450
Senior Vice Presidents	$235	$275	$400
VPs & Account Managers	$175—$195	$200-$225	$295
Account Executives	$150-$170	$175-$190	$245
Other Professional Staff	$115-$140	$145-$170	$195
Production/ Support/Clerical	$55	$75	$95

All Personnel

Travel:
One-half the applicable hourly rate, except:
(1) Travel overnight away from home, which is full rate, with a minimum eight hours per day, and

(2) Travel for crisis situations, which is full rate.

* Ongoing programs rate requires annual budget commitment of at least $96,000.
** Minimum advance payment for projects is $12,000.
*** Minimum advance payment for crisis is $25,000.
*** Minimum fee for special situations is $2,500.

cont.

PR Play 7-15 continued

Expenses:

Incidental out-of-pocket (OOP) expenses, such as postage, phone, travel and entertainment on client's behalf is billed as incurred, without markup. Costs for outside products or services, such as printing, photography, graphic design, artwork, production, materials, etc., are billed at gross cost which includes the standard 15% agency service charge. Charges for outside products or services in excess of $500 are payable in advance.

Terms:

Work will begin upon receipt of retainer and signed Letter of Agreement. Invoices are payable upon receipt. A service charge of 1.5% per month is imposed on all bills not paid within 14 days. If a bill remains unpaid after 30 days, Burwyn will discontinue work until payments are received to make your account current. Burwyn reserves the right to terminate an account for non-payment of bills. Additional terms and conditions are set forth in the Letter of Agreement. (See www.larrylitwin.com for examples of Letters of Agreement or email larry@larrylitwin.com.)

---

forecasting – Using economic models to plan budgeting increases and decreases in spending – taking into account the growth of the *national economy* and other macroeconomic factors. It must be based on expected costs. A good starting point for estimating cash requirements might be a review of the previous five to 10 years.

Because of *Integrated Marketing Communication* (and *cross promotion*), estimating sales levels and the impact of various budget decisions on sales could be a consideration for the PR practitioner. In other words, the PR practitioner, to justify the budgeting request, tries to determine what level of sales will be generated through various levels of promotion.

leftover – The least acceptable to the honorable PR practitioner. That's because this is the method whereby the public relations office gets whatever may be left after all other funds have been allocated.

percentage – A budget may be tied to gross revenues.

task or goal – Allocations are made on a task-by-task basis. This is used specifically in the build-up method.

EXERCISES

PR Challenge 7-1

Develop a mini plan for a special event of your choice. From the plan's tactics, compile a realistic budget. Only you and those involved can determine financial resources. Be certain to itemize your tactics once goal, objectives and strategies are determined and approved.

PR Challenge 7-2

As strategic communication director for a non-profit organization it is your responsibility to craft your department's budget. While there are recommended steps, how would you go about it? List the steps and explain the sequence. In the end, you will create your own line item (program or department) budget.

CHAPTER 8
You, Too, Can Conduct Successful Campaigns

Think one vote doesn't matter much? Just ask Al Gore (or George W. Bush).

Recently, in New Jersey, on the same election day, one race was decided by just 35 votes, another by 31 and yet another by 29. Those pluralities are huge compared to some others from that same day – a difference of 14 votes in one town, nine votes in another, seven, two, two, two in four other municipalities, respectfully, and amazingly, in Medford Township, N.J., the outcome was a dead heat. Thank goodness for absentee ballots. Oh, they were tied, too!

When it comes to conducting a campaign, there is one preliminary step that is even more important than the issues or key talking points – the budget. That translates into how much of an effort must be put into fundraising. However, this chapter focuses on the nuts and bolts of conducting successful campaigns from the grass roots level rather than raising money.

Conducting a successful campaign is not rocket science. By their very nature, campaigns are premeditated – carefully planned and executed integrated marketing communication (synergistic) activities to achieve communication objectives.

Both major political parties use a similar approach, as do the minority parties. State and local municipalities follow a similar formula and so do school districts in those states that must ask voters to approve budgets and building bond referenda. In fact, students who seek office in colleges and schools research and soon discover the steps they must take to get elected to student government or class office. Succinctly, those seeking office must communicate "who they are; what they think about themselves; what they are trying to do; and why they deserve voter support"— the same ingredients that go into a mission statement.

Below is a narrative plan summary used by a number of school districts that have run successful financial campaigns over the last four decades. It worked then and still works today.

Conducting a Successful Bond Issue Campaign Through Total Community Involvement

Getting people to vote for higher taxes is a real challenge to boards of education. Yet, in New Jersey, Pennsylvania, New York, Michigan, Iowa, California and some other states, voter support is needed to maintain sound educational programs in school districts.

Boards of education must realize that effective school communication is a year-round, two-way process. Effective programs seek community attitudes at the same time they disseminate the information (push polling). A program must reach everyone – not just teachers, parents or community leaders (Chapter 15 – Key Communicators). The audience is everybody including other community residents, students and support staff.

During a bond issue (or budget) campaign, a strategic communication program must be intensified, particularly during the six-week period before Election Day. If a school district conducts an "honest" year-round communication program, there should be no credibility gap during the campaign. By building confidence in the schools throughout the year with clear communication about problems, as well as successes, administrators establish rapport with the taxpayers.

Above all else, establish the need for a bigger budget – telling how the new building or program (thus the tax increase) will improve the educational program quality and environment. Remember, you are dealing with the taxpayers' two most prized possessions – their children and their money.

Following these introductory paragraphs is a list of steps on how one school district (Washington Township in Gloucester County, N.J.) conducted a successful bond issue campaign for a middle school. The campaign attracted the second highest voter turnout ever. The number of "yes" votes (2,341) was the most ever for a financial election in Washington Township. The number of "no" votes was reduced by 31 percent from previous middle school referenda.

Washington Township is a community of 22 square miles, half of which, at the time, was still undeveloped land. Its student enrollment had been increasing at approximately eight percent per year. Enrollment increased from 3,634 to more than 6,000 in just six years. Enrollment was close to 10,000 at the turn of the century.

Conspicuous by its absence is mention of a budget. In most states, school districts and school boards are *not* permitted to conduct a "Vote Yes" campaign. This, therefore, is designed as an informational campaign. It is paid for through the public relations office's budget. Such outside groups as parent-teacher organizations, service and "animal" groups (Rotary, Lions, Kiwanis, Elks, etc.) or political action committees – PACs – e.g., (527 or 501(c)4 organization) may endorse a plan and conduct their own campaigns.

> ### PR Play 8-1
> ### Campaigns – Defined
>
> Campaigns are premeditated – carefully planned and executed integrated marketing communication (synergistic) activities to achieve communication objectives.

By gaining support from outside groups, additional strategies and tactics can be implemented. Examples would include:

- Gaining third party endorsement (opinion leaders examining, discussing and endorsing the issues)
- Creating and then emphasizing widespread public support for the issue or candidate (bandwagon effect)
- Mobilizing that public support
- Encouraging outside supporters to conduct social media and letter to the editor campaigns
- Rallying support from ministerium (more third party endorsements/validation)
- Making maximum use of poll workers and poll watchers to assure that supporters do – indeed – cast their ballots
- Encouraging all groups (governmental and otherwise) on your side to pass resolutions supporting the issue

An important part of the bandwagon effect is *coalition building*. It is a tactic that emphasizes broad-based support for an issue or candidate. Coalitions encourage groups to coordinate their efforts and prevent duplication.

PR Play 8-2
How To Do It

Here are 35 easy and proven steps to follow when conducting a comprehensive two-way strategic communication campaign for a bond referendum – whether for a school district, municipality or state. (Many candidates for public office follow similar steps with adjustments and modifications):

1. Attempt to schedule the bond issue on a day when there are other activities in the schools, which would attract potential voters to the polling places.
2. Set a date for bond issue.
3. Receive board approval on resolution for bond issue.
4. Design an interactive website.
5. Design and encourage a downloadable app for smartphones.
6. Conduct a voter registration drive (include registering high school students).
7. Keep an indexed file (on computer) of your plan of action including all correspondence and news clips.
8. Designate one person as the chief spokesperson for the school district and campaign.
9. Plan your campaign on an easy-to-read Gantt Chart (spreadsheet) or calendar (See Gantt Chart example – Chapter 7).
10. Recruit bond issue volunteer workers.
11. Compile a comprehensive (electronic) "booklet" of information about the campaign (plan of action), which can be used as a ready reference "Fact Pack" for school district administrators, board members, other staff, bond issue volunteer workers and the news media. Link the booklet to the district's website. (The media can turn out to be partners in the public information effort.)
12. Have a summary of the "Fact Pack" prepared. It should contain a minimum number of pages. Link the "Fact Pack" to the district's website.
13. Compile other background information to be given to bond issue volunteer workers and the news media during in-service meetings. Update all information through emails and the district's website.
14. Kick off the campaign with an in-service session for the news media. Make this more than just a news conference. Make it a major special event. Have a well-briefed board member and/or

cont.

PR Play 8-2 continued

administrator available to meet with reporters on a one-to-one basis following the general announcement about the start of the bond issue campaign.

15. Prepare a series of news releases to be distributed from the initial stages of the campaign throughout the comprehensive campaign and make them available in the website's press room.
16. Hold in-service meetings for bond issue volunteer workers.
17. Keep bond issue volunteer workers informed through background bulletins published whenever needed and blast emailed.
18. Schedule meetings with individual PTAs and community groups. Teams of teachers and students should conduct them.
19. Distribute a brochure (via bulk mail and inline email [embedded in email rather than attached]) exclusively about the bond issue approximately 10 days before the election. ("Save the date" vote cards – reminders, which can be clipped to a calendar, should also be sent. Don't overlook the value of "blast" emails.)
20. Incorporate third-party validation and credible endorsement testimonial letters (known as source credibility) from respected board members and/or community (opinion) leaders (explaining the issue) and mail to residents – in hard copy and blast emails.
21. Schedule an issue of the school district's community newsletter so that it reaches the homes shortly before the day of the bond issue. (Publish both online and hard copy.)
22. Work with community groups who might be interested in sponsoring newspaper or billboard ads.
23. Work with teachers' associations who should be interested in quietly supporting the referendum.
24. Work with individual students and students' organizations who might be interested in supporting and carrying the message through WOM (word of mouth [free]) or viral marketing (paid for and called WOMM [word of mouth marketing]).
25. Keep in contact with the news media, to assure that at least one story appears each week in daily and weekly newspapers.
26. Work with TV and radio stations to assure campaign coverage on the several days before the bond issue. (Strive for saturation coverage on radio [all-news stations] and early television coverage on Election Day. It helps remind people to vote.)
27. Work with the editorial page editors of the local dailies and weeklies in an attempt to gain valuable editorial support from their papers. cont.

PR Play 8-2 continued

28. If positive editorials are printed, reproduce them from the newspapers and distribute them as widely as possible to show broad-based support.
29. Prepare and distribute a news release about editorial endorsements.
30. Work with students' organizations (endorsing bond issue) to schedule a parade or some other demonstration showing their support. (Students may go door-to-door [on their own] on Election Day.)
31. Be prepared to answer technical questions about the election process from residents on the day of the election. (Have professionals available on Election Day to answer phone calls.)
32. Hold a news briefing soon after the election to update the media on plans and alternatives.
33. Send thank-you notes to everyone who helped with the campaign.
34. Order sign to be erected on proposed site (if successful).
35. Arrange for groundbreaking (if successful).

Tips from Carville and Matalin

Philosophically, political consultants Mary Matalin and James Carville don't agree about much. Matalin works for Republicans (Presidents George H.W. Bush, George W. Bush and Vice President Dick [Richard B.] Cheney), and Carville for Democrats including President Bill (William Jefferson) Clinton. Carville and Matalin do, however, agree in two areas – their family (they are husband and wife) and their approach to winning elections.

Here are excerpts from one of Matalin and Carville's recent speaking engagements:

The Candidate

- The candidate must be *optimistic*.
- The candidate must possess a *passion* for the job and for campaigning.
- The most hopeful and optimistic candidates win. (Research shows, the optimistic candidate wins more than 90 percent of the time. In fact, since 1952, the only presidential candidate who fit this profile and lost was Hubert H. Humphrey. Given one more week to communicate his message, Humphrey might have defeated Richard M. Nixon. In fact, Matalin and Carville agree, Humprhey would have won – because he had momentum.)

PR Play 8-3
The Campaign

(Follow PR-Pie [Chapter 2])

1. Name a coordinator
2. Timing

Phase One

- Plan (strategic) campaign
  - o Learn the laws
  - o Research
    - Focus panels
    - Phone surveys
    - Intercept surveys
- Target audience
- Voter registration drive

Phase Two

- Information campaign/ Community education
  - o Liberal use of Internet
  - o News releases
  - o News conferences
  - o Public meetings
  - o Small group meetings (in-home coffees)
  - o Talk shows
  - o Paid advertising
- Face-to-face
- Speakers Bureau

Phase Three (climax)

- Endorsements
- More sophisticated printed and electronic (online) publications (brochures)
- Buttons
- Bumper stickers
- Neighborhood canvassing
- Telephone calls
- Emails
- GOTV (Get Out The Vote)
  - o Ground game or ground attack – using "ordinary" people to mobilize GOTV campaign (if they are paid it is viral marketing) – going door-to-door to get out the vote.
  - o "Amway®" your candidate or issue to a win – getting out the vote by organizing those ordinary citizens to make phone calls using a pyramid approach.

3. Financing
   - Corporate contributions
   - Individual contributions
   - Political Action Committees (PACs)
   - Service organizations
   - Carefully scrutinized budget

PR Play 8-4
"X" Records the Vote

Whether it is pulling the lever, drawing an "X" on a paper ballot, tapping the screen or clicking the mouse, voters must be persuaded to vote for a candidate or issue. Ed Ziegler (Chapter 2) stresses educating the targeted public – whether marketing a product or service. Everett Rogers (Chapter 2 – Innovation Diffusion Theory) and Floyd Shoemaker followed a similar model:

1. Knowledge – Individuals are exposed to a strategic message to better understand the product, service, candidate or issue.
2. Persuasion – Individuals develop an attitude (favorable or unfavorable) toward the product, service, candidate or issue.
3. Decision – Individuals engage in activities which lead to a choice of adopting or rejecting the product, service, candidate or issue.
4. Confirmation – Individuals seek reinforcement for their decision – but, if dissonance sets in they may have a change of mind – especially if exposed to conflicting messages.

Adopters – and Their Willingness

- Innovators – Venturesome, educated, multiple info sources.
- Early adopters – Social leaders, popular, educated.
- Early majority – Deliberate, many informal social contacts.
- Late majority – Skeptical, traditional, lower socio-economic status.
- Laggards – Neighbors and friends are main info sources, fear of debt.

PR Play 8-5
Questions to Answer Enroute to a Successful Campaign (Political or Issue)

Why make a change?
What must be accomplished?
What journey must be taken to reach the goal?
Who should receive the message (audiences)?
What must be done?
How should it be done?
What happened and why (evaluation)?
How effective was the campaign?
What changes must be made for future campaigns?

PR Play 8-6
Why Information Campaigns Fail

- Voter is generally uninformed.
- There are large groups in the population (passive audience) who admit to having little or no interest in public issues.
- People tend to expose themselves to material that is compatible with their attitudes and beliefs and to avoid exposure to issues, candidates and products that do not match their beliefs (selective perception).
- Selective perception and interpretation of content follows exposure: individuals perceive, absorb and remember content differently.
- Changes in attitudes – even following exposure to a message – are difficult to achieve. It may be a mistake to take too much time or spend too many resources in an effort to lead to a more favorable behavior. (Concentration should be placed on getting out the vote of those in agreement (active audience) with your candidate or issue.)
- Poor GOTV effort.

Two Rhetorical Traditions in Politics
- One looks at how bad things are.
- The other looks at how to make things better.
  [This candidate almost always wins.]

Each Issue (in politics and in life) has Three Segments:
1. Set Up
2. Conflict
3. Resolution

Points To Keep In Mind When Delivering the Strategic Message:
(SRR)
- **S**implicity (voice cuts/sound bites)
- **R**elevance (can audience relate?)
- **R**epetition (keep hammering away)

While Chapters 3 – Total Effort to Communicate and 7 – Public Relations Planning and Budgeting have already presented the Basic Planning Steps, it is important to repeat these steps (repetition is, after all, the "mother" of all learning) as a reminder and for those who have yet to read those chapters. These steps are important to any plan, but are a must when campaign planning:

1. Identify Issues (Determine purpose – Situation Analysis)
2. Design Research Questions
3. Conduct Initial Research (Research Actions)
4. Select Goal – must be attainable – realistic and reachable
5. Write Backgrounder (Case) Statement [Chapters 5 and 6]
6. Identify and Rank Audiences
7. Craft Messages
8. Determine Channels
9. Determine Aperture (Best time to deliver messages)
10. Write Objectives
11. Craft Strategies (what, to whom, how)
12. Select Tactics (Vehicles/Tools)
13. Prepare Budget
14. Design Gantt Chart (Calendar Time Line) [Chapter 7]
15. Measure Your Work (Evaluate) – an assessment
16. Further Research (What changes would you make?)

PR Play 8-7
Examples of S-R-R

"Do unto others as you'd have them do unto you."

Known as: *The Golden Rule*

"You can pick your friends, but not your family."

"You can't judge a book by its cover."

"Some people see things as they are and say why.
I dream things that never were and say why not?"

Robert F. Kennedy – Paraphrased from George Bernard Shaw

PR Play 8-8
Political Message
(According to Carville and Matalin)

- Develop your candidate's message and continually *repeat* it.
  - Limit key message points to five – preferably even fewer.
  - Don't be concerned with criticism that the candidate is being repetitious. Repetition is the foundation of learning and the philosophy behind successful advertisements and commercials.

- Determine your opponents' vulnerability and continually *attack* it.
  - Does this mean the use of negative ads? Only the campaign manager or Strategic (PR) Counselor can respond to that – let your conscience be your guide – or, it depends on how badly you want to win.

To win any election takes a well-thought out and well-executed plan. It must include all three corners of the *MAC Triad Plus – the P for Purpose and T for Timing.* It must consider various strategies, all available tactics and tools, and the channels to deliver them. A well-informed voter expects candidates to be competent. Prospective voters will support certain issues (referenda) once they are convinced – or at the very least, persuaded – of the need.

It is widely agreed, whether for a candidate or referendum on the ballot: crafting the campaign plan is essential; proposals must be sold – or related very well – to the voters; and involving as many people as possible (developing broad-based support) is key to winning.

PR Play 8-9
"Plans are nothing. Planning is everything."

Gen. Dwight D. Eisenhower

EXERCISES

PR Challenge 8-1

Which of the communication models discussed earlier in *The Public Relations Practitioner's Playbook for (all) Strategic Communicators* would you rely on before beginning the long road to a successful outcome and why?

PR Challenge 8-2

What steps would you take to help plan a Get Out The Vote (GOTV) ground attack for a local mayor's election?

CHAPTER 9

Media Relations – and –
The Impact of Public Relations
(Strategic Communication) on the News

The very first step toward becoming successful in dealing with the media is the ability to recognize *hard* news and understand the difference between *hard* news and features.

Hard news is something of interest to a segment (or fragment) of the public. It is (more) immediate. For the most part, it is timely and has a local "hook." It probably becomes outdated quickly unless it is updated. A more formal definition calls for *hard* news to be truly newsworthy, presented factually and objectively. Many times, it is breaking news.

Feature (or *soft*) news, on the other hand, covers many categories that don't fall under *hard* news – human-interest stories, personality pieces, etc. Feature stories are less timely and don't have the immediacy that hard news does. In many cases, they are "evergreens."

Hard news can often be controlled. (Announcing a major breakthrough, appointment or resignation.) This type of information can be announced through a news release or news conference. Other *hard* news events might be beyond your control – an employee walkout, a shooting, an industrial accident or the unexpected death of a key employee.

When unexpected news breaks, time may not permit preparing a news release. However, you can call the media (if possible, before they call you) and give them the full story (or as much as you have that can be on the record). Good reporters usually find out anyway, especially if the news is bad, and you will gain some powerful friends because *you* contacted *them* with the information. With the pressures of 24/7 news, it is more important than ever to be proactive.

As for features, many times you won't even have to write them. Just pitch the story ideas to reporters, who in turn will "sell" them to their editors (gatekeepers) – and voila' – they do the work for you.

On the subject of news releases – they should never be hit or miss. News releases and, depending on the event, media kits, should be part of an over-all communications program (see pros and cons of media kits in Chapter 5).

Never forget this simple "unwritten" rule: reporters like to talk to people who make news. They look for name recognition – whether in print, online or broadcast. Your job as a public relations practitioner is to make that person available and your responsibility as strategic adviser is to make certain that the newsmaker is prepared for the interview.

Recognizing Hard News

It has already been established that *hard* news is any event that affects or is of interest to a reasonable number of people. News is about change and how those changes are tracked and documented. Reporters – whether seasoned or rookies – will tell you, news is the search for truth. According to veteran editor and college professor Everett Landers, "Journalists rely on public relations and/or media spokespeople to provide facts and other information because writing from ignorance is the highest unethical act in journalism.

"People act on information that isn't true. Newspapers, especially, have an obligation to filter."

When deciding whether you have a newsworthy item, ask yourself these questions:
1. Is the item of consequence to a reasonable number of readers, listeners or viewers?
2. Will the readers be interested in reading it?
3. Does it have impact?
4. Is it timely?

An important event that occurs today or tonight must be reported in tomorrow's papers (or it might even find its way almost immediately onto the newspaper's website or a TV or radio station website). Missing the deadline for the next day's paper may cause editors to reject an otherwise good story. If something happens today, or is about to happen, prepare a news release or media advisory, sometimes called "an invitation to cover" (Chapter 5 – Basic Strategic [Persuasive] Writing) that could be emailed, faxed or "snail" (regular) mailed. Never play favorites with reporters. (Well, almost never.) [You might have to "use" a reporter for your benefit.]

Is your story local in nature – in other words, does it have a "hook" and does it relate to what people might have on their minds?

The local media thrive on news that originates within their circulation, listening or viewer areas. Try to emphasize the localness of the story by name-dropping.

No matter with what organization you are associated, developing good media relations is imperative. Failure to get along with the media can result in bad press even when conditions don't warrant it. It is a no-win situation for you if you decide the media are your adversaries. A "rule" to live by: "Never argue with anyone who buys ink by the barrel and paper by the ton."

Knowing how to communicate is essential. If reporters are regarded as intruders, they will react accordingly. If, however, you treat them with trust and consideration, their attitude will be positive and friendly, but still businesslike. View reporters as partners in the distribution of your organization's news, not as adversaries.

PR Play 9-1
Reporters like to talk to people who make news. It is your job to make that person available and your responsibility to make certain that newsmaker is prepared for the interview.

Treat Newsmen and Newswomen as You Would Want Them to Treat You!

Get to know reporters on a first-name basis. Results support the finding that a reporter on friendly terms with a source will make every effort to be fair to that source when controversial news develops.

However, even the most effective media relations programs won't always escape the wrath of the media. If you are criticized, don't jeopardize a longstanding relationship by "jumping" on the reporter. Rather, schedule an informal meeting, over coffee or lunch, and discuss the issue(s). If nothing else, you will ascertain whether or not the reporter and/or his outlet have an agenda.

Some Things You Ought To Know

Right or wrong, the media consider themselves watchdogs. The majority of reporters are not interested in sensationalizing the news. Essentially, they report controversy because they believe it to be in the public interest and because that is what their editors assign.

Reporters are charged by their editors to cover the news accurately and fairly. However, some reporters might enter into combat with an inherent bias – which leads to agenda setting.

Unfortunately, unless you are in a metropolitan area, staffs are small with few "beat" systems. All that adds up to the public relations practitioner dealing with different reporters whenever a story breaks – supplying the same background information time and time again. It can get frustrating. But remember, as the media relations contact, you are there to serve – to help assure that the reporter gets a factual story. The reporter is your first step toward getting your story to the target audience. The reporter – and newspaper – are intermediary audiences (message carriers).

As a media relations contact, you must remember – print is a space medium; television and radio are time media.

PR Play 9-2

"Never argue with anyone who buys ink by the barrel and paper by the ton."

Everett Landers – Former managing editor (Gannett) – News Coach and Professor – Temple (Pa.) University and Rowan (N.J.) University

---

Establish a Policy

Every organization, small and large, should have a media relations policy. It should underscore its commitment to be truthful and to give facts accurately when dealing with the media. The policy should also include a commitment to admit problems and mistakes when asked about them and to explain what is being done to solve them. The act of accepting responsibility when necessary must be included in any media policy. (Examples:

Positive – Johnson & Johnson®, which pulled all Tylenol® products from store shelves following product tampering [1982] blamed for seven deaths on Chicago's West Side; Negative – Ford® and Firestone®, which blamed each other for hundreds of deaths and injuries [2000] attributed to crashes involving Ford Explorers® and Firestone® tires; and Pennsylvania State University [2012], which was slow in reacting to the Jerry Sandusky child-abuse scandal (see Chapter 14). An example of mutual respect between a spokesperson and the media would be Connecticut State Police Lt. Paul Vance reacting to the mass shooting at Sandy Hook Elementary School in December 2012 (see Chapter 14).

Every person responsible for dealing with the media – in fact, every PR practitioner, strategic adviser and counselor – should have an understanding of how each vehicle or communication channel (newspapers, magazines, radio and TV news and the Web – podcasts, videocasts and blogs) works and the role it plays in the *convergence of distribution* (media convergence) and other *cross platforming* techniques (Chapter 10). When crafting a *media relations policy,* don't be afraid to discuss its contents with media representatives – editors, news directors, reporters, editorial writers, etc. Their involvement and recommendations add credibility and understanding to the policy because they partnered in drafting it.

What Editors and Reporters Expect of PR Practitioners

Editors and reporters embrace the concept of *relationship (management) marketing* when dealing with an organization's spokesperson or media relations contact.

Because of downsizing in print media, both in personnel and editorial copy space – known as the news hole – less space (fewer column inches) is being allocated for editorial copy. (However, as hard copy space decreases, Web content increases.)

On the flip side, TV has been increasing its news programming and providing more opportunities for features to fill time. Years ago, local stations carried only 6 and 11 p.m. (10 p.m. in some markets) newscasts. Today, it is common for local affiliates to carry early morning, midday (noon or earlier) and 4, 4:30, 5, 5:30 and 6 p.m. "shows" or a combination of late afternoon or early evening broadcasts. And, almost all affiliates and many independent TV stations and cable operators run 10 or 11 p.m. newscasts.

For public relations, staff cutbacks in print and broader programming on the television side translate into many more opportunities for organized and savvy strategic advisers to become "content providers" through well-written news releases and/or by providing professionally-produced video.

In all media, thanks to increased deadline pressures, reporters have come to rely on an organization's communication staff more than ever. In summary, these are the top criteria editors, news directors and reporters expect of PR practitioners and other strategic communicators:

- Relationships
- Know what news is
- Deadline awareness
- Accuracy
- Timeliness
- A climate of trust/honesty
- Understanding media limitations
- Accessibility (especially when bad news hits)

Making the "Pitch"

There are numerous opportunities to get stories into newspapers and on radio and TV using the news release as the foundation for a reporter's story. When presenting – "pitching" – your story to a reporter or editor:

- Use few words with a hook.
- Work in an action verb or two.
- Hot topics are best.
- Target it.
- Drop a familiar name or two.
- Ask yourself: Does my story have impact? (Reporters do not get paid for under-reported information.)
- Get to the point quickly – but don't forget the angle.
- Personalize it, if possible.
- Don't be afraid to offer facts in support of your "pitch" and story.
- If sent electronically, ask for receipt confirmation in lieu of follow-up call.

As in baseball, some "media pitchers" are better than others. But, when it comes to "media pitching," everyone can learn – because unlike baseball, strategic communicators don't "pitch" curves. All "pitches" are straight – although they do need a "hook." While that might sound contradictory, the bottom line is – "pitches" must be open, honest, thorough and valid (relevant).

PR Play 9-3
Preparing the "Pitch"

The "pitcher's" preparation should include more than just a familiari-ty with local news outlets.
- Read, read, read.
- Watch, watch, watch.
- Listen, listen, listen.
- Get story ideas *from* the media.
- Think trend pieces.
- Research who you are pitching.
- Create targeted media lists.
- Know the publication or news outlet before making the contact.
- Know which reporter to contact (rather than just a "cold call").
- Have all the facts at your fingertips.
- Craft a sample "pitch" or elevator speech (30 seconds maximum) before making the call.
- Practice your "pitch" before making the call.

It never hurts to think outside the box. As you do, ask yourself, "If I were a reporter, would *I* be interested?" Believe in your "pitch." Understand and know your client, product or service as well as you know your own name. You must convince yourself before you try to persuade others – a major step in your becoming a "content provider."

Practice being smooth and comfortable on the phone. Research an outlet's deadlines. websites and other electronic outlets – many 24/7 news providers – have a deadline a minute. No matter which newsroom you call, always ask, "Is this is a good time?" If not, ask *when*. Be persistent, but not rude. Everyone has a different "pitch-ing" style. Find the one that works for you and be consistent.

Here are more suggestions to help you get coverage for your phone "pitch":
- Identify yourself and who you represent.
- Ask about timing. Is reporter on deadline?
- Once you get the positive response you are looking for – start "pitching."
- At *that* moment "hit" the send button on your computer to re-mail your news release so that the reporter has it (again) at the top of his/her mails and won't have to search for it.
- Your "pitch" should be 30 seconds – maybe a bit longer.
- If you are interrupted with questions – it's a good sign. cont.

PR Play 9-3 continued

Don't get discouraged if you are rejected. In fact, learn from rejection. Hitters in baseball are considered successful if their average is .300 or better. Media relations "pitchers" should consider themselves "winners" if 30 percent or more of their story ideas make it into print or on the air.

PR Play 9-4
A Checklist
"Newsworthy Story Angles"

WHO
- **Celebrity**
  - Are famous people involved?
- **Human Interest**
  - Does it have a man or woman in the face of adversity?
  - Does someone have an unusual job?
  - Is it someone who makes a good story?

WHAT
- **Adventure**
  - Is there an adventure, experiment, exploration or voyage?
- **Hot News**
  - Does it relate to a hot news item?
- **Bleeds and Leads**
  - Does it involve hate, tragedy, love, sex, children or animals?
- **Mystery**
  - Does the mystery have suspense?
  - Will they find an answer?
  - Will they find a cure?
  - Will the community/world survive the onslaught (power shortage or water)?
- **New**
  - Is it new?
- **Novel**
  - Is it unusual, novel, peculiar, humorous, different or odd?
  - Is it the biggest, smallest, nicest, meanest, strangest or happiest?

cont.

PR Play 9-4 continued

- **Unknown**
  - Is it little known but interesting (desolate beach, unusual service/store/product/restaurant, etc.)?

WHEN

- **Timely**
  - Is it timely?

WHERE

- **Proximity**
  - Is it local?

WHY

- **Importance/Impact**
  - Is it important to a large number of people?
  - Is it important to a small number of people?
- **Consequence, Conflict, Controversy**
  - Does it have consequence, conflict or controversy?
- **Future**
  - Is it going to change the future?
  - Will it help you earn more money or live a longer/healthier life?

PR101: Media Relations and M. Larry Litwin, APR, Fellow PRSA

The "pitcher" has to intrigue the reporter or editor enough to pique his/her interest in the story. The reporter wants to hear why the story might be relevant to the news outlet's readers, listeners or viewers.

Use words and examples that paint pictures to bolster your "pitch." It's called "scene setting." Once the reporter or gatekeeper "buys" into your story, he/she still has to sell it to an editor at an editorial planning meeting also called an *editorial content, log* or *budgeting* meeting. Print (space) media rely on such meetings to plan their pages while broadcast (time) media rely on them to lay out their shows.

Meeting participants traditionally include editors or news directors, news planners and assignment editors. There are times when beat reporters and general assignment reporters might attend to "pitch" their own stories, which might include those "pitched" to them. News planners are critical to the space and time devoted to a story and, in fact, help reporters justify covering stories. News planners maintain the news files and work with assignment editors to set up stories a day or two in advance.

Anatomy Of A Newspaper

While this entire book could be considered an "anatomy" of strategic communication, the next several paragraphs home in on the "anatomy" (structure) of a newspaper.

First and foremost, it must be accepted that newspapers are a business. Just ask the local group – Philadelphia Media Holdings, LLC (PMH) – who purchased *The Philadelphia Inquirer* for $562 million from The McClatchy Company, which spun it off from its Knight Ridder acquisitions. Less than nine months later, PMH announced major layoffs – nearly 20 percent of its editorial staff, plus dozens of others in sales and support positions.

Daily newspapers rely on more than just the paper that hits the street every day to contribute to the bottom line. They generate revenue online, with such sister publications as weeklies and guides, and special sections. Approximately 75 percent of a daily's revenue is from display and classified advertising – half of that is from classified (rather than display) automotive and real estate ads – and 25 percent is from circulation. Market penetration (circulation) of 50 percent of the homes in a market is considered good. With all of the news sources now available, more than 50 percent is considered very good.

On any given day, dailies are made up of the following sections:
- Section A – Main news with a 95 percent readership. The front page is also referred to as Page 1A.
- Section B – Local and metro news with strong readership – more than 50 percent. Page 1B is referred to as the second front page or split page.
- Sports (section C in many papers) – Readership averages 55 to 60 percent.
- Business – (section D in many papers) – Readership averages more than 50 percent thanks to increased number of features.
- Lifestyle/Home – (section E in many papers) Heavy on features – considered "soft" and "fuzzy" news by editors. Its readership is in the 40 to 50 percent range.
- Classifieds (section F in many papers).

- Other sections (especially on Sundays and "lettered" for quick reference) could include:
  - Automotive
  - Books
  - Arts & Entertainment
  - Health/Well Being
  - Jobs
  - Opinion
  - Neighbors (Zoned)
  - New Homes
  - Real Estate
  - Travel

Daily and weekly newspapers have transitioned to online. A strong online presence – for both print and broadcast media outlets – serves to establish the Internet as a strong advertising vehicle. Web versions of newspapers mirror print. For example, *The New York Times* on any given day has the following "jump to" (links) sections:

- Front Page
- International
- National Report
- Obituaries
- Editorials
- Op-Eds and Letters to the Editor
- The Metro Section
- Business Day
- Sports
- The Arts

Newspaper sectioning started as an advertising strategy – attracting certain readers – thus targeting audiences. Each has its own editor and staff – many eager to develop relationships with an organization's media relations representative. Staff is comprised mostly of general assignment reporters, but a number are considered beat reporters, meaning their area of coverage is specialized.

During the evolution of sectioning, editors discovered that readers enjoyed the ease of finding the news they wanted. Sections have their own front and back pages. Many of the section fronts – called *cover pages* – carry banner or strip ads across the page bottom (footer) and occasionally across the top (header). Those section fronts carry *center packages* – a major (lead) story in the center also called the *centerpiece story*. *USA Today* commonly uses this technique.

Section back pages have become premier advertising space – often carrying dramatic full page ads. Sunday papers have the most sections and the largest circulation. News is in shortest supply for the Monday and Saturday editions.

A newspaper's corporate flow chart consists of its publisher, who serves as the chief executive officer (CEO). Other department heads include news, controller, advertising, circulation, production, human resources and marketing.

The news department is headed by an editor-in-chief or executive editor. Moving down the chart is the managing editor and news editor, who runs the desk – or slot, as it is known in some newsrooms. The section editors, who have the most impact on readers, report to the news editor. They include section A (front), city, sports, business, entertainment, lifestyle and travel. Many newspapers have weekend and special section editors. Special sections are usually run to generate revenue.

Instrument of Understanding

Newspapers view themselves as instruments of understanding – the muscle that drives journalism – even today with all of its editorial staff reductions.

Their first loyalty must be to their readers, listeners or viewers (now that print is cross platforming with blogs, podcasts, videocasts and tweets). To achieve that loyalty, reporters must never forget their job is to find the truth and report on it, according to Everett Landers, a news coach and former managing editor (Gannett).

That's where the strategic communicator/media relations specialist comes in – not only pitching stories important to his/her organization, but working with the enterprising reporter to help him/her report with *balance, accuracy, fairness* and *meaning* (keeping in mind what the reader will get out of the story). Said Landers: "Without meaning to the stories they carry, newspapers – as we know them today – cannot survive. To contribute to their quest for survival, *civic journalism* is now commonplace – stories about the critical issues on readers' minds; stories that reflect the community.

"The media relations specialist contributes to that *civic journalism* by working with reporters to develop a relationship and being able to explain why, what they are pitching is as it is and is news."

Strategic communicators must always keep in mind the newspaper's role in the community – mirroring life as it happens – reporting on stories and their reactions so that the people who read it learn about their neighbors, community, jobs and possible changes within their "section of town."

The *MAC Triad Plus* plays a vital part in placing a story. That's because the PR practitioner, who helps craft the strategic message and has chosen the newspaper as its channel, also targets the audience(s) (general and specialized), its geodemographics (where), demographics (who) and psychographics (personality, values, attitudes, interests, or lifestyles – also called IAO variables (Interests, Attitudes and Opinions).

Landers believed a strategic communicator's trust must be earned "always keeping in mind that knowledge is power and that knowledge and the knowledge of those you represent make *you* a valuable resource. The reputation and credibility of both the newspaper and the organization's strategic communicator must be first and foremost."

Landers and others recommend that the organization's media representative know his or her product as well as their own name, know the people behind it and the organization's philosophy, mission and vision.

According to Landers, "Newspapers often serve as *contrarians (skeptics)* – questioning whether the public receives what is promised. Ideally, ethical public relations, universally practiced, would eliminate the need for *contrarians*."

More than a century ago, newspaper (*Emporia* [Kansas] *Gazette*) editor and publisher William Allen White said, "A newspaper is an instrument of understanding – information that people want and need. Newspapers bring news to the people."

That concept holds true today. For newspapers to achieve that goal, said Landers, editors continually remind reporters that journalism's major purpose is to *inform*, *educate*, *inspire* and *entertain* – help readers make intelligent decisions. When pitching a story or reacting to a reporter's interview, a good practice would be for the PR practitioner to keep in mind the characteristics of a quality newspaper:

- It reflects values.
- It transmits culture.
- Its content is relavent.

With the rapid technological changes, Landers suggests that if television newscasts report the news, today's newspapers – in hardcopy and online – must define it. A well written news story is not unlike an "executive summary."

Understanding the difference between hard and soft news and the philosophies of William Allen White and Everett Landers are hardly enough for the public relations practitioner. The person responsible for media relations should also fully understand the make up of a traditional newspaper from the front page (1A) to that display ad on the back page of section E or whatever letter or title is on the final section. (Terms commonly used in newspaper newsrooms can be found beginning on page 290.)

Landers offers this advice to media specialists to help them better understand journalists and their outlets: "There has always been a special bond between the public and press. The average person has a preoccupation with the other person's trouble. It's called *human interest* and people react to *human interest*."

PR Play 9-5
Scheduling a News Conference

Scheduling of a news conference is dictated by the subject matter or its urgency. But when the luxury exists, think about selecting a "light" news day. For example, most public bodies, town councils or school boards regularly schedule their meetings for the first and third or second and fourth Mondays or Tuesdays in a month. Why not try to schedule your news conference or event for the "fifth" Monday or Tuesday in a month, for example? There are only a few such days in a year, and editors have available space the day after. It is a wonderful public relations tactic that doesn't take a great deal of strategic planning.

PR Play 9-6
News Conference or News Availability Checklist

Purdue University, Rowan University, reporters and others offer these suggestions to assure a successful news conference:

[ ] Reserve a room large enough to accommodate the expected number of media representatives and invited guests. The meeting area must contain electrical outlets and space for television crews.

[ ] Have tables, chairs, lectern, pencils and paper.

[ ] Arrange to have microphone and amplification.

[ ] Have water and glasses for speakers.

[ ] Arrange for parking.

[ ] Notify phone receptionists, security and others who might have to respond to calls or to media when they arrive.

[ ] Use banner, sign and/or logo behind the lectern and on the front of it.

[ ] Provide visuals for television.

[ ] Alert/remind the media by phone or email no later than the day before.

[ ] Invite public officials and VIPs who have an interest.

[ ] Brief participants about format and possible questions.

[ ] Post signs directing news media to the conference site.

[ ] Arrange to have someone meet the media.

[ ] Take notes and/or record for reporters unable to attend or for follow-up calls.

[ ] Be prepared to help get things going following the initial statement, by having someone ask the first question if no one else does.

[ ] Prepare a media kit (Chapter 5).

[ ] Make the media kit available on your website for media outlets who did not send representatives to the conference and for follow up.

cont.

PR Play 9-6 continued
Media Kit Contents

- Cover memo (list of media kit's contents)
- List of participants
- List of partnering or cooperating organizations
- Media Advisory/Media Alert/News and Photo Memo/Invitation to Cover (There is little difference. Choose one heading and stick with it for all of your media kits and media announcements.)
- News Releases
- Straight (hard stories)
- Features (soft stories)
- Biographies of speakers and key personnel
- Fact Sheets
- Backgrounder
  - Historical
  - Statistical
- Pictures and other graphics and visuals (suggested captions)

- Public Service Announcements (on CD or flash drive [USB])
- Position Paper(s)
- Op-Ed piece(s)
- Letter(s) to the Editor
- Texts of speeches
- Quote sheet
- Testimonials
- Fillers (newsy notes)
- Clip sheets (news clips)
- Logo repros or slicks – include on Flash (USB) drive, CD or DVD
- Collateral materials – Brochures/Publications
  - Annual reports
  - Magazines
  - Newsletters
  - Videos (DVD/Flash [USB] drive)
  - Free samples (if ethical)
  - Entire media kit should be duplicated on Flash (USB) drive, CD or DVD

With the advent of the Internet and other technology, the debate over media kits and their effectiveness has grown louder. Don't allow the cons to be a deterrent. Prepare a media kit for the Web just as you would for hard copy (Chapter 5). Those reporters interested in this resource would be encouraged to take advantage of it by downloading it from the website's "Newsroom." For those who attend the news conference, the media kit should contain a version on disk or Flash (USB) drive – known as electronic press kit (EPK) – as well as hard copies of such major components as news releases and fact sheets. For those organizations that really want to impress, think about distributing the kit on a low capacity, inexpensive "flash drive" that plugs into a computer's USB port.

The News Conference Compared to a News Availability

The news conference is an effective media relations' tool when properly used. It gives members of the media an equal opportunity to ask questions about a variety of topics or just the subject matter at hand.

While some organizations hold regular news conferences, it is more advisable to call them only when making major announcements, announcing important developments that need detailed explanations or to clear up a major controversy. Most times it is prearranged.

A news availability, on the other hand, is an opportunity to make someone available for questions from the media. It is less formal with no prepared statement – although the experienced strategic counselor has worked with that "someone" on key message points.

When scheduling a news conference, keep these suggestions in mind:
• Unless under pressure of time, give at least 24 hours notice.
• Let editors know why the news conference is being called.

PR Play 9-7
In-service For Reporters

A rarely used, but accepted and encouraged method among strategic communicators is the "in-service" for media members covering a long-term story or special event. A New Jersey school district that had lost nearly a dozen bond and budget referenda over several years determined that neither the public nor the media understood the issues. The public relations professional and school administrators invited media to a series of workshops spread out over several weeks. The workshops, over lunch (reporters do have to eat), lasted 45 minutes to an hour. Media outlets were encouraged to send any reporter who might cover the next referendum. A number of handouts – electronic and printed – were distributed and visuals were used freely. Attendance was excellent. The message was communicated to the reporters who in turn took it to the public in terms the audiences could understand. Those in-services – cutting edge at the time – were considered successful because the district went on a "winning streak" at the polls. (A number of media outlets were so impressed, they decided to run [side bar] stories on what they considered a unique approach.)

- Hand out a statement, background paper or fact sheet covering the main topic.
- Allow for a question period once the statement has been delivered.
- Don't allow the chief executive to handle the questioning alone. Staff members familiar with the topic should also be present.
- Anticipate questions and be sure the main participants have been fully briefed.
- If some of the questions stray, try to answer them. If they cannot be answered, be diplomatic. If not, reporters grow suspicious (skeptical) – it's their nature.
- End the conference as soon as interest lags. Be sure to thank the reporters for attending.

When and How to Complain

Errors are bound to occur – at least once in a while – no matter how hard you try to prevent them or the reporters try to avoid them. Remember, reporters and editors are under tremendous pressure. Never complain about minor errors. Save those complaints for the big mistakes.

If you must complain, get together with the reporter and discuss the error. There may have been a misunderstanding about a point or fact. There is even the possibility that the change was made by an editor without consulting the reporter.

If it is felt that a reporter slanted a story unfavorably, discuss the matter openly with him or her. The misunderstanding will probably be cleared up and a new improved long-standing relationship may be developed.

If errors occur frequently, or if the reporter continues to slant stories that might be embarrassing to your organization, discuss it (agenda setting) with the editor. But be prepared to document your argument with clippings, releases, fact sheets and other data.

If an editor gets the impression you are complaining without justification, he/she will probably instruct the reporter to step up his hard-hitting tactics. Never demand that an editor replace a reporter on your beat or fire him/her. Simply lay the facts on the table and let the editor decide how to handle the situation.

PR Play 9-8

Never hold a reporter responsible for an editorial stand his/her newspaper may have taken even if you believe the reporter had input in the action. Unfortunately, a paper has the right to take any stand it wishes and usually has an editorial board who establishes the opinion.

Some DOs When Dealing With Reporters

- Always be available to give information at any time.
- Give reporters your home or cell phone number and get his or hers – and also exchange email addresses. These numbers and addresses come in handy when unexpected news breaks during off-duty hours.
- Compliment a reporter when he or she has done an exceptionally fine job and on occasion, it doesn't hurt to drop a note or email to the editor.
- When a reporter isn't available to attend an event, a meeting or a speech, take notes and call immediately with the information.
- Be sure to let the media know if an event has been cancelled.
- When discussing news with reporters, always put facts in perspective and give as much background information as possible – but remember, you are always on the record.
- Always respond promptly to a reporter's question. If you don't have the information available or want time to think before answering, tell the reporter you will call back in a few minutes. *Then, make sure you do.*
- When giving a reporter an impromptu statement on the phone concerning a controversial issue, jot down or record your side of the conversation so you can recall what you said. The notations can also come in handy if another reporter calls about the same topic. It can also help if you are misquoted.
- According to the *Los Angeles Times*, it is acceptable to offer a reporter the opportunity to have him/her fact check and back check story content with you to make certain quotes and other facts are accurate.

Some DON'Ts When Dealing With Reporters

- Don't expect newspapers or other media to publish or air every word you write or say. Papers will rewrite your releases to conform to style and fit into limited space. Radio and TV stations will edit your material – many times taking a 10 or 15-minute interview and reducing it to a 25-second sound bite.

PR Play 9-9
On and Off the Record/For
Background Only/Not for Attribution

Remember – when talking with reporters you are always on the record – even during informal or chance meetings. Avoid casual comments or "off the record" remarks unless you specify first that what you are about to say is not for publication or air. And be sure the reporter will accept "off the record" information before volunteering it. *Background* ("*on background*") information is just that – for *background only* – not to be used and not to be attributed until such a time (if ever) that the *newsmaker* gives the go ahead. It is purely an act of educating a journalist about the subject without saying anything that can be used in a specific story until it is released. "Not for attribution" means that the information can be used, but the source may not be identified.

- Don't complain to an editor if a story isn't published or aired. If compelled to ask when a story will be published or aired, be diplomatic.
- Don't ever ask a reporter to see a story before it is published. (The very best and more secure reporters might go over strategic points in a story to assure the facts are correct [fact checking and back checking].)
- Don't ask reporters for clippings, tear sheets or recordings of stories after they appear or are aired. (If they practice good relationship marketing, they might just send them to you.) It is your responsibility to track *hits* and *impressions* (see pages 293 and 294). Set up online "alerts."
- Don't ask a newspaper to return a photo unless it is a very rare print – most are emailed, anyway.
- Don't try to suppress unfavorable news. Any attempt to do so usually ends up with the story receiving greater prominence.
- Don't tell a reporter how to write the story. If you want certain points emphasized, do that during the interview.
- Don't stress your title or position. Just be certain the reporter is given such information as corporate heads, key officers and "key" players.

Getting Coverage In Print and On The Air

Persuading the media to cover your business can be exasperating – both for you and for the journalists you approach. Contacting your local media with poorly researched story ideas is likely to result in no coverage and may even turn off reporters and editors who will consider future coverage.

"When business owners turn to the media, they think they can clobber them over the head with an idea and that the reporter should do it," says Greg Matusky, president of Gregory Communications, Inc., a

---

PR Play 9-10
Twenty-five Ways to *Deal* with the Media

- Make the CEO responsible for *media relations*.
- Face the facts.
- Consider the public interest in every operating decision.
- Respond quickly.
- Return calls.
- Know to whom you are talking.
- Be a source before you are a subject.
- If you want your views represented, you have to talk.
- Be prepared.
- Know your message.
- Put your story in context.
- Use everyday language.
- Don't speculate.
- Slow down.
- You are always on the record.
- Cage your lawyers.
- Tell the truth – or nothing.
- Be available.
- Don't expect to bat 1.000 (to be perfect).
- Be realistic.
- Don't take it personally.
- Control what you can.
- Know with whom you are dealing.
- Avoid TV unless you feel you can speak candidly.
- Be human.

Purdue University
M. Larry Litwin, APR, Fellow PRSA

---

media communications firm based in Ardmore, Pa. "Business owners must understand that good media coverage is like good sales – it starts with relationships."

Matusky and other communications professionals offer these tips for approaching the media:

- Get to know your local media. That means read, watch and listen to the news sources in your market.
- Understand that journalists have specific coverage areas – called beats. If you need help determining which reporter covers your business area, contact an assignment editor at the media outlet.
- Determine how you can help reporters do their job – such as supplying them with relevant statistics or relating what may be an emerging trend that you've noticed among your customers.
- Call the appropriate reporter with your story idea, and ask to schedule a telephone appointment.
- Expect to spend six to 12 months developing contacts in the media before you get results; and, remember, you are likely to see coverage only if a reporter considers your information to be a legitimate story angle.
- Be prepared for rejections.
- Tell the truth.

Check with your local chamber of commerce or other business groups to see if they offer media relations training seminars. Ideally, seminars include a panel of media representatives from your market.

Meg Whittemore – *Nation's Business/September, 1994*

Twenty-five Ways to *Deal* with the Media

- **Make the CEO responsible for media relations.** That means he/she must often speak for the corporation – routinely and in times of crisis – and must delegate enough authority to make the public relations spokesperson a credible source.
- **Face the facts.** If you screw up, admit it candidly. Avoid hedging or excuses. Apologize, promise not to do it again, and explain how you're going to make things right.
- **Consider the public interest in every operating decision.** Your reputation depends far more on what you do than on what you say. Act accordingly. Try giving your senior public relations expert a seat at the table when decisions are made.

- **Respond quickly.** You can't influence a story once its deadline has passed. Stalling can tarnish or destroy credibility. In a crisis, figure you have a day – at most – to get your story out.
- **Return calls.** Reporters are always writing on a deadline. Delays could mean that your side of the story may not be told.
- **Know to whom you are talking.** Ask the reporter who he or she represents and the nature of the story.
- **Be a source before you are a subject.** The time to make friends with reporters is long before trouble hits. Get to know the people who cover your company. Educate them. Help them with their stories and give them reason to respect you. Determine which journalists deserve your respect and trust.
- **If you want your views represented, you have to talk.** Reporters are paid to get stories, whether you help or not. When you clam up, they must depend on other sources – often people like that marketing VP you fired last month.
- **Be prepared.** Review the topic and have notes.
- **Know your message.** Predetermine your main points and stick to them.
- **Put your story in context.** Briefly provide any relevant background or anecdotes that explain the problem or situation.
- **Use everyday language.** Avoid jargon or specialized technical terms.
- **Don't speculate.** If you don't know an answer to a question, don't guess. Offer to get the answer later if you can, or refer the reporter to someone who can answer it. (Know the reporter's deadline.)
- **Slow down.** Speak clearly and concisely. Encourage questions for clarification.
- **You're always on the record.** There's no legal obligation for a reporter to keep anything off the record. Never say, "no comment."
- **Cage your lawyers.** They will (almost) always tell you to keep your mouth shut. But in many crisis situations your potential legal liability may be trivial compared with the risk of alienating your customers, employees or regulators.
- **Tell the truth – or nothing.** Nobody likes a liar.
- **Be available.** Offer to answer follow-up questions or help clarify problems that might develop as the story is being written and edited. (Editors and reporters list as a complaint, organizations' spokespeople not being available, especially when bad news breaks.)

- **Don't expect to bat (a perfect) 1.000.** Strategic communication is a game of averages, so be content if you win most of the time. Even the most flattering story will likely have a zinger or two, and even the best companies get creamed now and then.
- **Be realistic.** Be aware a reporter's job is to get news, not necessarily to make Rowan University or you look good.
- **Don't take it personally.** The reporter is neither your enemy nor your friend. He or she is an intermediary between you and the people you need to reach. And forget about your ego – nobody cares about it but you.

PR Play 9-11

H O W A R D   J O F F E

BEST EVIDENCE

EXECUTIVE MEDIA RELATIONS • CRISIS COMMUNICATIONS • VIDEO DEVELOPMENT

Top 10 List of Media Relations Mistakes

© COPYRIGHT 2001 BEST EVIDENCE, INC.
ALL RIGHTS RESERVED.

10. Lack of preparation/plan

9. Failure to identify audience

8. Reluctance to accept responsibility

7. Inability to show compassion

6. Failure to focus

5. Natural bias against reporters

4. Inability to shut mouth

3. Natural tendency to want to sound more intelligent than we really are

2. Fear & loathing

1. Panic

100 Springdale Road, Suite 120 Cherry Hill, NJ 08003-3398 Voice: 609.795.9229 Fax: 609.795.3990 Email: BestEvid@aol.com

PR Play 9-12
Building Strong Reporter Relationships

Learning more about the beat reporter or columnist who covers your industry for your local newspaper, radio or television station is an integral first step. After all, research is a key component of every public relations process.

There is no reason reporters should intimidate you. Many times, they need the company spokesperson as much as the company needs them. Former Gannett editor Ev Landers said, "Don't be afraid to make the first move. Once reporters know you, they will have an interest in what you know, develop a mutual trust and maybe even write about you."

Landers and others suggest picking up the phone and inviting the reporter for lunch or coffee. Offer to pay, but know that company policy may prohibit the reporter from accepting a "free lunch." (Let them pay for your meal if they offer – or split the check.)

1. Become familiar with the kinds of stories they cover so you can discuss them.
2. Take a media kit, background information or fact sheets they might find interesting. (Put them on a CD or "flash" drive they can keep.)
3. Offer yourself and your organization's employees as local experts for national stories.
4. Ask about other "areas" they cover or stories they are working on.
5. Don't talk off the record unless you fully understand the ramifications (PR Play 9-9.)
6. Ask about the reporter's personal interests, family, hobbies (relationship marketing).
7. Suggest story ideas and offer to do the "leg work" (research). Offer to provide names of those with opposing points of view.
8. If they write about you or your company, send a thank-you note (inside front cover) but never a gift.
9. Offer your home phone, cell phone and beeper numbers. If you are serious about your job, invite them to call you 24/7.
10. Ask, "How else can I help you?"
11. Exchange business cards.
12. Mail a thank-you note within 24 hours.
13. Keep in touch regularly. Offer feedback on their stories. Email helpful articles about their areas of expertise or their hobbies. Share news tips and story ideas.
14. Do lunch again in about six months.
15. Contact another reporter, from another news outlet, for the same kind of "mindshare" meeting.

- **Control what you can.** Release the bad news yourself – before some reporter digs it up. Use your selective availability to reporters as a tool. Set ground rules every time you talk. If the public isn't buying your message, change it.
- **Know with whom you are dealing.** The press is not a single entity. TV is different from print. Magazines are different from newspapers and the *Fairfield Daily Ledger* is different from *The Wall Street Journal*. Within any news organization there will be a normal mix of individuals, some honorable and competent, some not. Do your homework on journalists before you talk to them, reviewing their past work or talking to other executives they have covered. It's called "due diligence."
- **Avoid TV unless you feel you can speak candidly.** Even then, learn to present your views in the 10-second sound bites that are the building blocks of TV stories. Use simple declarative sentences and ignore subtleties. Whenever possible favor live TV shows over those that can edit your remarks.
- **Be human.** Reporters – and the public – usually will be more sympathetic to a person than to a corporation. If you can do it without lying or making a fool of yourself, show that you are a person with feelings. Then, the media may minimize your mistakes. Insist on being judged on a human scale, with normal human fallibility taken into account. Remember, people love to root for underdogs.

Purdue University
M. Larry Litwin, APR, Fellow PRSA

Print Media Terms Every Practitioner Should Know

ABC – Abbreviation for Audit Bureau of Circulations, an organization that compiles statistics on circulation.

art – Photograph(s) or other graphics accompanying a print or Web story.

attribution – A line identifying the source of a quote.

back story – In both print and broadcast journalism, it is the copy or information toward the end of the story – but is still important.

banner – A headline stretching across the top of a page; also called a *"streamer"* or *"banner line."*

banner ad – Ad that stretches across the top of a printed page or horizontally across part or all of a Web page. Also called a *header*.

beat – A specific topic that a reporter usually covers (e.g., business, education, police, a municipality, a sports team, etc.).

blurb – A quotation or statement that is separated from the rest of a news story and sometimes set off with borders above and below – for emphasis. The quote is usually taken from the story it accompanies. Also called a *liftout quote* or *pull quote*.

boxcar – A teaser or banner head that runs above the nameplate is called a skybox or skyline. If they are boxed (with art), they are called skyboxes or boxcars. If they are only a line of type, they are called *skylines*.

broken display ad – Display ads usually disguised as editorial copy where an ad is inserted over the copy – sometimes "interrupting it" as an attention getter. Also known as an *interrupted display* ad.

bullet – A type, usually a big dot, used to highlight items listed in the text. Also called a *dingbat*.

byline – The reporter's name (or author's name), usually at the beginning of a story.

caption – A line or block of type providing descriptive information about a picture. Headline or text accompanying a picture or illustration. Also called a *cutline*.

center package – The major (lead) story in the center of a main page of a newspaper. Also called the centerpiece story. *USA Today* commonly uses this technique.

centerpiece story – The major (lead) story in the center of a main page of a newspaper. Also called the center package. *USA Today* commonly uses this technique.

classified advertising – Advertising arranged according to the product or service advertised, and usually restricted in size and format. The ads are "classified" into various categories such as help wanted, autos for sale, apartments for rent, etc.

column inch – A unit of measurement one inch deep and one column wide. Generally speaking, a 250-word release, double spaced, 12 point type, would become six column inches in the typical newspaper.

copy desk – The desk where copy is edited, headlined and placed on the page it will appear in the newspaper.

cover page – The first page in a section. Also called section front.

cutline – The copy (usually only a few lines) that accompanies and gives necessary information about a picture or "cut." Not as in depth as a caption.

dateline – Line at the beginning of an out-of-town story that indicates both the place and the date of origin of the story.

deadline – The last moment to get copy in for an edition.

display ad – Advertising matter other than in-column classified ads. They usually have a border.

dot whack – An ad, usually on front page of newspaper attached to as if it were a Post-it® or sticky note. Also called *popper* or *press-on* ad.

double truck – A two-page spread in a print publication, where the ad (editorial copy) runs across the middle gutter. It could be the center fold ("center spread") or any two full side-by-side pages (facing each other). If it prints across the gutter between the two pages, and if the pages are on the same sheet, rather than two adjacent sheets, it might be called a "true" double truck. This name comes from the days when the heavy forms for newspaper pages, largely filled with lead type, were rolled around the composing room floor on heavy carts called trucks. Two pages for one project meant a double truck.

ears – Space at the top of the front page on each side of the newspaper's name where weather news, index to pages or announcement of special features appears.

edition – A press run of a newspaper. A daily generally has more than one edition a day – for example, "City Edition," "Lakeshore Edition," "Early Edition," "Late Edition."

editorial – An article that expresses the opinion of the newspaper's editors and usually also reflects the opinion of the publisher or owner of the newspaper. The department of the newspaper where news is gathered, written, edited and readied for publication.

feature – Any story that has human interest value, even though it is not news in the strict sense.

filler – Short informational stories or advertisements, usually timeless, used to fill small spaces where needed.

first-day story – A story published for the first time and dealing with something that has just happened, as distinguished from a "follow-up" story.

First Amendment – The first article of the Constitution's Bill of Rights, guaranteeing Americans freedom of religion, speech, press, assembly and petition.

five W's – Who? what? when? where? why? – the questions usually answered in the lead of a news story.

flag –The printed title (i.e., name and logo) of a newspaper at the top of the front page. Also called a *nameplate*.

folio – Newspaper name, date, and page number that appear at the top of each page.

follow-up – Story giving later developments of an event already reported.

footer ad – Display ad that stretches across the bottom of a printed or Web page. Also called *strip ad*.

general assignment – A reporter who covers a variety of stories rather than a single "beat."

graf – Newsroom slang for paragraph.

halftone – A picture or drawing that has been concerted into a pattern of tiny dots for reproduction in a newspaper or other print medium.

handout – A press (news) release – prepared material given to news people in the hope that it will be printed without change or that it will be helpful in preparing news stories.

hard news – (important news) – Straight news reporting without interpretation or background material.

head/header – Headline or special label for any regularly appearing section, page or story. Also called a *standing head*. Also, a *banner* ad that runs across the top of a newspaper page.

headline – Large type running above or beside a story to summarize its contents. Also called a *head*, for short.

hit – Each time a news story appears in or on a different media vehicle. In an Internet sense, it is a visit to a particular page on a website by a Web visitor. See *impression*.

hold – "Hold for release" instruction to hold a story until the editor releases it for publication.

hook – The stylistic device used by a reporter to draw a reader into the story.

hot – A label given to an important story.

human interest – Emotional appeal in the news. A "human interest" story, as compared with a "straight news" story, bases its appeal more on the unusual than on consequence.

impression – The number of potential readers, listeners or viewers who could see a printed or broadcast story, ad or commercial or number of visitors to a website. Impressions are based on a publication's circulation or a radio or television program's unduplicated audience. Some consider an impression the number of pairs of eyes or ears that will be exposed to a media vehicle. See *hit*.

index – Table of contents of the newspaper, usually found on Page One.

insert – A flyer or magazine that is placed into the folded newspaper after it has been printed.

interrupted display ad – Display ads usually disguised as editorial copy where an ad is inserted over the copy – sometimes "breaking it" as an attention getter. Also known as a *broken display* ad.

inverted pyramid – The standard news story structure in which facts are arranged in descending order of importance.

jump – To continue a story from one page to another.

jump line – The continuation instructions of a story that is jumped to another page (Continued on page 10; Continued from page 1).

kicker – Small headline, often in italics and sometimes underlined, above and slightly to the left of the main head. Usually, one line. In broadcast, the last or tagline of a commercial or public service announcement (PSA). Also called a *tagline* or *stinger*.

kill – To eliminate all or part of a story.

letter to the editor – A letter in which a reader expresses his or her views in the newspaper; usually printed on the editorial page or the page opposite the editorial page.

liftout quote – A quotation or statement that is separated from the rest of a news story and sometimes set off with borders above and below – for emphasis. The quote is usually taken from the story it accompanies. Also called a *blurb* or *pull quote*.

localize – To emphasize the local angle in an out-of-town story.

masthead – Statement of ownership, place of publication, executive personnel and other information about the newspaper, generally placed on the editorial page.

nameline – See *cutline*.

nameplate – The printed title (i.e., name and logo) of a newspaper at the top of the front page. Also called a *flag*.

news hole – The amount of space left for news after advertisements have been arranged on the page.

news services – News-gathering agencies such as the Associated Press or Reuters that distribute news to subscribing newspapers.

newsprint – A grade of paper made from recycled paper and wood pulp, used primarily for printing newspapers.

nut graph – The explanation paragraph that generally follows the lead *graph*. It explains the significance of the story and gives its news "peg." Some public relations practitioners also refer to *boiler plates* as *nut graphs*. However, boiler plates should be the final paragraph in a story.

obit or obituary – A biography of a dead person. Sometimes "canned obits" are kept on file in the newspaper's library to be used at the time of a prominent person's death.

offset press – A printing press in which the inked image is transferred from a plate to a rubber roller, which in turn puts the ink onto the paper.

op-ed – Commentary traditionally printed on page opposite the editorial page (Chapters 5 and 6) of a newspaper.

overline – The caption above a photograph.

Page One (or Page 1A) – The first page of the newspaper. Also refers to the importance of a story – as in "page one news."

pagination – Computerized newspaper page design.

piece – The general term applied to any newspaper article written by a reporter. Also called "*story*."

pix – Abbreviation for pictures.

popper – An ad, usually on front page of newspaper attached as if it were a Post-it®. Also call a *dot whack*.

population – In marketing research, the total group that a researcher wishes to study. The individuals whose opinions are sought in a survey. The population can be as broad as every adult in the United States or as focused as liberal Democrats who live in the Fifth Ward of Chicago and who voted in the last election. The sample is drawn to reflect the population. Sometimes called the *universe*.

porkchop – Half-column picture. Synonymous with *thumbnail*.

pox – Police.

promo – An eye-catching graphic element, usually on Page One or section front, that promotes an item inside. Also called a *teaser*.

public relations (journalist's definition) – The art or science of developing understanding and goodwill between a person, firm or institution and the public.

publisher – The chief executive and often the owner of a newspaper or other publishing firm.

pull quote – A quotation or statement that is separated from the rest of a news story and sometimes set off with borders above and below – for emphasis. The quote is usually taken from the story it accompanies. Also called a *blurb* or *liftout quote*.

put to bed – Printer's term meaning all the pages of an edition are completed and the presses are ready to roll.

Q and A – Copy in question and answer form, as in verbatim reports of court proceedings.

quotes – Quotation marks. A quote is a portion of a story that consists of direct quotations.

register or registration – Correct placement of printing on the sheet. In color printing, register means the correct placement of each plate so that the colors are laid down properly, without running "off-register."

ROP – Run-of-paper news and advertising that appears in any part of the paper. Convenient to the make-up of the paper.

second-day story – A "follow– up" story giving new developments on one that has already appeared in the newspaper.

second front page – The front page of a second section. Also called the "*split page.*"

section – Separate parts of a newspaper.

section lead – Top story in a section.

sectional story – A major news story with different aspects, featured under two or more headlines.

series – A group of related stories generally run on successive days.

shirt tail – A short, related story added at the end of a longer one.

shoot – To take photographs. As a noun, a *shoot* is a photo session.

shot sheet – A list of photo opportunities that can be provided to a newspaper or magazine photographer, videographer, or one hired by the public relations practitioner coordinating an event.

sidebar – A secondary news story that supports or amplifies a major story.

skybox/skyline – A banner head that runs above the nameplate. Serves as a teaser. If they are boxed (with art), they are called skyboxes or box-cars. If they are only a line of type, they are called *skylines*.

slant – An angle of a story. A story is "slanted" when a certain aspect is played up for policy or other reasons.

soft copy – Copy seen on a computer screen.

source – A supplier of information. A person, document, etc.

split page – Usually the first page of the inside or second section (section B) of the newspaper carrying local, metro or area news; the second front page.

spot news – News obtained on the scene of an event, usually unexpectedly.

spread – The display given to an important story; a double spread is one across facing pages.

squib – A short news item; a filler.

stand-alone photo – A picture that doesn't accompany a story, usually boxed to show it stands alone. Also called *wild art*.

standing head – Headlines that do not change and are usually kept in a library file on a computer so they are ready for instant use. Also a special label for any regularly appearing section, page or story. Also called a *header*.

steeplechase ad – Ad that runs vertically up one side of a page or the other.

stet – A Latin term meaning "let it stand" – stetundum, Proofreader's notation instructing the printer to ignore a change marked on a proof.

story – The general term applied to any newspaper article written by a reporter. Also called "*piece*."

straight news – A plain account of news facts written in standard style and structure, without coloring or embellishments.

streamer – A multi-column headline leading a page, but not necessarily across its full width. Synonymous with *banner*.

stringer – A correspondent for a newspaper or a news agency, usually part-time, who often covers a certain subject or geographic area. The person is usually paid according to the number or length of stories printed by the newspaper.

strip ad – One or two inch-wide ad across the bottom of a page. (Example would be front page of *Courier-Post* or *USA Today*.) Also called a *footer ad*.

style book – A compilation of typographical and other rules formulated by a newspaper to make uniform its treatment of spelling, capitalization, abbreviations, punctuation, typography, etc. Most newspapers provide style books for their staffs' use.

subhead – Small, one-line headline inserted in the body of a story to break up the monotony of a solid column of small type.

summary deck – A sentence or two below a headline that introduces a story. Many times, summary decks are set in italics.

table – A graphic or sidebar that stacks words or numbers in rows so readers can compare data.

take – A portion of copy in a running story sent to the composing room in sections. Each page would be a *take* – Take 1 (page 1), Take 2 (page 2), etc. (In broadcasting, a "take" is each attempt at recording a story.)

tearsheet – A full page of the paper, including the folio, which has been clipped out and sent to an advertiser as proof that his or her ad has appeared.

teaser – An eye-catching graphic element, usually on Page One or section front, that promotes an item inside. Also called a *promo*.

text – The verbatim report of a speech or public statement.

think piece – A background or opinion article.

thumbnail – A half-column picture. See *porkchop*.

tie-back – The part of a story that ties it back to something that has already been published.

PR Play 9-13
'Journal' tries to start anew

By Al Neuharth
Founder of USA Today

The new year this week saw a highly publicized attempted regeneration of a 118-year-old newspaper which once was No. 1 in the nation. This year also will mark the 25th anniversary (Sept. 15) of the new kid on the block who dethroned the former champ.

The past 25-year history of both:

In 1982, *The Wall Street Journal* was tops in circulation with 1,925,000 copies sold each day. *USA Today* started then with zero.

Now, *USA Today* has 2,269,000 circulation; the *Journal* 2,043,000.

This week's "new" *Journal* hyped its content, but behind a still bland face. It reminded me of the fateful meeting noted pollster Lou Harris had with our Gannett board of directors after his extensive and expensive research in 1981 about a possible new national newspaper.

cont.

PR Play 9-13 continued

With copies of *The Wall Street Journal* spread in front of him, Harris said:

"A good newspaper is not necessarily dull. The TV generation will not fight its way through gray, insipid newspapers no matter how good they are." (Ditto the Internet generation.)

When we launched *USA Today*, a short page-one note highlighted these goals:

"Enlightening and enjoyable to the nation's readers."

"Challenging and competitive to the nation's journalists."

In last weekend's *Journal*, publisher L. Gordon Crovitz touted the "new" *Journal* in a lengthy letter, which read in part:

"We understand the concern at a time when so many once-authoritative news outlets have fallen to "journalism lite,' with fads and entertainment as news. Rest assured — as others dumb down, we intend to increase the amount of exclusive, highly distinctive coverage in the *Journal*."

Dumbing down, or dumbing up? "Enlightening and enjoyable" or "exclusive, highly distinctive"? As long as the competition for No. 1 continues, readers and advertisers will benefit. Stay tuned.

Feedback

"Readers don't give a fig if the paper they read is No. 1 on the Hit Parade or not; nor, luckily for them, do they really have to choose between the "either/or" attributes cited by Al. Long live the (enlightening) *Wall Street Journal* and the (highly distinctive) *USA Today*.

— Gloria Cooper, deputy executive editor,
Columbia Journalism Review

"Stay tuned, but not because one newspaper or the other wins the circulation war. Stay tuned, because now more than ever we need the best in quality, fearless journalism."

— Marvin Kalb, senior fellow at Harvard's Shorenstein Center on the Press, Politics and Public Policy

Published: January 7, 2007

PR Play 9-14
Differences Among Media

	__Magazine__	__Newspaper__	__Television__	__Radio__
Deadline	Weekly/ Monthly	Morning/ Afternoon	Live/ Morning/ Afternoon/ Evening (Cable – 24/7)	Live/ every minute (24/7) for all news/ hourly for others
Needs	Photos/ Quotes	Photos/ Quotes	Scenes/ Sound bites	Natural sound/ Sound bites
Story Length	50-1,500 words	50-1,500 words	60-90 seconds	10-35 seconds
Reporter	Weeks on a story	A day or week on a story	A few hours on a story	20-30 minutes on a story

PR101: Media Relations
Mary Ortega and M. Larry Litwin, APR, Fellow PRSA

PR Play 9-15
Anatomy of a Newspaper – Typical Sunday Web version – *The Philadelphia Inquirer*

World
U.S.
Washington
Business
Technology
Sports
Arts
New York/Region
Editorials
Op-Ed

PR Play 9-16
Anatomy of a Newspaper – Typical Sunday traditional hardcopy – *The Philadelphia Inquirer*

Sections

National/Foreign	**A**
City & Region	**B**
Currents (Editorials/Opinions)	**C**
Sports	**D**
Business	**E**
Automotive	**F**
Jobs	**G**
Arts & Entertainment	**H**
Real Estate	**J (I is omitted)**
New Homes	**K**
Neighbors	**L (Targeted to specific regions)**
Image	**M**
Travel	**N**

PR Play 9-17
Why send news releases?
(Here are just a few reasons.)

- Accomplishments
- Appointments
- Breakthroughs
- Honors and awards
- Workshop presentations
- Anniversaries
- Major special events
- Death of key personnel
- Product launches
- Organization expansion
- Grants received

- Official announcements
- Survey results from polls you conducted or reaction to another's survey and your tie-in
- Retirements
- Event partnership(s)
- Position paper or op-ed offering
- Visit by VIP

---

tie-in – Used to connect one (possibly a sidebar) story with some other, perhaps more important, story.

total market coverage – If a newspaper covers only a percentage of its market through paid circulation, then a supplement has to be published/printed that would go free to the rest of the market.

trial balloon – A project or idea tentatively announced in the news media to test public opinion.

trim – To reduce the length of a story; same as boil down.

typo – Typographical error – a mechanical error in typing a story.

underline – See *cutline*.

universe – In marketing research, the total group that a researcher wishes to study and measure. Also, all people who are prospects for a specific product or service. See *population*.

wild art – A picture that doesn't accompany a story usually boxed to show it stands alone. Also called *stand-alone photo*.

wx – Weather.

zoned editions – Geographic region served by a newspaper. For example, *The New York Times* and *Los Angeles Times* publish a city edition and zoned editions for their many suburbs.

Portions from *Newspapers In Education Partners In Education*
with modifications and additions by M. Larry Litwin, APR, Fellow PRSA –
Rowan University, Glassboro N.J.

Broadcast Media Terms Every Practitioner Should Know

actuality – The recorded words of someone who is part of a radio news story.

anchor interview – An interview conducted live by a television news anchor with a newsmaker either inside or outside of the studio.

assignment editor – Supervises and coordinates coverage by radio or television news gathering staff: Maintains contact with outside news agencies, police and fire departments, and other news sources to obtain information regarding developing news items. Determines priority and assigns coverage to news units. Works closely with the *news planner* at many television and radio news outlets.

B-Roll – Video accompanying a television story.

breaking news – News that is happening right now.

cop shop – Police headquarters.

cross platforming (media convergence) – The convergence of distribution – print, radio, television, broadband, wireless and digital signage. Also called *multiple platforming*.

doughnut (sandwich) – A reporter's on-location, live intro and close with pre-recorded video or audio. Also called a *wrap*.

live shot – An on-scene television or radio news story reported as it is happening.

media convergence – See *cross platforming*. Also called *multiple platforming*.

multiple platformting – See *cross platforming*. Also called *media convergence*.

narrowcasting – Targeting niche audiences through electronic media.

nat sound – Audio that's part of a television or radio news story but is not the sound of someone speaking directly into a microphone or to the camera (background sound).

news planner – Oversees daily and long-range newsroom planning Creates and maintains planning systems that help develop stories while working with newsroom journalists. Develops and executes planning systems day ahead, week ahead, month ahead and longer range planning and oversees planning meetings to review these events. Today's news planners use social media to find events/contacts that will lead to stories across multiple platforms. Works closely with the *assignment editor* at many television and radio news outlets.

newser – A news conference.

package – A pre-recorded television news story voiced by a reporter. It usually consists of standup or bridge, sound bites and B-roll.

phoner – An interview taped over the phone by either a radio or TV reporter.

reader (talent reader) – A TV news story with no accompanying video.

PR Play 9-18
Critical Thinking for Media Relations Specialists/News Release Writers

1. Why does your story matter? (The hook?)
2. What's the Point?
3. What does it say about Life? The World? The times we live in?

Connecting with Readers

1. What's the story about – in ONE word – sometimes, TWO?
   - Economy
   - Education (local schools)
   - Environment
   - Health Care
   - Social Security (two words)
   - War
   - Neighborhood (theirs)
   - Relationships (love)
   - Social Media
2. All about readers (target audience[s])
   - What surprised them?
   - What did they learn about themselves?

sandwich (doughnut) – A reporter's on-location, live intro and close with pre-recorded video or audio. Also called a *wrap*.

sound bite – The recorded words of someone who is part of a television news story.

take – Each attempt at recording a story is considered a "take."

talent reader – A TV news story with no accompanying video.

talking head – Close-up video of a newsmaker or newsperson speaking.

voice over sound or VO/SOT (sound on tape) – A television news story with accompanying video read by the anchor that leads into the recorded words of a newsmaker. (Similar to actuality except it is for TV.)

voicer – A pre-recorded radio news story voiced by a reporter.

wrap – A radio or TV news report voiced by a reporter and containing the voice of a newsmaker. (Similar to a *sandwich* and a *doughnut*.)

Courtesy of Kathy Kerchner – Interspeak, Scottsdale, AZ, and Debra Gelbart – Mercy Healthcare Arizona, Phoenix, AZ, with modifications and additions by M. Larry Litwin, APR, Fellow PRSA – Rowan University, Glassboro N.J.

EXERCISES

PR Challenge 9-1

As a public relations practitioner or media relations director, new to a job and to a region, what immediate steps would you take to develop relationships with the local media? List the first five steps that are absolute and then five you would take as time permits.

PR Challenge 9-2

Referring to PR Play 9-9, how do you justify to your "boss" that he or she should go "off the record" in discussing certain issues? If you are opposed to going "off the record," why?

PR Challenge 9-3

If you decide to hold an "in-service" for reporters, what strategic message would you send to persuade them to attend?

PR Challenge 9-4

PR Play 9-17 lists a number of reasons to prepare and send a news release. Can you list five others?

PR Challenge 9-5

Please respond to the following questions using as many or as few words as necessary. You may refer to other chapters in *The Public Relations Practitioner's Playbook for (all) Strategic Communicators* to support your responses:

1. How would you develop relationships with the media?
2. Once you establish a relationship with a reporter, editor or news director, how would you maintain it?
3. What might be the biggest obstacle you would encounter when dealing with the media?
4. What skills are necessary for dealing with the media?

5. How do you feel about so-called transparency and open communication?
6. Is open communication essential to public relations and when might it have to be avoided – at least temporarily?
7. Do you feel public communication is essential to public relations?
8. What do you feel is the most essential, effective or efficient form of public communication?

CHAPTER 10
Cross Platforming – The Digital Networked Age
Radio, TV, Internet and *Non*broadcast Video
[Collaborative Media]

Forty years ago it was said that broadcast media was among the most overlooked media as far as public relations practitioners and other strategic communicators were concerned. Not much changed as we entered the 21st century. But those same practitioners who have ignored broadcast media have shifted their focus from mainstream media to the Internet – websites, e-newsletters (as attachments or inline – inserted into the body of an email message), blast emails, texts, tweets, podcasts, videocasts, phonecasts, streaming, blogs, etc.

The networked age – digital and otherwise – and cross platforming or collaborative media – when properly used – can be a bonanza for communicating strategic messages. Cross platforming is the convergence of distribution (media convergence) – print, radio, television, broadband, wireless (Wi-Fi), digital signage, special events and face-to-face. Strategic communicators should think in terms of multi (multiple) platforming – full media convergence or collaboration – to acheive their goal – synergy.

Rather than *media convergence*, Jessica Gisclair, Elon (N.C.) University communication professor, advocates *collaborative media* (IMC – integrated marketing communication). "Media really has not converged into one or something new," she says. "However, legacy (traditional) media uses 'new' or digital (social) media in *collaborative* efforts to reach and engage audiences. One does not supersede the other."

Collaborative media – used strategically – complement each other (work together) to achieve synergy (e.g. CBS collaborating on "March Madness" with TBS, TNT and truTV).

Originally, cross platform was a term referring to computer programs, operating systems, programming language and computer software. The term now refers to using available *(collaborative)* media to carry a strategic message.

Included are mainstream and alternative media – print, radio, television, Internet (and interactive – blogs, tweets), iPod®, (Podcasts, etc.), Vcasts®, cell phone, iPhone® and other smartphones, iPad®-type tablets and devices, digital signage, aroma marketing, WOMM (word of mouse marketing) and silent publicity. Add to these, the "two-screen (multi-screen) experience" – people watching television with a mobile device (smartphone or tablet) in their hand or on their lap to access additional information. (More about "two-screen" under Web 2.0 on Pages 317, 319 and 320.)

Effective strategic communicators have embraced Twitter – describing tweets as "an incredible forum to magnify a person or organization's voice." Viviana Hurtado, blogger-in-chief of the website *The Wise Latina Club*, says, "I've ended up really embracing Twitter, in particular, after adopting social media, in general. But (using) Twitter, Latinos are just booming."

For an example of Twitter's speed, power and impact one need only to look at Oreo® cookies' rapid response to the 34-minute blackout during the 2013 Super Bowl featuring the 49ers and champion Ravens. Soon after Baltimore opened the second half with a 108-yard kickoff return, the New Orleans (Mercedes Benz®) Super Dome went dark. Minutes into the delay, Twitter lit up – with the advertising agency representing Oreo® demonstrating how social media can be a game changer with an "instant ad."

Like many other agencies, Oreo's® digital team was monitoring the online buzz (about the game and commercials) in a "war room" and "thumbed" into action immediately crafting a print-like ad showing a picture of an Oreo® surrounded by darkness. While the tagline in the attached display ad says "You can still dunk in the dark," it was the tweet that broke through the clutter – "Power out? No problem." (Those 22 characters say it all.)

While 15,000 re-tweets pales in comparison to 111 million people watching the Super Bowl on TV, the buzz created sent its own message to strategic communicators: "This needs to be done all the time," says Ben Winkler, chief digital officer at OMD, a New York City ad agency.

Bob Dorfman, executive creative director of Baker Street Advertising in San Francisco, told NPR's Neil Conan, Audi®, a Super Bowl advertiser, took a jab at Mercedes Benz® when it tweeted, "Sending some LEDs to the @MBUSA Superdome right now..."

Not to be outdone, Tide® tweeted, "We can't get your blackout. But we can get your stains out." (59 characters)

But let's not get ahead of ourselves. Three decades ago, the problem rested in the laps of the broadcast executives who didn't quite understand how to *work together* with public relations and other strategic communication practitioners. For the most part, they viewed them (us) as nothing more than publicists. Today, the blame lies with the PR professional who is not savvy enough to get his or her client's message on radio or TV. In fact, many are more educated about the use of the Internet, which is relatively new in comparison, than they are about the workings of TV. We are now approaching 80 years since the first commercial TV stations went on the air.

As strategic communicators, the time is now to take advantage of both radio and television. While many radio stations still look for good stories and programming for so-called "down time" or off hours, it is those TV stations that could prove to be a bonanza. With the advent of cable (TV and radio), many communities now have access to literally hundreds of stations or cable "networks" just by touching a button on their remote. But local stations – network affiliates of ABC, CBS, FOX and NBC – have expanded their news programming to include early morning, midday (noon or earlier) and 4, 4:30, 5, 5:30 and 6 p.m. "shows" or a combination of late afternoon or early evening broadcasts. And, almost all affiliates and many independent TV stations and cable operators run 10 or 11 p.m. local newscasts. Electronic news, such all news radio stations as *KYW* (Philadelphia), *WCBS* and *WINS* (New York) and *KFWB* (Los Angeles), *CNN*, *FOX News Channel* and *MSNBC* on cable, and many newspaper, radio and TV news websites now offer 24/7 news. Succinctly, those outlets need appealing stories to fill time (radio/TV) and space (Web).

While all forms of electronic media are hungry for programs and topics of interest, they have one major criterion in common – messages must have a "hook" to get the audience to listen or watch, or in the case of the Internet, to drive the audience to a website in which the content is appealing enough to be read.

That "hook" is the *news* that a news or program director is looking for before deciding whether to carry the story, program or public service announcement (PSA) that you are pitching.

News directors and editors define *news* as "anything of interest to a great number of people." But those who deal on a regular basis with the "gate-keepers" fully understand that *news* is also "whatever the news director says it is." It is the responsibility of the media relations specialist to convince a news director or news editor of a radio or television station that a story being pitched is *news*.

There are proven persuasive steps that story pitchers have used to get the approval of the *gatekeeper*. But it all begins with *relationship (management) marketing* – developing sound relationships and loyalty by making media outlets and their reporters feel good about working with you. Depending on skill and likeability, it could take weeks or months to develop a (mutually trusting) relationship. Many times, relationship marketing leads to a subliminal feeling that is the major ingredient in persuading a media outlet to cover your event or to consider your firm or organization a credible news source.

Be an *Advance Person*

It is commonplace for an advance person to precede the president of the United States or a cabinet secretary into a city or country to "get a lay of the land." As the strategic communicator in charge of getting the story on electronic media, you have the same responsibility. Whether it be radio, commercial TV or cable, there is one basic rule to follow to get your story on the air – *get to know the local stations*. Know the types of programming they carry, preferred lengths and especially their preferred format.

How do you find out? Do your research. Start by conducting your own informal surveys (anecdotal research) – using the Internet to visit station websites and by watching and listening to the news sources in the markets where you are trying to acquire coverage.

If radio is your goal, listen to stations either at work or while driving to and from your job. If it is television, pay attention to the types of programming (including cable) on TV. Because of the impact of TV and radio, the public relations specialist, who knows how to use area stations to his or her advantage, will be viewed as a "star."

Advantages of Radio

Radio relies on the listener's mind to fill in the visual element, delivers a high level of frequency and lends itself to repetition. Radio targets audiences, is affordable, offers frequency (number of times a listener is exposed to a message), is available in dozens of formats and is viewed as credible.

- **It's immediate** – Even though television can go "live" at the drop of a hat, the distance from head to toe is much further for TV than radio. All that is needed to go "live" on radio is a cell phone. TV, even with fiber optics, still requires set up time and, if using a microwave, it must require a signal. Skype®-type broadcasts – using laptops, smartphones or tablets – are quick and easy to set up, but the video and audio quality fall short of looking and sounding professional.

If there is an emergency, radio can get your message to the masses faster than any other form of communication, although cell phone alerts, blast emails and TV are not far behind in speed. More people have more immediate access to a radio than they do to either a television or computer. Think about it, where do you turn during a snowstorm to find out whether you have to report to work that day or your children have school? If you are like the overwhelming number of others, the response is your local radio station. (Unless you have Internet access or have subscribed to a cell phone notification service.)

- **It's comfortable** – People who are listening to the radio can do something else at the same time. They are comfortable, too, because their favorite radio stations have become their "friends."

- **It's focused** – Audiences are narrowly defined – niched. Your message will reach a particular (target) audience.

- **It's captive** – Many listeners are confined to a limited space, such as a car or office. It has become commonplace to see joggers, walkers and bike riders listening to radios – even if they are part of their iPod® or similar device. (Where do you think Sony® came up with the brand name Walkman® as in MP3 Walkman with FM tuner?)

- **Mental imagery** – Listeners subliminally enjoy envisioning what they hear.

Advantages of Television

Television brought journalism to life like only TV can. No other medium has the emotion and impact of TV. No other medium, except for motion pictures viewed in a theater, keeps your attention. Pictures – seen on TV – can be riveting. Whether it is a "live" shot of a child being rescued after falling into a well, or video of a plane crash or a dramatic sports victory, those pictures speak much louder and with far more impact than any number of words.

Observers believe, in the not too distant future, there will be thousands of networks, thanks largely to the advent of computers and Web TV. Properly produced and distributed, your message can get on the air. And if getting on radio makes the strategic communicator a princess, getting on TV makes her a queen.

TV is:

- **Nearly as immediate as radio** – With the use of electronic news gathering (ENG) equipment, satellites, microwaves and fiber optics, the only thing keeping TV from being as immediate as radio is the time needed to transport the equipment to the site and setting it up. But TV is becoming more immediate every day. Radio is absolutely immediate because the only piece of equipment needed is a cell phone. All of us know how to use a phone. Some of us might need assistance in setting up the ENG equipment or computer and cables. With wireless phones, radio transmission is 100 percent portable. Wi-Fi has almost eliminated the gap. A laptop and small video camera (or Skype® — although not as sharp) are all one needs to transmit a crisp broadcast signal, which can be transmitted live on TV. (Newspaper websites are now taking advantage of the same "live" technology to broadcast breaking stories.)

- **Accessible to your audience** – No other medium can reach the masses that TV can. Nearly 115 million homes in the U.S. have at least one TV set. Most have multiple sets. Those sets are turned on an average of more than seven hours per day in each American home. The average person watches approximately five hours of TV a day.

- **Comfortable** – Like radio, viewers are usually watching TV because they want to – in the comfort of their homes or at work. It's the strategic communicator's responsibility to provide programming that will interest them. When it comes to local newscasts, *comfort* is the key.

Viewers develop a strong habit of watching one local newscast. As a communication specialist, your advance work should include determining which station's programming (demographics) matches your target audience and how many viewers can be reached.

- **Pervasive/Captive** – While it is true that a viewer can get up from the sofa or chair and walk away from the set, TV is still considered a captive medium even with the advent of technology that allows for time shifting (recording television shows for purposes of viewing them later at a more convenient time) and personal instant replay. TV can and does deliver the message. That's why billions of dollars are spent each year in TV advertising. (Current numbers show, more than $70 billion is spent on network, local and cable TV. That's more than 30 percent of all advertising dollars compared to $20 billion and more than 7 percent for all forms of radio.) Like advertisers, the strategic communicator is delivering a message. To help assure the message is being absorbed, you must first engage the viewer's mind (get his or her attention). To accomplish that, think "hook" or local angle. It is pervasive because television is everywhere – homes, restaurants, airports, retail stores, doctors' offices, etc.

- **Impactful** – No other medium has the influence or effect that TV has. Video can be, and is, emotional and compelling.

- **Cost-efficient** – While TV vehicles (VNRs, films and commercials) are expensive to produce and broadcast, the cost per thousand could be relatively low. TV reaches 10s of millions of viewers simultaneously.

Advantages of Cable

Nearly 90 percent of all homes in the United States are wired for cable. However, with Internet, Wi-Fi, and smartphones and other devices, the number of subscribers has been decreasing. Demographically, cable can reach just about every audience segment. In addition to carrying commercial stations, the same ones that can be received with an outdoor antenna, cable provides – in digital format – thousands of specialized programs on hundreds, approaching thousands, of channels with very specific (fragmented) target audiences. Many cable operators offer excellent opportunities for *local origination programming*. Potential programming opportunities abound for such professionals as physicians, dentists, attorneys, other professional experts, non-profit organizations, school districts and hospitals.

Depending on financial resources and expertise, programs may be professionally produced at a substantial cost while others are obviously "low-budget." However, low budget does not necessarily mean poor quality. Cable staff, college students or community volunteers may be willing to assist with a production. Take advantage of offers. Profit-making organizations, or professionals, may have to pay production costs, but the key word here is *may*. Because the professional is providing a service-type program to the cable operator, barter could be negotiated to cover production costs and college students may be willing to take on projects for college credit and/or internships. Cable TV advertising revenue remains in the $27-$30 billion range.

PR Play 10-1
PR Opportunities in Radio, TV and the Web

- Actualities or Sound Bites
- Blogs
- Twitter®
- Podcasts
- Vcasts
- Community Calendars
- Creative programming
- Discussion programs
- Editorials
- Expert availability
- General-interest films or videos
- News releases and story pitches to news departments
- Newscasts
- Protest demonstrations
- Public Service Announcements (PSAs)
- Silent Publicity
- Talk (Call-in) Shows
- Videotapes for news programs or mini Video News Releases (VNRs)

Advantages of the Internet

Even though the Internet is more than 50 years old, it is still considered to be in its infancy. With its rapid expansion and the evolution of technology, the Internet has become increasingly more effective as a tool and vehicle for public relations practitioners. Corporations, media outlets and other organizations must have a strong online presence to prove credi-

---

PR Play 10-2
Websites Should Include:

- Listing of contents
- Company information
  - About the company or organization
  - Management/key personnel
  - Company or organization history
  - Awards/professional affiliations
  - Directions to physical site
  - Contact information
  - Job postings
- Marketing and sales information
  - Calendar of events
  - Product descriptions (use words, pictures, video, podcasts)
  - Online catalog
  - Customer testimonials
  - Common questions (FAQs) with answers
  - Order forms
- Customer service information
  - Product updates
  - Training resources
  - Support phone numbers
  - Common questions (FAQs) with answers
- Other information
  - Newsroom for media and public
    1. News releases
    2. Announcements
    3. Calendar of events
  - Related links
  - Resources of interest (books, videos, contacts)

---

bility and attract advertisers (if they sell space). During the 2000 Republican National Convention in Philadelphia (and repeated in 2012 at both major political party national conventions), one exhibitor promised no fewer than one million separate and distinct "networks" on *Web TV*. We are not there yet, but the industry moves closer almost every day.

Web 2.0 – Participatory Media

The concept of Web 2.0 and social media – once referred to as "new media" is targeted to the I-generations. But these – two-way – innovations

---

PR Play 10-3
Popular Social Networking Sites

43things.com	flickr.com	myyearbook.com
about.me	foursquare.com	orkut.com
bebo.com	friendster.com	pinterest.com
blackplanet.com	graduates.com	reddit.com
cardomain.com	hi5.com	reunion.com
care2.com	hulu.com	stumbleupon.com
classmates.com	instagram.com	thestudentcenter.com
facebook.com	Linkedin.com	tumblr.com
facebox.com	mog.com	xanga.com
faceparty.com	myspace.com	YouTube.com

---

are hardly new. If Web 1.0 is about connecting computers then Web 2.0 is about digitally connecting people – and the most popular and growing method is through social networking sites – *participatory* media.

Web 2.0 is a phrase coined by O'Reilly Media in 2004. It refers to a perceived or proposed second generation of Internet-based services. Chris Shipley, co-founder and global research director for Guidewire Group, is considered the first person to have coined the term "social media."

Three of the more popular social media are Facebook®, Twitter® and YouTube®. Social media are the online tools and platforms that people use to share opinions, insights, experiences and perspectives with each other. Social media can take many different forms, including text, images, audio and video. Popular social media include blogs (online diaries), Twitter®, message boards, podcasts, wikis (websites that allow the visitors themselves to easily add, remove and otherwise edit and change available content, and typically without the need for registration), mash ups (blending of computer applications), videologs and folksonomies (Internet-based information retrieval methodology consisting of collaboratively-generated, open-ended labels that categorize content such as Web, online photographs, and Web links) that emphasize online collaboration and sharing among users.

O'Reilly Media, in collaboration with MediaLive International, used the phrase – Web 2.0 – as a title for a series of conferences, and since 2004

---

the phrase has been adopted by technical and marketing communities. Its exact meaning has been open to debate.

The number of blogs created worldwide has exceeded 250 million – about 95 percent of which are "personal" journals, according to Derek Gordon of Technorati Inc., which tracks blogs, podcasts, vcasts and photo-sharing – all social media. He says technical and gossip-oriented blogs are the most popular on the Web. There are more than 1.6 million blog entries being added daily along with 175,000 additional blogs. Many do become inactive after a time.

Moorestown, N.J. blogger, Chris Pesotski told *Courier-Post* columnist Kevin Riordan, "If an opinion is worth having, it's worth sharing. And, if it's not worth sharing, it's not worth having. It's the first time that the printing press is in the hands of the writers. It's incredibly powerful."

Chloe Sladden (@ChloeS) is head of media at Twitter®. She says, "Once upon a time, there was one screen that TV broadcasters needed to fill. These days, it's all about the two-screen (multi-screen) experience.

"People have been watching television with their laptops, smartphones and tablets in hand for a while now. But this year (2012), big business tried harder than ever to bring television to a second screen."

"This year, I think we've seen a maturity in the social television space, which is still very nascent," says Mark Ghuneim of Trendrr TV, which keeps track of social media around television. "Just looking at this year versus last year, there's been an 800 percent growth in the commentary around TV, real time."

In other words, says Ghuneim, social media chitchat about TV shows was nine times louder in 2012 than in 2011. According to Nielsen, in 2013, more than 40 percent of people who own tablets and smartphones watch TV with them every day.

As more and more people join in "electronic conversation," more and more brands are pushing toward the second screen.

According to "two-screener" Roxane Gay, "Take a show like *Survivor*. They have a hashtag (pound or sharp sign before a word or phrase) for something like #ImmunityChallenge, so that you can see other people talking about it. And so television shows are realizing that people are starting to consume television differently."

Every tweet with #ImmunityChallenge will fall into one, searchable feed. So when CBS places a hashtag on Screen No. 1, they're essentially creating a chat room on Screen No. 2, which offers additional (unfiltered) information, reaction and conversation.

Online chatter is just one of the things that second screens are used for. Ghuneim says people also want to learn about what they're watching.

Millions of viewers tweeted while watching the 2012 presidential debates. Even more tweet about their fantasy football teams while watching NFL (National Football League) games.

The possibilities for public relations practitioners and other communicators are endless. A.C. Nielsen is partnering with Twitter for the industry-standard metric based entirely on Twitter data called "Nielsen Twitter TV Rating."

"As the experience of TV viewing continues to evolve, our TV partners have consistently asked for one common benchmark from which to measure the engagement of their programming," says Nielsen. "This new metric is intended to answer that request, and to act as a complement and companion to the Nielsen TV rating." The possibilities are endless and nearly impossible to keep pace.

PR Play 10-4
Getting On The Air

The National Association of Broadcasters (NAB) suggests that if your appeal is to be effective, you should have the answer to some key questions before contacting local stations: (Some refer to it as the *MAC Triad – message, audience, channel.*)

- What is your message? [**message**] Are you sure of the basic idea you want to communicate?
- Who should receive your message? [**audience**] Is it of general interest to a large segment of the audience? Can it be tailored to reach a specific audience?
- How can you best put your message across? [**channel**] Does it have enough general interest for a special program? Would a PSA serve just as well?

Your answers to these questions should help you determine in advance whether your pitch will work.

PR Play 10-5
Radio Spot – PSA Example No. 1
Washington Township Jaycees (Listen to *Playbook* CD)

Public Service Announcement

Burwyn Associates

FADE IN MUSIC		COPY
Panel Moderator	1	And now ladies and gentlemen, four concerned
	2	parents will tell us all they've done
	3	in the last year to make their community a better
	4	place to live.
	5	
(MUSIC FADE OUT)	6	
	7	
Parents	8	(SILENCE)
	9	
Panel Moderator	10	Thank you parents.
	11	
FADE IN MUSIC...	12	
UP AND OUT	13	
	14	
	15	
COMMERCIAL	16	
ANNOUNCER	17	What have you done lately for your town?...make
	18	your community a better place because you live
	19	there. Fight drugs.
	20	
	21	The preceding announcement brought to you by
	22	(ORGANIZATION) The Washington Township
	23	Jaycees and this radio station. Check out
:30	24	W-T-J-A-Y-C-E-E-S.com.
Washington Twp. Jaycees	25	
Clyde Cool,	26	
856-555-1212	27	
cool@wtjaycees.com	28	
Run thru: 12/31	29	
	30	

Communications Specialists • P. O. Box 692 • Cherry Hill, NJ 08003 • 609-428-9049

PR Play 10-6
What makes Radio so special?

Radio creates visual images through audio communication. PSAs (public service announcements) use sound to create an image that stimulates listener reaction.

Communication adage:

Supply **Information TO** create an **Attitude TO** motivate **Behavior**

Writing PSAs Specifically For Radio

- **Differences from print media**:
  - Time is a controlling factor.
  - Uses fewer words to relay the message.
- **Know your target audience**
  - Whom do you want to reach?
    - Give benefits to the target audience.
    - Address their needs and concerns.
- **Defining the message**
  - Identify the key information.
  - Develop the message so it focuses on and reinforces the key information.
- **Structuring the PSA**
  - The Opening
    - Develop a strong, short opening sentence directed at the target audience.
    - Focus on the key information and the benefit to the listener.
    - Do not overload with a multitude of facts and figures.
  - The Body
    - Use correct number of words:
      75 words = 30 seconds
      150 words = 60 seconds
    - Supply a limited number of facts and figures that support the message.
    - Address the needs and concerns of the target audience.
  - The Ending
    - Summarize the message.
    - Repeat key information.
    - Tell the listener where to get more information.

cont.

PR Play 10-6 continued

- **Live reads should end**:
  "For more information call 1-800-555-1212 or online at rowan.edu. That's 800-555-1212." (Put phone number of the organization in the PSA header, which could run vertically on left side of copy sheet with other instructions or on the top half of the traditional 8½ x 11 sheet of paper with the actual PSA on the lower half [see examples below].)
- **Pre-recorded reads should end:**
  "For more information call XYZ Organization at 800-555-1234 or visit rowan.edu."

Portions by Bonnie Hart – Rowan (N.J.) University Graduate

PR Play 10-7

Cabrini College Radio PSA (Listen to *Playbook* CD)

Public Service Announcement Example No. 2

Cabrini College/Eagle Road/Radnor PA/610-555-1212

Cabrini College Flower Show King of Prussia and Eagle Roads Radnor, Pennsylvania Exit 5, from the Blue Route **Start date**: April 28 **Run thru**: May 2 **Contact**: Gregory Potter **Phone**: 610-555-1212 **Fax**: 610-555-1214 **email**: gpotter@cabrinicollege.org 30 seconds, 70 words (phone number is listed twice) Recorded CD enclosed Also sent as MP3 file	ANNCR: Spring is in the air...and Cabrini College is celebrating the season with its annual flower show on May 2nd. Fill your senses with flowers from around the world and tour the Cabrini campus in beautiful Radnor, Pennsylvania. Take Exit 5 off the Blue Route for the Cabrini College Flower Show...Friday...May 2nd from 10 until 5. Call 610-555-1212 for information. That's 610-555-1212 for the Cabrini College Flower Show...or...cabrini.edu.

PR Play 10-8
Public Service Announcement for Radio Example No. 3

AMERICAN EDUCATION WEEK IOWA

FROM: Doug Pocock
Chief Communication Officer

For Use: Monday, Nov. 11
thru Friday, Nov. 15

Fairfield Education Association
Fairfield High School
Fairfield, Iowa 52556
515-555-1212
media@fea.com
www.fea.org

AMERICAN EDUCATION WEEK IN IOWA
Nov. 10 - Nov. 16 (official dates)
Time: 30 seconds
Words: 78

ANNCR: Drive by a school. Watch the faces on the hundreds of students as they come and go…young men and women who one day will govern this nation. During American Education Week – November 10th to November 16th – public, parochial and private school teachers in Fairfield invite you to watch this vital form of freedom in action. Visit your local school and observe techniques of instruction that help prepare our children for tomorrow.
It's American Education Week…in Fairfield.

- End -

What makes the Internet an *advantage*?
- It reaches the millions of consumers who have access to computers at home or work and in libraries, cyber cafes and Wi-Fi (wireless) locations, as well as cell phones, etc.
- Email is easy to use.
- Web page usage continues to expand.
- Users share information in online discussion groups and on message boards.
- Web pages offer links to immediate information about your company or organization.

Some *disadvantages*:

- Available *only* to individuals who have computer access (there are still many hold outs)
- Difficult to drive audiences to the website
- Looks unprofessional
- Frustration by some who have trouble accessing your information
- Difficult to navigate
- Keeping information current (one person or a small team of individuals should be assigned the task)
- Security
- Has a link that doesn't work
- Is sometimes unexpectedly unavailable
- Has typographical errors
- Doesn't include contact information
- Failure to provide quick responses to customer service questions

The Internet is an ever-developing form of mass communication that fascinates participants. For some, it still must pass a trial and error period before its effectiveness as a PR tool can be fully measured. Advertising revenue continues to increase. It is approaching $62 billion annually, up from $32 billion in 2011.

Types of Vehicles – Broadcast – Internet – Other Platforms

- **Actualities or Sound Bites** – The recorded words of someone who is part of a radio news story (newsmaker).

- **Blog** – Web log, online diary or journal. It is unfiltered opinion.

- **Community Calendar** – A list of upcoming events that appears in many newspapers and magazines. Entries are brief and usually contain only the name of the sponsoring organization and a very brief description of the event.

- **Creative programming** – Such as medical updates, gardening, geriatric reports or education. These are effective for either radio or TV because they can be targeted to specific demographics.

- **Discussion programs** – Short programs offered in non-prime time that could give your organization or firm exposure in a particular area of expertise. This type of program may be self-produced, meaning the

moderator and the interviewee are provided by the organization –
much like an infomercial but not quite as blatant. These types of programs are usually heard or viewed early on Sunday mornings. Don't
discount them. Although limited, there are audiences out there. Radio
and TV have loyal audiences who listen and watch all night and others who can't live without these media early on a Sunday morning.

- **Editorials** – Opinion, as opposed to an objective news article, appearing in a newspaper, magazine, on an Internet site, radio or television.

- **Expert availability** – Make available to the media a staff person who
has a special skill or knowledge in some particular field. A specialist
– someone with source credibility.

- **General-interest video or films** – TV or non-broadcast. These, too,
must be well produced. Recently, a number of Rowan (N.J.)
University professors and graduates combined efforts to produce a
documentary about Seabrook Farms. During the 1940s and 1950s,
Seabrook brought together families of many different cultures, nationalities and languages to live and work side by side in the only rural
global village of its size in the country to process fruits and vegeta-
bles that fed America's armed forces during World War II.

- **News releases** (printed and video) – **Story pitches** to local and network news directors. When pitching think – few words with a hook;
hot topics are best; target stations; get to the point quickly, but don't
forget the angle; personalize it, if possible; don't be afraid to offer
facts in support of your pitch and story; if sent electronically, ask for
receipt confirmation in lieu of follow-up call.

- **Newscasts** – A broadcast radio or TV program offering stories with
solid news value. On radio, all news stations and some talk or talk-
plus (news) formats will carry your stories. However, most radio outlets today, because of format, provide little, if any, airtime for local
news. Instead, those stations depend on network programming (local
affiliates throughout the country that receive their programming
simultaneously via satellite or hard wire from such networks as ABC,
CBS, NBC and CNN). Local TV stations are always looking for stories with a hook and even well-produced *video news releases (VNR)*
(more on *VNRs* later in this chapter) because they now carry several
hours of local news each day and they must fill the time.

- **Protest demonstrations** – Well-orchestrated, they can attract attention. But remember, you are trying to communicate a positive image. Stay in control.

- **Public Service (spot) Announcements** – Whether radio or TV, 10, 15, 30 and 60-second announcements can get on the air. They are produced much like commercials, except they are provided free or with the assistance of corporate dollars ("cause-related marketing") to help assure they get aired (time is actually purchased). On radio, an announcer – called a talent reader – may read PSAs live. (Much more below.)

- **Silent Publicity** (similar to product placement, but it is free) – Use (or video) of your products or facilities for a TV (or radio) program.

- **Talk (call-in) or interview shows** – Talk radio and cable TV channels provide many opportunities to communicate your message. Don't arbitrarily discount Kimmel, Leno, Letterman, Oprah, "The Daily Show" or Colbert. Your spokesperson must not only be an expert in his or her field, but must also be a good communicator.

- **Twitter**® – Personal social media websites that allow subscribers to have their messages – both sent and received (called *tweets*) – posted for everyone to view or they may be password protected. *Tweets* are limited to 140 characters. Tweets are considered a form of "voice magnification."

Public Service Announcements (PSAs)

PSAs are a valuable tactic to inform audiences about charitable, educational or other non-profit programs. Just as you would for other types of programming, check with your local stations for PSA guidelines. Some radio stations might want you to record your PSA at their station. Others prefer you produce an MP3 file for them to use, and some might want just the paper copy provided so the station's radio personalities can do a "live" read – from the copy you provide.

PSAs are usually transmitted by radio or TV in a spot that runs 10 to 60 seconds. When planning a PSA, it's important to cover the five W's (who, what, when, where and why) in the short amount of time you have.

PSAs are known as "mobilizing information." PSAs should contain mobilizing information, such as the location of a meeting and a number to call or a place to write for more information (PR Play 10-7).

PSAs are not advertisements – they are provided free by stations making time available.

PSAs should contain vital public information that makes the audience act – a "call to action" – just as it should with any other strategic message.

Public Service Announcement Templates

Many organizations have created templates for consistency. Among them is Purdue University. Three of their templates, which are online, are below.

Preceding the templates is the disclaimer: "The following PSAs are provided for your use in working with local *radio* stations. Purdue University suggests you feel free to adapt them to your needs."

Public Service Announcement No. 1

Hello, I am _____ a Purdue Extension Educator in _____ County. Using research from Purdue University, I provide all members of this community opportunities to improve their lives through learning. Purdue Extension in _____ County has **Knowledge to Go** for you. Find out what we offer in _____ _____ and _____. Helping you and your neighbors improve life through knowledge is a way of life for me. Call me, _____ , at 555-EXT-INFO or 555-398-4636*** or visit PEE.edu.

Public Service Announcement No. 2

At Purdue Extension of _____ County , we have research-based information you can use now. That's why we call it, **Knowledge to Go**. Hello, I am _____, a Purdue Extension Educator in this county. My goal is to bring knowledge to you and your neighbors in the areas of _____, _____ and _____. It is my pleasure to live and work in this county and watch it grow. Education is an important part of that growth. I invite you to visit or call us at 555-EXT-INFO or 555-398-4636*** or visit PEE.edu.

PR Play 10-9
Keys To Keep In Mind When Trying To Get Your Message On Radio and Television

- Responsibility
- Contacts
- First meeting
- Timeliness and relevance
- Be brief
- Controversy
- Teamwork
- Suggestions and criticism
- Limitations
- Make appointments

- Write for the ear
- Plan ahead
- Be on time
- Follow instructions
- Sending news releases
- Feedback
- Relate your image, don't sell it
- Thank-you letters

Public Service Announcement No. 3

Hello, my name is _____ a(n)
(Consumer & Family Sciences, 4-H/Youth Development, Agriculture &
Natural Resources, Leadership & Community Development,
Horticulture) Educator for _____ County.

Using research from Purdue University, I have the opportunity to
encourage youth, strengthen families, and assist others in improving our
community and the environment. Purdue Extension in _____
County, specializes in education that is ready for you to use now. That's
why we call it, ***Knowledge to Go***. We are the place to find information
about: _____ _____ and
_____ . As an educator, with Purdue Extension in
_____ County, helping others learn is a way of life for me. For
more information call me at: *** or visit PEE.edu.

* Pick up to three or add your own: 4-H, natural resources, agriculture,
animal sciences, horticulture, food safety, nutrition, health and wellness,
parenting, family relationships, finances, leadership, biotechnology,
environment.

*** Use 555-EXT-INFO or add your own number.

PR Play 10-10
Standard Radio Dayparts

Morning Drive	6-10 a.m.	5-10 a.m.	5-9 a.m.
Mid-day	10 a.m.-2 p.m.	10 a.m.-3 p.m.	
P.M. Drive	2-6 p.m.	3-7 p.m.	4-8 p.m.
Evenings	6 p.m.-Mid.	6-11 p.m.	
Overnights	Mid.-5 a.m.	Mid.-6 a.m.	11 p.m.-5 a.m.

Standard Television Dayparts

Early morning	M-F 7-9 a.m.
Daytime	M-F 9 a.m.-4:30 p.m.
Early fringe	M-F 4:30-7 p.m.
Prime access	M-F 7:30-8 p.m.
Prime time	M-Sa 8-11 p.m. and Su 7-11 p.m.
Late news	M-Su 11-11:30 p.m.
Late night	M-Su 11:30 p.m.-1 a.m.
Saturday morning	Sa 8 a.m.-1 p.m.
Weekend afternoon	Sa-Su 1-7 p.m.

Note: All times are local.

Whether using radio or television, these steps should be followed:

1. One person should be responsible for the news of your organization. That person must be familiar with the capabilities and limitations of the electronic media.

2. Your representative should contact the program director or general manager of each local radio or TV station being considered as outlets for your message. The station representative will suggest the types of programming most likely to be broadcast; the appropriate time limits

for spot announcements and programs; and who (your organization or the station) will physically produce the programming.

3. During the first meeting between your representative and the station representative, guidelines will be established for proper microphone and recording techniques. If your organization does not have access to professional broadcasting equipment, it should ask the station for help. If assured good programming, many stations will offer staff assistance and studio time. It must be understood from the start that all programs will be professionally produced. Follow-through is essential. Once your group or organization has made a commitment, there is no turning back. Remember the importance of deadlines. Most stations schedule their programming days, if not weeks, in advance.

4. Messages should be timely and relevant. They must be of local (hook) interest. In other words, listeners should identify with the programming. It must be relevant.

5. Broadcast presentations should be succinct. Your firm or organization should try for a variety in program content and presentation. However, do not pad it with unnecessary or unimportant content. To the stations, time is money.

6. Controversial topics don't have to be avoided. Problems, innovations and current involvement should be presented and explained. Solutions to problems should be offered. At all times, be honest and tell the whole story.

7. All types of programming, from 90-minute spectaculars to brief spot announcements, require planning and cooperation with local (or network) stations. You might want to consider podcasts – self-styled audio productions recorded in digital format and downloaded to computers, iPods®, tablets, smartphones or other digital (music) players. No matter which tactic is chosen, teamwork is the key to success in any project.

8. Accept suggestions and constructive criticism. You may be working with experts in a field foreign to you.

9. Your firm should know its limitations. A half-hour interview program might seem ideal, but spot announcements, if well produced, can be more effective than a long program that is inadequately prepared.

PR Play 10-11
*Helpful Hints for Broadcast Writing**

1. Write simple spoken English.
2. Never use a long word when a short one will do.
3. Try to keep one thought to a sentence.
4. Vary sentence length.
5. Use verbs. Do not drop verbs. Listeners need verbs.
6. Use picture nouns and action verbs.
7. Use the active voice.
8. Try to use the present or the present perfect tense.
9. Avoid using "today." Try to give *your* news story or release the most up-to-date peg you can.
10. Do **NOT** use synonyms – avoid synonyms. Synonyms can confuse the listener.
11. Do **NOT** use pronouns. Repeat proper names.
12. Avoid direct quotes – paraphrase (it's safer).
13. Always find a way of repeating location. Repeating the location toward the bottom of the story (or throughout video news release) is important to the listener or viewer.
14. Keep adjectives to a minimum. Adjectives tend to clutter speech and obscure the main line of the story.
15. Don't use appositions. (A construction in which a noun or noun phrase is placed with another as an explanatory equivalent – example: Litwin, the public relations specialist, was born in Philadelphia.) Please **DO NOT** use appositions. Most appositions are not natural to speech. Appositions often confuse the listener because he/she cannot see the necessary punctuation.
16. Use simple sentences. This would usually mean not starting a sentence with a prepositional phrase or a participle phrase.
17. Attribution. Almost always comes at the beginning of sentence...**NOT** at the end. (Example: Use – Company spokesperson Daniel O'Neill pointed out that this year's contributions will be the biggest ever. **Don't use** – "This year's contribution will be the biggest ever," said Daniel O'Neill, company spokesperson.
18. Place yourself in a story or two. If you are writing the newscast (or release) for air in Philadelphia and the story is about a college in Philadelphia, say...*Here in* Philadelphia.
19. When you write a broadcast release or a news story this way it must follow that it be delivered naturally – but with authority – and if delivered naturally, it means proper names may not always be emphasized – often the verb is emphasized – *natural* inflection.

*Portions adapted from "Writing - here at ABC"

PR Play 10-12
Sample Storyboard

Gail O'Hara
Rowan University, Public Relations Planning class
Story Board - 60-second spot

"In the News"
CCTS School Spirit Week

20 seconds   Male V/O

Broadcaster reads:

"Breaking news just in...
A new activity all CCTS students can participate in.
CCTS's very first SCHOOL SPIRIT WEEK!
A festivity designed for students to express their school pride and celebrate CCTS."

School SPIRIT WEEK...
(Start date) - (End date)
5 days to celebrate:
☺ **you,**
☺ **your accomplishments and**
☺ **your school**

20 seconds   Male V/O
Blinking blue screen/ white writing

"School Spirit Week begins (insert date) and ends (insert date).
The grade with the most participants wins a free lunch of choice.
Five days for all students to participate.
Five days of fun.
Five days to celebrate you, your accomplishments and your school."

Let's Go CCTS!!

20 seconds   Male V/O
Small blue corner screen – blinking

"Go down in CCTS history.
The first CCTS school spirit week.
Let's go CCTS.
Let's celebrate!"

"Visit – C-C-T-S.com"
(superimpose: CCTS.com)

10. People who work for radio and television stations are usually pressed for time. Do not drop in on them unannounced. Phone first to make an appointment.

11. When writing for radio, use simple, descriptive words that form pictures, give dimension and add color. Radio reaches only the ear. The listener must be able to sketch in his or her own mind (imagine) the picture you are trying to create. When writing for television, allow the pictures to tell the story. Depending on the situation, some narration may have to be more detailed than others. Every production is unique.

12. Make sure all spot announcements (public service announcements) are accurately timed. Ten-second spots usually contain 25 words; 30-second-spots contain about 75 words; 60-second spots usually contain 150 words (PR Play 10-6).

13. Submit all program copy and ideas to the program director or station manager as far in advance as possible. Ten days is not too soon.

14. Be on time for a live program or recording session. The clock waits for no one. Arriving an hour in advance may not be too early. Most stations have a "green room." (The author believes, "If you are not early, you are late.")

15. When preparing for a live broadcast or recording session, accept instructions for proper microphone technique – distance from microphone, voice projection and how to avoid extraneous noises (paper rustling, chair squeaking, etc.) during the production. For video, suggestions will be made about proper attire (colors, styles, jewelry, etc.).

16. After the production has been broadcast, send a letter (or email) to the station expressing appreciation for its help. This practice will strengthen the relationship between your organization and the station and will increase your chances of getting airtime.

17. Your organization should let the station know of any reactions received about the production. Positive written comments (included in a thank-you note) can benefit a station when it applies for its license renewal.

18. News releases for the electronic media should be about one page long, double-spaced. They should be typed (word processed) to fit on one side of an 8 ½ x 11 piece of paper. Sending releases electron-

ically may not be appropriate for some stations. Check with each station to determine how it prefers releases be sent. (Note: News people don't usually look on the back of a sheet of paper.) The copy should be readable and legible. Releases should be mailed (emailed), delivered, electronically transmitted or faxed (some still accept faxes) one week prior to the event. This gives the editor ample time to plan. (The same holds true for a *media advisory* or an *invitation to cover*. See Chapters 5 – Basic Strategic (Persuasive) Writing Techniques – and 9 – Media Relations.)

19. And remember, you are trying to *relate* your image, not *sell* it. This, after all, is public relations – not advertising.

Ten Tips for the Use of Television by Public Relations Practitioners

Though production costs are higher in television, it still offers great potential as a communication vehicle for many organizations and corporations. TV is more than radio with pictures, but many of the suggestions for the use of radio can be applied when working in the visual media. Consider these 10 tips for the use of TV by an organization, firm or business:

1. Be simple. Messages can be highlighted and the best camera work done when backgrounds are plain, participants are few and movement is minimal. Quick or sudden movements can be distracting and may draw the viewers' attention away from the focal point.

2. Check with the program or public affairs director on the use of video and pictures and even films that can help communicate your message. (Many stations would prefer shooting their own video – using a format compatible with their equipment.)

3. Make sure the text (copy) written to accompany visual aids fits. In other words, if a video or film runs 30 seconds, the text should contain about 60 words. A one-minute video should contain about 125 words of text.

4. Keep in mind that pictures (JPEG) should be transported electronically or emailed, making for easier integration into programming. Older photographs should be scanned, stored and electronically sent or transported.

5. Provide one photo, illustration or other visual, for each 10-second spot; two for a 20-second spot and so on.

6. When discussing such statistical topics as budgets or surveys, use charts. Be sure they are large enough to be easily read. Use vivid colors on bar graphs and pie charts. Do not use line graphs.

7. If you are providing props, take them with you after the "shoot" or live program. Otherwise, they may be discarded.

8. When your representatives go on the air, they will want to look and sound their best. TV personnel will give participants helpful suggestions and appreciate cooperation in return. During the appearance, the director and floor managers will need additional cooperation. They may find it necessary to give hand signals during the show to control the speed of the presentation. Your representatives should ask the director any questions about the show before the show goes on the air.

9. Participants should not worry about the role they are playing. They are appearing on the program not as an actor or actress, but rather as an interesting person, representing your firm or organization.

10. For both TV and radio, be on time. In producing a TV program, many things must be accomplished in a short period of time and every minute is important.

Once productions are complete, and letters of appreciation sent to TV and radio stations, your organization should go a step further. A good starting point for a continuing relationship (*relationship [management] marketing*) with local radio and TV stations is to ask them to consider your personnel as experts in your particular geographic area. The radio and TV exposure could be worth thousands of dollars (known as *ad value*) if the time had to be paid for. It is also excellent silent publicity.

You might suggest to the media they check your website for a current list of experts or mail them updated personnel sketches several times a year. Be sure to keep your website current. Few things are as irritating as outdated information that appears to be current. It could also prove to be embarrassing, not only for the media using the information, but also for you. After all, you did provide it.

Writing for Broadcast Media – and Other Video
When writing for radio, television or non-broadcast video, the text or scripts must be tailored to listeners or viewers who might not be paying full attention (passive listeners or viewers). Bearing that in mind, refer back to

Chapter 5 – for news release writing style – noting the differences between print and broadcast writing. PR Play 10-11 contains some general suggestions from Nicholas George, former ABC Radio News managing editor.

Cross Platforming – Media Convergence – Collaborative Media

Much more on television techniques, preparation and training comes later in this chapter. But TV is just one component, vehicle or platform used in cross platforming – the *convergence of distribution*. As mentioned earlier, specifically, *cross platforming* and *media collaboration* include mainstream and alternative media - print, radio, television, Internet (and Interactive – blogs, Twitter®), iPod®, (Podcasts, etc.), Vcasts®, cell phone, iPhone®, tablets, digital signage, aroma marketing, WOMM (word of mouth marketing) and silent publicity.

Cross platforming is the transfer of information into different media. Adrian Miles is a lecturer in Cinema and New Media in the School of Applied Communication at RMIT University, Melbourne, Australia. During an interview with the Australian Broadcasting Corporation (ABC), Miles said that when crafting strategic messages, strategic communicators and others must keep in mind the various media and media outlets that will use the content and anticipate how that content will be received.

Newspapers and magazines now send their reporters on interviews with camera in tow (smartphone) – still and/or video – so the interview can be downloaded to the Web and stills can be used both in the newspaper itself and on the website. Using the same content for different outcomes saves time and resources – reasons why more and more media organizations are choosing to cross platform.

Many newspapers, and radio and television stations consider the website to be an interactive extension of their primary purpose – print, radio or TV. The *Courier-Post* (Camden, N.J.) and many other newspapers have "new media" (digital) editors who are responsible for their Web extension. KYW Newsradio (Philadelphia) has a director of digital news and media.

According to ABC, in terms of television's future, all employees, no matter the role, need to know how digital media affects them and how content can be repackaged as "new media and digital services" filters into the other divisions or components.

Says Miles: "Employees in traditional occupations such as producing, researching and operating have to rethink the way they approach their work and digital media's effect on it. Employees within the script department, for example, need to collaborate with employees in the new media (digital) department to consider how content will work on the website, an aspect they did not have to previously consider."

Podcasts and Podcasting for Communicators

Diane Holtzman, public relations/advertising instructor at Rowan (N.J.) University and Richard Stockton College of New Jersey and a long time PR practitioner, specializes in podcasting. She says podcasts offer communicators a new way of reaching their audiences – by using audio files instead of text to send messages. *Podcasts* are self-styled audio productions recorded in digital format and downloaded to computers, iPods® or other digital music players. *Podcasting* is a method of publishing sound files to the Internet, allowing users to subscribe to a feed and receive new audio files automatically.

"Podcast" is a combination of the words "broadcast" and "iPod®" and was voted word of the year in 2005 by the *New Oxford American Dictionary*. The derivation of the word gives us clues as to its use. A podcast is an audio form of content that consumers can download from an organization's website and listen to on computers or upload the information from computers to iPods®, MP3 players or cell phones.

Another definition of podcasting by Watlington (2006) states that a podcast is a multimedia file that may contribute sound, visual, and textual information, distributed over the Web via syndication feeds. In technical jargon, a podcast is an RSS (Really Simple Syndication) news feed but one that contains an MP3 or audio file within the enclosure tag. It brings all the advantages of RSS distribution, including syndication and ease of access, to audio content. No matter which definition is used, according to VNU Business Publications (2006), the podcast gives the listener control over *what* they hear and *when* they hear it.

A podcast can cover any topic that would be enhanced by offering live voices presenting information on a subject. Many companies, organizations and media outlets offer downloadable podcasts.

Television and radio stations, limited to the constraints of time, use podcasts (or vcasts) to offer additional video and audio content online. Nearly all TV newscasts – network and local – provide vcasts of major stories. One example can be seen at the *CNN* podcasting site www.cnn.com/services/podcasting, which presents updated news clips of the stories being covered by the news network.

KYW Newsradio (Philadelphia), *1010-WINS* (New York) and *KFWB News 980* (Los Angeles) rely on podcasts even though they are "All news. All the time." – 24/7. They, like many other radio stations – music, talk, all news, etc. – supplement their programming (podcasts) in an audio format that consumers can upload from the website to their iPods® or MP3® players, which allows the consumers to take the news or other programs to work with them.

Sharing updated news is one way podcasting aids communicators. Another is the way companies and organizations are using podcasts to communicate with consumers in their brand marketing.

For example, GM® was innovative in offering a podcasting program in the style of talk radio – the show is described as "FastLane Radio" and presents 12-minute podcasts of telephone interviews with various GM® personnel throughout the company to discuss the latest innovations in the GM® family throughout the world. One example of a GM® podcast can be heard at http://fastlane.gmblogs.com/podcast/solstice_interview.mp3 which features an interview/conversation with the Director of Design for Small and Mid-Size Vehicles about the development of the Pontiac Solstice® car – including discussion on its features, why it might appeal to people and how the car will further develop in the future.

According to a July 14, 2006, posting in *PodWorkx*, podcasting is a marketer's dream. According to the posting, there are 10 reasons to podcast:
1. Provides an additional communication tool for your business.
2. Offers increased online contact with your target market.
3. Increases Internet visibility from the search engines.
4. Increases Internet visibility and traffic from the RSS, blog and podcasting directories.
5. Provides a communication medium that is more powerful than text. This means increased potential results for your marketing message.
6. Improves the level of perceived expertise from your target market.

7. Offers "value added" components of presenting your product that can only be done through audio format.
8. Increases mind share from your target audience. People listen to podcasts while doing other tasks online. They can also take your messaging with them on their portable media player such as an iPod®.
9. Provides more frequent touch points and more frequent "top of mind" participation from your target audience.
10. Increases consumers' perception of your product, service, brand or value in the mind of the customers.

Also presented in the *PodWorkx* July 14, 2006, posting, podcasts can be used in the various strategic communication disciplines as presented below:

Public Relations: Audio press releases, messages from company executives, expert interviews and other industry-related material, all delivered directly to the media.

Direct Marketing: Sales letters and other vehicles from "ad creative," delivered in audio and directly to your prospects.

Customer Relationship Management and User Support: Personal messages and greetings from company executives, personalized messages to key clients by key account managers, educational content and industry interviews, seminar or conference recordings, product support information and tutorials.

Promotion: Achieving additional company/brand/product exposure by providing podcasts and promoting them via podcast directories and search engines.

E-commerce: Audio product announcements and presentations, delivered to prospects that opt-in to receive the latest product information. In the case of audio products, podcasts can also carry short excerpts or previews of new editions, thus enticing prospects to order.

Branding and Prospect Conversion: Educational content and industry interviews that help shorten the sales cycle or generate/improve company credibility and enhance its brand.

In addition, podcasting is used in delivering lectures on college campuses, political messages to stakeholders, corporate newsletters to stakeholders and consumers – both news about products/services or for training.

According to Angelo Fernando in an article in *Communication World*, communicators need to stay on the forefront of the incorporation of newer technologies into the marketplace. When Apple® entered the cell phone market, it marked the arrival of the wireless iPod® and the iPod® incorporated into cell phones.

Says Professor Holtzman: As strategic communicators we gather, create, package and distribute information. What warrants watching is how podcasting is poised to become a whole new territory of communication, and how other media are forced to adapt with this revival of radio. Podcasting moves radio into the narrowcasting age – thus allowing customizing the message to narrower segments – fragments – of an audience. We need to consider how using podcasts enters into our communication and marketing mix. For more information about the available tools for podcast users and creators, visit www.podcasting-tools.com

Info Snacking

Mainstream media no longer have broad-based appeal. Audiences, across all demographics, are more passionate and opinion-based. They rely on narrowcasting – opinions that validate their own. Many younger news consumers, who use the Internet as their primary source for news, want that news in "chunks." Yahoo!® refers to it as info snacking – "consumers reading a piece or part of a piece and then following link after link – known as tagging – (until they are satisfied)."

In broadcast, "chunks" are known as "bites." Either way, they are designed for the 30-second reader, listener or viewer. Yahoo® and its proponents believe that by "chunking" pieces into multiple (usually two to four) shorter segments they give the consumer a much richer experience.

Info snacking is just one more tactical approach to keep in mind when developing a strategic plan. Do not shy away from the question, how will the target audience (end user) receive the message? Info snackers, e-readers and e-papers are not the future. They are the here and now.

The Video News Release

A video news release (VNR) can be an expensive but effective vehicle to assist in getting your message on TV. According to *The ABCs of Strategic Communication* – AuthorHouse, a VNR is a broadcast version of a news release – a video program produced to promote or publicize a product, service or viewpoint. VNRs are designed to resemble the same style as traditional television news reports (packages or wraps). Their purpose is to educate, inform and influence (if necessary).

VNRs usually include a packaged news story – approximately 90 seconds (some packages may run longer) – ready for on-air use and ample B-roll (background or scenery "footage") to allow producers to edit and create their own stories – also called pieces. News directors and producers who use VNRs say they fill in the gaps in news coverage.

Effective VNRs are timely, newsworthy, have a local connection or can be localized, are excellent quality, contain powerful visuals, and include B-roll, real people, extra voice cuts and sound bites, names and titles, and a script.

To the novice, a VNR can be compared to a "package" or "wrap" on a TV news program. Whether it be network or local newscasts, every program carries "packages." A *package* is usually an anchor introducing a reporter who might be providing a live or recorded lead in (stand-up – known as *fronting the story*) to a piece that includes bites of interviews (the face and voice of a newsmaker), B-roll (scenery shots) with the reporter's voice over the video, a few seconds of the reporter on camera (known as a bridge), back to a bite or more B-roll and finally the sign off, also known as a lock-out. The entire package usually runs from one minute to two and a half minutes (longer on some magazine programs). Producers say 90 seconds would be ideal.

Local stations may carry it in total or in part and some networks have been known to carry portions of VNRs on their evening newscasts. It is quite an accomplishment for a public relations staff to get a VNR on a network news program. But generally, the smaller the station, the better the chance the VNR will be carried unedited.

A well-produced VNR should contain more than just the "package." That's because many local stations have multiple newscasts throughout the day and need material to fill the time, especially on "light" news days. That's where the extra materials come in – extra video of the newsmaker (sound bites), extra video or scenes of the area (B-roll), titles of the reporter and newsmakers that can be superimposed on the screen and in some instances, an anchor-type person introducing the *package*. On a separate track on the video, the narrator (in this case, your reporter) may record an entire "voice-over" narration.

It is also suggested the VNR open with printed instructions that can be seen on the screen. The instructions should also be included as hard copy (printed on paper) or emailed along with a copy of the script so both may be reviewed prior to the news director clicking the computer mouse or popping the VNR in the DVD player. Stations should be surveyed to determine which video (electronic/digital) format is preferred.

VNRs can cost anywhere from a few thousand dollars to more than $50,000 to produce. And there are additional fees for distribution. The least expensive method is the DVD, followed by uploading to the computer for electronic transport, followed by YouTube®, fiber optic transport and finally via satellite. It is not unusual for a firm to charge $5,000 to uplink a VNR on a satellite. In all cases, television stations must be made aware of how the VNR will get from you to them. If it is by satellite, let the station know so it can "lift it off" or downlink it.

Because of the expense, it is important to determine whether the video release will be used. If stations don't "buy" into your pitch, VNRs are not a very sound investment.

In the case of video news releases relating to new product launches, TV stations must weigh the value of the news against giving the time for free. Television stations must wrestle with just how biased the presentation might be and whether to identify the "package" when it runs as "provided by XYZ Company." You might suggest, for ethical reasons, that stations disclaim that the VNR or part of its content has been provided.

According to A.C. Nielsen, health and medical releases are the most frequently used VNRs. Business stories rank second, followed by political news, fashion and lifestyle, and sports.

In Philadelphia, for example, a top five TV market, it has become commonplace for two of the major network affiliates to carry VNRs provided by "Consumer's Report" and "Good Housekeeping."

TV news directors and news producers now face the same dilemma that print editors have faced since Ivy Lee hand delivered his first typewritten release in the early 1900s – whether to use and how to attribute material gleaned from VNRs. Does the VNR contain news value or is the station giving away free publicity through free air time?

When new tamper-proof packaging for Tylenol and when such products as Celebrex (arthritic relief drug) or Viagra (male potency drug) were launched, the pharmaceutical manufacturers produced effective VNRs. How far a station goes in identifying a manufacturer and showing its logo is a decision that rests with individual stations.

Often, newspapers use quotes from printed releases without mentioning the source. In other cases, newspapers attribute the quotes to a company statement. Many major newspapers make the determination on a case-by-case basis. TV stations now must do the same.

Getting Your Video News Release on TV

A number of recommendations have been made by news directors and producers over the years to help strategic communicators get their VNRs aired. Among them are:

- **Timely** – VNRs cannot become outdated too quickly. While they don't have to be evergreens, they do need a moderate shelf life.

- **Newsworthy** – Not necessarily spot or "hot" news (a breaking story, but wouldn't that be nice), but certainly it should be of current interest and relevant.

- **Local "hook"** – Sometimes difficult to accomplish. Using an earlier example, tamperproof caps of medicine bottles or safety devices on hedge trimmers are subjects that are local almost anywhere. The video should show how the subject affects the average viewer.

- **Sexy** – In the news sense, the topic should be a grabber with a hook – something to pique the "gatekeeper's" attention. News people refer to those topics as "sexy" because your message should be excitingly appealing as it relates your organization's image. It is a common newsroom term.

- **Excellent quality** – Programming sent to commercial TV stations must meet the same professional standards as programs produced by those stations or networks.

- **Visuals** – Television is a visual medium. The video and graphics should be interesting and eye-catching.

PR Play 10-13
For The On-Camera Interview

DO	DON'T
• Use first names	• Let the topic/subject drift
• Speak to the interviewer and not to the camera	• Assume anything
• Stand up for your rights	• Be afraid to take a compliment (but keep your guard up)
• Deliver your message early	• Consider the interviewer a friend – or an enemy
• Be prepared from the time you leave your office/home	• Gossip, criticize or speculate
• Couch your position as necessary (avoid specifics)	• Use YES and NO answers
• Speak only the truth; be ready with facts	• Put the interviewer on defensive without good cause
• Be aware of and sensitive to time	• Forget the importance of body language
• Know what the interviewer wants	• Speak too fast or too slow
• Be big enough to learn from your mistakes	• Go into any situation without preparation
• Thank the interviewer and crew for their time	• Be too hard on yourself
	• Ever say "NO COMMENT"
	• Ask for a copy of the final interview

PR Play 10-14
In Front of the Camera

Unless you are an expert in front of the camera, DO NOT look directly into the camera. Look at the interviewer or if the interviewer is remote, pick a spot that is slightly off-camera.

If there is a TV monitor within view, ask that it be removed out of view. If that cannot be done, DO NOT look at the monitor at all.

If you must look into the lens of the camera, pretend that the person who you most want to convince is behind that lens. If that makes you uncomfortable, then pretend that your mother, best friend, daughter or son, or anyone else you feel comfortable with is behind that lens.

- **Real people** – Those newsmakers you are providing as "bites" or "talking heads" must relate to the viewer. In other words, the company spokesperson who is telling the story should be a "real person."

- **Commercialism** – Avoid it. Your VNR is not a commercial because you are not paying to have it aired. Limit corporate identification to the *silent publicity* that will be communicated through the message.

- **Brief** – Keep the wrap or package to 90 seconds.

- **"B-roll"** – Include extra "B" (background) roll.

- **Extra cuts** – Include extra sound bites (voice cuts or actualities with identification).

- **Names and titles** – Include super-imposed names and titles. To avoid errors, in addition to listing each name and title on separate "frames," consider including a brief still shot – with identification – on the video. This will assure the proper name goes under the newsmaker it is intended for, especially if your VNR contains more than one male or female newsmaker. Many times, stations will use their own logotype or typeface to superimpose names and titles under a sound bite so that it appears that they have actually conducted the interview and it is their "tape."

- **Script** – Include hard copy of the package's script and other contents. This will greatly assist the news producer with editing and preparation, especially if the station chooses to carry the package on one program and the story as a "wild" on another.

- **Experienced professionals** – For the very best results, hire proven professionals to assist with the production and distribution. While it might appear expensive on the surface, their experience in this area will probably be cost effective.

- **Truth** – Above all, tell the truth. It is your production, so "gatekeepers" fully accept that the contents will be subjective and one-sided. However, it is still your obligation to be factual, provide attribution and to use disclaimers if any of the video is a simulation and not an actual portrayal (see PR Play 10-13).

The First Step

Experts suggest answering three questions before proceeding with a *VNR*: What is the purpose; what strategic message are you trying to communicate; and through which vehicle? Once it has been decided the *video news release* is the vehicle, what's next?

- Determine your **goal.** What do you want to communicate to the audience?

- Once you determine the goal, write down exactly what you want to say to reach the goal (**message**).

- Gather your thoughts leading to your goal. You might want to use focus groups to assure you are developing background information and facts.

- Focus panel members might serve to provide the types of questions needed to help you reach your goal.

- As you write down the supporting points that will lead to your goal, continually refine the facts to short sentences.

Any one or more of the following angles could help you reach your goal as a script is being written (each has its own hook):
- controversy
- conflict
- competition
- consequence
- familiar people
- humor
- heartstrings/emotion
- problems
- progress
- success
- unknown
- unusual
- wants/needs

Tips for Talking to the Electronic Media

Chances are Chris Matthews, Bill O'Reilly, Jimmy Kimmel or Oprah Winfrey will never interview you or a representative of your firm. But whether it is an interview by a network correspondent, local radio talk show host or a cable local access reporter, a number of suggestions are recommended (*Media training* begins on page 351):

1. Be prepared.

2. Anticipate sensitive questions.

3. Be open and honest.

4. Never say "NO COMMENT."

5. Try to avoid OFF THE RECORD statements. The operative word is try. (Chapter 9).

6. Think before you speak.

7. Never lose your temper.

8. Don't let a reporter put words in your mouth.

9. Don't use jargon.

10. Emphasize the benefits of your project by pointing out its features.

11. When dealing with television:

    a) Talk in "sound bites" (10- to 20-second responses).

    b) Think visually.

    c) Dress conservatively.

    - Wear suits or dresses of soft, medium colors (although women may wear bright, solid colors – see page 349). Avoid sharply contrasting patterns and colors. Men should consider wearing blue dress shirts although, thanks to technology, white is acceptable. Solid or striped ties are preferred.

    - Jewelry should be simple and uncluttered. Pearls and dull-finished metals reflect less light than sparkling and highly polished jewelry.

    - Don't worry about glasses. The studio crew will arrange lighting to avoid glare.

    - The program's director or floor manager will discuss makeup. Pancake makeup is advisable for men with heavy beards. Women should avoid heavy makeup or overuse of lipstick (see page 349).

    d) Be natural.

    e) Forget about the camera (it will follow you).

Looking Your Best on Television – Women

According to the National Women's Business Center, Washington, D.C., and the Pond Group, Indianapolis, Ind., there are a few guidelines that will help you put your best foot forward and ensure that the viewing audience focuses on your message and not on your pocket scarf! Knowing how to look good on camera is as much know-how as good looks. On a television newscast, the most effective look is professional and contemporary. People are far more likely to believe you are important when you look important.

Clothing – What should I wear?

• Women look best on camera in bright, solid colors. Choose rich colors such as a royal or deep navy blue, hunter or kelly green, deep purple, chestnut brown or maroon.

• Women should choose smart, tailored, business-like attire like suits, dresses and pantsuits. Be a professional!

• Women should avoid red, white, ivory and light pastel colors in dresses, jackets and suits. These colors, however, are fine for blouses (under a jacket), ties and scarves. Hint: If you have a few days' notice, watch what female TV news anchors wear.

• Both women and men should avoid small, busy patterns, such as small plaids, tiny checks, mini-stripes and paisley patterns.

• Women should not wear any shiny fabrics.

• Women should not wear overpowering scarves or other accessories.

• Women should avoid wearing large amounts or large dangling pieces of shiny jewelry, including necklaces, earrings and pins. (Unless, of course, you're the jewelry designer!) Choose dull finished jewelry or pearls instead.

Hair and Makeup Tips

• Whether female or male, if offered the services of a makeup professional at a studio, take them up on it. Professionals understand how to make any skin type look good through a camera's eye.

• Women should wear their makeup as they normally would for every day. Avoid overdoing it!

• Brush on some loose powder to help eliminate shine.

- Choose a long-wearing matte lipstick.

- Even if you normally don't wear makeup, powder and lipstick will help you avoid looking "washed out" by the bright lights.

- Women should consider a hairstyle that emphasizes their face and doesn't hide it. On the air, your hair should look smooth and sleek. Mid-length styles tend to look best. Very short hair makes you look too bare and long hair looks too cluttered. Keep your hair in a contemporary style and update it at least every three years. Classic hair, with some new angles, looks fresh. Avoid anything too extreme.

Looking Your Best on Television – Men

- Most men look best in dark jackets – black, charcoal and navy. When you contrast a deep jacket with a crisp, white or light blue shirt and a handsome, bright tie, the clothes contrast with one another and skin coloring so you appear crisp and professional. A deep khaki suit in spring, with a light blue shirt, looks great for most men. Patterned jackets or suits that are heavily textured do not work well on camera. For the most part, stick with solids. Focus groups still prefer white and light blue shirts over gray, ecru or patterned colored shirts and matching ties. It may sound boring, but a dark jacket, a white or vivid blue shirt and a bright tie are what viewers, news directors and general managers prefer.

- Men should wear professionally laundered, standard straight collars. Avoid button-downs which always look wrinkled on camera – unless well-laundered. Avoid turtlenecks, cowl sweaters or any style that comes up high on the neck. Both men and women should wear clothes that fit. Any extra fabric translates into excess weight on camera.

- Men, as well as women, look better in makeup. Good coverage that matches your skin tone is a must. An oil-absorbing powder is essential to eliminate any shine. Contouring helps nearly all men and women photograph better. Don't hesitate to ask TV station personnel for advice.

- Men's ties are a man's most important accessory and noticed first. The trend in ties is more diplomatic, small, neat, repetitive patterned or handsome solids. Choose red rather than maroon, or a bright gold rather than a soft yellow. The brighter and more clear or highly contrasted the tie (like navy, white and red), the better it will photograph.

Media Training

Television interview techniques and general interview techniques require training. A complete course follows. While all of it won't be absorbed, even by the best executives or potential newsmakers, it offers an excellent foundation as they become more involved with the media.

It is imperative that everyone involved knows the difference between *media training* and a *media interview rehearsal*. *Media training* is providing coaching to individuals specifically targeted to dealing with the news media. Participants are taught guidelines, strategies and skills to work effectively with media – electronic *and* print – for public relations purposes. Those techniques are below.

Media interview rehearsals are specific to the interview or news event – news conference, editorial board meeting, one-on-one interview, etc. Generally, a rehearsal is a session of exercise, drill or practice, usually private, in preparation for a public performance, ceremony, etc. *Media interview rehearsals* are walkthroughs practiced at the site or venue (if possible) – in the room or venue – of the interview or news event to help reduce or eliminate surprises. Specific questions are raised with suggested responses – practiced to sound as though they are being delivered naturally.

To prepare for a media interview, first you must perform an *audience analysis*. Media coach Maria McCabe (Veritas Communication – www.veritascommunication.net) suggests:
* Identify your audience.
* Analyze your audience demographically.
* How well does your audience understand the issues (or topics) you wish to discuss?
* What is your audience's attitude toward your agenda?
* What does your audience need to know or believe in before you can change its behavior? (What's in it for them?)
* To what type of arguments is your audience likely to respond?

Establish *interview goals*:
* What outcomes do you want from your *target* audience as a result of your *strategic* message?
* What outcomes do you want to prevent (if any) from your *target* audience?

- What points or arguments are your opponents or competitors likely to make?

Think *sound bite*:
- Short and sweet
- Visual
- Simple
- Compelling

Avoid the Media Traps
- Stay calm and composed.
- Stay on message.
- Don't provide answers that could have a negative impact on your reputation or your organization's reputation.
- Don't be caught off-guard by questioning that you want to declare off-limits.
- Listen carefully to the reporter's choice of words and don't repeat the negatives.
- Don't be tempted to speculate or engage in hypothetical thinking.
- Don't feel obligated to fill a silence.
- Don't allow yourself to be drawn into disparaging your competition.
- *Listen* carefully to each question to better determine the reporter's agenda in asking it.
- Correct inaccurate perceptions and facts.

Media Training Techniques

1. **Know the facts – don't guess**
   There is no such thing as a pleasant surprise on television. Get the latest information available on the subject before the interview.

2. **Rehearse your message**
   Know what you are going to say, and equally important, know how you are going to say it. Don't over-rehearse and lose spontaneity.

3. **Say it in 20 seconds or less**
   Remember, your time within a TV news story is very valuable and very limited. Economize to maximize.

4. **Help set the "ground rules"**
   Journalists need help getting the story. Assist them with background, locations for good visuals and find out exactly what the story is to be about.

5. Answer questions – stay alert – listen

Listen to your interviewer. Don't start formulating the answer to a question that is not being asked.

6. Prepare for the worst – do your homework

Don't hope that maybe the journalist won't ask *that* question. Assume that he or she will and prepare for the worst case.

7. Admit mistakes

No one will fault you for being honest and forthright. But follow the admission with how you have corrected the situation. Place the mistake in its proper perspective.

8. Relate to the viewer, not the interviewer

Think about how the viewer will receive your information – not how the interviewer posed the question. Talk directly to the journalist, not the viewer at home. The camera will provide the subjective angles.

9. Strive for informality

Remove the stiffness from your presentation and let the warmth of your personality come through.

10. Humanize yourself

The audience will relate to a real human being, no matter what the subject matter.

11. Think like the reporters think

What kind of story are *they* after? How will *they* most likely tell it? How can you present it in the best possible context?

12. Know journalists' language

Use their language. Don't say "film" when all that is being used today is video. You may be asked for a "sound bite" which is a few comments. "Cutaways" are visuals that support your story – possibly "B" roll.

13. Be politely persistent, but don't get angry

Try to always finish your statement without being constantly interrupted. Smile, be patient and allow your overall grasp of the situation to come through. Remember, you will always know more about the story than the reporter.

PR Play 10-15
Friedman's Bill of Rights

Former WPVI-TV (Philadelphia) reporter Karen Friedman is now a media coach. Here is Friedman's Bill of Rights:

1. You have the right to *tell* your side of the story.
2. You have the right *not* to answer questions.
3. You have the right to *correct* someone who is putting words in your mouth.
4. You have the right to *share* your credentials, so it is clear you are the expert.
5. You have the right to *take* time to prepare.
6. You have the right to *ask* questions.
7. You have the right to *decline* to talk.
8. You have the right to *explain* your point of view.
9. You have the right to be *human*.
10. You have the right to make a mistake and *correct* it.

Karen Friedman Enterprises – Blue Bell, Pa. –
www.karenfriedman.com

---

14. Localize your story

If there is a national story that the media is airing locally, give them the local significance of that story. Many times, your efforts will be either better than the national average, or at least have a positive impact on local citizens.

15. Lean forward slightly – positive body language

Don't lean back, don't swivel and don't fidget. Look interested and professionally aggressive in your body language.

16. Tell it like it is – look at the interviewer

Candid responses, when thought out, and presented in a professional, warm manner directly to the reporter are most effective. The interviewer is your audience. The person in command of the interview is you.

17. Stick to the subject – don't gamble

Don't open other situations unnecessarily. Answer the questions with enough information to get your side of the story told.

---

18. Dress for the occasion

Conservative dress and a professional image go a long way on television. Solid color jackets and blue shirts preferred. No plaids or distracting patterns.

19. Almost never go "off the record"

The rule of thumb is, "if you don't have an outstanding working relationship with a reporter and a true understanding of what 'off the record' means, don't go 'off the record.'" It has often been said, "If you don't want to see it on the evening news, don't say it." (See Chapter 9)

20. Keep it on a one-on-one basis

The interview is with one person in the audience, through the interviewer. Keep it personal and direct.

21. Never say "no comment"

No matter what anyone says about your right to silence, it is not golden in the media, and a no-comment is generally perceived as a "guilty" plea. At the very least, tell the reporter that you are not at liberty to discuss it. Try not to use the word comment, at all. (See "Sandy Hook" in Chapter 14.)

22. Maintain solid eye contact

Don't look to heaven for guidance before answering. Remember, your facial language tells more about you than what you are actually saying.

23. Avoid arguments and hostility

It is impossible to win an argument with a person who has the editing equipment. The old adage, "Never argue with a person who buys ink by the barrel" is very appropriate.

24. Provide advance biographical and background data

If time permits, provide the correspondent with information on you as well as the story. Things that he may not know, that would flesh out the story for the interviewer and make a better and more objective story.

25. Be direct and friendly

The directness of your words in those 20 seconds must be balanced by the friendliness of your delivery.

26. Don't fold your arms

Avoid body language that is defensive. Don't look down. Most interviewers prefer you look at them when responding. The camera will follow you.

27. Don't clench your fists

Remember, the camera can isolate on the various ways that you release tension. Poise yourself before the interview. Then relax and enjoy.

28. Don't squint at the lights

Give yourself enough time in the studio before the interview to adjust to the set and the lighting.

29. Suggest talking points before the interview

Again, help set the agenda. You know the story, the reporter only knows what he or she has been told – often, not very much. Help them to help you tell the story.

30. Always have at least two themes going into each interview

Know what the interview is about and have two positive themes that relate to the subject – and get those themes out front.

31. Anticipate questions to be asked

If you have done your homework on the subject, you should be able to anticipate areas of tough questions within the story and answer them in the best possible light. Work with a media pro and tape your responses to questions in a mock session.

32. Know the reporter

Watch a different channel or news program every night. Get to know the reporters' styles. Know their beats – politics, education, business, etc.

33. Develop a single sentence/catchy phrase to make a point

Audiences have a difficult time remembering comments by interviewees, and you can help make the interview memorable by coming up with a catchy sentence.

34. Never guess and never, ever, lie

Having to retract or alter your comments is awkward and damaging. Your comments on tape are the essence of your reputation.

35. Advance work – do it

It may seem like extra work to have your staff assist you in preparing for the worst, but it is worth the effort.

36. Arrive early for questions and pre-talk interview (warm-up) with the reporter

Pre-talk about the other stories that the reporter has done (if known) and establish a rapport with him. Establish yourself as a professional in your field early, before the interview begins.

37. Edit yourself as you speak

Be concise, correct and conversational. Don't ramble.

38. Practice talking about 125 words per minute

Any faster and the audience will lose you – any slower and you will sound dull or overly cautious to the audience.

39. Use reporter's name in an interview

Use sparingly, but use it in front of the statement that you want to get on the air. It is a "point of sale" technique that we all use at the time we want that person to take notice of what we are going to say.

40. Practice the art of bridging

Bridging is being able to move from a topic you do not want to deal with to one that you do.

41. The inconsistency trap

Avoid spending a great deal of time on questions that ask you old data. ("That was 10 years ago…we have to look at today.")

42. Be prepared

Preparation and practice are the key elements. Winging it will not do. *Preparation is the key.*

43. Prepare yourself mentally before the interview

Much like an athlete, you must be physically and mentally prepared for the television interview. This may require relaxation exercises and the mental exercise of answering questions in your mind.

44. Above all – be yourself

Audiences are inundated with TV news magazines and are more sophisticated than ever. They can usually detect when someone is making an appearance to promote a personal or business interest. Audiences prefer watching someone who is being herself – not someone whose sole purpose is to impress. Remember – be observant, concise and ready to deliver short, sharp statements.

EXERCISES

PR Challenge 10-1

Using broadcast writing techniques learned from both Chapters 5 and 10, write a 30-second PSA using the information below. Your PSA should follow one of the two suggested formats illustrated in this chapter.

WHAT: Gov. S. William Kramer will lead state, county and local officials in a groundbreaking ceremony for the new Cherry Hill Public Library.

Other dignitaries include:
* New Jersey Secretary of State Linda Alexander
* New Jersey Community Affairs Commissioner Mark Marmur
* Cherry Hill Mayor Arianna Stefanoni
* Dr. Stephen C. Barbell, president of the Cherry Hill Library Board of Trustees
* State legislators, Camden County freeholders, township council members and representatives from community organizations

WHEN: Sunday, Dec. 15, 2013
11:30 a.m.

WHERE: Next to current Cherry Hill Library
1100 Kings Highway North

PR Challenge 10-2

Your CEO has asked that you lead a media training session. Prepare an agenda for a full-day media training and media rehearsal workshop for your organization's top executives.

CHAPTER 11
What Public Relations Practitioners and Other Strategic Communicators Should Know About Advertising

What does advertising have to do with *public relations*? Plenty. To achieve *synergy*, the advertising and public relations campaigns for a product, service or issue must complement each other in such a way as to make each other more effective.

At larger corporations and institutions, advertising departments or staffs are commonplace. But such is not always the case at "non-profits." That makes it imperative for public relations practitioners to have at least a cursory knowledge of *advertising*. Many times, at "non-profits" and smaller organizations, the responsibility of researching and placing advertising falls to the public relations practitioner. In fact, many carry the title, director of strategic planning and evaluation. They are strategic communicators.

What's the Difference?
Advertising is paid, (non-personal) communication from an identified sponsor using (mass) media to persuade or influence an audience. The operative word – *paid*. Because advertisements are paid for, the firm or organization paying the bill has *control* over the message and the time or location of placement. Direct marketing using regular and email has made advertising "personal."

Public relations, on the other hand, is *un*controlled because there is no direct payment for the placement of news releases or other information – sometimes referred to as *publicity*. Practiced properly, *public relations* is two-way communication. *Advertising* is almost always one-way.

No matter the organization or company – it is a *brand*. Ultimately, it is the firm's reputation. *Branding* is everything the public thinks of when it hears the organization or company's name. Public relations drives the brand. Advertising sustains it. Both approaches should be consistent. For any organization or firm to prosper it must continually seek new business opportunities, sell additional services to existing clients, and relate its image to its many publics.

Both public relations and advertising must be included in a company or organization's *integrated marketing communication (IMC)* – collaborative media – program. For an organization to experience *synergy* though, its IMC should include more. Because *synergy* "is the whole being greater than the sum of its parts," some other ingredients in the marketing mix could include sales promotion, direct-response marketing, personal selling and packaging (the last opportunity to persuade the consumer to "buy" your product).

PR Play 11-1
Synergy

The whole is greater than the sum of its parts...
or
Each part makes the other more effective.

PR Play 11-2
Ad Exposure

While there is no consensus, experts estimate that the average person is exposed to 1,500 to 3,500 ads and commercials each day and upwards of 25,000 in a given week.

While the strategic communicator does not have to be an expert in advertising, it is important to know and understand the major types and the mechanisms or techniques used. PR practitioners must know that print media deal in *space* and broadcast media in *time*.

PR Play 11-3
Marketing Mix...[or Mix Marketing]

- Advertising
- Sales Promotion*
- Public Relations*
- Direct-Response Marketing
- Cause-Related Marketing [Positive Association]
- Sponsorship (Partnering) Marketing
- Positioning* (Place)
- Personal Selling* (Face-to-Face)
- Price* (Pricing strategies [Play 11-19])
- Product* itself
- Packaging*
- Policy*
- Politics* (Interaction of people/brain storming/sometimes controversial)
- MindShare – Intellectual Property (Staff members sharing information/brain storming)
- Brand Identity (a product or service's reputation)
- Interactive (Communication flow in all directions and use of the Web)

* Litwin's 9 P's of Marketing

The 11 Basic Types of Advertising:

- **Brand** – Also known as *national consumer advertising*. It focuses on the development of long-term brand identity and image.
- **Retail** – Also known as *local advertising*. It focuses on a store – bricks and mortar or online – where a variety of products can be purchased or where a service is offered. Many times, prices are included in the ads. It tries to create a distinctive image for the store.
- **Directory** – People refer to it to find out how to buy a product or service – advertisers are usually listed alphabetically (e.g., Yellow Pages advertising; online classifieds and other directories – Craig's List; Angie's List).
- **Direct-Response** – Can use any medium to try to stimulate a direct sale. The advertisement usually calls for an immediate response with the product being delivered directly to the consumer's residence or place of business. If purchased online it is called "mouse to house."

PR Play 11-4
IMC Definitions

[For a glossary of more than 8,000 terms, tips and techniques, see *The ABCs of Strategic Communication* – AuthorHouse]

1. **Public Relations** – A [two-way] strategic communication process [management and counseling function] that builds and maintains mutually beneficial relationships between organizations and their publics – through an understanding of audience attitudes, opinions and values. It is planned and deliberate. Public Relations/Strategic Communication succeeds when it fills three key roles – as an organizational conscience (chief integrity officer), as an overseer of the corporate brand and/or reputation, and as a manager of relationships with internal and external audiences.

2. **Advertising** – Paid, (non-personal) communication, from an identified source (sponsor), using (mass) media, to persuade or influence an audience. Using direct mail and the Internet has allowed advertising to be *"personal"* – 1-to-1 (*addressable advertising*).

3. **Brand** – A name, sign, symbol or design, or some combination of these, used to identify a product and to differentiate it from competitors' products. A brand is a product from a known source (manufacturer, product or service).

4. **Branding** – The process of establishing the elements of a brand, including its name, identifying symbols and related marketing messages. The promise to customers.

5. **Marketing** – a) The matching of a product or service to the needs of consumers as discovered through research to determine attitudes, opinions and behavior. b) Business activities that direct the exchange of goods and services between producers and consumers. Also, strategies that employ the various elements of the marketing mix to achieve marketing objectives – traditionally, this is taken to include the original "4P's" – Product, Place, Price and Promotion. **"Product"** refers to market requirements and ensuring that those requirements are seen in the products and/or services offered by the company. appropriate prices for the products/services. **"Place"** is determining the best geographic areas to sell in – taking into account the competition (positioning) and also the best "channels" for distributing to those markets. **"Price"** is determining and setting the most appropriate prices for the products/services. **"Promotion"** refers to all activities involved in making potential customers aware of the company, its products and services and their features and how those features benefit the consumers and encourage them to buy the product or service.

cont.

PR Play 11-4 continued

6. **Marketing Mix** – A plan that identifies the most effective combination of promotional activities. (Sometimes referred to as *Integrated Marketing Communication – IMC.*). It is a blend of designing, pricing, distributing and communicating about the product or service. The goal is to achieve *synergy.*

7. **Public Service Announcement** – A type of public relations communication that deals with public welfare issues and is typically run free of charge. The media once provided time and space free. Now with competition keen for so-called available space and time, non-profits have been forced to turn to corporations to help underwrite the costs.

8. **Publicity** – Information supplied to a news medium without cost.

"Items you want to get into a newspaper and are willing to pay for are called advertising. Items you don't want in a paper are free and are called news."

- **Business-to-Business** – Messages directed at retailers, wholesalers and distributors, as well as industrial purchasers and such professionals as physicians and lawyers.

- **Corporate** – Messages used to enhance the image or identity of an entire corporation (i.e., Kellogg's® which would include many of its individual cereal brands; Campbell Soup Company®, which would include many of its brands in the same advertisement – condensed soups, chunky soups®, V8®, SpaghettiOs®, Prego®, Pepperidge Farm®, Swanson® etc.). This type of advertising is also used to communicate a particular point of view that a corporation has about an issue or cause, or to put a face on the corporation for those who may not be familiar with its multiple brands.

- **Institutional (Product)** – Messages used to enhance a product rather than a brand or corporation (i.e., "pork, the other white meat." Some other products might be milk, beef and the "institution" of New Jersey farms, which refers to itself as *Jersey Fresh®.*) The other definition of *Institutional* would be for such entities as museums, hospitals and educational institutions so long as they are *non*-profit.

- **Recruitment** – Display or broadcast messages used to recruit new employees. The U.S. Army and Navy use recruitment advertising as do colleges and schools trying to attract new students. Businesses

---

PR Play 11-5
Steeplechase (Tower) Ad

Ad that runs vertically up one side of a printed or Web page.

PR Play 11-6
Banner Ad

One or two inch-high ad that runs horizontally across (or partially across) the top of a newspaper or Web page.

PR Play 11-7
11 Major Types of Advertising

- Brand*
- Retail (Local)*
- Directory*
- Direct Response*
- Business-to-Business*
- Corporate
- Institutional (Product)*
- Recruitment
- Political*
- Issue (Advocacy)
- Public Service (Charity/Non-profit)*

*Among original eight basic types of advertising

PR Play 11-8
Strip Ad/Footer Ad

One or two inch-high ad that runs horizontally across the bottom of a printed or Web page (front page of *Courier-Post* or *USA Today*).

---

using the classifieds as their vehicle are using *recruitment* advertising.

- **Political** – Using advertising to persuade people to vote for politicians. Political advertising's requirements are different from all other types (see page 380).
- **Issue (Advocacy)** – A message aimed at bringing about legislative change. Many of the guidelines for *political advertising* may be applied.
- **Public Service** – Used to communicate a message on behalf of a cause or non-profit organization. The media once provided time and space free. Now, with competition keen for so-called available space and time, non-profits have been forced to turn to corporate dollars to help underwrite the costs.

The 26 Major Advertising Mechanisms or Techniques

Companies appeal to consumers in many different *mechanisms* or *techniques* to persuade them to buy their products or services. The *mechanisms* or *techniques* carry the basic *types* of advertising:

- **Co-op** – A form of advertising in which a national manufacturer reimburses the retailer for part or all of the retailer's entire advertising expenditures for ads carrying the manufacturer's brand(s).
- **Per Inquiry** – A technique in which the advertiser pays for the time or space based on the number of bona fide inquiries made about the product or service being advertised. (Pay-per-click would fall under Per Inquiry. 800 and other toll free numbers used on direct response radio and TV ads and on some *direct-response* cards are a possible indication of a *per inquiry*.)
- **Tie-in** – Two (usually related) brands/products advertised together. The intent is the incentive that the purchase of one will inspire the purchase of the other (e.g., a discount coupon for a jar of peanut butter inside the cap of a jar of jelly). Many times the brands/products complement each other.
- **Piggyback** – Two or more (not necessarily related) advertisers combine their resources to purchase large blocks of space or time which they divide among themselves. By "piggybacking" their resources, they should save money (e.g., Four advertisers purchase a full newspaper page at the full-page rate. Each runs a quarter page ad. Dividing the full-page rate by four saves money over the cost of each advertiser buying a quarter of a page individually).
- **Competitor** – Messages that compare brands, stores or service companies. This type of advertising must be based on fact.
- **Product Placement (Embedded Ads/Advertainment)** – Advertisers pay to place their product brands or service in a motion picture, on a television program, as a "cheater" in video games or in a print article.
- **Product Integration** – Takes *product placement* to the next level – when a brand becomes inextricably identified with the content of a motion picture, television or live (Broadway) show. The brand (name) is written into the script (and spoken). Company marketers hope viewers and/or listeners make a subtle association between shows they like and their products – and that might form your behavior the next time you're thirsting for a beverage or contemplating a new ride. That's why network and movie executives use words such as "natural" and "organic" when they talk about *product integration* and scripted TV — adjectives more

often associated with high-end environmentally friendly groceries. They don't want it to be so blatantly obvious that it overwhelms the programming (*vampire creativity*). But they don't want you to miss it, either.

- **Silent Publicity** – (The best of PR tools other than *word of mouth*) Product or service company's logos appear free (many times – passively – in news stories).
- **Advertorial** – Print ads that resemble editorial copy or newspaper stories. They should be labeled as paid advertisements. (See page 370)
- **Infomercial** – Television or radio programs that sell a product, brand or service. Normal broadcast commercials run 30 seconds or a minute. Infomercials may run anywhere from five minutes to one hour.
- **Endorsement** –A message containing a statement by a well-known individual in a commercial or advertisement that encourages people to buy the product brand or service. These third party endorsers need not have used the product or service. If they have, their *endorsement* becomes a *testimonial.*
- **Testimonial** – A message in which a person talks about his or her personal use of a product, brand or service. (The key is – personal experience with the product or service.)
- **Informational** – A message that contains a great deal of information (pharmaceutical ads). Many times, *advertorials* are *informational ads.*
- **Partnering (Partnership)/Affinity Marketing** – Advertising in which numerous (usually unrelated) advertisers combine their resources in one ad to promote an event or an issue. (e.g., Philadelphia's Fourth of July celebration "Welcome America!" The logos of more than two-dozen advertisers are included in newspaper, outdoor and electronic ads. Unlike *piggyback* where ads are separate, in *partnering,* logos and other identification share the same space – co-mingled.) Sometimes known as *sponsorship marketing.*
- **Cause-Related (Positive Association) Marketing** – Corporate sponsorship of such fundraising events as golf tournaments (e.g., signs on tees or greens on a golf course). Many times, *partnering* is *cause-related.* Also called *sponsorship marketing.*
- **Co-authoring** – Two brands sharing the same TV commercial sell their products – either related or unrelated. (e.g., Maytag repairmen riding around in a Chevrolet; A young man puts money in a vending machine to purchase a Pepsi and out come keys to a Mercedes Benz, which is then shown on the screen.) View this link: http://www.youtube.com/watch?feature=player_embedded&v=EvFul32xKCs

- **Co-branding** – An ad or commercial for one product that has two distinct brand names (e.g., Kellogg's® Rice Krispies®; McDonald's® Big Mac®; Burger King® Whopper®.)
- **Interactive** – Delivered to individual consumers who have access to a computer and the Internet. Advertisements are delivered via Web pages, banner ads, pop ups, talking cutaways (superstitials), etc. Computer "click ads" and print "scratch and sniff" ads are *interactive.*
- **Scent or Aroma Marketing** – The subliminal use of scent or smell to suggest the purchase of a product. ("Got Milk" ads in bus shelters in San Francisco infused the scent of freshly baked chocolate chip cookies (using adhesive scent strips within walking distance of a bakery. Years ago, movie theatres learned that popping popcorn near the auditorium's doors would increase sales of popcorn along with Coca-Cola®.)
- **Virtual** –Technique used by television. Banners or billboards electronically appear on the screen. Viewers at home see the ads while spectators inside the sports venue do not. Virtual ads can actually cover a billboard that has been erected inside a sports stadium or arena. (The yellow first-down line and direction arrows on football fields use the same technology to help entertain home audiences by making it easier to follow the game.)
- **Specialty** – Advertising that uses such promotional items as pens, cups, balloons, matchbooks, etc. to carry their logo and/or message. They are company giveaways. (www.adspecialtiesinc.com)
- **Street Marketing** – Distribution of free samples on city streets or in supermarkets and other type stores. When food samples are offered in stores, the intent is similar to *direct response* – to stimulate a direct sale. Often used in product launches. (see *flash mob* in *The ABCs of Strategic Communication* – AuthorHouse.)

PR Play 11-9
An Example of
Corporate Advertising

- **Viral Marketing** – An advertising and/or marketing technique that spreads the strategic message like a virus. The message gets passed on from (so-called) "consumer" to consumer and market to market by

PR Play 11-10
Selling Premises

Copy Strategy – Sales logic behind an advertising message.

Creative Platform – A document that outlines the message strategy decision behind an individual ad, commercial or an entire campaign. It is based on the *creative brief* (page 378).

- **Product-centered strategies** – Ads that focus on the product itself. Should be based on fact. Often a scientifically conducted test or other research technique provides support for a claim.
  - **Claim** – A statement about the product's performance – its *features or attributes*.
  - **Brag and Boast** – An advertising strategic message written from a company's point of view to extol its virtues and accomplishments. If a claim is made, it must be supported by fact.

- **Prospect-centered strategies** – Ads that focus on needs and wants rather than on what the company can produce.
  - **Benefits** – Statements about what the product can do for the user.
  - **Promise** – A benefit statement that looks to the future.
  - **Reason Why** – A statement that explains why the feature will benefit the user.
  - **Unique Selling Proposition (USP)** – A benefit statement about a feature that is both unique to the product and important to the user.

PR Play 11-11
Co-op Advertising

A form of advertising where a national manufacturer reimburses the retailer for part of or all of the retailer's entire advertising expenditures for ads carrying the manufacturer's brand(s).

people hired to use the most effective advertising or public relations tactic – word of mouth. The ethics of *viral marketing* are in question because the person spreading the message usually does not reveal he or she is being paid. (A growing number of brands, including those owned by Proctor and Gamble®, are among the manufacturers who

PR Play 11-12
26 Major Advertising Mechanisms or Techniques

- Co-op
- Per Inquiry
- Tie-in
- Piggyback
- Competitor
- Product Placement (Embedded/Advertisement)
- Product Integration
- Silent Publicity
- Advertorial
- Infomercial
- Endorsement
- Testimonial
- Informational
- Partnering (Partnership)/ Affinity Marketing/ Sponsorship Marketing)
- Cause-Related (Positive Association/Sponsorship Marketing) Marketing
- Co-authoring
- Co-branding
- Interactive
- Scent/Aroma Marketing
- Virtual
- Specialty
- Street Marketing
- Viral Marketing (Word of Mouth – WOMM)
- E-viral Marketing – E-WOMM (Word of Mouse Marketing or Mouse to Mouse)
- Promotainment
- House

PR Play 11-13
Back End Marketing

Ads or other messages printed on the back side of shorts or pants to draw attention. Whether the vehicle is a bikini or sweat pants, the message must be brief – a few words or just a logo. Also called a *butt print.*

have employed *viral marketing.*) If email is the tactic used to spread the message, it is called **word of mouse marketing**.

- **Promotainment** – Commercials produced specifically for theatres scheduled to run before the feature film – either prior to or during the previews.
- **House** – Sometimes referred to as promos. They are ads promoting the vehicle in which they are contained (print), heard on (radio) or on which they are viewed (TV).

Public relations practitioner, Susan Hardy Brooks of Tuttle, Ok., challenges today's professionals to learn as much as possible about the advertising and marketing changes that affect them.

PR Play 11-14
Advertorial – Example

Advertisement

Stress No More – Find Lost Files in a Flash

FAIRFIELD, Iowa – Find lost files on a flash would be a more appropriate headline. Burwyn Associates has developed a USB device smaller than the average thumb that holds five terabytes or 5,000 gigabytes (GB) of memory – many times greater than the average hard drive and infinitely larger than what had been the highest capacity flash drive.

Burwyn calls it "The Master Key," because you carry it on your key chain. Reasonably priced at $49.95, "The Master Key" eliminates the stress of lost files. And you can't misplace it. An embedded code can be accessed from your cell phone or smartphone. Dial the code and hear "The Master Key" beep.

To order "The Master Key" or for more information, call 555-555-1212 or visit www.themasterkey.info.

PR Play 11-15
Alternative Media – More Than Ever Before

- Radio
- Television
- Internet (and Interactive – Web 2.0/Blogs/Wikis/Twitter®)
- iPod® (Podcasts, etc.)
- Vcasts®
- Cell Phone/Smartphone
- iPhone®/Droid
- Digital Signage
- Aroma (Scent) Marketing
- WOMM (Viral)
- Convergence of Distribution
  - Cross Platforming
  - Print
  - Digital Signage
  - Wireless/Tablets
  - Broadband (Web 2.0)
  - TV

PR Play 11-16
The Effects of Advertising on the Web

Ask yourself these questions:

- *How intrusive are online ads?* Will the ad lead users to not return to the site hosting the ad?

- *Are some forms of online ads more intrusive than others?* Will it make a difference if the ads are not related to the subject matter of the site?

- *Will online ads interfere with users' ability to remember site content?* Which types or techniques of ads most interfere?

Scott McCoy – Assistant Professor – College of William and Mary – Williamsburg, Va.

PR Play 11-17
"Fish where the fishes are"

Whether advertising or public relations, a key is delivering the message to the target audience at a time it is paying attention (aperture). Otherwise, it is "wasted coverage." Think *MAC Triad Plus*.

Advertisers have more choices than ever before to communicate their message to their target audience through a particular channel (making use of the *MAC Triad Plus*). Depending on the purpose for the ads, speed may be a necessity. Thanks to technology, that should not be a problem. Brooks, like others involved in both advertising and public relations, stresses the importance of keeping messages simple.

Why Advertise?

A major purpose of public relations is to *relate* an image. Advertising's purpose is to *sell* it. Most times advertising will cost more than many of the other components of the marketing mix. So – why spend that money? Here are just a few reasons:

- To enhance an image
- To increase consumer awareness
- To increase sales traffic and sales
- To move excess inventory
- To increase goodwill/community involvement
- To reach your customers at home, at work and in their cars
- Because if you don't, your competition will!!!

These are the advertising spending prjections for 2016:

eMarketer Digital Intelligence projects total U.S. advertising spending to reach $196.7 billion by 2016 thanks in no small part to the rapid rise of digital advertising, national elections, Summer and Winter Olympics and brands' continued confidence in television advertising despite increasingly fragmented viewership. Other projections range from slightly below eMarketer to nearly $215 billion by Pricewaterhouse Coopers.

Broken down, 2016 projections show: $72 billion on all forms of TV – network, local and cable; $19.2 billion on radio – network and local;

```
┌─────────────────────────────────────────────────────────┐
│                                                           │
│                     PR Play 11-18                         │
│              Know the Product Life Cycle                  │
│                                                           │
│   A concept which draws an analogy between the span of a human │
│   life and that of a product, brand or retail store (outlet) suggesting │
│   that, typically, a product's life consists of a sequence of five stages: │
│   • Introductory – Product/brand is born and introduced (launched). │
│   • Growth – Demand develops for the product and/or brand. │
│   • Maturity – Product/brand gathers "steam" as it ages. │
│   • Decline – Competition or other factors have a negative effect on │
│     demand and bite into market share.                    │
│   • Withdrawal – Product/brand (or retail store) dies or goes out of │
│     business.                                             │
│                                                           │
│   The concept is used as a tool to form marketing strategies appropri- │
│   ate to each of the stages. Also, the history of a product from its │
│   introduction to its eventual decline and withdrawal.    │
│                                                           │
└─────────────────────────────────────────────────────────┘
```

$21.5 billion on local and national newspapers (including both display and classified [$17 billion] and online [$4.5]); $62 billion for online (digital [up from $32 billion in 2011 and only $1.7 billion in 2000]); $15.4 billion for print magazines; $6.6 billion for digital ad spending at magazines; $8.7 billion for outdoor; and $5.2 billion for directory advertising.

Philadelphia advertising executive Steve Schulman takes a reverse approach to educating communicators about the importance and effectiveness of advertising. He offers *How to Kill Business in 10 Easy Steps:*

1. **DON'T ADVERTISE.** Just pretend everybody knows what you have to offer.
2. **DON'T ADVERTISE.** Tell yourself you just don't have the time to spend thinking about promoting your business.
3. **DON'T ADVERTISE.** Just assume everyone knows what you sell.
4. **DON'T ADVERTISE.** Convince yourself that you've been in business so long customers automatically come to you.
5. **DON'T ADVERTISE.** Forget that you have competition trying to attract your customers away from you.
6. **DON'T ADVERTISE.** Forget that there are new potential customers who would do business with you if they were urged to do so.

PR Play 11-19
Pricing Strategies

Customary or Traditional – A single, well-known price for a long period of time. Movie theaters and candy manufacturers employ this pricing strategy in the hope that the customer will become less sensitive to price. It's the price that consumers expect to pay for a certain product.

Odd – Strategy of having prices that end in an odd number, as in $5.95, $19.99; sometimes referred to as odd-even pricing.

Line – All products sell for same price. For example, Southwest® Airlines charges the same for all seats on a flight – unlike other airlines.

Psychological – Strategy intended to manipulate the customer's judgment process. Two common forms of psychological pricing are odd pricing ($9.97) and *Prestige Pricing*. There are also psychological price breaks such as – $9.99; $19.99; $24.99; $99.95; etc.

Price lining – The strategy of pricing different products in a product line at various price points, depending on size and features, to make them affordable to a wider range of customers – good, better, best. (Sears® has been using price lining for years. State Farm® Insurance has implemented this strategy.) Also, targeting a specific market segment based on price – a retailer who practices price lining only carries goods that sell within a defined price range.

Prestige or Image – A strategy where prices are set at a high level, recognizing that lower prices might inhibit sales rather than encourage them and that buyers will associate a high price for the product with superior quality – certain cars, appliances and clothing brands (see Play 11-20).

Value – A strategy where the selling price of a good or service is based on the company's assessment of the highest value of the product to the consumer – what the consumer is willing to pay for it – what the market will bear. Many times, it is predicated on supply and demand.

7. **DON'T ADVERTISE.** Tell yourself that it costs too much to advertise and that you don't get enough out of it.
8. **DON'T ADVERTISE.** Overlook the fact that advertising is an investment – not an expense.
9. **DON'T ADVERTISE.** Be sure not to provide an adequate advertising budget for your business.
10. **DON'T ADVERTISE.** Forget that you have to keep reminding your establishment (customers/clients) that you appreciate their business.

PR Play 11-20
For the Advertising Skeptic

Why Is It? (a/k/a The Advertising Poem)
A man wakes up after sleeping
under an advertised blanket,
on an advertised mattress,
pulls off advertised pajamas,
bathes in an advertised shower,
shaves with an advertised razor,
brushes his teeth with advertised toothpaste,
washes with advertised soap,
puts on advertised clothes,
drinks a cup of advertised coffee,
drives to work in an advertised car,
and then, refuses to advertise,
believing it doesn't pay.
Later when business is poor,
he advertises it for sale.
Why is it?

Advertising vs. Public Relations

Again, advertising is *paid* and therefore *controlled*. Public relations is *unpaid placement* and therefore *uncontrolled*. Research is clear, public relations is more credible – although credibility can't accurately be measured – and more believable. For IMC to be successful, public relations must support and complement an advertising campaign. In fact, *Television Week* has reported that public relations "drives sales."

PR Play 11-21
Examples of Prestige Pricing

Example #1 – Philadelphia area hair stylist Barry Leonard, known as "Barry The Crimper" charged more because his clients were willing to pay for the privilege of going to his salon for his expertise. Long before Leonard cut hair from the heads of Marilyn Monroe, Richard Nixon, Diana Ross and many others, he developed a reputation for "being the best." He says it was he who convinced the Beach Boys to go blonde while styling their hair in the '60s.

Example #2 – Personal Shopper: Be a Sexy Little Thing

Victoria's Secret gives new meaning to V-Day with its Sexy Little Things beauty collection.

Add a little spice to the lovers' holiday with a spritz of Sexy Little Things eau de parfum for $39. Prep that pucker with Just Kiss Me! glossy lip balm in Sexy Bomb and Little Devil for $12 each.

Dust on Love Me, Sexy Blush for $18 or get all-over glow with Give Me the Shimmers Body Powder for $28. Bejewel your bod with Adore Me, Adorn Me Body Bling for $7.

Get these goodies at Victoria's Secret stores. Buy them for yourself or that special someone.

Julie Haverman – *Courier-Post* – Feb. 1, 2007

Mark Weiner in *Unleashing the Power of PR: A Contrarian's Guide to Marketing and Communication* (Jossey-Bass) cites one market segment (Miller Brewing Company) study that compares advertising to public relations. "Trade (industry) advertising delivers roughly $2.20 for every dollar ($1.00) spent, and TV advertising delivers $1.06. Public relations, by contrast, delivers $8, the best of any marketing agent tested."

Ries and Ries, in their book, *The Fall of Advertising & The Rise of PR* (New York: Harper Collins) stress that advertising is the "self-serving" voice of a company anxious to make a sale. Brands need public relations as a brand-building tool to maintain credibility with target audiences.

Now that we have examined advertising's *Basic Types, Mechanisms and Techniques*, here is a summary of Ries and Ries' main points:

PR Play 11-22
Political Ads – Deception is Legal

Here's a fact that may surprise you: candidates have a legal right to lie to voters just about as much as they want.

That comes as a shock to many voters. After all, *consumers* have been protected for decades from false ads for commercial products.

The *First Amendment* to the US Constitution says, "Congress shall make no law...abridging the freedom of speech," and that applies to candidates for office especially. And secondly, in the few states that have tried laws against false political ads, they haven't been very effective.

According to the Annenberg Public Policy Center of the University of Pennsylvania and FactCheck.org, laws protecting consumers from false advertising of products are enforced pretty vigorously. For example, the Federal Trade Commission (FTC) took action in 2002 to protect the public from the self-proclaimed psychic "Miss Cleo," whom the FTC said promised free readings over the phone and then socked her gullible clients with enormous telephone charges. The FTC even forced a toy company some years ago to stop running ads showing its "Bouncin' Kid Ballerina Kid" doll standing alone and twirling gracefully without human assistance, which the FTC said was video falsehoods used "to arouse interest, excitement or amusement."

- Advertising seldom works (alone) as a brand-building tool
- Ideally, credible brands are established through PR and then maintained through advertising
- Most advertising focuses on being creative, not effective, and is seldom noticed by the consumer
- Clients love creative advertising because it makes them think they are doing something edgy when in fact most are simply wasting their time and money

Advertising Research
By conducting research (Chapter 4), the target *audience(s)* will be identified and matched with the proper *message(s)*, *channel(s)* and best time to reach them to deliver the message. The research should reveal the composite of the audiences – demographics, psychographics and geodemographics.

PR Play 11-23
Federal Communications Act

(US Code: Title 47, Sec. 315. - Candidates for public office)

"...there's *no* such truth-in-advertising law governing federal candidates. They can legally lie about almost anything they want. In fact, the *Federal Communications Act* even *requires* broadcasters who run candidate ads to show them uncensored, even if the broadcasters believe their content to be offensive or false."

PR Play 11-24
Equal Time

. . . If any licensee shall permit any person who is a legally qualified candidate for any public office to use a broadcasting station, he shall afford equal opportunities to all other such candidates for that office in the use of such broadcasting station: Provided, That (sic) such licensee shall have no power of censorship over the material broadcast under the provisions of this section.

Demographics are the vital statistics about the human population, its distribution and its characteristics. Examples include gender, age, education, occupation, income, family size, etc.

Psychographics are all the psychological variables that combine to shape our inner selves, including: activities, interests, attitudes, opinions, personality traits, needs, values, decision processes and buying behavior. Properly executed, research will reveal the targeted audience's sensitive measures of motivation and behavior, lifestyles and preferences for products, services and entertainment – based on self-evaluations.

*Geo*demographics is a contraction of *geography* and *demographics.* They are the demographics of individuals or groups who reside in the same geographic area. Specifically, according to Middlesex (London) University Business Research Services, geodemographics is the analysis of information about people's locations and how this information can be put to use in marketing, human resource development, resource planning, service delivery and other areas of business.

PR Play 11-25
The Creative Brief
A framework for developing and evaluating marketing materials

Just as the *situation analysis* is used as the primary reach "template" or tool prior to developing a comprehensive public relations plan the *creative brief* – sometimes called a *client needs analysis* – is the tool used to gather and evaluate information on internal and external environments and to assess a brand's strengths, weaknesses, opportunities and threats (SWOT), and to guide its goals and objectives. It sets the table for ad planners and marketing directors by detailing necessary information acquired through scientific and anecdotal research.

According to Sanestorm Marketing (Columbus, Ohio), the Creative Brief is a planning tool widely used by advertising agencies and marketing personnel when designing or implementing a marketing program. It can be used when creating communications directed at clients, employees, shareholders, potential investors, the media or any other target group.

The Creative Brief is a cooperative tool by which the various people and groups involved in a project focus their thoughts and analyze the best method(s) of approaching a program. When used properly it can also reduce the time and cost associated with marketing projects, as it requires all the key participants to agree on important factors at the onset of the project.

Many organizations and agencies have a very refined, occasionally bizarre, possibly even copyrighted *Creative Brief* tool that is specific to how they do business. Most, though, have a few important elements in common:

- **Objective:** What is to be accomplished by this program? Is the goal to create awareness, knowledge, preference, or purchase? One traditional tool used for this purpose is the definition of **SMART** objectives: Specific, Measurable, Agreed Upon, Realistic, and Time-based.
- **Primary audience:** Whom is this campaign meant to reach? The more specific and detailed the better. When possible, list details like title(s) of audience members, industry, size of company, revenue, number of employees, geographic details, affiliations, key behavior attributes (i.e., do they make the buying decision or influence it?).Demographics and psychographics go here.   cont.

PR Play 11-25 continued

- **Attitudes/Beliefs/Objections of audience:** Another way to state this element is: "Why hasn't the audience already done/thought what you want them to?" If you were hired to argue against the purpose of this campaign, what would your points be? What is the status quo?
- **Current/Proposed behavior:** What is the audience doing now? How are they thinking/dealing with the situation about which you are addressing them? What do you want them to do differently?
- **Call-to-action:** What do you want the audience to do/think? Again, the more specific the better. One of the 10 Commandments of good advertising is: tell the audience what you want them to do. If you don't know, don't advertise until you do. Examples of good calls-to-action include: "Call today"; "Visit our Web site for more information"; "Complete and return this form."
- **Tone:** Should this be a friendly, relaxed message, or a hard-sell with a sense of urgency? Should the audience feel like a confidant, pal, victim (in need of rescuing), partner, controller, etc.? Should the ad convey a rich, textured impression or something more Spartan and utilitarian?
- **Key message:** What is the one thought that the audience should be left with (take-away message)? The initial level of regard given to most print advertisements has been measured at between one and two seconds. If you absolutely had to, how would you state your message in seven words or less?
- **Secondary message(s):** If the advertisement does draw in a reader, what are the other one or two points that should be conveyed? Another advertising commandment: people never remember more than three things.

Creative Brief/Client Needs Analysis

Project name:_____

Version: _____Date: _____

Participants: _____

_____

_____

cont.

PR Play 11-25 continued

Objective(s): _____

_____

Time Frame: _____

Primary Audience Demographic: _____

Primary Audience Beliefs:_____

Current Behavior: _____

Desired Behavior: _____

Call to Action: _____

Tone: _____

Key message:_____

_____

Secondary message(s): _____

_____

Approval requirements at stages:

Brief   Concept(s)   Drafts   Finals

_____   _____   _____   _____

_____   _____   _____   _____

_____   _____   _____   _____

_____   _____   _____   _____

Types of Advertising of "Special Interest" to Public Relations Practitioners

Issue Advocacy Ads – These ads try to influence public perceptions of proposals being debated in Congress or state legislatures, often by putting public pressure on lawmakers. Like political ads that aim to defeat or elect a candidate, for the most part, issue ads are not regulated. Sponsors are neither subject to spending limits, nor must they disclose sources of funding.

Political Advertising – The purpose of *political ads* is to persuade people to vote for a candidate, or in some cases, an issue. While the Federal Trade Commission and Federal Communications Commission view *political ads* liberally when it comes to "truth in advertising" and "deceptive" practices, there are certain guidelines that must be followed:

- Political advertising does not have to adhere to truth in advertising as other types of ads do. They may use deception and misleading information (PR Play 11-21).
- If a printed piece is mailed, the name and address of the candidate or representative must be on the ad.
- All printed pieces, brochures, fliers, and newspaper and magazine ads must indicate who is paying for them.
- Radio commercials must contain the candidate's voice and television commercials must show the candidate's face (even a still shot). They must also state who is paying for the commercial.
- Candidates for federal office must disclaim their radio and television ad – either at the beginning or end – stating their name and saying "I approve this message." On TV, they must be shown saying it.
- Generally, both print and electronic media charge the lowest rate on a rate card for a section or page in the newspaper or magazine, or "day part" in radio or TV. (Congress is considering legislation related to political pricing charged by TV stations.)
- As a safety precaution, most media outlets require that payment is made at the time ads are placed.

Purchasing Media Space and Time

Public relations practitioners experienced in the counseling, writing and researching aspects of their profession might want to consider outside help if they embark on an advertising campaign. Many practitioners should be able to handle the creative functions of advertising. And while hiring an advertising agency may be financially out of the question, it might be prudent to investigate a media consultant before purchasing the ad space or time.

Buying media is foreign to many in the profession. Even the most astute advertising executives admit that buying advertising has become a specialty. For example, one must be knowledgeable about such terms as:

- **Exclusive audiences** – Estimated number of people in a market who listen to one and only one radio station during a particular daypart or read just one newspaper.
- **ROP (Run of Paper)** – The placement of advertising at the discretion of the newspaper instead of the advertiser.
- **ROS (Run of Schedule)** – The purchase of spots by an advertiser for which the broadcast station selects the time. ROS spots or commercials always cost less than spots designated for a particular daypart. Also called *floating time* and *run of station*.
- **Daypart** – Any of the time segments of a broadcast day for which listening or viewing estimates are calculated and recognized in the industry. Television dayparts are usually early morning, daytime, evening, primetime, late night and overnight. Radio dayparts are morning drive, mid day, afternoon drive, evening and overnight (Chapter 10).
- **Contract Rate** – A discounted rate given to an advertiser upon the purchase of a specific number of ads or spots in a given time period.
- **Open Rates** – Also called *one-time rate*. The basic cost for a single advertisement: one that does not earn a frequency discount. Also called a *basic rate*.
- **CUME** – An abbreviation for *cumulative audience*. An estimate of the number of different television households or radio listeners who view or listen at least once during the average week for five minutes or more during the reported time. This is an unduplicated audience.
- **Cost Per Thousand (CPM)** – The cost to reach 1,000 television viewers, radio listeners, newspaper or magazine readers or direct mail households.
- **Sworn Statements** – Statements filed by newspapers and magazines certifying their circulation.
- **Mechanical (Camera ready copy)** – A final layout of photographs, copy, proofs, and so on, ready for a newspaper or magazine.

PR Play 11-26
Advertising Vehicles

While no one knows for certain, it is estimated that the average person is exposed to as many as 25,000 ads and commercials a week. Below is a lengthy but partial list of vehicles that carry ads. If you know of one that is not listed, please email larry@larrylitwin.com. It will be posted on the larrylitwin.com blog link.

Address books
Adopt-a-highway
Ads in fortune cookies
Airline seatbacks
Airplane pulling ad
Airplane writer
Airport baggage belts
Airports
Aprons
Arena advertising (scoreboards, etc.)
Ash trays
Auto skins
Backs of cereal boxes
Bags (sports; designer; make-up)
Balloons
Bank deposit bags
Banks (toys)
Banners/pennants
Barf bags on planes
Barns (signs painted on)
Barrettes
Basketball backboards
Basketball court
Bathroom stalls (inside door)
Bathroom urinals
Batting gloves
Beach balls
Beach chairs
Beach towels
Beach umbrellas
Bibs
Big erasers
Bike helmets
Bill inserts
Billboards
Billfolds

Binders/Notebooks
Blankets
Blimps
Bluetooth [those wearing hear
    commercials when on hold]
Boats
Bobblehead dolls
Body painting
Book covers/school
Book marks
Book matches
Bottle caps
Bottle openers
Boxing ring (center of it)
Boxing ring (posts)
Brand names on products
Bridges
Brochures and publications
Bumper stickers
Bus shelters
Bus wraps (skins)
Business cards
Buttons
Cabs – Smart signs (LCDs) on roof
Cabs (interior on backs of seats)
Cafeteria trays
Calculators
Calendars
Candles
Candy
Caps and jackets
Car dealer stickers (on backs of cars)
Car mats
Car tires (brand name in white letters)
Car wraps (skins)
Casino chips
Catalogues

cont.

PR Play 11-26 continued

CD giveaways
Ceilings
Chair backs
Chair cushions
Channel One (at schools)
Checks
Chip bag clips
Christmas stockings
Church bulletins
Church-type hand fans
Clipboards
Clock or watch faces
Closed Circuit TV
Clothing
Coasters
Coffee mugs
College course guides
Coloring books
Combs
Comic books
Company cars
Computer disks
Condoms
Consumer guides (ad on back)
Contact lens solution bottles
Contact lenses (Wesley Jessen®
    inscribed)
Convention badges
Conveyor belts at super market
Checkouts
Coupons
Cross promotions
Cue sticks
Dartboards
Decals
Delivery vehicles
Dental floss
Desk sets
Diaries
Digital signage
Direct mail
Doggie blankets
Door-to-door
Dot Whacks/Poppers/Post-it Notes®
    (Front page of newspaper or

magazine cover)
Dry cleaning bags
Dry cleaning hangers
Dumpsters
Earrings
Electronic billboards (on cab roofs)
Electronic mail
Elevators (inside) [Computer video]
Emery boards
Enhanced billboards
Event sponsorships
Exercise bikes
Eyeglass cases
Eyeglass cleaners
Eyeglass frames
Fashion shows
Fast food kids' toys
Fax machines (actual faxes)
Field/Court/Ice ads
Finger nail art
Finish line ribbons
First aid kits
Fishing vests
Flashlights
Fliers
Fly swatters
Folders (manila)
Frisbees
Gasoline stations
    (video screen on pumps)
Gift boxes
Give-aways (free samples)
Glassware
Go karts
Golf balls and tees
Grocery bags
Hair scrunchies
Haircuts (sculptured)
Hangers
Hockey ice
Hot air balloons
Hotel "smart" keys
Ice scrapers
Ice sculptures
In-store or office closed circuit TV   cont.

PR Play 11-26 continued

Internet
Internet cookies
Internet to "Smart Market" movies
  (WOM)
Jar openers
Jewelry (watches, etc.)
Jingles
Jitneys
Kazoos
Key tags
Knives
Labels
Lamp shades
Lamp shades (beer in bars)
Lawn signs
Letter openers
Libraries
License plate frames
Lifting gloves
Lighters
Litter bags
Luggage tags
Magazine wraps
Magazines
Magnets (refrigerators)
Mall directories
Manicure kits
Maps and map cases
Mascots (team)
Matches
Memo pads
Milk cartons
Mints/Candies with logos
Mirrors
Mobile billboards
Money clips
Motorcycles
Mouse pads
Movie theatre (on screen prior to
  movie)
Movie trailers
Mud flaps on trucks
Music CDs
Musical instruments

Napkins
Neon signs
Newspaper plastic bags
Newspapers
Nighttime silhouettes
Notebooks
On computer games (Product
  Placement/Integration)
On rented or purchased videotapes
  (Pre-roll)
Outdoor trashcans
Overpasses (on highways)
Paint mixer sticks
Park benches
Patches for backpacks
Paycheck inserts
Pens and pencils
People in costume
Pet collars
Phone cards
Photo paper
Picture frames (with logo around
  them)
Pillows
Pins
Placemats
Plastic newspaper bags
Playbills
Playing cards
Pocket calendars
Point-Of-Purchase
Poppers/Dot Whacks/Post-it Notes®
Post-it Notes®/Dot Whacks/Poppers
  (Newspaper front page or
  magazine cover)
Postcards
Posters (movies and sports)
Post-it® (sticky notes)
Post-it® attached to front page of
  newspaper
Posts that hold basketball
  backboards
Pot holders
Pre-paid phone cards   cont.

PR Play 11-26 continued

Pre-roll Internet commercials
Prescription pads
Promotainment
Promotional announcements on
    TV shows
Public transit
Race car driver (uniforms)
Race cars
Radio (various demographics)
Rain bonnets
Rain coats
Restaurant placemats
Roof top signs
Rulers
Sales receipts
Sand imprinting (for beachgoers)
Sandwichboards
Seashells
Sewing kits
Shelf talkers (printed and literal)
Shoelaces
Shoes/sneakers
Shopping carts
Shower curtains
Shrubs (topiary)
Ski lifts
Sky writing
Smart signs – on roofs of cabs
Snow globes
Socks
Soda can covers
Soles of Shoes [Boxers]
Special events
Sponges
Sponsors of major sports events,
    concerts, blimps
Sports equipment
Sports schedules
Sports uniforms
Stadium cushions
Stadium seats (seat backs)
Stamps/Stickers
Statues (dolls—Pillsbury Dough Boy)
Stickers

Straws
Street maps with ads
Stress balls
Stress indicators
Stuffed animals (Hush Puppy dog)
Stuffed animal's clothing
Subway underground flashes –
    on walls
Suit bags
Sun shades for cars
Sunglasses
Supermarket checkout dividers
Supermarket/Pharmacy tile floors
    (slotting)
Suspenders
Sweat bands
Swimming pool floats
Swizzle sticks (drink stirrers)
Table billboards (table tents)
Table Tops (Restaurants)
Table clothes
Tape measures
Tattoo ads on eggs
Tattoos (on bodies/fruit/vegetables)
Team sponsorships
Teeth braces
Telemarketing
Telephone on hold
Theatre marquis
Thermometers
Ticket backs
Ticket stubs
Tic-tac containers
Tie-tac
Toiletpaper
Toilets (inside toilet bowl)
Token cups at casinos
Toll booth (video screen)
Tools
Toothbrushes
Towels
Trade shows
Trams

cont.

PR Play 11-26 continued

Transit (taxis)	magazine programs
Trash bags	Wall ad reflections
Truck wraps (skins)	Watchband calendars
T-shirts and other specialty items	Water bottles
TV (Cable)	Water coolers on sidelines
TV (Commercial)	Water towers
TV (Educational)	Web pages
TV (Public)	Welcome mats
TV (Sports)	Whistles
TV (online streaming)	Window signs
Umbrellas	Word-of-mouse (electronic viral
Urinal cakes/screens	marketing)
Urinal talkers	Word-of-mouth (bird-dogging)
Vanity credit cards	Yardsticks
Vending machines	Yearbooks
Videos as P-O-P	Yellow pages
Virtual ads in sports and news	YouTube (pre-roll commercials)

Making the Buy

Here are some reasons why public relations practitioners and others not experienced in media buying should consider a Media Planner and Buyer (MPB).

MPBs:
- provide information gathered through primary and secondary research
- assist with media vehicle selection
- negotiate media prices
- perform post-campaign analysis

MPBs possess such special skills as expert knowledge of media opportunities, media content, audience habits and media trends.

Success Through Research and Experience

Public relations practitioners and other strategic communicators must take a "page" from their marketing and advertising counterparts. All must recognize that a *synergistic* or *integrated marketing communication* approach or campaign is key for the overall success of a program, organization or company.

PR Play 11-27

General Motors Corporation ran this quintessential *Corporate* ad in 1952. From left – counter clockwise – are: Pontiac, Chevrolet, Oldsmobile, Buick, Cadillac.

The effective use of public relations, complemented by a thoroughly researched and well thought out advertising campaign, can help your audience develop trust in your organization – a trust that can lead to them visiting your website, buying your products and becoming loyal and lifetime clients and/or customers.

Be certain to set clear, definable and obtainable objectives that lead to goals. Be realistic. Know as much as you can about your target audience(s) and the size of your market. Ask, "How can I reach them in the most cost efficient way?"

It is important to keep in mind that when targeting Generation Yers (Millennials), you provide them what they want, where they want, when you want and how they want. (See all Generations in *The ABCs of Strategic Communication* – AuthorHouse)

Review the 80/20 (Pareto's Principle – see *The ABCs of Strategic Communication* – AuthorHouse) rule to analyze your efforts – which means (for profit-making firms) that 80 percent of revenues comes from 20 percent of the clients or customers. To be effective and successful, do not fall into the trap of wanting to implement every strategy in "the book." Be selective. Choose only strategies that will work for your company, product or service. How will you know? Successful practitioners know through research and experience.

PR Play 11-28
QR Code

Quick Response (QR) Codes are quirky squares with an intricate black and white design inside. The design is actually a matrix code that stores a large amount of information in a small, square space. When scanned, it quickly and accurately decodes such data as URLs (websites) and text. With the advent of smartphones, iPads®, other tablets and devices using barcode-scanning apps, resourceful marketers (advertisers and other strategic communicators) use QR codes (also known as 2D barcodes) as a portable way to promote/connect their businesses or organizations.

EXERCISES

PR Challenge 11-1

Explain the difference between product placement, product integration and silent publicity. Watch a television sitcom and an evening news program and cite examples of each of these tactics.

PR Challenge 11-2

What are the major advantages and disadvantages of product placement/product integration over traditional ads and commercials – whether in motion pictures, on television or in print. Why can product integration not occur in print? Argue the pros and cons of each.

PR Challenge 11-3

Clip an advertorial from a newspaper or magazine. Argue the ethics behind placing advertorials in print or infomercials on television.

CHAPTER 12
Designing Effective Publications – Print and Electronic (Online)

Designing effective and enticing publications requires the same skills and techniques as other media used by the successful strategic communicators.

The first step is to consider the *MAC Triad Plus P and T* – Message, Audience, Channel, Purpose and Timing (Chapter 2). Ask yourself and/or your superior, the *purpose* (*P*) of the publication. Once you have an answer, determine the target audience so that an appropriate type of publication can be chosen and a message or messages crafted.

Format or type of publication is the *C* in the *MAC* Triad. The *channel* might be a newsletter – hard copy, inline (inserted into the text of an email message) or online, brochure, booklet, magazine, annual report, direct mail piece or point of sales (POS) display. No matter the format, it must achieve its goal of communicating with the target audience in a clear and concise manner. If it does not, the publication's purpose has been defeated and can be considered "wasted coverage."

The *T* is for timing. Determine the most effective time (aperture) to communicate the message to your target *audience(s)*. Once again, if the proper message is sent to the target audience, using the correct channel, but at an inconvenient time or the wrong time, the publication is a waste of time and money and falls into the category of "wasted coverage" (see *The ABCs of Strategic Communication* – AuthorHouse). Neither informization nor synergy is being achieved.

Successful editors and publishers include a number of elements on their checklist when designing publications. Among them are layout and design. No matter which type of publication is chosen, it must be designed using the *30-3-30* principle (Chapter 5). Never assume all readers are going to read every word of copy and look at every picture and other piece of artwork.

Instead, create a design that offers something for the 30-second reader, 3-minute reader and 30-minute reader (headline reader, skimmer, in-depth reader). *The Public Relations Practitioner's Playbook for (all) Strategic Communicators* follows the 30-3-30 principle.

Research is clear – while some of your audience will read every word in a publication, the numbers are small when compared to those who scan or skim it (3-minute readers) or those who only glance at it (30-second readers). Effective publications reach all three types of readers.

According to Karen Jurgensen, the national newspaper *USA Today* reaches all three types of readers – but refers to its concept as the *5-15-2* principle. Says Jurgensen, a former *USA Today* editor, "*USA Today* wants people to be able to read the paper in 5 minutes, 15 minutes or two hours. The choice is theirs."

To accomplish its goal, over its more than 30 year history, *USA Today* has gone through, what Jurgensen calls, three generations or phases; expanding its "reader-friendly" format to include unique stories and graphics that aren't available anywhere else. As a result, she says, the paper offers something for everyone whether they want to just glance at the headlines or sit down for a leisurely read. Your publications coordinator should be of the same mindset.

Al Neuharth founded *USA Today* with two concepts in mind: It should be "enlightening and enjoyable." Your publications should do the same.

Albert Holliday, publisher of *Journal of Educational Communication,* says the purpose of good layout and design is to direct the reader's attention to the message – not to dazzle him with artistry. Keeping the *30-3-30* principle in mind, three goals can be achieved and the publication will be:
- Attractive
- Convenient
- Easy to read

PR Play 12-1
Types of Publications
(Print – Inline – Online)

- Newsletters – E-newsletters
- Magazines – E-zines
- Handbooks
- Brochures
- Booklets
- Direct Mail
- Annual Reports
- Point-of-Sale (POS) Displays

Copybreaking Devices

In the 1970s, Rowan University graduate student, Ralph Burgio, developed the copybreaking device he called "blurbs." Today, they are commonly referred to as "pull quotes" – quotes or high-lights taken from an article or section of a publication to accommodate the 3-minute or 30-second reader.

Burgio, former Roanoke College publications director, was also an early advocate of shorter paragraphs, "boxed" items (information of interest), extra subheads, summary decks and expanded photo cut lines that tell an entire story.

He also recommended strategic communicators develop general all-purpose design formats, which he referred to as "logo formats." Burgio believed consistency in format would make a firm or organization's design immediately recognizable to its audiences. Admittedly, his idea was derived from Westinghouse Broadcasting's all-news radio formats. Gannett's *USA Today* was among the first newspapers practicing a similar format.

PR Play 12-2
Who Uses Publications?

- Advertisers
- Marketers
- Journalists
- Small Companies
- Large Companies
- Non-profit Organizations
- Government

Once it has been established that the three corners of the *MAC Triad* plus *purpose* and *timing* have been achieved, other steps on the list must be checked off. They are commonly referred to as the *Seven Steps in Creating Effective Publications*:

- Writing
- Design

PR Play 12-3
Dollar Bill Test

The *Dollar Bill Test* is simple: take a dollar bill and turn it on a page of copy. To pass the *Dollar Bill Test*, it must touch at least one copybreaker. If it does, your publication passes. If not, it fails.

Rowan University Professor Claudia Cuddy has her own list of copybreakers to assure publications pass the *Dollar Bill Test*:

- Heads
- Subheads
- Pull quotes (Blurbs)
- Rules
- Initial (or drop) caps
- Shaded (screened) boxes
- Pictures
- Art (line art)
- Bullet lists

- Production
- Typesetting
- Printing
- Distribution
- Evaluation

Getting People to Read Your Publications
Writing
Writing, for the most part, has been covered in Chapters 5 and 6. As a reminder, though, strategic/persuasive writers should write to communicate (express), not to impress. Keep the copy simple, related to the tar-

geted audience, actively written and to the point. Write only as long as you must to make a point or communicate your crafted message.

Publisher Holliday stresses that good publications must say something to someone. They also must say it well.

Design
Design starts with a design brief – clarifying objectives and making certain that a firm or organization's key points are included.

The next step is creating thumbnails or small sketches of the concept, inside and out. Always present at least three versions to the decision-maker. It helps to use focus panels for opinions.

Production, Typesetting, Printing
The third, fourth and fifth steps are *production, typesetting* and *printing.*

Typesetting and *printing* are major components of the *production* step. *Typesetting*, today, may be the simplest step. Unlike just a few years ago when an editor had to work closely with a printer on type font selection, it can and usually is done right on the desk top by the publication editor. In fact, many organizations and individuals design their publication and set their type using a desktop publisher such as *InDesign®*, *QuarkXPress®* or *PageMaker®*.

Choosing the right commercial printer can save hundreds and possibly thousands of dollars and hours of time. Marilyn Trocket and Dean and Teri Pugh of CRW Graphics, Pennsauken, N.J. suggest "thinking backwards" when planning – know your budget, decide on quantity needed and select the format or design.

Dean Pugh tells every editor to create a "dummy" or *design brief* before spending money. He advises finding vendors who will be "partners" – not adversaries – who are willing to answer questions about unfamiliar terminology and who offer design and cost-saving suggestions.

Working With Printers
Selecting a printing firm or organization that's right for your organization's projects is much more than simply evaluating equipment and price. Successful long-term client/printer relationships are built on rapport, communication and knowledge.

PR Play 12-4
Making Your *Thumbnail* or *Design Brief* Effective

- What is the *purpose*?
- Identify *target audience*
- Decide on type of publication (*channel*)
- Plan a realistic *budget*
- Plan a realistic schedule with firm deadlines
- Include your corporate profile
- Highlight your corporate/organization/brand identity
- Include your market position
- Clarify organization's objectives

Example of *Design Brief*

[ ] Thumbnail – Layout sketches of each page
[ ] Purpose – Communicate to organization's members
[ ] Corporate profile/mission – The Public Relations Student Society of America and this chapter aim to foster the following:
  - Understanding of current theories and procedures of the profession
  - Appreciation of the highest ethical ideals and principles
  - Awareness of an appropriate professional attitude
  - Appreciation of Associate Membership in PRSA and eventually accredited membership

Today, nationally, the Public Relations Student Society of America has more than 10,000 members in 300 chapters on college campuses in North America.

[ ] Identity – Rowan University Chapter has been named Outstanding Chapter eight times – more than any other, nationally.

[ ] Market position – Rowan University PRSSA is one of four chapters in New Jersey and one of five in Greater Philadelphia Region.

[ ] Objectives – The objectives of this chapter shall be to encourage the understanding of current theories and procedures in the practice of public relations; provide students with the opportunity to become acquainted not only with their peers, but with professional practitioners as well; encourage students to adhere to the highest ideals and principals of the practice of public relations and to instill in them a professional attitude; and to

cont.

PR Play 12-4 continued

provide each member with knowledge of the practices of public relations beyond the college community.

[ ] Type of publication – 4-page printed newsletter (also placed on website)
[ ] Budget - $250 per monthly issue (all for printing)
[ ] **Public Schedule – Editorial Calendar** (work backwards)
[ ] Publication (issue) date = Dec. 10
[ ] Download to website = Dec. 3
[ ] Blueline corrections returned to printer = Dec. 3
[ ] Bluelines (a printer's proof, blue in color made from an offset negative) or laser proofs = Dec. 1
[ ] Final camera ready publication emailed to printer = Nov. 20
[ ] Computer/Desk Top layout = Nov. 16-20
[ ] Final copy editing = Nov. 15
[ ] Copy returned to writers (if necessary) = Nov. 10
[ ] Copy editing = Nov. 2-9
[ ] Copy due = Nov. 1
[ ] Stories assigned = Oct. 1

There are many types of commercial printers – ranging from "houses" that do only single-color-quick printing like a FedEx Office® or Staples® to high-quality multi-color sheet-fed presses to web (large rolls of paper) press shops. The key is finding the printer that meets your needs.

Meeting Your Needs

The ideal situation is to build a rapport with at least three sources for each type of printing capability.

If your firm or organization makes an investment in investigating and choosing a printer, a long-term relationship may be cost effective and certainly more productive. Take time to tour facilities, obtain a copy of policies and check references. Identify your needs and expectations. Discuss your criteria for service, quality, supervision and approval.

Chemistry between client and the printer's representative is essential. Whether you deal with a salesperson or an account representative, teamwork and shared goals are necessary to achieve consistent quality printing. The printer's representative should be as concerned as you about your jobs every step of the way.

Knowledgeable sales people can offer suggestions of alternative ways to print a job that can save you time and money. Let them know that you expect to receive estimates quickly and be fully informed on job status and changes throughout the printing process. You should be notified immediately of any problems that arise during the printing process. *Increase your knowledge of the printing process so you can clearly communicate your specifications and concerns.*

Meeting Deadlines

Printers must adhere to schedules to keep jobs moving smoothly through their plants. Quality suffers and price overruns occur when rush situations force a print shop to pull out all the stops to meet the original deadline. Avoid creating crisis situations. Mistakes occur because of deadline pressures or poorly-communicated instructions. Establish a firm deadline for delivery and work with the printer to develop a schedule. Insist that all parties abide by the schedule.

Capabilities

Find out the full range of services offered by each printer:
- What type of equipment do they have?
- What size runs are necessary to use that equipment?
- Are they an integrated shop (can the shop perform all that is needed from shooting the negatives [if necessary] to plating, binding, mailing and/or distributing [if necessary])?

These and other services may save you time and money on some jobs. Other suggestions to save time and money include:
- Written specifications (PR Play 12-11) and delivery instructions save time and money and avoid confusion and delays.
- Decide what you want to accomplish and what your priorities are. This information helps the printer determine exactly what type of equipment and "personpower" is best suited for your project.
- Insist on a blueline proof (a printer's proof, blue in color made from an offset negative). Many printers now make laser proofs available. This quality control process is the final step before publications are plated. It protects the interests of both parties. Give the proof serious time and attention. Errors missed at this stage invite disaster in the finished product. Prompt turnaround of a blueline or laser speeds the process.

Price alone, however, should not be the deciding factor. Print shop reputations are built on service, quality and dependability. What you should be seeking from printers is the best value for your investment dollar. Therefore, you cannot compare a quick print shop to one that specializes in six-color, sheet-fed jobs.

Comparable printers of comparable quality should not be far apart on price. If they are, check again to determine if everyone is working under the same assumptions and specifications. Also, check to see what process each printer has in mind.

When asking for bids or quotes, let the printer know if this type of project is scheduled to be done periodically and ask for the bid to include a full year's printing. Because the printer can count on your business on a regular basis, you may receive better scheduling, pricing and/or service.

Shopping for printing companies does take an investment of time, money and effort. The reward is the development of a network of loyal print suppliers you can depend on.

Basing your selection of printers on their ability to sustain conscientious service, produce consistently high-quality products and meet deadlines will be cost effective and more productive over time than a shotgun approach to choosing a printer, based on low bid.

Distribution

Publisher Holliday of *Journal of Educational Communication* says efficient *distribution* using an organized, updated system is crucial to the publication process.

That system must include:
* Assigning a staff member to take responsibility for distribution and mailing – whether regular or electronic (email).
* Building a master data base system of names, by categories or audiences – various publics, key communicators, news media, government officials, etc.
* A mechanism for continually updating the list as new listings and/or changes come in. This prevents "wasted coverage."
* Determining how specific audiences can be reached quickly and economically.
* Knowing the best times to mail or email so that heavy mail times can be avoided (just before Christmas, at income tax time, first of the

month billings, etc.). Remember, you want your organization's message to be received with clarity – the way it is intended to be received.

- Possibly contracting with a "mailing house" could be cost effective and save time. (Mailers know how to package mass mailings to get the cheapest postal rates and many times the quickest service at the post office.)
- Checking and reevaluating distribution and mailing lists frequently. You must control the system rather than allowing it to control you.

Remember, not all publications have to be snail (regular) mailed. Email, either as attachments or inline, continues to grow in popularity and preference. Many times publications are linked to an organization's website, distributed internally or placed in strategic locations throughout a business environment or community – doctor and attorneys' offices, supermarkets and other retail stores, realtor offices, etc. The importance of a well-coordinated distribution system cannot be measured. Holliday says, "Your distribution system will work in proportion to the attention given it."

Evaluation

The final step in Creating Effective Publications is also the final step in the *Public Relations Process – evaluation.*

Obtaining feedback, whether for a publication (print) or one of the other major media (face-to-face, broadcast, Internet or special events) is a necessity of our profession. An honest sampling is the only true method for determining whether goals and objectives are being met.

Frequent sampling of audiences is a must – whether random or otherwise. Encourage email responses, letters to the editor and phone calls or provide postal card inserts with prepaid postage asking for feedback. Only by using open, honest, thorough and valid research can you assure that your approach is totally objective and not a reflection of your biases. Based on feedback, be prepared to make changes. The evaluation process also enforces what readers like and enjoy.

Give your audiences what they demand. As Holliday points out, "Your audiences deserve the best you can produce for them."

Rowan University's Professor Claudia Cuddy offers these suggestions to make publications more appealing:

PR Play 12-5
Plan Before You Publish (Print)

- Save time and misunderstanding by creating a design brief or *thumbnail(s)* (Play 12-4)
  - Clarify your objectives
  - Provide designers (if you use them) with key organization points

A number of other considerations fall under *production*:
- Choosing the right paper
  - Weight, texture and size affects look and feel
  - Paper can account for up to half the job's cost
  - Seek printer's advice
  - Ask how printer purchases, uses and charges for paper
  - Use printer's advice to limit waste and save money
- Choosing colors
  - Increases readership
  - Adds cost
  - Spot color is less expensive than process color because the color separation work is less tedious
- Folding
  - Publications should be designed with folding and binding in mind
  - Think in terms of "signatures" (a folded sheet containing 4, 8, 12, 16 and so on, pages that are folded to form a part of a book or pamphlet. Also called a "section.")
- Choosing the proper binding
  - Plan binding before printing
    - Saddle stitch
    - Side wire
    - Spiral
    - Perfect (book)
  - Consider margins, staples, etc.
  - Ask whether it will be done in-house

- Add white space
- Use multiple columns (depending on width of page)
- Don't center more than three lines of type
- Type one space after periods
- Use only 10 to 20 percent screens (tints) behind copy.

PR Play 12-6
A Professional Checklist to Assure Quality

- Recruit your own personal "board of directors" to serve as *your* advisory council. Use them as a focus panel – to suggest ideas and critique your work.
- Design publications to meet the needs of target audiences, not to satisfy someone's ego.
- Write to communicate (express), not to impress.
  - Successful writers suggest that the first draft come from the heart with successive drafts coming from the head.
- Rely on the *Associated Press Stylebook* for a proper consistent style that follows clear and simple rules. Refer to it often. *A.P. Style* and its proofreaders' marks are universally accepted.
- Consult frequently with your superiors and other members of your firm or organization to gather suggestions and reactions.
- Develop a distinctive style ("logo design") in all publications from your organization. This will help create an identity.
- Closely monitor the distribution process to assure publications reach their intended destination.
- Exchange publications with other public relations practitioners to share ideas and techniques and to gather additional feedback.
- Implement an effective evaluation mechanism. Every publication should be evaluated before it is printed and after it is distributed.

- Use pictures to attract readers to a story
  - Pictures reproduce best when in a ".tif" or tiff format (tagged image format file – high quality image)
  - Research says:
    - Picture stories or pages entirely devoted to photos attract attention and score higher in readership than regular news pages
    - Thumbnail photos (headshots) increase readership of a column
    - Photos attract more attention than line drawings
    - More attitude changes occur with a story and an accompanying picture than a story that stands alone

Professor Cuddy suggests purchasing a book that defines such common printing terms as font, point, leading, word spacing, reverse, bleed, spot color, process color, cropping and drop/initial cap. She also encourages practitioners to ask questions of printers when unfamiliar terms are used.

Cuddy's 30 years of experience as both public relations practitioner and publications specialist dictates using a serif (Roman) type font for body copy and sans serif (Gothic) for display or headline type.

Serif examples:

Times Roman is the most versatile

Bookman is a big type.

Palatino looks friendly.

Cooper Black is strong

New Century Schoolbook is easy to read

Sans Serif examples:

Arial is a little smaller than Helvetica

Arial Narrow is a variation of Arial

Avant Garde has a modern look

Helvetica is popular

Helvetica Narrow is a variation of Helvetica

Univers is similar to both Arial and Helvetica

Popular novelty type examples:

Comic Sans is a pleasant change

Broadway can be difficult to read

Cooper Black is popular for informal titles

STENCIL SHOULD BE USED SPARINGLY

Andy is the display font on this book's cover

Producing Newsletters

Newsletters, whether internal or external, – printed or electronic – are powerful and proven methods to tell your audiences – clients and prospects – or staff what is going on in your organization. The right mix of words and graphics can help make the newsletter entertaining as well as informative.

PR Play 12-7
Some General DOs

- Covers of publications other than newsletters should be 1/3 type and 2/3 white space with illustrations.
- Pull reader from panel to panel.
- Strive for a balanced or equal format.
- Use boxes or borders.
- Use color wisely.
- Make it look like your firm or organization's other pieces.

PR Play 12-8
Brochure Design and Production

- Determine budget.
- Determine purpose.
- Determine audience.
- Decide what to say and how to say it.
- Choose cover and text stock and other design materials.
- Supervise production and printing.
- Determine quantity.
- Establish distribution method (mailing, envelopes, free-standing, etc.).
- Verify content.
- Plan design.
- Decide production.
  - Paper stock (weight)
  - Ink
  - Type
- Create layout.
  - Who provides?
    - Your firm or organization
    - Freelance graphics artist
    - Printer
- Final production.
  - Type-setting
  - Printing
  - Folding
  - Stuffing
  - Distribution

PR Play 12-9
Printing Tips

- Scheduling – Conception to blueline/laser (page proof) to completed product.
- How costly are changes/corrections?
- Where is the job to be delivered?

PR Play 12-10

Amy Ovsiew – *PRomo* Editor – Rowan Unviersity

Ingredients of an Effective Newsletter – Printed or Electronic

Lead Story
Have one main or lead story on the front page. Don't try to be many things to many people. Decide what you want to communicate and go with it on the front page. The lead story should carry good graphics including at least one photo that grabs the reader. The lead story may jump to an inside or back page.

Secondary Stories
Stories that surround the lead story on Page One don't have to be related to it, but should complement it. As space permits, one or two secondary stories should be used. It's encouraged that one of them be a sidebar to the lead.

Photos
Organizations are about people, and the newsletter should be, too. With that in mind, use the most successful technique for getting the public to first look at your newsletter and then read it. Use photos and/or graphics about people. They can be real grabbers. Research shows that readers do not want to look at the front page of a newsletter and see headshots or table shots of people working. Be sure to limit the number of people in a picture to three or four.

Boxes, Screens and Screened Boxes
The newsletter can be dressed up by using screens, boxes, boxes with screened inserts and tinted drawings. But don't overdo it. Too much in the way of graphics can defeat the purpose, which is to break the monotony for the reader and to make the publication more appealing.

Moving to the Inside
The four-page newsletter is the most popular. The centerfold may be devoted to a main feature with a number of sidebars, or pages two and three could be a potpourri of short stories. Successful newsletters have gone with a large feature in the centerfold, spiced up by good photos and other graphics. Again, discretion should be used when dealing with screens, boxes, graphs and pie charts.

Back page
Don't use the back page as a dumping ground. It can't hurt to start a story on the back page and jump it to the inside. This has been done successfully by many major publications including the New York and Philadelphia *Daily News* and *The Sporting News*.

Color

Color can make or break a publication. Color used properly – whether in a brochure or newsletter – will attract the usual 30-second reader who might otherwise have glanced over it. Do not use a color for a headline or blurb (pull out quote) unless it is dark enough to be read. Don't laugh – poorly planned publications have printed headlines in yellow.

Headlines and Type fonts

Use no more than two fonts for the newsletter's headlines. More than two clutter the publication. Body type should be from the Roman (serif) family – at least 10 pt. (Many publications are going to 11 pt. type with 12 pt. leading [spacing between lines]).

In Summary

Every effective publication evolves from a plan. The proper mix of words, pictures, other illustrations and graphics and pleasing layout help assure it is being read.

The national newspaper *USA Today* is proof positive of a plan. According to Lisa Singhania of the Associated Press (Sept. 9, 2002), "When it (*USA Today*) debuted, the industry turned up its nose, doubtful that a newspaper with a national focus and a penchant for short, easily-digested stories could succeed."

Nearly 30 years and hundreds of millions of dollars later, the skepticism has been replaced by general, if sometimes grudging, admiration. *USA Toay* is now the nation's largest-circulation daily. Its use of colorful graphics quickly became, and still remains, a driving force in design at papers across the country.

"They've really set the standard for color and snappy, tight writing," says Barton Crockett, an analyst at J.P. Morgan Chase. *"USA Today* really answered skeptics and has a newspaper that not only is No. 1 in terms of readership, but is also profitable and very influential."

With a plan, you, too, can achieve success similar to *USA Today* and its parent, Gannett. While the Pulitzer Prize may not be in your future, you will achieve your goal and objectives, reaching your target audiences with strategic messages using an effective tactic to bring about the desired behavioral change.

PR Play 12-11
Typical Specifications Sheet for Commercial Printers

1. Your name, address and other pertinent information about your organization
2. Printer's name, etc.
3. Job Title/Item
4. Quantity
5. Creative Art
6. Layout
7. Typesetting
8. Mechanicals
9. Page Size
10. Proof
11. Stock for Text
12. Stock for Cover
13. Ink
14. Customer-furnished Materials
15. Bindery and Finishing
16. Packing
17. Shipping
18. Half Tones
19. Quote Deadline
20. Job Delivery Deadline
21. Miscellaneous
    a) bleeds
    b) die cuts
22. Price
    a) price breakdown for additional quantities

Keep in mind, publications provided to the printer as camera ready still need specification sheets. They serve as contracts. However, many of the items are simply marked – supplied by customer (you). They are known as "customer-furnished material."

PR Play 12-12
A Dozen Tips to Produce Top Publications

1. Never lose sight of your audience
2. Know the purpose of your publication
3. Have your design enhance the message, not obscure it
4. Be judicious in use of color
5. Use photographs well
6. Don't print over designs unless you are certain it will enhance the product
7. Avoid using too many type fonts in the same publication
8. Design your publication for different types of readers
9. Use informative headlines
10. Avoid large tinted or screened boxes
11. Avoid a layout that looks "busy"
12. Read your writing aloud and determine if it sounds conversational

PR Play 12-13
CAUTION!!!!
"Author's Alterations"
may be hazardous to your invoice.

One of the most frequent sore spots between printers and customers is the "Author's Alterations." If, through customer's error or change of mind, work has to be redone a second time or more, such work carries an additional cost, charged at current rates. Such costs usually appear on the invoice as "Author's Alterations" or simply "AAs." "AAs" are supported with documentation.

Dean Pugh – CRW Graphics – Pennsauken, N.J.

Printing Terms Every Practitioner Should Know

bleed – Running a picture or graphic off the edge of a page.

blurb – Pull quote.

body – The consistency of a printing ink.

body copy – The main text of any communication vehicle (a message).

Blueline/dylux – A printer's proof, blue (ink) in color and made from an off-set negative. This is typically the final step before publications (jobs) are plated. Many printers now make laser proofs available. Laser proofs can be provided in full color although the colors may not be the exact PMS (Pantone Matching System) colors that will be used on the completed publication.

budget – Allocation of space for stories in a publication.

bullet or dingbat – Dot or small graphic used as ornamental device.

caption – Short, but full, descriptive copy accompanying a picture or illustration. (See cutline.)

copybreaker – Anything that breaks up long blocks of copy (subheads, pull quotes, pictures, bullets, boxes).

cropping – Changing the shape or size of a photo or illustration to make it fit in a designated space or to cut out excess or undesirable elements.

customer-furnished materials – Hard copy, emailed or Flash drive containing material ready for print.

cutline – A name and title under a picture – briefer than a caption. (See caption.)

display type – Large type for headlines or display ads; usually larger than 14 points.

drop cap (initial cap) – When the first letter of a story (or paragraph) is larger then the rest of the type.

font – An assortment of type faces in one style and sometimes one size.

headline – Title of a story.

InDesign® – Layout and design program by Adobe®.

jump – To continue a story from one page of a publication to another.

justify – Spacing the type so the left and/or right margins are aligned.

knockout – Same as reverse.

knockout and fill – Same as overprint (fill in reverse with colored ink).

laser print/proof – A printer's proof made from an off–set negative. This is typically the final step before publications (jobs) are plated. Many printers now make laser proofs available. Laser proofs can be provided in full color although the colors may not be the exact PMS (Pantone Matching System) colors that will be used on the completed publication.

legibility – The visual contrast between one type font and another and between text blocks, headlines, and the surrounding white space. How pleasing is the layout to the eye?

mechanical – Also called a (finished) paste up. A finished layout that is photographed for offset printing. With desktop publishing, the *mechanical* stage is skipped, because the laser print *is* the *mechanical,* which can be emailed.

mortis headline – Also referred to as a *mortis head*. It is a headline or display type printed on a picture (not a reverse).

orphan – One line of type at the end of a column or page that begins the next paragraph.

overprint – Same as knockout and fill – fill in reverse with colored ink.

over runs (or under runs) – Printed copies in excess of the specified quantity.

PageMaker® – Layout and design program.

pagination – Using a design program to electronically layout pages.

point size – A relative measure of the size of a type font – the higher the number the larger the font.

process color – Use of all four colors primarily in photographs – a special printing process that enables you to employ high-quality photos and illustrations.

proofs – Copies of type and visuals that eventually become the finished printed product.

QuarkXPress® – Layout and design program.

quote – Estimate of costs.

PR Play 12-14
When planning...Think sdrawkcab (backwards)!

---

readability – The reading (grade) level of written material.

reverse – To print text or art in white on a dark background.

sans serif – Type fonts without hands and feet (Gothic type).

score – To crease the paper or cardboard in the printing process so that it can be folded easily and without damage.

screens – Boxes that are shaded.

serif – Type fonts with hands and feet (Roman type).

spot color – Colors used in addition to black for highlighting purposes on a page. One widely used color numbering scheme is known as the Pantone® Matching System – or PMS.

thumbnail photo – Small version of a photo.

---

trapping – Print slightly over the knocked-out area or white.

widow – White space at the end of a paragraph when the last line does not fill the entire width of the column.

EXERCISES

PR Challenge 12-1
Select an organization's newsletter – print, electronic or inline – and evaluate its effectiveness based on what you have learned from this chapter. Be certain to consider both legibility and readability.

PR Challenge 12-2
Using PR Play 12-4, select a publication of your choice and prepare a *Design Brief.*

CHAPTER 13
Researching, Writing and Delivering Effective Speeches

So, you have to prepare a speech for an executive in your firm or organization. What should a strategic communicator/public relations practitioner do to guarantee the speech won't disappoint the audience?

Opinion surveys consistently reveal that public speaking is the number one human fear – even more than death. In fact, at least one poll shows twice as many people are more afraid of speaking in public than of dying.

Are you up to meeting the challenge of researching and preparing a speech that effectively communicates the intended message by hitting the bull's eye or will it be uninspiring and miss the mark?

Communications trainer and television host, Steve Adubato says superior public speaking skills are learned. He and such other television executives as, Roger Ailes and his associate, Jon Kraushar, earn their livings evaluating people and working with them to overcome their fears, build confidence and develop a "can-do" attitude.

Organization is crucial. Most speeches have three parts: an introduction, body and conclusion. Start by explaining to the audience what your message will be, deliver the message and conclude by reminding them of the two or three major points (key messages or key message points – KMPs) they were just told.

One of your challenges as the organization's communication specialist is that you are probably writing the speech (personalizing it) for someone other than yourself. Therefore it takes another one of those *step-by-step* plans that public relations practitioners prepare for such situations.

David R. Voss of Voss and Associates, Sarasota, Fla. suggests establishing a speech objective:

- If I can persuade them that _____
- And can help them _____
- Then they will _____

The next step, according to Voss, is to list the conclusions your *audience* must reach for you to reach your objectives.

Before you read another word, go online and watch, listen to and/or read The Rev. Martin Luther King Jr.'s "I Have a Dream" speech delivered at the Lincoln Memorial in Washington, D.C. on August 28, 1963. It is arguably one of the great historical speeches.

Ingredients of a Successful Speech

- What message do we want to get across (communicate)?
- Who is your audience?
  - Why are they here (did they choose to attend or were they forced)?
  - What are the demographics?
  - Are they expecting a particular topic?
  - Are there any subjects to avoid (be politically correct)?
- What type of speech are "we" going to deliver? (Will it inform, entertain, inspire or all three?)
  - **Informative** – Offers information that can be easily understood by the audience.
  - **Persuasive (or promotional)** – Attempts to convince an audience of an idea or action or to support a person.
  - **Goodwill** – Leaves listeners feeling good about the company, organization, topic or product and it helps to build audience confidence. Uses numerous positive examples.
  - **Entertaining** – Intended to entertain by giving the audience a pleasant experience while communicating your organization's message.
  - **Technical** – Goes beyond basic information. It might need visuals to support oral presentation.
  - **Brief remarks** – Might be welcoming remarks, thank yous or words of acceptance.
- Where is our speaker on the agenda?
  - Is he/she first, middle, last or the only speaker?
  - Will the audience still be listening when it is our turn to speak?

- Now it is time to sit down with the person actually giving the speech (the person you are writing for). Interview him or her.
- Research
  - View and listen to previous speeches.
    - Delivery cadence
    - Mannerisms
    - Idiosyncrasies
- Writing the speech itself (style is important).
  - Put yourself in the deliverer's shoes.
  - Get a feel for the audience and localize the message to meet its needs. (It doesn't hurt to flatter or play to the audience.)
  - Establish the speech with some light humor early. (More may be interspersed throughout body of the speech, as well.)
  - Humor:
    - Creates interest.
    - Makes speaker appear more human.
    - Must be relevant.
    - Should help reinforce a point rather than confuse it or interrupt the train of thought.
    - Should be in good taste and politically correct. (Know your audience.)
    - Should be current.
  - Establish subject matter (*Introduction*).
  - Be a namedropper of local people known by many.
  - Go deeper into subject matter (*Body*).
    - Stress the points that must be made.
    - Use real-life situations or experiences to stress some points.
    - Use some more light humor, but don't belittle the subject matter.
  - Intersperse simple and complex sentences – long and short sentences.
  - Choose the "right" words.
    - Speak to communicate (express), not to impress.
    - Use easy-to-understand words.
    - Avoid jargon (unless research indicates that is what the audience expects – usually in technical speeches).
    - Repetition – don't be afraid of repeating to stress some points.
    - Identify with the audience by using "we," "our," "us."
    - When using statistics, keep them simple and use visuals. The ear cannot process as quickly without the assistance of visuals.

– Use only to enhance the speech.

– Be certain of effectiveness.

– Must be easily seen and read by audience (sometimes difficult with large audiences).

– Use bullets to make visual information more organized.

– Today's speeches are interactive – short bites, flip charts, PowerPoint®, Q&A, etc.

– Wind down.

– This is the homestretch (*Conclusion*).

  • Summarize, by stressing those main points the audience should remember most. In other words, bring the audience back – much as radio and television news writers do. Some refer to this as a "tie-back" to the introduction.

  • Rephrase the statement of purpose.

  • Give the audience a challenge, a plan of action or something specific they can do.

– End on a very positive UP note.

PR Play 13-1
Components of an Effective Speech

• Beginning (Introduction)
• Middle (Body)
• End (Conclusion)

PR Play 13-2
Types of Speeches

• Informative
• Persuasive
• Goodwill
• Entertaining
• Technical
• Brief Remarks

Will your speech
• Inform
• Entertain
• Inspire
or
• All three

As part of the training and preparation for giving the speech, which should include using video, have the speech giver practice eye contact with someone or several people in the audience. Many people have difficulty focusing on others. If (your) speaker can't look someone directly in the eye, use the practice of focusing on one's nose or chin. When delivering a speech, by selecting one or two people to look at in each section of the room, it communicates to the audience that the speech giver is talking directly to each of them.

Delivering a Speech

Former KYW-TV magazine host, Ray Murray once said, "Television is about a single viewer. The producer (or host) and viewer have a direct relationship." Much the same can be said for the person who delivers the successful speech. Look back at Presidents Obama, Clinton, Reagan and Kennedy. Each has been dubbed a "great communicator" because of their special ability to engage viewers in what some thought was a one-on-one conversation.

PR Play 13-3

"Television is one on one. It's just you and me, my friend."

Fred Rogers – Mister Rogers' Neighborhood

"Most of the time, public speaking is a learned skill which people are trained to do well," says Adubato. It requires what he calls the three P's: preparation, practice and a positive "can-do" attitude.

Melissa Connell and Joseph White, Rowan University master's degree graduates and who went on to successful careers, compiled basic techniques to consider once the decision has been made to craft and deliver a speech:

* Show your pearly whites
  - Typically, a smile deems the speaker intelligent and confident.
  - A smile indicates warmth and compassion.
* Eye contact
  - Speaker should focus on individuals, not the audience as a whole.
  - Implies speaker respects audience and views them as individuals.
  - Allows presenter to read the audience's reaction.
* Have a course of action
  - Know what action the speaker wants the audience to take as a result of the speech.
  - Use examples to stress a point is good, but be careful of going off on tangents that could cause a loss in focus.
* Be honest
  - Audiences forgive almost anything if the speaker conveys sincerity, candor and frankness, and an obvious interest in the topic.
  - Don't force the audience to relate to the topic.
  - Effective speakers develop their own style.

PR Play 13-4

T.J. Walker of Media Training Worldwide® suggests there are roads to take in speech preparation:

The Hard Way (lol) or the Easy Way

The hard way...

1. Gather every fact you can on the subject.
2. Ask all of your colleagues for all of their files and documents on the subject.
3. Create giant file folder to hold all of the documents and charts.
4. Digest all of your subject matter into 279 specific bullet points.
5. Cut and paste all of the bullet points and place into a PowerPoint document.
6. Email the PowerPoint to all of your colleagues around the world and ask for input.
7. Gather and collate the additional 1079 bullet point suggestions given by your thoughtful colleagues.
8. Sift through the new and old bullet points to narrow it down to a mere 356 bullet points that fit on 72 PowerPoint slides.
9. Tinker with the size of each bullet point.
10. Tinker with color of the PowerPoint background.
11. Tinker with dissolves, builds and other special effects to swish the PowerPoint bullets onto the screen.
12. Redo entire PowerPoint presentation.
13. Rewrite PowerPoint presentation to make it "flow" better.
14. Schedule rehearsal session for speech from 9 p.m. to midnight the night before you are to give the speech.
15. Have every intention of rehearsing your speech.
16. Gather more input from colleagues on additional PowerPoint slides to add from 9 p.m. until midnight the evening before you give your speech.
17. Proclaim to everyone that you meant to rehearse your speech but that you "just ran out of time."
18. While feeling anxious and nervous, give your speech, which consists of you dumping data very quickly because you thought you would have more time.
19. Bore your audience and communicate nothing.
20. Cement your reputation as a mediocre speaker.

Approximate time: 100 hours.

Or

cont.

PR Play 13-4 continued

The easy way...

1. Brainstorm on every important message you could say on the topic.
2. Narrow the list to no more than five messages.
3. Think of an example for each message.
4. Think of a story involving a real conversation with a real customer, client or colleague that vividly demonstrates each message point.
5. Find a picture, image or graph (without any text) that makes each message come alive and use that for your PowerPoint.
6. If you can't come up with a visual for a PowerPoint slide for any one point, then you just do without.
7. Create a final one-page outline that lists your five key points, your main examples, and a one or two word phrase that reminds you of the relevant story for each message.
8. Rehearse your speech in front of one or two colleagues.
9. Ask your colleagues what they remember from your speech.
10. Throw away any slides they didn't remember.
11. Give your speech, confident that you are going to be interesting and memorable to your audience.
12. Bask in the glory of knowing you have enhanced your reputation as a great communicator.

Approximate time: 3 hours.

www.presentationtrainingworkshop.com

- Watch the "ahs," "likes," "ums" and "you knows"
  - Avoid "space-fillers" or voice detractors that do nothing but distract from the speech.
- Avoid aggravating mannerisms
  - Speakers shouldn't "play" with glasses, tap a pencil, scratch their head, adjust their clothing, wobble from side to side or "play" with change in their pocket.
- Homework (research, research, research)
  - Know the audience's background and interests.
  - Preparation communicates sincerity, enthusiasm and confidence.

– Make it a point to visit the actual room in which the speech will be given to become familiar with its environment, layout, sound system and other equipment, etc. (Gives the opportunity to request changes if necessary.)

Walker and others have developed procedures speechwriters and their subjects should follow to assure success:

- About a month before the speech or as early as possible, have an initial meeting about the three to five key message points (KMPs) you want conveyed to the audience.
- Hold a brainstorming session to gather examples, stories and personal conversations the speaker has had that are relevant to the KMPs in the speech.
- Establish deadlines for both the speaker and speechwriter understanding that the speech will go through a series of drafts.
- Once the speech is completed, the speaker should do a videotaped rehearsal of the speech with the speechwriter in the room as part of the rehearsal team. Together, the speaker, the speechwriter and others on the team can evaluate what works and doesn't work so that the speech can be edited and improved.
- Do at least one more rehearsal with the final speech. (The speechwriter should be present.)
- When the speaker gives the speech, the speechwriter should be present. If that is not possible, the speechwriter should be provided with a videotape of the speech for evaluation.
- A post-speech analysis with the speaker and the speechwriter should always be held. Three major questions should be asked: What worked? What didn't? How can we improve things for the next speech?
- The more time the speechwriter spends with the speaker and the more previous speeches he views, the more the speechwriter can capture the natural voice of the speaker and incorporate real stories from the speaker's life. For best results, the speechwriter should try to meet informally – over lunch, dinner or coffee – with the speaker. It can help gain certain insights.
- If you treat your speechwriter like he or she is the cleaning lady who is delivering a commodity service like emptying your trash cans, then that is what you will get: a commodity speech. And it won't make you look good or enhance your career.

- The final product should be a collaborative effort resulting in a speaking performance to change, maintain or enhance the audience's behavior – after all, that should be your goal.

Presenting the Speech

Memorizing the speech
- Only for those who are comfortable doing so.
- Not necessarily recommended.
- Could take too much time.
- Risky for the inexperienced.

Reading the speech
- Could be boring.

Using note cards
- Good compromise for many presentations.
- Serve as physical and psychological crutch.
- Demonstrates speaker has done his or her homework.
- Speaker is able to maintain eye contact.

The very best speakers memorize their "script" or use bulleted talking points. But they are the minority. That means most will use 8 ½ x 11 sheets of paper or index cards. Here are a few musts:
- Never use staples to keep speech together. If staples are used, remove them before beginning the speech. Carrying the speech in a folder or loose-leaf book (three-ring binder) is acceptable. But try turning the pages inconspicuously. Do not allow the sheets to make noise as the pages are turned.
- Number the pages whether using full sheets or note cards. (What could be worse than a speech that is dropped or whose pages are out of order?)
- Use larger type. It is much easier to read. It makes no difference to the audience whether the speech is 10 pages or 20 or 100 note cards rather than 50. They do care that it doesn't run too long (20 minutes is a good goal), that the speaker is persuasive about the topic and that it is a pleasant experience for all involved (not boring).

Keep in mind that reporters might be covering a speech. In that case, give them a copy – but remind them that the actual speech may differ from what they've been given. And, if reporters do not stay for the actual speech and major changes are made, be sure to notify them so that neither

---

PR Play 13-5
Mayo Clinic

Public speaking is the number one fear for most people. But the Mayo Clinic HealthQuest newsletter offers simple steps to ease the jitters.

- Determine your audience and the message you want to deliver so that it is received with clarity (exactly as you intend it to be interpreted).
- Research your topic and find out what people want to know about it.
- Outline what you want to say.
- Practice your presentation – in the room where you will be giving the speech, if possible. Tape the rehearsal and play it back.
- Shortly before your presentation, make sure the equipment and props are ready.
- Take a short, brisk walk before your presentation. Breathe deeply and slowly. Drink water.
- Have confidence you will do well.

---

side is embarrassed as occurred some years ago when a New Jersey state senator completely left her text, changed her KMPs and an incorrect story appeared in newspapers only to be corrected the next day – not with a small correction, but with entirely new stories explaining the mix up.

If reporters do cover the speech, offer to give them one-on-one interviews after the speech. (TV reporters appreciate it.) Remember, KMPs must be stated in sound bites that run no more than 20 seconds (see Chapter 10).

Elevator Speech

An elevator speech is a strategic message delivered quickly and simply (no more than 30 seconds – 75 words – about the duration of an elevator ride) that communicates a brand promise, mission or other main element about you or your organization. The elevator speech or "pitch" must be clear and concise and communicate the core aspects of your business – touch briefly on the products or services you sell, what market you serve, and your competitive advantage. It must be brief and clear. Employees and stakeholders should know their organization's elevator speech.

If the elevator speech is about you, identify your personal attributes and quickly explain their benefits – benefits that might just get you a job or a promotion. The challenge: selling yourself in 30 seconds.

According to author and business coach, Rhonda Abrams, it takes quite a bit of thinking and practicing to decide what to mention in an elevator speech. Because it must be short, you have to decide what must be left out. "Often," she says, "these can be the things you are most excited about."

You'll find you use your elevator speech more than just in elevators. Says Abrams, "You will turn that 30-second speech into emails to prospective customers and investors, to introduce yourself at organizational meetings or when running into an old friend at a ballgame. Who knows? You may even use it if you meet a potential customer in an elevator."

PR Play 13-6
Sample Elevator Speech

Rowan University is a dynamic Top Tier regional university serving high-achieving students through a combination of teaching, research and project-based learning. The school's reputation for academic distinction is aided by its small class size, focus on inter-disciplinary work and technologically-advanced facilities.

"So," she advises, "go out and find a three-story building with an elevator, ride up and down and practice your pitch. That way, you'll be prepared the next time someone asks you, 'What do you do?'"

Political consultants James Carville and Mary Matalin are married to each other, although Carville advises Democrats and Matalin, Republicans. While their political philosophies differ, their approach is the same. As mentioned in Chapter 8 – You, Too, Can Conduct Successful Campaigns, they suggest, "Speakers must be optimistic and communicate a passion for their topic."

Each issue should be approached in three segments:
• Set up
• Conflict
• Resolution

They suggest some points to keep in mind while delivering the speech (message):
• Simplicity

- Relevance (can audience relate?)
- Repetition (keep hammering away)

Television executive Roger Ailes offers these four essentials of a great communicator: Be prepared, make others comfortable, be committed and be interesting. He suggests, "You will get what you want by being who you are."

In Closing

The effective speaker will communicate to an audience that he knows his topic as well as he knows his own name. If you are the strategic counselor and your speaker leaves that impression, you have "hit a home run." It is a wonderful feeling.

PR Play 13-7
Examples of S-R-R messages are:

"Do unto others as you'd have them do unto you."

The Golden Rule

"You can pick your friends, but not your family."

"You can't judge a book by its cover."

PR Play 13-8
10 Tips for Successful Public Speaking

Feeling some nervousness before giving a speech is natural, healthy and even beneficial. It shows you care about doing well. But too much nervousness can be detrimental. Here's how you can control your nervousness and make memorable presentations:

Some proven tips on how to control your butterflies and give better presentations – from Toastmasters International:

1. **Know the room.** Be familiar with the place (layout, environment and culture) in which you – or your "client" – will speak and/or present. Arrive early, walk around the speaking area and practice using the microphone and any visual aids. Walk the room to get a feel for its ambiance. cont.

PR Play 13-8 continued

2. **Know the audience.** Greet some of the audience members as they arrive. It's easier to speak to a group of friends than to strangers.

3. **Know your material.** If you are not familiar with your material or are uncomfortable with it, your nervousness will increase. Pick a topic you are interested in. Know more about it than you include in your speech. Use humor, personal stories and conversational language – that way you won't easily forget what to say.

4. **Practice. Practice. Practice!** Rehearse out loud with all equipment you plan on using. Revise as necessary. Work to control filler words. Practice, pause and breathe. Practice with a timer and allow time for the unexpected (anticipate).

5. **Relax.** Ease tension by doing exercises. Begin by addressing the audience. It buys you time and calms your nerves. Pause, smile and count to three before saying anything. ("One one-thousand, two one-thousand, three one-thousand." Pause. Begin.) Transform nervous energy into vitality, positive energy – enthusiasm.

6. **Visualize yourself giving your speech.** Imagine yourself speaking, your voice loud, clear and confident. Visualize the audience clapping – it will boost your confidence. When you visualize yourself as successful, you will be successful.

7. **Realize that people want you to succeed.** Audiences want you to be interesting, stimulating, informative and entertaining. They're rooting for you. They don't want you to fail.

8. **Don't apologize.** If you mention your nervousness or apologize for any problems you think you have with your speech, you may be calling the audience's attention to something they hadn't noticed. Keep silent.

9. **Concentrate on the message – not the medium.** Focus your attention away from your own anxieties and concentrate on your message and your audience. Your nervousness will dissipate.

10. **Gain experience.** Mainly, your speech should represent you – as an authority and as a person. Experience builds confidence, which is the key to effective speaking. A Toastmasters club can provide the experience you need in a safe and friendly environment.

http://www.toastmasters.org or email: tminfo@toastmasters.org

PR Play 13-9
Speech Evaluation Form – No. 1
SPEECH EVALUATION FORM

Speaker's Name _____

Evaluator's Name or Code No _____

PART 1: THE SPEAKER (circle the appropriate number)

1. Eye contact: 1   2   3   4   5

        poor   effective

2. Voice: 1   2   3   4   5

        monotonous   varied

3. Posture: 1   2   3   4   5

        poor   natural

4. Gestures: 1   2   3   4   5

        distracting   appropriate

S. Self-confidence: 1   2   3   4   5

        nervous   poised

PART 2: THE SPEECH (circle the appropriate number)

A. Overall performance

1. Speaker's knowledge of the subject – carefully researched; factual errors; missing details:

           1   2   3   4   5

           poor   superior

2. The speaker's language – too technical; filled with clichés or slang expressions; or crisp and descriptive:

           1   2   3   4   5

           poor   superior

cont.

PR Play 13-9 continued

3. Use of visuals – too many or too few; well-placed; appropriate size; handled with care; interfered with speech:

   1   2   3   4   5

   poor   superior

B.   Parts of the speech

1. The introduction – brief and attention getting; informative about topic:

   1   2   3   4   5

   poor   superior

2. The body – carefully organized and easy to follow; appropriate amount of information; message developed and conveyed clearly:

   1   2   3   4   5

   poor   superior

3. The conclusion – brief, effective summary of the main points:

   1   2   3   4   5

   poor   superior

PART 3: YOUR FINAL REACTION

1. The speaker's main strengths were:

2. The speaker needs to improve on:

PR Play 13-10
Speech Evaluation Form – No. 2

SPEAKING AND PRESENTATIONS   Presenter:

MEASUREMENT TOOL   Session/event:

Group/audience:

TOTAL SCORE _____   Date:

Score each element on a scale of 1 through 5 representing the following:

5 = Superior. Exceeded all criteria and expectations.
4 = Excellent. Met all criteria and expectations.
3 = Good. Met most criteria and expectations.
2 = Needs improvement. Met some, but not most, criteria and expectations.
1 = Poor. Met none, or very few, criteria and expectations.

Criteria

1. A strong opening   Score _____

The opening statement grabbed the audience's attention. People knew what the speech was about and why they should listen. The audience had a road map for where the speech was going. The opening included a clear and memorable message.

Comments _____

2. Direct eye contact   Score _____

The speaker's eyes supported and helped communicate the message. The speaker made contact with members of the audience one at a time. The speaker looked at people on both sides of the room, front and back. The eye contact was sincere and penetrating.

Comments _____

cont.

PR Play 13-10 continued

3. Vocal energy and variety   Score _____

There was sufficient energy to match the importance of the message. The speaker's words flowed easily with natural breaking points. Key messages were highlighted by changing pace or pitch. Silence was used effectively to break up key elements or to bracket main messages.

Comments _____

4. Gestures and facial expressions   Score _____

Hands and body movements enhanced the message and helped achieve the presentation's goals. Facial expressions changed to accurately reflect different messages. The speaker usually had a natural and open face. There were no major distractions, such as pacing, bad habits or noises.

Comments _____

5. Organization   Score _____

The content of the speech or presentation was delivered in a logical order. The audience was able to follow the direction. The speaker appeared to put some thought into the organization.

Comments _____

6. Visual aids   Score _____

Visual aids were used and they supported and supplemented the words. (When no visual aids are used, give a score of 4 if that was a good decision and 2 if it was not.) The visual aids were large enough for everyone to see. They were simple enough for everyone to understand. The audience moved easily from the visual aid to the speaker.

Comments _____

cont.

PR Play 13-10 continued

7. Content for audience   Score _____

The speaker's words indicated he/she had analyzed and understood the audience. The needs of the audience were addressed. The content provided the right amount of depth, information and major points. The speaker adjusted, if necessary, to the reaction of the audience.

Comments _____

8. Language   Score _____

The speaker delivered a clear and memorable message. The speaker used short conversational sentences. Word pictures, concrete terms, stories or analogies helped the audience relate. The speaker avoided jargon, acronyms, inappropriate jokes or off-color language.

Comments _____

9. Strong closing   Score _____
The speaker provided a review, reminder or reference to major points. If appropriate, the speaker provided action steps for the audience to follow. The speech ended on a positive, upbeat or hopeful note.

Comments _____

10. Final impression   Score _____

The audience knows and understands the main message. The audience has a feeling about the speaker that supports the main message. The audience would be favorably inclined to take action.

Comments _____

Adapted from Voss and Associates – Sarasota, Fla. – www.vossandassociates.net

---

PR Play 13-11
Communicating With Older People

Communicating with older people often requires extra time and patience because of physical, psychological and social changes.

Some suggestions:
- Reduce background noises.
- Talk about familiar subjects.
- Keep your sentences short.
- Give the person a chance to reminisce.
- Allow extra time for a response.

Speech Examples (with pauses and emphases noted)

Speech Example No. 1
Teamwork Speech (Delivered by M. Larry Litwin on Sept. 12, 2001)

Before yesterday's vicious attack on New York City and near Washington, D.C. – the attack on the United States – I had already decided to talk tonight...about **Teamwork**.

It's a term that we hear so much about, but too many times, we do not fully grasp its meaning. **Teamwork** is a cooperative effort by members of a team to reach a common goal. Yesterday, in New York City and at the Pentagon, we witnessed **true...Teamwork**.

Firefighters, police officers, paramedics, by-standers, hospital personnel and others...working together to achieve a common goal – attempting to save lives.

Rowan University's PRSSA (Public Relations Student Society of America) members, who are enrolled in our capstone courses – Case Studies and Public Relations Planning – heard this word – teamwork – in class last week.

If they didn't know the importance of it last week, they do tonight. As you enter your careers as public relations professionals, your success WILL depend on that word – TEAMWORK. Thank goodness, more times than not, your reaching a common goal will not be a matter of life or death...as it was yesterday. But let's talk for a few moments *about* **TEAMWORK**. To communicate my message, I will be dropping in a number of key words.

The first of those key words is **success**.

To be a success in our profession, IT IS going to mean being a part of a team. Let's put it into perspective.

Might I ask,...how is your teamwork going on your team? Is everybody working together? Or do you have some superstars who think they're a little bit better than somebody else? Or worse, do you have some players who refuse to carry the ball and depend too much on others?

Like yesterday, teams that are successful in sports don't allow that to happen. Historically, there are the New York Yankees, Dallas Cowboys and Boston Celtics. How about those Philadelphia Flyers from the Stanley Cup years?

Like rescuers in Manhattan and at the Pentagon, those teams believed in teamwork. Everybody – part of his or her team. No one more important than anybody else. No one less important than anyone else. Everyone...making a contribution in his — or her — own way. **Teamwork** is vital. No superstars. Just everybody...a part of the team.

Jim Tunney, a former schools' superintendent in Los Angeles and a former NFL Referee once suggested — Sometime when you're feeling important, sometime when your ego is in bloom, sometime when you've taken for granted you're the best qualified in this room, sometime when you feel that *your* going, would leave an unfillable hole, follow this **simple** instruction and see how it humbles your soul.

Take a bucket, fill it with water, put your hand in it up to the **wrist**...pull it out...and the hole that's remaining is the nature of how **you** will be **missed**.

You see, said Dr. Tunney, you can splash all you please when you enter. You can stroke the water galore. But stop, you'll find in a minute...that it looks quite the same as before.

The moral of this example is to do just the **best** you can, be proud of yourself...but remember...there is **no** indispensable man. Be proud of yourself, but remember...there is **no** indispensable person.

Everybody is part of that team. And, in the professional world, we must play to win – or we may not be able to feed our families. Unfortunately, yesterday, winning or losing was a matter of life or death.

Let's a take quick look at some other key words as we work together to reach our public relations goals and goals in life –

In all of my years working with successful professionals – whether it be in sports, radio and television, education or public relations – they've taught me to practice the meanings of these six words:
- **Sacrifice**
- **Respect**
- **Desire**
- **Discipline**
- **Passion**
- **Commitment**

The **sacrifice** is of yourself. Because as an athlete or…as a successful person in business, there are certain times when you must make self-sacrifices to be a success. Just look at those firefighters, police officers and rescuers in Manhattan.

Respect – You must respect others…your coaches, your teammates, your bosses, your clients – but especially you must have respect for yourself.

You must have **desire** – the desire to always try to be the best at what you do. Without the desire, you probably don't deserve to succeed.

Discipline – Winning and being a success means disciplining yourself. There are times, when you'll probably have to do things that you won't want to do…and more importantly…there are times when you won't want to do some things that others may want you to do for your own good.

Passion – It's been said that you should never love anything that can't love you back. But in this instance, loving what you do for a living – your profession – will make life so much better…and fulfilling…for you.

And how about **commitment**? Most importantly, there's **your** commitment. You must commit yourself to specific goals in life so that you will have something to strive for.

Never make the goals easy ones to achieve. Make your goals difficult, **but** achievable. Make them something that you must work hard at…in order to achieve them.

Even though thousands of lives *were* lost yesterday, the members of those rescue teams *were* successful…because they did save thousands more lives…because **THEY** made a commitment to others and to themselves. **THEY** worked together. Like those rescue workers—**Your grasp should always exceed your reach.**

Those six words:
- **Sacrifice**
- **Respect**
- **Desire**
- **Discipline**
- **Passion**
- **Commitment**

were words taught to me by my coaches – by my teachers – by my bosses – by my parents – people instrumental in helping me to be a success in my career.

I'd like to close today by singing you a little song – but – as many of you know...I can't sing.

The song is a great one...that talks about your **confidence**, your **trust**, and the **ability** and the **competence** and the **integrity** that you must possess – those of you...those of us – who are strong. Those of us who want to be successful. This song is about those rescue workers who, yesterday, risked **THEIR** lives to save others.

As Dr. Tunney has said in the conclusion of his speeches and Frank Sinatra sings...Here's to the winners, lift up the glasses. Here's to the glory still to be. Here's to the battle...whatever it's for...and asks of the best of ourselves...then give much more. Here's to the heroes...those who move mountains. Here's to the miracles that make us see. Here's to all others. Here's to all people. But especially...here's to the winners that all of us can be.

Speech Example No. 2
(Written for Cherry Hill, N.J. Mayor – June 2004)

Thank you all for being here today to hear from our former mayor and now Commissioner of the Department of Community Affairs, Susan Bass Levin. Commissioner Levin will discuss Governor Jim McGreevey's proposals for badly needed property tax relief and reform. I want to personally thank the Commissioner for being here on behalf of the Governor so that residents of Cherry Hill Township have the opportunity to express their views about property tax reform and to learn more about the Governor's plans.

A number of Cherry Hill residents...maybe some of you here today...have expressed their concern to me over rising property taxes. My administration has gone to great lengths to try to alleviate the burden of property taxes on our residents. We have introduced new and innovative ways to increase our municipality's non-tax revenues. We work every day to increase efficiency in government and to find new ways to stretch our limited dollars. We do it through prudent spending, grants – many from the DCA – corporate sponsorships, competitive bidding, and cooperative purchasing agreements.

I commend Governor McGreevy for taking the lead to help municipalities lower the tax burden faced by their residents. The efforts he has made to reach out to municipalities across the state to seek their input on how best to combat this problem has been remarkable.

Last year, the governor began a series of property tax forums...similar to this one...in different regions of our state. In January of this year, I wrote a letter to the governor asking him to host one of these forums here in Cherry Hill so that our residents could have the opportunity to communicate their views on this subject. I'm so glad that he responded to my letter by sending Commissioner Levin to Cherry Hill so that our residents know that their views count and that their voices are being heard.

Soaring property taxes are a state-wide problem. I look forward to working with the governor, the commissioner and our legislators as they tackle the challenges of property tax reform, school funding and new and alternative revenue sources. I am confident Governor McGreevey will lead the way to a more equitable tax plan – a plan most of us can live with.

Now I would like to introduce the chairman of the Cherry Hill Committee for Property Tax Reform, Mark Markos. Mark has been the Chairman since the committee's inception in 2002. This committee joined the state-wide coalition of Citizens for Property Tax Reform shortly after they formed. Mark has been a Cherry Hill resident for 39 years and an active and valuable member of this community. I praise him for his efforts in making sure that residents and taxpayers have a voice in changes that could be a benchmark for many other states. Mark...

Speech Example No. 3

Remarks of M. Larry Litwin, APR – Chair, New Jersey Privacy Study Commission – Dec. 20, 2004

The time has come for me, as chair, to thank every member of the commission for their **dedicated** service as we worked hard to research, debate, recommend and adopt a number of reports that are the framework for a **final** report to be sent to the Acting Governor and then – onto the Legislature.

The Privacy Study Commission was created under the Open Public Records Act – OPRA – to study the privacy issues raised by the collection, processing, use and dissemination of information by public agencies – balancing the recognized need for openness in government with concerns for personal privacy and security.

Over nearly two years, **all** of us participated to study the privacy issues in light of the recognized need for openness in government – while, at the same time – protecting the privacy rights of individuals.

As charged by the Governor, we studied home addresses and telephone numbers, the use of personal information by commercial entities for title searches, mortgage and other loan applications, **and** information used by private investigators and other firms that use personal information for such publications as printed and on-line directories. We spent a great deal of time studying technology and **its** effect on the way government operates.

We are making specific recommendations that we deem appropriate to strike a balance between openness in government and – protecting the individual.

We appreciate all the assistance of staff members, Marc Pfeiffer, Paul Dice, Susan Jacobucci and Erin Mallon Knoedler, but especially, **early on** – our attorney...Catherine Starghill – who compiled a matrix consisting of legislation in **every** state and ranked them by **effectiveness**. I could not place a value on Catherine's help.

In drafting, debating and adopting our reports, we reviewed the collection, processing, use and dissemination of information by State and local government agencies here in New Jersey and in many **other** states.

My personal objective was for us to work together – as a commission – so that we would achieve the overall goal of striking **that** balance between an individual's right to privacy and the public's right to know. It was a **major** challenge – one this commission has met.

Thank you to all of the chairs – Grayson Barber for chairing the Special Directive Committee on Home Addresses and Telephone Numbers – and for presenting a document that met with unanimous approval, Tom Cafferty for his work as chair of the Commercial Use Committee and Bill Kerns for Chairing the Technology Committee.

Judge Rosemary Karcher-Reavey chaired the Public Interest Committee, which handled the public hearings and made recommendations for the website. Also, Karen Sutcliff for chairing the Committee on New Jersey Practices and Ms. Barber, again, for chairing the Committee on Practices Outside of New Jersey.

While they are the chairs, none of our work could have been completed without the input of George Cevasco, Richard DeAngelis, Edithe Fulton, John Hutchison, Pamela McCauley, Jack McEntee and Lawrence Wilson.

And, thank you to any DCA – Department of Community Affairs – staff members I may have missed. Thank you to Commissioner Susan Bass Levin for the confidence she has shown in us – and my personal thanks to Tara Bennett, the Rowan University graduate who served as my intern and became a DCA staff member.

Every person in a leadership role should have a Tara.

While our final report may not be perfect in everyone's eyes, I see it as a benchmark that other states could emulate.

It has been an honor to serve as commission chair.

EXERCISES

PR Challenge 13-1
Select a topic of your choice and research and write a 20-minute speech. Select the audience and venue.

PR Challenge 13-2
Your instructor will select a topic for you to research and have you write a speech to be delivered by your superior. Your instructor will select the audience, venue, time and the "person" for whom you are writing the speech.

CHAPTER 14

Being Ready For A Crisis
[Tell it *First* – Tell it *Fast* – Tell it *All* –
Tell it *Yourself*]

Crisis is defined in *The American Heritage Dictionary* as "a crucial point or situation in the course of anything; a turning point." It is also defined as "an unstable condition...in which an abrupt or decisive change is pending."

The same publisher defines *communication* as "the exchange of thoughts, messages...speech, signals or writing."

Successful public relations practitioners view a crisis as "a situation you plan for but hope never occurs – but if it does, you are prepared."

Firms and organizations should develop two types of *crisis plans* – an *operational* plan and a *communication* plan. Operational plans are designed to keep organizations functioning. This chapter concentrates on the communication plan – successful communication techniques used during an unstable period or during a surprise situation that might have a short decision time.

A lack of crisis planning could make a bad situation worse, could have dangerous side effects or it could even spell doom. The book, *Public Relations...Strategies and Tactics* (Wilcox, Ault and Agee), states, "How an organization responds in the first 24 hours (of a crisis) often determines whether the situation remains an incident or becomes a full-blown crisis."

Strategic communication guru, Anne Sceia Klein, APR, PRSA Fellow, of Anne Klein Communications Group (Mount Laurel, N.J.), has years of experience that prove the first hour or two following a crisis are the most crucial. "After that," she says, "It's a whole different ballgame." Her advice, "Be prepared for that first news media call" (no matter how qucikly it comes).

Practice Your ABCs

Those first few hours (two to four) are considered the communication director's Golden Hours. Successful strategic counselors think about their "ABCs" –

- A=Anticipate
- B=Be prepared
- C=Communicate clearly, calculatingly (measure each word), concisely, consistently, completely (specifically and simply) – and correctly.

Tell it **FIRST** – Tell it **FAST** – Tell it **ALL** – Tell it **YOURSELF**.

Like so much in our profession, the key to a successful crisis communication plan is *anticipation*. Anticipation is not predicting, but rather being prepared beforehand. Even the best communicator can boast all he or she wants about having advance knowledge or a premonition. But whether or not the practitioner possesses that innate ability isn't the key. The key to a successful reaction is planning – being ready for that event "just in case it happens." However, it must be kept in mind that a plan is just that – a plan.

Live and YouTube videos and case studies of the 2013 Boston Marathon bombing are proof positive – and reinforce – that well- planned crisis organizational and communication plans do work. Federal, state, local law enforcement and other officials (more than 30 agencies) did their best to collaborate and cooperate so that Plays 14-1 and 14-3's rules could be followed as closely as possible – maintaining the proper emotional tone.

Klein suggests that one way for practitioners to anticipate is to answer the question, "Is there anything that keeps me awake at night?"

No matter the response, practitioners must recognize that no two crises are the same. Thus, there is no "cookie-cutter" approach.

"Nothing is more important during a crisis than good, quick, effective, accurate communication," says J. William Jones, retired corporate public affairs officer at PECO® (an Exelon® Company) in Philadelphia and the former director of public affairs for the School District of Philadelphia. "Effective management response is the key to credibility."

That was evident on Dec. 14, 2012 – a day most will never forget. Soon after classes began on that Friday, a mass shooting occurred at Sandy

Hook Elementary School in Newtown, Conn. Twenty first graders – 6- and 7-year-olds – and six teachers and other educators were brutally murdered by a 20-year-old gunman who earlier had shot his mother to death in her house and eventually took his own life inside the school.

The details of the horrific event – a tragedy of unspeakable terms – remained in the news for months. The following paragraphs are not about the tragedy, but rather about textbook crisis communication led by Connecticut State Police Lt. Paul Vance, whose years of experience were obvious. He followed the "Three Rules of Crisis Communication" by immediately controlling the message, getting the information out quickly and in his own terms (See Play 14-1) and link to:

http://newyork.cbslocal.com/video/8069787-gov-dan-malloy-and-lt-paul-vance-brief-on-connecticut-school-shooting/

http://www.youtube.com/watch?v=VFWA29yhTuE

http://www.youtube.com/watch?v=KfW9cBnHeJ0

It was evident from the moment Connecticut Gov. Dannel Malloy turned the news briefing over to Lt. Vance the media respected and trusted him. Vance was direct and forthright. Like other first responders, he was making extraordinarily difficult decisions under time pressures – fully understanding his responsibilities.

Said Vance soon after arriving on the scene: "This is an active, ongoing investigation. There's a great deal of work to go. And there are a lot of things we cannot confirm or discuss as of yet."

He recounted what he knew detail by detail commencing with the first 911 "call for help at the Sandy Hook Elementary School" shortly after 9:30 a.m. He said the response to the first call "was instantaneous."

Showing compassion, he said first and foremost police were concerned for the safety and welfare of everyone inside the building "knowing it was a potential active shooter situation. They (first responders) immediately entered the school. Their focus was to search for students, faculty and staff and remove them to a safe area outside of the school."

"They did search every nook and cranny, every room, and every portion of that school and accomplished that task. They took the rescued to a 'staging area' to reunite them with family members. As has been reported, there were fatalities," he said.

Lt. Vance went on to painstakingly describe the gruesome details including the death of the shooter who was found inside the school. He said there is a "great deal of work going on" including identifications and crime scene examinations.

"We need to establish identity," he said. "We need to document the entire scene. Simply stated, we need to answer every single question so we know how and why this incident occurred. We are not even putting a time stamp on when we will complete this project."

Lt. Vance then took questions reminding the media, "This is an active on-going case and there are things that we cannot and will not discuss at this time."

While he did attempt to answer all of the questions, he clearly demonstrated his crisis communication expertise in employing the "pseudo no comment." Not once did he say "no comment" or even mention the word "comment" as he dodged sensitive questions or those for which he did not have the facts.

Lt. Vance explained why he could not discuss certain aspects – often reiterating what had been said explaining, "that's as much as we want to go into detail." At no time did the media appear dissatisfied.

He said a final report would contain answers to all questions. That initial briefing and those that followed ended with Lt. Vance scheduling the next briefing – some within "60 minutes at which time I will try to have answers to some of your questions and more detail." When a scheduled briefing did not start promptly, media appeared patient because of the trust he evoked, his preparation and thoroughness. He was both credible and believable.

As he was leaving the first briefing, Lt. Vance turned back to the microphones stating, "One thing I would like to say is we have been meeting with all of the family members. It's a very difficult scene for the family members – all of the first responders. It's a tragic scene. We have been asked by the family members to ask the press to respect their privacy and to please leave them alone at this time. They are going through a tremendous amount of grief, which I am sure you can appreciate."

In response to a question about the scene, he said out of respect to the families and others he would not describe what he saw: "I have been a trooper a long time and my lieutenant to my left has been in law enforcement a long time and describing it serves no useful purpose. It is a horrific scene. Between our mutual experience we have never seen anything like this. It is heart wrenching for us as it is for the families. I would just like to leave it at that."

Throughout each briefing, Lt. Vance's compassion and incredible patience with the media never wavered. As he responded to many of the same or similar questions, he repeated the facts, as he knew them, about the "massive investigation."

"An investigation like this," he said, "is like a puzzle. We want to put this puzzle together and form a complete picture so that everyone without any doubt what so ever can truly understand what occurred. We will send you out a news release, a press release. If you are not on our email list get it off the Associate Press (wire service). Primarily, it will contain all the details of all the briefings." Reporters were assured that fact sheets and releases would be available at the media "staging area," on the state police website and on (the) AP.

He made a point of commending the partnership between Newtown Police, state police, federal law enforcement and local police from other states and then urged the media "not to read anything (speculate about other police jurisdictions) into what he was saying. We are not going to hide anything from you."

Lt. J. Paul Vance

Lt. Vance's concluding statement from that – lengthy – first briefing illustrated the mutual respect he, his colleagues and the media had for each other: "(It's) all hands on deck. We will get this done in a timely fashion. Give us until morning. Hopefully we can tie up some loose ends first thing in the morning. We will fill in the voids tomorrow as much as we possibly can."

During the briefing, which was quintessential crisis communication, Lt. Vance touched on the crisis operation plan – a description which could be used for the communication plan, as well: "First responders who were first in the door with surrounding police departments and the troopers – this is something that you train for…you plan for. You work towards. You hope they'll never have to use. Their training kicked in. They saved a lot of lives. They did a great job. They did a great job."

Connecticut State Police Lt. J. Paul Vance and other state and local police fielding questions near Sandy Hook Elementary School during the first of many news briefings. Such impromptu media conferences are described as "media scrums."

Another example of how the ABCs of strategic communication was implemented would be actions taken prior to and during the October 2012 Superstorm Sandy, which struck much of the coast from the Carolinas to New England. It, especially, wreaked havoc on the New York and New Jersey coastlines. New Jersey Gov. Chris Christie, New York Gov. Andrew Cuomo and dozens of mayors demonstrated their crisis communication prowess by holding news conferences days in advance – unveiling their operational plans.

Gov. Christie

While property damage was in the billions and more than 110 died, the consensus was clear – without **Anticipation**, preparation (**Be** prepared) and clear **Communication**, human loss and suffering would have been far worse.

The nonpartisan cooperation – established days before Sandy hit New Jersey – is best illustrated by Gov. Christie, staunch backer of Republican presidential candidate Mitt Romney. "It's been very good working with the president," Christie said on MSNBC's *Morning Joe*. "He and his administration have been coordinating with us. It's been wonderful."

On NBC's "Today," Christie said the president had been "outstanding" and FEMA's response has been "excellent."

The Republican governor also sent out a thankful tweet: "I want to thank the president personally for all his assistance as we recover from the storm."

Christie said, "The president has been all over this and he deserves great credit. I've been on the phone with him personally (sometimes) three times a day including midnight. He gave me his number at the White House, told me to call him if I needed anything. And he absolutely means it."

It was 17 years earlier that PECO's Jones had to deal with tragedy. He was a member of the strategic counseling team that advised PECO® management to accept blame after a 1995 gas explosion in its service area left two people dead and rocked a neighborhood in Suburban Philadelphia. PECO's® president and CEO uttered the magic words, "It was our fault." At the time, other than Johnson & Johnson® taking the direct approach, few organizations had. The PECO® team received universal praise as evidenced by some of the newspaper headlines below:

Some Headlines from PECO® December 1995 residential gas explosion

SORRY

Peco prez: Response in fatal gas blast was 'unacceptable and regrettable'

Philadelphia Daily News – December 20, 1995

PECO: It's our fault

Daily Times – December 21, 1995

PECO does the right thing

Philadelphia Daily News – December 26, 1995

PECO takes blame in fatal blast

The Reporter – December 20, 1995

Peco's mea culpa hailed as 'brilliant'

Savvy PR, Despite firm's blast liability

Philadelphia Daily News – December 22, 1995

That same direct approach was evident when with both engines out, a cool-headed pilot (Chesley Sullenberger) maneuvered his crowded jetliner over New York City and splash landed in the frigid Hudson River (January 2009). Miraculously, all 155 on board were pulled to safety as the plane slowly sank. One victim suffered two broken legs, a paramedic said, but there were no other reports of serious injuries.

New York Governor David Paterson called it "a miracle on the Hudson."

STEVEN DAY / Associated Press

Passengers and crew wait on the wings of a jetliner that safely ditched in the Hudson River in New York after geese knocked out both of its engines.

The plane, a US Airways Airbus A320 bound for Charlotte, N.C., struck a flock of geese during takeoff three minutes earlier at LaGuardia Airport and was submerged up to its windows in the river as rescuers converged from both sides of the Hudson – Manhattan and Newark, N.J. Rescuers arrived in Coast Guard vessels, ferries, water taxis, tugboats, inflatable rescue craft and ships from Circle Line. By the time the first vessels arrived – within 90 seconds of the plane hitting the water – passengers were exiting onto the partially submerged wings while others waded in water up to their knees. The crash took place on a 20-degree day, one of the coldest of the season in New York. The water temperature was 36 degrees.

Within two hours, Mayor Michael Bloomberg and his crisis team leaders – with his gathered facts in hand and for distribution to reporters – faced the media on national television from the New York side of the

Hudson. He opened: "Let me tell you what we know happened and what we don't know, yet. We have just witnessed grace under pressure."

It was clear, both his operational and crisis communication plans had been carried out flawlessly.

Even before Bloomberg spoke, about 90 minutes after the plane "ditched," US Airways Chair and CEO Doug Parker was addressing the media from company headquarters in Phoenix, Ariz. He did not take questions so he could immediately fly to New York City. His strategic statement follows:

> I can confirm US Airways Flight 1549 was involved in an accident. The Airbus A320 was en route to Charlotte from LaGuardia. It had 150 passengers on board. The flight was operated with a crew of two pilots and three flight attendants. US Airways is confirming passenger and crew names and will issue those as soon as possible. At this point, no additional details can be confirmed. Our preliminary report is that everyone is off the plane and accounted for.

> We've activated our US Airways care team of specially trained employee volunteers to assist those affected by this accident. Individuals who believe they may have family members on board Flight 1549 may call US Airways at 1-800-679-8215 within the United States. The number can be reached toll free from international locations through AT&T's U.S.A. Direct. To contact an AT&T operator please visit www.usa.att.com/traveler for U.S.A. Direct access codes. Others are asked, please, not to call this number so the lines can be kept available for those who truly need them.

> It's premature to speculate about the cause of this accident. Out of respect for those affected we would ask that you also resist the temptation to speculate.

> The National Transportation Safety Board will conduct a thorough investigation to determine the probable cause with our complete support and the support of many others. Further, we are working with and will continue to cooperate fully with the N.T.S.B., local, state and national authorities and answers will emerge during the course of that investigation.

Right now we're working to care for those who have been touched by this accident. Members of our airline family will come together with these families to help however we can. I am on my way to New York shortly.

In closing, safety is, has been and forever will be our foremost priority at US Airways. All of us at US Airways are committed to determining the cause of this event and to assisting in every way possible in preventing a similar occurrence.

US Airways will continue to release information as it becomes available. Please monitor usairways.com for the latest information.

Pennsylvania Gov. Mark Schweiker also used the direct approach when he took control of a crisis in Pennsylvania (July 2002) after nine coal miners were trapped underground. Schweiker, the point person, was described as responsive, forthright and compassionate throughout the ordeal. His care and concern were visible at every news briefing. When it was determined that all nine miners were alive and relatively healthy, it was Schweiker who delivered the good news enthusiastically, raising his arms in triumph. Pennsylvania had a plan.

In contrast, it soon became apparent Pennsylvania State University followed none of the crisis communication rules in the Jerry Sandusky child sex-abuse scandal. Penn State did not react within the Golden Hours. In fact, its administration and ultimately its board did not respond to the crisis for days and in some cases, weeks.

A scientific survey conducted by *The Philadelphia Inquirer* proved perception is reality. The phone survey of 601 likely Pennsylvania voters conducted from Aug. 21 through 23, 2012 had a statistical margin of error of plus or minus 4 percent.

"*The Philadelphia Inquirer* Pennsylvania Poll found the state's voters widely disapproved of the way figures such as former Pennsylvania State University President Graham Spanier, head football coach Joe Paterno, and Gov. (Tom) Corbett handled allegations against the former assistant coach convicted in June 2012 of molesting 10 boys.

"Only 10 percent of those polled said they approved of Spanier's handling of the crisis, as opposed to the 77 percent who thought he had bungled the job.

PR Play 14-1
Three Rules of (Damage Control) Crisis Communication

1. Get information out early.
   - Respond within 2-4 hours (quicker, if possible) – if only as an acknowledgment that you are on top of the situation.
2. Get it out yourself.
   - The spokesperson should be a high profile representative of the organization.
3. Get it out on your own terms – control the message.

   - Tell it *First*

   - Tell it *Fast*

   - Tell it *All*

   - Tell it *Yourself*

"Paterno fared slightly better with a 28 percent approval rating and 65 percent who said they were disappointed by his actions.

"Only 17 percent of poll respondents said they approved of how Corbett had approached the investigation, while 61 percent found his decisions lacking."

Public Deserves Answers

Whether the crisis is the 2013 Boston Marathon bombing, child sex-abuse at Penn State University or some less visible organization, or a mass shooting at a school or movie theater, a major charity executive embezzling funds, the (seven) Tylenol-related deaths in 1982, or a space shuttle tragedy, the public wants and deserves answers.

As J. William Jones says, those answers must be based on accurate information and should be given by "unflappable" professionals who know what they are talking about.

The need for crisis management policies has become a major priority for many corporations and other organizations. Thanks to effective plan-

---

ning, victim organizations can control a crisis through rapid systematic dissemination of information – being proactive rather than reactive – so long as that information is factual.

> ### PR Play 14-2
> ### Phases of an Emergency
>
> - Initial Crisis
> - Successive Events
> - Follow-up Management

Strategic counselors and reporters alike agree there is no substitute for believability (truth) and credibility (trust). Once lost, they are nearly impossible to regain. Avoid any instincts to minimize or cover up bad news. If not totally truthful and trustworthy, the media will eventually discover your unprofessional approach. Whatever trust you once had will be gone forever.

Keep in mind, when dealing with a crisis, the goal should be more

> ### PR Play 14-3
> ### Communicate Early and Often
>
> - Contact the media before they contact you.
> - Communicate internally first, then externally.
> - Put the public first.
> - Take responsibility.
> - Be honest.
> - Never say "No comment."
> - Designate a single spokesperson.
> - Set up a central information center (staging area).
> - Provide a constant flow of information.
> - Be familiar with media needs and deadlines.
> - Monitor news coverage and telephone inquiries.
> - Communicate with key publics.
> - Be accessible.

than just "damage control." If the crisis communication plan is carried out properly and successfully, the damage control will take care of itself.

When a crisis hits, your publics want to know: what happened; how it will affect them; what is going to be done about it.

For the most part, there are two major categories of crises – *natural* and *man-made*.

Examples of *natural crises*:
* Created by acts of nature – tornados, hurricanes, blizzards
* Flood
* Flu epidemic

Examples of *man-made crises*:
* Terrorism
* Bomb threat
* Stock market crash

Developing a Crisis Communication Plan

No matter under which category your crisis falls, you will need an effective, proven, near-flawless (proactive) plan.

* The first step in any well-crafted strategic plan is research. But during a crisis, there may not be time enough to find the source or cause. If resources permit, appoint someone on staff to try to locate the cause. Meanwhile, others should be gathering the facts. Those facts will greatly assist in communicating accurate information and minimizing rumors. No matter the magnitude of the crisis, only one person should be designated as a spokesperson. This helps assure control of the situation, which should sway public opinion to your side.

* Gathering the facts and implementing your plan should be simultaneous. During the first session (within those Golden Hours) with the media or the first communiqué from the public relations office, it may have to be explained, "This is the information we have thus far. As additional facts are gathered we will continue to keep you informed or we will schedule media briefings." This will help manage and control the flow of information. Operating from a "staging area" or "situation ("war") room" – possibly at an alternate site (to help control the situation and maintain calm) – has proven successful. It could be a small conference room or a large office. No matter where you choose to locate your staging area, a central facility should be used to gather and disseminate information. It should be a room equipped with hardline phones, wireless technology (Wi-fi), computers, copiers, etc. (See Emergency Management Kit, PR Play 14-11.)

- All employees should be aware, in advance, that management does have a crisis plan. They don't have to know how the plan works unless they are part of its implementation. However, if a crisis hits, that plan should be publicized, first internally and then to outside publics. It is the internal family who helps communicate calm and control to external publics. That internal family should include more than employees. It may include stakeholders (possibly neighbors of an oil refinery that may be emitting fumes into the atmosphere).

- If you have the luxury of running *crisis drills*, do so. During the drills, gather feedback from people you trust. They could be employees, reporters, key communicators (Chapter 15 – Other PR Tools), independent evaluators or crisis management personnel from other organizations.

PR Play 14-4
The Role of Public Relations in the Johnson & Johnson® Tylenol® Crisis

The public relations decisions related to the Tylenol crisis and the product's strong comeback came in two phases.

Phase one was the crisis phase, which began on the morning of September 30, 1982, with the grim news of the cyanide poisonings. Since the extent of the contamination was not immediately known, there was grave concern for the safety of the estimated 100 million Americans who were using Tylenol. The first critical public relations decision, taken immediately and with total support from company management, was to cooperate fully with the news media. The press was key to warning the public of the danger.

Later it was realized that no meeting had been called to make that critical decision. The poisonings called for immediate action to protect the consumer, and there wasn't the slightest hesitation about being completely open with the news media. For the same reasons the decision was made to recall two batches of the product, and later to withdraw it nationally. During the crisis phase of the Tylenol tragedy, virtually every public relations decision was based on sound, socially responsible business principles, which is when public relations is most effective.

cont.

PR Play 14-4 continued

Almost immediately, planning began for phase two, the comeback, and this involved a more detailed and extensive public relations effort that closely followed important marketing decisions and reached out to many audiences. The comeback began officially with a 30-city video press conference via satellite, an innovative approach suggested by Burson-Marsteller, the public relations agency responsible for Tylenol product publicity.

The video conference and all other key decisions were discussed and debated by a seven-member strategy committee formed by Chairman and CEO James E. Burke to deal with the Tylenol crisis. The committee included a public relations executive and met twice daily for six weeks. The decisions it made dealt with every aspect of the problem – from packaging to advertising to appearances on network television. Many required follow-up by the public relations staff at corporate and at McNeil Consumer Products Company – the subsidiary that manufactures Tylenol.

The Tylenol tragedy proved once again that public relations is a business of basics, and that the best public relations decisions are closely linked to sound business practices and a responsible corporate philosophy.

Lawrence G. Foster
Corporate Vice President-Public Relations
Johnson & Johnson

- Just as research is the first step in any plan, evaluation is the final step. As Jones puts it, "All crises have at least one thing in common. Eventually, they end." That's when you evaluate your plan, its successes and its failures. If you made a mistake, do as PECO® did, admit it. Just don't let it happen again. By recognizing mistakes or shortcomings, you should be able to build a better plan for the next crisis.

Every step should be reviewed (keep a minute-by-minute diary). Don't be afraid to ask everyone involved for feedback – staff, reporters, key communicators, other members of the public, etc.

PR Play 14-5
Lessons Learned

- Don't duck the issue.
- Take responsibility.
- Offer to make good on broken promises.
- Cover all the bases.
- Measure results.

KDPaine & Partners, LLC • www.measuresofsuccess.com

PR Play 14-6
Get Down to Basics

1. When a crisis breaks, first, before anything else, get the facts – gather information.
2. Once you have the facts, determine which changes must be made in the strategic plan to best manage this particular crisis.
3. Communicate your plan, first internally, then externally.
4. Seek feedback.
5. Evaluate your plan.

PR Play 14-7
The 10 D's of Crisis Communication

- Direct
- Distance
- Deflect
- Distract
- Divert
- Diffuse
- Defuse
- Dilute
- Dissolve
- Dodge

Initial Crisis

- Recognize there is a crisis.
- Inform staff of the crisis.
- Put both crisis plans – communication and operational – into action ("everyone to their stations").

- Establish command post (staging area – situation room) and begin gathering facts (first true step):
  1. Extent of the disaster
  2. Names of all involved
  3. Are there injuries and if so, at what locations
  4. Retrieve information from computer
- Activate communication network:
  1. Smartphones, tablets, PCs and laptops
  2. Establish contact with team members (your so-called crisis cabinet)
- Establish communication with emergency agencies
- Decision making:
  1. Assign and reassign staff depending on type of crisis
  2. Schedule news briefings
  3. Determine need for such support services as food, shelter, security, counseling, etc.

Successive Events

- Determine who will communicate with families of victims (injured or killed).
- Maintain contact with media through briefings, news conferences, releases, interviews and continuous blast texts. (Do not play favorites.)
- Deal with rumors (as resources permit, one staff member should be assigned the task of dissolving rumors).
- Be prepared for additional emergencies.

Follow-up Management

- Continue the flow of information.
- Continually evaluate and adjust your plan.

Knowing the difference between media training and presentation training could be pivotal. Media training is more concerned with looks, gestures and mannerisms. Actual presentations need rehearsals to work on delivery, key message points and tone setting. Rehearsals and presentations should be video and audio taped – and viewed and listened to – so that adjustments can be made (Chapter 10).

Hindsight is 20-20. But one thing has been proven time and again — the lesson to be learned when dealing with a crisis is to adopt a philosophy similar to that of KDPaine & Partners, LLC headquartered in Berlin, N.H. (www.measuresofsuccess.com):

- *Don't duck the issue* – Every time a company tries to "stonewall" or deny the story, the media will gather information and print or air it. Companies that take a forthright approach to their crises reduce publicity almost immediately.

- *Take responsibility* – It is important to accept responsibility immediately and offer to fix the problem. Take a page from Taco Bell®. In December 2006, an E.coli outbreak struck a relatively small number of its 5,800 restaurants, but sent dozens of customers to hospitals – some seriously ill. Taco Bell® took action. "We immediately notified health officials and voluntarily closed several restaurants in New Jersey, New York, Pennsylvania and Delaware," said Greg Creed, Taco Bell® president. "The public's safety continues to be our utmost concern, and we will actively support an industry coalition including government regulators, competitors, suppliers and other experts to develop improved guidelines and procedures to safeguard the product supply chain and public health." Taco Bell® established a toll-free number to answer questions and deal with concerns. That's the kind of decisive action that must be taken.

- *Cover all bases* – In the Tylenol tragedy, J & J® removed its product from store shelves and warehouses nationwide, absorbed the losses, eventually developed an improved product with several safety devices on the packages and offered consumers "gift certificates" for any product they disposed of. Simultaneously, J & J®, through its corporate public relations office, cooperated fully with the news media (using a single spokesperson).

PR Play 14-8
Crisis Management Tips from Professionals

1. Even the most carefully laid plans must be constantly re-evaluated and refined.
2. Planning is just the beginning.
3. Every crisis is different and when one occurs, it is a mistake to assume a plan will handle all the answers.
4. In a crisis, the best defense is staying on your toes.

- ***Offer to make good on broken promises*** – During alleged "profiling" of minority drivers on the New Jersey Turnpike, Gov. Christine Todd Whitman promised to correct it. When it became apparent that wasn't happening, she called for the resignation of the state police superintendent. (He sued the state and governor for forcing him out of office. The courts found in favor of the governor.)

- ***Measure results*** – Monitor the news media – using search engines and alerts. Press clipping services are more efficient than ever. This is also a wonderful opportunity to tap your key communicators (feel their pulse [Chapter 15]) to help determine whether your approach is on course. Kathryn (Katie) Paine of KDPaine & Partners, LLC, reminds us, "In a crisis, the goal can never be to squelch negative coverage completely. Rather, it must be to shorten the life span of the bad news, to minimize those messages you don't want to see in print and get as many of your key messages out there as possible."

Almost immediately after a crisis hits, management must determine which of the so-called 10 D's it is going to use in its approach to communicating. Whichever is chosen, credibility must never be in doubt.

- ***Direct*** – to take charge with authority. (This is the newest approach to dealing with a crisis. It is a head-on approach to controlling or managing a situation. NASA's top administrators took the ***Direct*** approach [at the four hour mark] following the disintegration of the space shuttle Columbia in February 2003.)

- ***Distance*** – attempt to separate itself from the cause. (During Vice President Al Gore's presidential campaign, every effort was made to distance himself and other Democrats running for office from President Clinton because of Mr. Clinton's involvement with White House intern Monica Lewinsky.)

- ***Deflect*** – attempt to shift the blame. (In the Tylenol case, law enforcement officials did the deflecting for J & J®. Investigators determined that the tainting of the capsules was not done on J & J® premises and J & J® was not to blame.)

PR Play 14-9

Considerations Your *Single* Spokesperson *Must* Keep in Mind (During *A Crisis*)

- Do your homework.
- Be accessible.
- Be prompt and dependable.
- Avoid being pushed into easy solutions.
- Accept responsibility.
- Be responsive and forthright, and show compassion for victims and their families.
- Bluffing an answer is not acceptable – wait until you have the correct information.
- Speak and write your information clearly.
- Be prepared to respond to incorrect information.
- Remain calm and confident – at all times maintaining the proper emotional tone.

- **Distract** – attempt to divert focus or attention from a firm or organization. (Also called "The Tail Wagging the Dog," meaning an item of minor importance is created to intentionally influence events or gain more attention than the larger and more important event [in this case, the crisis]. This is not recommended. J & J® never attempted to side-track the media or consumer by placing blame elsewhere. It took quick, forceful and responsible action. In contrast, Penn State did not communicate for several days and its board of trustees avoided blame.)

- **Diffuse** – attempt to soften the blame on yourself by spreading out the cause. (In May 2000, the National Highway Transportation Safety Administration issued a letter to Ford® and Bridgestone-Firestone® requesting information about the high incidence of tire failure on Ford Explorer® vehicles. During July 2000, Ford obtained and analyzed the data on tire failure. "The data revealed that 15 inch ATX and ATX II models and Wilderness AT tires had very high failure rates: the tread peels off. Many of the tires were made at a Decatur, Illinois, plant. Worse, when the tires fail the vehicle often rolls over and kills the occupants." Initially, Bridgestone-Firestone and Ford Motor Company attempted to shift the blame to each other. In the end, they did the right thing. Even though they eventually accepted responsibility, the diffused approach was taken, with both companies attempting to ease

---

PR Play 14-10

Successful Crisis PR Depends on Planning and the Practitioner's Mindset. Needed Are:

- A strategic communication process in place
- Support from senior management
- Communication with the chief strategic counselor or someone with direct access to senior management
- Good relations and credibility with the news media
- Effective internal communication
- Strong peer relations, especially with attorneys
- Ability to "fly the plane" so to speak

C. Fernando Vivanco – The Boeing Company – and
Kathleen L. Lewton – Fleishman-Hillard, Inc.

---

the pain and prevent a similar crisis. Penn State's board could be accused of diffusing blame.)

- **Defuse** – attempt to prevent the "explosion" before it occurs. (J & J® did defuse the situation by accepting, or giving the perception of accepting, full responsibility whether or not it was fully at fault. J & J® manufactured the product. That was enough for upper management to do what it could to pull the plug [fuse] on a popular product, make good on consumer losses and maintain the public's confidence.)

- **Dilute** – to weaken. This is similar to *diffuse*, but isn't necessarily the spread of blame. It is an approach that clarifies a situation by demonstrating that it is not as "bad" as perceived. (In the Lewinsky matter, President Clinton was asked a number of questions about his relationship with Monica Lewinsky. Mr. Clinton attempted to weaken the interrogator by asking him to define "sex" and convincing enough senators that he should remain in office and not be convicted on impeachment.)

- **Dissolve** – to cause to disappear or vanish. (It is nearly impossible to dissolve a crisis or alleged crisis. That is why rumors can be so damaging. Too many times, people remember the first thing they hear about a topic. [Who was it that said, "We get only one chance to make a good first impression"?] Johnson and Johnson® did *dissolve* its Tylenol® crisis by launching the "caplet," which replaced the "capsule." J & J® not only regained its market share for Tylenol, but increased it – almost unheard of.)

PR Play 14-11
Emergency Management Kits

No matter the industry or profession, when a crisis or emergency hits, you should be just as ready with your own Emergency Management Kit (EMK) of communication-type items as you would be with a first-aid kit containing bandages, antiseptics, alcohol, etc. Below is one strategic counselor's suggestion for an EMK. Its contents might depend on the type of company or organization and staff size. You or your staff should customize your own, determine quantities and keep it current. Emergency Management Kits and copies of a Crisis Communication Plan should be in several locations so that if an emergency hits, the plan and kit will not be in a quarantined area. It should be quickly accessible by smartphones, tablets and other devices.

At the very minimum, it should contain:
1. Copy of Crisis Communication Plan (keep the plan on a password protected website link, USB "flash" drive, CD and hard copy.) Be certain it is up to date. The website could be kept "dark" until a crisis hits – known as a "dark website."
2. Legal pads.
3. Pens (ballpoint, felt tip [Bic® and Sharpie® brands are dependable]).
4. Large felt-tip markers.
5. Plain white peel-off stickers (used to identify injured staff at the emergency site).
6. List of (electronically accessible) phone numbers for various offices and satellite company locations, local law enforcement agencies, emergency medical services, fire department and other agencies that need to know of the crisis. Include cell phone numbers and email addresses on this list. Fax lines and emails at major offices should also be included.
7. List of cell and beeper numbers for staff.
8. Local phone directory with email addresses.
9. Current staff directory.
10. Floor plans showing locations of all exits, telephones and wall jacks, computers, and other devices that may be useful in communication during an emergency.
11. Fully charged battery-operated bullhorn.
12. Local street and zone maps.
13. For all trips from the site, a map showing the most direct and safest routes to be traveled to and from the destination.
    (For GPS navigation purposes, all addresses should be complete with street number and zip code.) cont.

PR Play 14-11 continued

14. List of assigned roles for personnel.
15. Summary of information that can be made public during an emergency. Include Freedom of Information Act summary, company policy and others.
16. List of professional and community contacts for organizing a crisis care team of counselors, clergy and others.
17. Laptop computers and tablets (iPad®) with fresh batteries.

• *Divert* – a combination of *deflect* and *distract*. It is both shifting blame and turning attention away from the issue(s) at hand (not a responsible approach). (Turner Broadcasting System's Cartoon Network® – either planned or unintentional – attempted to *divert* attention when its marketing campaign for the *Adult Swim* show "Aqua Teen Hunger Force" caused a massive panic in Boston – LED signs of Ignignot and Err [Mooninite Marauders characters from the show] were mistaken as explosive devices. Boston authorities may have overreacted when it shut down part of the city and detonated the cartoon publicity devices, but TBS and its Cartoon Network® should have taken immediate and *direct* responsibility for guerilla marketing that went bad and caused "panic.")

PR Play 14-12
An Award-Winning Crisis Communication Plan

To view the award-winning plan, "Philadelphia Phillies – A Crisis Communication Plan Commissioned by *Courier-Post*" go to www.larrylitwin.com and click on Student Resources, Classroom Handouts, No. 49. Plans use a decimal system for easy reference. The plan earned the 2006 Pepperpot Award from the Philadelphia chapter of the Public Relations Society of America for Crisis Communication and the Frank X. Long Achievement Award for "excellence in writing and creativity."

• ***Dodge*** – avoid answering questions or use of excuses (not always truthful).

The Pennsylvania School Boards Association suggests that the chief spokesperson must do his or her homework. The spokesperson must be prepared and knowledgeable about the situation.

Accessibility is important. Reporters must be able to contact the so-called "point person." Editors and reporters have been heard to complain that key personnel are not available when bad news breaks. Remember, if you want your strategic message heard, you have to say or write it.

Promises made to the media must be kept. But don't allow reporters to push you into a corner or into easy solutions. Many times, reporters and their editors are looking for "quick-fix" answers. Remember though, no matter the medium, there are deadlines.

The spokesperson is expected to act responsibly. It is recommended that legal advice be readily at hand.

If you don't have the answer to a question or are lacking some information, say so. Promise to get whatever is needed and provide it as soon as you can.

While much of the information the spokesperson is disseminating is verbal, it is advised to back it up with written copy. In all cases, avoid jargon that might be pertinent to a particular industry or profession. Communicate in terms that everyone can understand.

If there is incorrect information floating, be ready to respond. But first, ask this question: "Should a response be made?" If resources permit, attempt to locate the primary source of this incorrect information or rumor.

Other Suggestions

As you prepare for the worst, hoping it never happens, follow the advice of *BusinessWeek* magazine: "Be visible, be sympathetic, be responsible." Gov. Schweiker (coal mine crisis) was all three. He also followed the magazine's other suggestions: "Don't delay, don't deny, don't hope it will go away."

Remember to keep your firm or organization's website current. Get information on it rapidly. In fact, many firms have what they refer to as "dark sites" – available only in the event of a crisis or some other emergency. It links from the main website. Remember too, if there is no "new" news, say it on the website. Include the date and time of the latest update.

Dealing With the Media When a Crisis Strikes

One instance in our business or private lives when you cannot ignore the presence of the media is during a time of crisis. When a crisis hits, in a matter of seconds, it can forever change the course of your business – or someone's life.

In the moments and days following a crisis, the media will be a part of your life – visiting your facility, talking to employees, neighbors, government officials, self-proclaimed "experts" and more importantly, wanting to talk to you. Yes, you, the public relations practitioner – the center of the crisis. Should you grant an interview? Yes. All of the people involved in the situation will present their points of view. This is your opportunity to tell the story as you see it.

Here are some tips from Peter J. McCarthy, vice president, public affairs, Elf Atochem North America, Inc. They are designed to help you manage the crisis:

- Boil down your message to no more than two or three points and make certain you deliver those points no matter what else the reporter wants to talk about. You have every bit as much right as the reporter to set the agenda and terms of the interview.
- A word of caution – the reporter is not your friend. He or she is a professional who, no matter how personally charming, will get all points of view into the story. So don't feel betrayed when that "nice guy" reporter also presents your opponent's point of view – that's his or her job.
- Your job is to use the interview as an opportunity to hammer home – simply, briefly and repeatedly – those messages that you believe are important for your audience to understand.
- One last thing – in every relationship someone is in charge. During the interview, make certain the public relations practitioner is in charge. During a time of crisis, damage control is the reason for giving the interview. Making certain that you are in control maximizes the likelihood of successful damage control.

The message is simple: Be prepared; anticipate the crisis; know your message; and most importantly ask yourself, "Who is in charge here?"

Peter J. McCarthy – Vice President – Public Affairs
Elf Atochem North America, Inc.
The Philadelphia Inquirer/Feb. 24, 1997

PR Play 14-13
Bernstein's 10 Steps of Crisis Communication

"Crisis communication's function is to preserve the value of the brand. That's accomplished by minimizing the impact of the crisis."

1. Identify your crisis communication team
2. Identify spokesperson
3. Train spokesperson
4. Establish communication protocol (notification systems)
5. Identify and know your stakeholders
6. Anticipate crises
7. Develop holding statements (quick response)
8. Assess the crisis situation
9. Identify key messages
10. Riding out the storm

Jonathan Bernstein – Bernstein Crisis Management LLC – www.bernsteincrisismanagement.com

Anne Klein Communications Group, strategic counselors, takes the guesswork out of what should be said during a crisis:

1. **Description of the general nature of the incident**, i.e., fire, injury, lawsuit, etc.
2. **Time of occurrence.**
3. **Location and description of the facility or geographic area involved.** Supply maps and diagrams of the site, if they are available.
4. **Whether the incident** (e.g., fire) **has been controlled**. This description should be in general lay terms. Don't go into technical details that might lead to confusion on the part of the media and the public.
5. **Policies**, particularly safety and training – already adopted or approved.
6. **Corrective measures being taken at present** and, if you know for sure, what will be done in the long term. Example: "The fire department has the blaze under control. Everyone has been evacuated from the building. While the damage is being repaired, we will move our operations from this site to another location."

PR Play 14-14
Jack Welch's Five Stages of Crisis Management

1. **Denial** – Denial in the face of disaster is human. It is the main and immediate emotion people feel at the receiving end of any really bad news. That doesn't excuse any official from not reacting quickly and staying "in front of the story." Rather than denial, the reaction should be forthright, calm, fierce and bold.

2. **Containment** – In companies and other organizations, containment usually plays out with leaders trying to keep the "matter" quiet – a total waste of energy. All problems, and especially messy ones, eventually get out and explode.

3. **Shame-mongering** – This is a period in which all stakeholders fight to get their side of the story told, with themselves as the heroes at the center.

4. **Blood on the floor** – Too many times, officials believe that someone has to pay for the crisis with his or her head.

5. **Galvanizing effect** – The fifth and final part of the pattern – the best part – is the awareness raised by a crisis.

Jack Welch – Former Chairman and CEO – General Electric®

7. **Emergency officials on the scene**, including fire, police, highway transportation department.

8. **Presence or absence of injuries**, but do not give names of individuals involved.

9. **Name(s) of hospitals being used** in case of injury.

10. **Identify organization officials coming to the scene** (in general, by type or title rather than by name). The key message is to express management concern.

11. **Details of the media briefing process, time and place of the next update and/or continuing media briefings.**

12. **Name and phone number of an organization official to contact for further information.**

PR Play 14-15
Bill Jones' 10 Commandments of Crisis Communication

1. *Perception is reality.* If your audience thinks it is, it is.
2. *Response is control.* The community wants access to information, and no crisis is unmanageable if you give clear, cool facts.
3. *Information is power.*
4. *Credibility is survival.*
5. *Body language is crucial.* If you behave like you have something to hide, people will think that you do.
6. *Calmness is essential.* Unflappability is your best asset. Always act knowledgeable and calm.
7. *Give a confession.* The public and the media want a confession; so don't be afraid to admit mistakes.
8. *Tell the franchise what happened.* It is in the best interest of the community to keep them informed.
9. *Preparation is 99% of success.*
10. *Out of every crisis comes the chance to "build a better mousetrap."* From every crisis there are major lessons to be learned.
11. *Pray like hell that you never have to handle numbers 1 through 10!*

Here are some of Klein's **"Important DON'Ts in Dealing With the Media"** during a crisis:

1. **Do not speculate about anything.**
2. **Do not give out unconfirmed facts.** Give only the facts you are sure of until further information can be obtained.
3. **Do not speculate on the potential impact of the incident** on employees, neighbors, the community-at-large, etc., unless you know, for sure.
4. **Do not estimate on dollar figures for damage that occurred.**
5. **Do not release the names of anyone injured or killed until family members have been notified.**
6. **Do not give out any medical reports on condition(s) of the injured.** This is the responsibility of the attending physician or hospital spokesperson and is restricted by the federal medical privacy laws outlined in HIPAA (Health Insurance Portability and Accountability Act).
7. **Do not assume liability for the incident or guess how the incident occurred.**

8. **Do not ever respond to a question with "No comment."** It is never an acceptable answer. Say you don't know if you are unsure of the answer or that you will put reporters in touch with someone who can answer their questions. If a question requires an answer that you feel is proprietary to the organization or would violate confidentiality, just explain that fact.

9. **Do not speak "off the record," "not for attribution" or "on deep background."** This is an area of high risk, and it is best not to venture there. (See Chapter 9.)

10. **Do not get angry with a reporter or raise your voice.**

Anne Klein and others who have been successful in dealing with the media during crises agree on the importance of remaining calm. Take time to compose yourself and craft your message as you formulate your answers. Remember, you are a professional doing your best to be helpful. Practice the highest ethical standards. Succinctly, you want to be open, honest, thorough and valid (relevant) in your responses and dissemination of information. Above all, never lie to a reporter, but do not answer a question if you don't have the answer and don't offer unsolicited information unless it is to your benefit.

Klein recommends you notify the media before they contact you when the community is in danger; your organization's operations are affected; if having the media first learn about the situation from someone else would damage your organization's image or credibility; a good number of employees know or could possibly know about the situation; or if there are regulatory infractions that would embarrass your organization if the media learned about them in some other way.

Crisis Communications Since 9/11: Where Do We Stand Now?

Op-ed submitted by Howard J. Rubenstein, *Founder, Rubenstein Associates* – New York
First published on Sept. 11, 2006, and reprinted from "Expert Recommendations" – *Crisis Communication Plan – Philadelphia Phillies*

On September 11, 2001 a few hate-filled individuals changed history for millions by destroying the World Trade Center (owned and operated by my longtime client, Larry Silverstein). Not only the larger sweep of history, but also the mindset of millions of individual Americans was forever transformed.

This change directly affects my approach to public relations. No longer can we wait in relative security until there's a new crisis. Instead, public relations professionals have to begin advising clients on how to anticipate and prepare for a crisis that doesn't yet exist — and that could take any number of forms, including terrorism, pandemics and economic downturn. We now need to be more serious and attentive than ever before. This transformation increases the value of having ready at hand a list of "DO's" and "DON'Ts" for meeting a crisis of any type.

First off, when you see early signs of a brewing crisis, take them seriously. These signs might take various forms: information from an outside source, warnings from whistleblowers or disgruntled employees within a company, media calls, inquiries from government entities, etc. Whatever form they take, don't ever assume they'll go away if you avoid them. To the contrary, be as proactive as possible.

In other words, prepare in advance. Put together a crisis team composed of management, legal personnel, communications experts and human resources professionals. Designate one or two people who will respond to media calls. Once the team is together, ask yourselves, "What's the right thing to do?" rather than, "What do we say?" Gather all the facts you can and identify the audiences you want to communicate with. These could include readers, public officials, stockholders, employees, the general public, etc. Respond quickly and, most important, accurately to all queries. Set the ground rules with reporters before you talk and, wherever possible, prepare written responses rather than winging it. But get the bad news out quickly – avoid "water torture."

What you don't want to do is lie, adopt a bunker mentality, automatically say "no comment" (doing so implies guilt) or make up answers. Never fight with reporters or gossip with them. Remember: The reporter has the last word in print and gossip almost always gets out.

If you put together your own aggressive crisis communications plan along the above lines, you'll have a good chance of minimizing the damage of negative news. An Oxford University study found that corporations that managed crises effectively enhanced their stock prices while those that handled the crisis poorly damaged them.

Sept. 11 (2001) got public relations professionals thinking about survival in a whole new way. You could say that because of the larger crisis in which the world is locked right now, we have more responsibility than ever before to manage those crises that can be controlled as professionally and effectively as possible. Public relations has become a key back-up system, like an emergency generator, that more and more people realize they can't do without.

Howard Rubenstein founded Rubenstein Associates in 1954. The agency has an extensive list of more than 450 clients, including the New York Yankees, The New York Post, the Guggenheim Museum, BMW, the Mt. Sinai/NYU Health System, the Bowery Mission, Rockefeller Center, Columbia University and the Empire State Building.

EXERCISES

PR Challenges 14-1 and 14-2

Below is one, all encompassing challenge fashioned after those that too many institutions have had to face in recent years:

How would *you* handle the following?

You are strategic communication director for a private college in a small Iowa town. The college has an enrollment of 7,000 students in a town with a population of 8,000. The 105-year-old Fairfield College had been planning an expansion – possibly opening a satellite college on the east coast.

As luck would have it, Fairfield College appeared to hit the jackpot. A graduate offered to contribute $150 million to the college. The only catch – the school's new convocation center be named after her. College President S. William Kramer calls you (the strategic counselor) into a one-on-one meeting for advice. During that meeting, Dr. Kramer informs you naming the new convocation center after Louise Roberts seems hardly enough. He proposes that Fairfield College become Roberts College of Iowa – with one goal in mind – becoming a nationally, if not, internationally known university.

a) Your assignment is to develop a "plan" with a strategic message or two on how the contribution will be handled and announced.

Some issues to keep in mind:
• Audiences
  1. Internal
  2. External
  3. "Townies"
  4. Alumni

- Tradition of name
- Rebranding plus brand expansion
- How do you propose Dr. Kramer respond to the "townies" who have given long-time personal and financial support to the college that carries the local name?

This just in...

After all is said and done, the college has the money. It has changed its name, built a new convention center and named it and the college, which became a university, after Dr. Roberts.

However, about three years after all of this was done, it becomes known that Dr. Roberts earned 10s of millions of dollars, including what she gave for the endowment, through illicit means. She is found guilty and sentenced to prison.

b) As strategic counselor, what advice do you give Dr. Kramer about the money in the endowment, about the name change and the university's overall image?

CHAPTER 15
Public Relations Potpourri – Other Strategic Communication Tools

This chapter is devoted to the many strategic communication tactics and tools used by successful strategic counselors that didn't quite fit into any other chapter. While they are in no particular order, all are integral to the profession.

SWOT Analysis
Understanding Your Strengths, Weaknesses, Opportunities and Threats

Mind Tools (www.mindtools.com) believes in helping people who are starting or advancing their careers to better understand the essential skills and techniques needed for them to excel in their chosen profession. Making the right decisions is crucial. Among the tools that help with judgment and decision making are the SWOT Analysis and Force Field Analysis (PR Play 15-18).

Why Use The SWOT Analysis?

SWOT Analysis is an effective way of identifying your *strengths* and *weaknesses*, and of examining the *opportunities* and *threats* you face. Carrying out an analysis using the SWOT framework will help you to focus your activities into your stronger areas, where the greatest opportunities lie.

How to Use SWOT

To carry out a SWOT Analysis, write down answers to the following questions. Where appropriate, use similar questions under the other categories:

Strengths:
- What are your advantages?
- What do you do well?
- What do other people see as your strengths?

Consider this from your own point of view and from the point of view of the people you deal with. Don't be modest – be realistic. If you are having any difficulty with this, try writing down a list of your characteristics. Some of these will hopefully be strengths!

Weaknesses:
- What could you improve?
- What do you do badly?
- What should you avoid?

Again, consider this from an internal and external basis – do other people seem to perceive weaknesses that you do not see? Are your competitors doing any better than you? It is best to be realistic now, and face any unpleasant truths as soon as possible.

Opportunities:
- Where or what are the good opportunities facing you?
- What is your awareness of interesting trends?

Useful opportunities can come from such things as:
- Changes in technology and markets on both a broad and narrow scale.
- Changes in government policy related to your field.
- Changes in social patterns, population profiles, lifestyle changes, etc.
- Local events.

Threats:
- What obstacles do you face?
- What is your competition doing?
- Are the required specifications for your job, products or services changing?
- Is changing technology threatening your position?
- Do you have debt or cash-flow problems?

Carrying out this analysis will often be illuminating – both in terms of pointing out what needs to be done, and in putting problems into perspective.

You can also apply SWOT analysis to your competitors – this may produce some interesting insights.

Example:

A start-up small consulting business might carry out the following SWOT analysis:

Strengths:

- We are able to respond quickly as we have no red tape, no need for higher management approval, etc.
- We are able to give good customer care, as the current small amount of work means we have plenty of time to devote to customers.
- Our lead consultant has a strong reputation within the market.
- We can change direction quickly if we find that our marketing is not working.
- We have low overhead (fixed expenses), so we can offer good value to customers.

Weaknesses:

- Our company has no market presence or reputation.
- We have a small staff with a shallow skills base in many areas.
- We are vulnerable to vital staff being sick, leaving, etc.
- Our cash flow will be unreliable in the early stages.

Opportunities:

- Our business sector is expanding, with many future opportunities for success.
- Our local town council wants to encourage local businesses with work where possible.
- Our competitors may be slow to adopt new technologies.

Threats:

- Will developments in technology change this market beyond our ability to adapt?
- A small change in focus of a large competitor might wipe out any market position we achieve.

The consultant might therefore decide to specialize in rapid response, good value services to local businesses. Marketing would be in selected local publications, to get the greatest possible market presence for a set advertising budget. The consultant should keep up to date with changes in technology where possible.

Key points:
SWOT analysis is a framework for analyzing your strengths and weaknesses and the opportunities and threats you face.

This will help you to focus on your strengths, minimize weaknesses and take the greatest possible advantage of opportunities available.

For more, go to: www.mindtools.com/swot.html

Special Events and Workshop Planning

Strategic Communication for Special Events

Some events just *happen*. Others are *created*. Created events, especially, need ingenuity and organizing ability to attract coverage in the news media. This extra dimension of creativity is the difference between *acting* to make news and merely *reacting* to news that happens. If your event *is* newsworthy, the coverage will come.

Strategic communication for *special events* would fall under *events management*. Special events include news conferences, anniversary celebrations, rallies, parades, yearlong celebrations, fundraisers, symposiums, grand openings, groundbreakings, ribbon cuttings and national conferences. Others examples include organ donor week, college/high school homecoming, parents' weekend, etc. Weddings and funerals are special events, too.

Four of the most successful special events ever created and carried out (executed) are the *2013 Presidential Inauguration* attended by more than a million people and the recurring *Super Bowls*, *Olympics* and *Academy Awards Ceremonies*.

Attracting attendance at an event requires a well-planned strategic campaign that includes the dissemination of a great deal of news and publicity. An advance information or publicity campaign informs readers, viewers and listeners that an event will occur and stimulates a desire to attend it.

A primary goal of a special event might be to attract large numbers of people. If ticket sales are involved, a goal is to sell those tickets.

Unfortunately, in metropolitan areas, news outlets usually won't serve as shills – in other words, the stories they carry will be more news stories than advertising type of stories. Rather than concentrate on ticket prices and event times, the outlets will look for a news angle, which would include features on participants, or on the reason the event is being held in the first place.

Presumably, every time the event is mentioned, public awareness grows. The astute strategic communicator should search for as many different angles as possible to produce a story.

PR Play 15-1
Special Events

Stimulating an interest in a person, product or organization by means of a *focused (noteworthy)"happening."*

Also, activities designed to interact with publics and to listen to them.

Newspapers are devoting more and more space to entertainment listings – both in hard copy and online. Because the so-called news hole is getting smaller, and because more of us in public relations are competing for the same space and time, the print media are listing events in agate (very small) type. And, research shows, dating back to the earliest days of movie listings, the public searches for various *events guides*. Take advantage of them.

And, just in case you haven't noticed, more and more network and local newscasts are carrying entertainment-type stories. They are no longer relegated to news magazines.

Drip-Drip-Drip Technique of Publicity

The *Drip-Drip-Drip* technique is the steady output of information from the time a decision is made that an event is going to take place or a product launched. As the event draws closer, the release of information intensifies. The heaviest barrage of information is released shortly before the actual event or launch.

The *Drip-Drip-Drip* technique builds anticipation and demand.

Once the event is completed, strategic communicators should evaluate its success or failure. The most common technique is an evaluation sheet that participants – not the people producing the event, but rather the attendees – fill out at the end of the event.

PR Play 15-2

Nov. 18 – CHEDCO* List of "Things" to Remember (Think Backwards)

Week One Oct 21-25	❑ 1	Create flier – Get final approval!
	❑ 2	Print envelopes for next meeting
	❑ 3	Update database with new CHEDCO members
	❑ 4	Make certain hotel is reserved
	❑ 5	Send detail letter to sponsor
	❑ 6	Update the website • New Program • Sponsor

Week Two Oct 28-Nov 1	❑ 1	Sponsor information/mailers
	❑ 2	Request staff
	❑ 3	Write News Release/get approval
	❑ 4	From speakers: Get resumes/ biographies Request additional invitation list
	❑ 5	Mail and Blast email THE INVITATION!!!!!!!!
	❑ 6	Finalize speaking points • Who is speaking for sponsor? • What is next month's topic? • Information on speakers
	❑ 7	Send detail letter to speaker

Week Three Nov. 4-13	❑ 1	Create name tags
	❑ 2	Money from petty cash
	❑ 3	RSVP list
	❑ 4	Fax/email Media Alert
	❑ 5	Make receipts
	❑ 6	Detail email to staff
	❑ 7	Flier – 2 copies/speaking points – 15 copies Media Alert (for reporters who might attend)
	❑ 8	Contact hotel and give RSVP numbers on 11/15
	❑ 9	Request specifics from • Hotel (caterer) • AV • Head table
	❑ 10	Reminder email to CHEDCO list on 11/12

Week of Event Nov. 18-22	❑ 1	Thanks to sponsor
	❑ 2	Where is the money?
	❑ 3	Thanks to speakers
	❑ 4	Create Financial Report for event
	❑ 5	Send hotel (caterer) voucher for the bill

* Cherry Hill (N.J.) Economic Development Council

PR Play 15-3

The Primary goal of any *Special Events Campaign* is to attract people. If the sale of tickets is involved, an objective is *to sell tickets.*

PR Play 15-4
First Step for a Special Event

Develop a *Strategic Plan* ...a list of DOs.

What do I have to do to reach my goal/objectives? Which strategies and tactics am I going to implement?

PR Play 15-5
Planning Our Special Event

- Goals
  - Why are we having this event?
  - What do we want to accomplish?
- Research
  - How will we accomplish our goals?
  - How will we tell if we've accomplished our goals?
- Budget
  - How much is appropriated?
  - How much does it make sense to spend?

A simple form asking people to rate such items as location, costs, facilities and program on a scale of one to five (one being the best) can be used. Other forms may ask people to rate aspects of a conference or a meeting as **(1) excellent, (2) good, (3) average or (4) could be better.**

Evaluation forms also can ask how people heard about the program and what suggestions they would make for the future.

An important step to remember is the release of the *media advisory* (Chapter 5 – Basic Strategic (Persuasive) Writing Techniques).

Some Special Events Tips
Itemize as you would with a budget. Where called for – be specific.

- Some events are to generate publicity – others are to get publicity.
- Shot list – Tell the photographer what types of pictures must be taken and who should be in them.
- Develop a Gantt Chart (Chapter 7).
- Staff the event.
  - Who to go to when there is a problem
- Have a back-up plan.
- Keep excellent records/diary.
- Create agenda for emcee.
  - What to say
  - What to wear
- It is your event. Try to enjoy it.
- There are no new ideas in our profession – just try to put your own fingerprint on it.
- Sponsorships should be visible to the media.
- Corporate sponsorship
  - Putting your name on an event is one thing – What you do with the sponsorship is another.
  - Sponsors need an answer to the question: "What is our return on the investment?"

Kate Sullivan, former public relations director – Morris Arboretum of the University of Pennsylvania, offers a number of suggestions she calls, "What's so *Special* about *Special* events, anyway?" She says special events are to:
- Celebrate accomplishments
- Mark significant occasions
- Encourage fellowship or camaraderie
- Raise money
- Garner public attention

You already know why – purpose – you are producing the special event. Now, the *MAC Triad Plus* must be employed not only to determine the *message, audience, channel* and *timing*, but to identify the who, what, when and where. Sullivan calls it "getting started."

Sullivan recommends working with reputable vendors willing to sign specifically written contracts. They lead to fewer misunderstandings.

Who?	What?	When?	Where?
Know your audience	Determine appropriate time frame	Timing is crucial Consider holding your event on the fifth Monday, Tuesday, etc. of a month. That would avoid regularly scheduled events. Organizations may choose a first and third Monday or Tuesday, but no group regularly schedules a fifth Monday of a month.	Make it convenient
Other publics	What will it finally look like?	Research possible conflicts	Be creative
Decision-makers/Influencers		Work in the future	Is it fun?

Some suggested "itemized line items" might include:

Venue	**Program**	**Decorations**
Indoors/outdoors	Speakers/speeches	Flowers
Yours or somewhere else	Entertainment	Balloons
	"Why we are here"	Favors/goody bags
		Theme?

She advises, "Always have a contingency plan."

Here are some "bonus" words of wisdom: be reliable with payments; be realistic with expectations; if there is a problem, share the blame; and learn from every event.

You are the special event's planner/producer and should be aware when glitches occur – but unless you point them out, chances are no one will notice. Remember, "The plan is nothing. Planning is everything. (But hope is not a plan)." Because you crafted the plan, you know what is in it – including those contingencies.

PR Play 15-6
Kate's 10 Key Points to Event Planning (Summarized)

1. Decide what you want to plan.
2. Organize the volunteers.
3. Be ready for anything.
4. Create a timeline (think backwards).
5. Create an incentive for participation in the event.
6. Communicate with your participants.
7. Make it a learning experience for attendees (what will they take away with them?).
8. The event – if well planned – will run itself (planning is everything).
9. Evaluate plan (and event) after it is finished (exit survey).
10. Have fun!!!

Kate Sullivan – Former Public Relations Director – Morris Arboretum of the University of Pennsylvania

---

Planning Effective Presentations

Houston-based strategic counselor Eileen Weisman stresses that effective presentations and special events take time, discipline and thorough planning. Effectively presenting information and material so that it is interpreted as intended (*clarity*) is vital. This section deals with key elements used by anyone who must stand in front of large groups and share information. It also proves quite helpful for the practitioner who is called on to plan special events.

Weisman, along with Phillip E. Bozek, Ph.D., author of *50 One Minute Tips to Better Communication*; Steven Mandel, *Effective Presentation Skills*; and Bert Decker, author of *The Art of Communicating,* are event planning specialists. Much of what follows are their proven techniques.

Tips for Organizing Effective Presentations

1. Emphasize Benefits in Your Introduction to Gain the Audience's Attention

Audiences tend to pay the most attention to the introductions and conclusions of business presentations. Therefore, they must be extremely powerful! Think carefully about your audiences' interests and concerns. Find ways your presentation will benefit them and make sure they know about it right from the start of your talk.

2. Use "Quick Specifics" for High Credibility

In professional presentations, especially those taking the persuasive approach, state specific names, facts, examples, statistics, stories or analogies, in rapid fire sequence early in your presentation. Your audience will assume your evidence must be overwhelming, and therefore your point must be valid. Follow-up with more in depth evidence. You must be prepared to provide supporting information on any piece of data you present to maintain your credibility.

3. Use the *B.E.S.T.* Recipe to Organize your Points

B = Bottom Line

To open each section of your presentation, state in 25 words or less the point you wish to make in that section. Use a signpost phrase to move from one to the other. For example, "The next point I would like to make...."

E = Evidence

After stating your point, list the best specific evidence, examples, statistics or stories you have to support it.

S = Summary of Bottom Line

Restate your point so the audience knows you are emerging from specifics into a general statement. You can use a signpost here, such as "To summarize this point...."

T = Transition to Next Point

Lead your audience to your next point with a transitional statement like, "That leads me to the next point," or "Now, let's move on." If you are making many points, rehash your key messages midway for your listeners, as you move through points four or five of a long presentation.

4. Conclude with Optimism, Challenges and Pronouns

The conclusion is an especially important part of your presentation. An ideal conclusion summarizes the main points of a presentation and also answers a very important question: "So What?"

The best answer to "so what?" involves translating the presentation's ideas into audience involvement. In some high-powered presentations, this may involve a dramatic rallying of the audience to action. But even in relatively low-key presentations, you may often find that an optimistic, team-building feeling would be appropriate as you conclude. To achieve this motivational effect, experiment with the following ideas in your conclusion:

- **Challenge** – Review your key points, possibly rephrasing them in a final perspective. Tell the audience that the ideas you have proposed may not be easy to implement. Challenge them to take on the ideas anyway.
- **Optimism** – Express as much sincere confidence as you can. Be willing to take on the challenges yourself. Predict a realistic success.
- **The future** – Refer specifically to times to come. Even use the word *future* as you predict a brighter day.
- **Pronouns** – Make your talk personal. Use the words, *I, me* or *mine* – referring to your own commitment and resolve. Tell how you feel. Risk a bit of self-disclosure. Also, use the word *you* to refer to the audience – or even better yet, *we, us* or *our* – referring to yourself and the audience as a team.
- **A final, uplifting phrase** – Make the very last words you say turn the group upward, not downward. End on a very strong, positive note. This is the one line most people will remember from your talk.

Working with Visual Aids

Visual aids help your audience understand the information you are presenting because it is now coming to them through both auditory and visual channels. We recommend keeping the physical format of your visual aids consistent and use the **"Three B's."**

BIG! The content of a visual should be written or drawn large enough to be seen by the entire audience. Fill the space of your visual aid. If it is a flip chart or white board, work it top to bottom, and leave space to create a comfortable border.

BOLD! Visual content should be prominent and clear. The lines should be striking and sharp. Avoid fancy lettering. If using colored markers, use the broad side of the tip for a bolder line.

BRILLIANT! Use more than one color per visual. Colors trigger emotions and help emphasize key points. Some colors are harmonious with each other; others contrast. Darker colors "come forward" visually while lighter colors "recede." Yellow doesn't show up well against white, but yellow against blue (in PowerPoint® slides, for example) is very intense and vivid. Use color in consistent patterns to tie ideas together.

Ten Tips for Planning Successful Visual Aids

When considering what type of visual representation to use for your data or ideas, there are some rules to consider:

1. **Use visual aids sparingly** – One of the biggest problems in technical presentations is the overuse of visual aids. A useful rule of thumb is one visual aid for every two minutes of presentation time.
2. **Use visual aids pictorially** – Graphs, pictures of equipment or buildings and flow charts. All give the audience an insight that would require many words or columns of numbers.
3. **Present one key point per visual** – Keep the focus of the visual simple and clear. Presenting more than one main idea per visual can seriously detract from the impact.
4. **Make text and numbers legible** – Minimum font size for most room set-ups is 18 pt. A sans serif font such as Arial or Univers is preferred. Can you read everything? If not, be prepared to provide additional explanation in handout material or highlight the areas of the chart where you want the audience to focus.
5. **Use color carefully** – Use no more than three to four colors per visual aid to avoid a cluttered rainbow effect. The colors used should contrast with each other to provide maximum visibility. Avoid "busy" graphics in color presentations. They quickly become hard to distinguish.

6. **Make visuals big enough to see** – Walk to the last row where people will be sitting and make sure that everything on the visual can be seen clearly.

7. **Graph data** – Whenever possible avoid tabular data (columns) in favor of graphs. Bar graphs and pie charts allow viewers to picture the information and data in a way that numbers alone can't do.

8. **Make pictures and diagrams easy to see** – Too often pictures and diagrams are difficult to see from a distance. The best way to ascertain this is to view it from the back of the room where the audience will be. Be careful that labels inside the diagrams are legible from the back row, also.

9. **Make visuals attractive** – If using color, use high contrast such as yellow on black or yellow on dark blue (reverse) for PowerPoint® slides. Avoid clutter and work for simplicity and clarity.

PR Play 15-7
Ten Tips for Planning Successful Visual Aids

1. Use visual aids sparingly
2. Use visual aids pictorially
3. Present one key point per visual
4. Make text and numbers legible
5. Use color carefully
6. Make visual big enough to see
7. Graph data
8. Make pictures and diagrams easy to see
9. Make visuals attractive
10. Avoid miscellaneous visuals

PR Play 15-8
Try to involve your audience if you can!

People retain:

23% of what they hear

43% of what they hear and see

70% of what they hear/see and do

---

10. **Avoid miscellaneous visuals** – If something can be stated simply and verbally, such as the title of the presentation, there is no need to use a visual aid.

Nine Audience Involvement Techniques

Adapt the following list to all your communications and you will definitely involve your audience.

1. Drama

Create a strong opening by announcing a serious problem, telling a moving story, or asking a rhetorical question to get each person thinking. You can also make a startling statement.

Include a dramatic element – such as a long pause – to emphasize a key statement, vocal tone and pitch changes, or higher-intensity emotion such as anger, joy, sadness or excitement.

Add visual and kinesthetic detail such as color, smell, temperature and other sensations to vividly recreate a story or experience for your listeners.

End your communications with a dramatic or inspirational quote, or a firm call to action.

2. Eye Communication

Survey all of your listeners when you start speaking before beginning extended eye communication with any individual.

Keep your listeners involved and engaged by maintaining a three to six second contact with as many as possible. Don't forget "orphans" at the far edges of a room or along your side of a conference table during small meetings.

Gauge the reaction of your listeners throughout your presentation. Do they agree?

Are they bored? Do they have questions?

3. Movement

Change the dynamics of your presentation with purposeful movement. Whenever possible, move around the room.

Never back away from your audience. Move towards them – especially at the beginning and the end of your communication.

4. Visuals

Add variety by using visuals. Give your audience something to look at in addition to you.

Use different types of visual aids in a formal presentation – for instance, use overheads, flip charts or brief PowerPoint®. Rehearse in advance so the transitions are smooth and non-distracting.

Involve the audience by using such techniques as writing audience concerns on a flip chart, filling in an overhead transparency or interactive white board (SmartBoard®) as you go.

5. Questions

There are three types of questions you can use in a group setting. Each allows you to obtain a deeper level of involvement:

- Rhetorical questions will keep your listeners active and thinking. This is especially valuable when you don't have time or it's not appropriate to actually discuss an issue.
- Ask for a show of hands to get listeners more involved and to give you a quick way to measure their reactions.
- Ask for a volunteer. Even though only one will speak or act, you can feel the adrenalin rush through the others as they consider whether they might be the volunteer.

6. Demonstrations

Plan ahead for every step or procedure and be sure to accurately time the demonstration before you use it.

Have a volunteer from the group help you in your demonstration.

7. Samples/Gimmicks

Have fun with your listeners. Get them involved, but you should always stay in control of the session. Keep topics appropriate for your profession as well as for your listeners.

If you are promoting a product, consider using samples to "reward" volunteer participants.

Use creativity. Gimmicks can be used effectively in most business settings. But keep things in good taste.

8. Interest
Before you speak, review what you plan to say by asking yourself, "How does my presentation benefit my audience?"

Recognize short attention spans. Use eye contact to gain interest. Use examples, drama, humor, visuals and movement to engage your audience.

Maintain a high level of personal interest. If you make the same presentation repeatedly, consider changing examples, getting listeners involved in different ways, or changing the order of your presentation without detracting from any of the elements.

9. Humor
Begin with a friendly, warm comment. A personal remark will start the ball rolling and relax things. Be professional while allowing your "humanness" to appear.

Develop a sense of humor and use it. Make your humor appropriate to your audience and relevant to your presentation. You might tell stories, refer to current events, include one-liners, poke fun at yourself or even play off a listener's comments.

Be willing to laugh at yourself if you make a mistake.

Workshop Planner
Draw up a *Memorandum of Agreement* in advance that clearly defines each partner's role and level of responsibility.

Criteria for successful workshop
• Confident and enthusiastic workshop chairs and facilitators
• Recruit strong partners: a professional team with experience in delivering workshops – a viable corporate or societal partner

Where to begin?
• Form a planning committee
• Obtain sponsorship
• Hold planning sessions

Form a planning committee
The first step in planning a workshop is to form a planning committee. The group should be comprised of people with different perspectives and expertise and with a stake in the workshop.

PR Play 15-9
Presentation Skills Self Assessment

Read the following statements carefully. Use the following scale to indicate how often the following apply to your presentations.

1. Never • 2. Rarely • 3. Sometimes • 4. Often • 5. Always

1. I set well-defined objectives for my presentations.
2. I do my homework before a presentation, making sure I thoroughly understand the audience's needs, interests and wants.
3. I completely understand the conclusions that my audience must reach for me to be successful.
4. I make sure that I provide persuasive content so my audience can reach those conclusions.
5. When preparing for presentations, I focus on my audience's needs rather than my needs.
6. When preparing for presentations, I organize my key message points (KMPs) in a sequence that will have the maximum impact on those I am trying to persuade.
7. In my presentations, I use words and phrases appropriate to my audience.
8. At the beginning of my presentations, I develop audience interest.
9. At the beginning of my presentations, I prepare my audience for the material ahead, setting clear expectations.
10. My presentations always have at least one clear and memorable message.
11. The structure of my presentations makes them easy to deliver and easy to follow.
12. I use vocal energy and variety to keep the audience's attention.
13. I use appropriate and timely gestures and facial expressions.
14. I maintain eye contact with my audience.
15. I control my nervousness during my presentations.
16. I set a friendly tone to my presentations.
17. The visual aids I use provide powerful reinforcement to my presentations.
18. I control the visual aids, rather than the visual aids controlling me.
19. I allow constructive dialogue and answer questions during the presentations in such a way as to maintain rapport and audience involvement.
20. I conclude my presentations with an effective summary, action steps or memorable line.
21. I seek constructive feedback on my presentations from my peers.

David R. Voss – Voss and Associates – Sarasota, Fla.

The necessary range of resources and expertise may not be contained within a single organization. It may be necessary to identify other organizations that may be suitable partners.

Key criteria will include:
• Knowledge of the subject
• Contacts at a senior level within government, the legislature and civil society
• Expertise and contacts in the media

The planning committee will:
• Establish the purposes and objectives of the workshop.
• Plan the activities leading up to delivery of the workshop.

PR Play 15-10

The composition of the planning committee is critical. Criteria include recruiting strong partners with experience in delivering workshops.

In addition, useful questions are:
• Who can be counted on or motivated to give time, to contribute actively, to come up with new ideas?
• Who is needed to make or facilitate key decisions?
• Who is needed to facilitate the practical arrangements for the workshop?
• Who will act as secretary to the group (this can be decided at the first meeting)?

PR Play 15-11

Where there is doubt about the willingness or ability of individuals to participate, sound them out before formally inviting them to the first meeting.

Obtain Sponsorships
• Identify potential sponsors
  – Visit chamber of commerce, economic development council or municipal government websites for corporate listings.

– Pay particular attention to firms and organizations bullish on *cause-related marketing (positive association)*.

– Ask key communicators for their valuable input. (Those involved with major firms may be interested themselves.)

PR Play 15-12

A memorandum of agreement should be drawn up between partners to clarify the roles and responsibilities of the organizations.

Budgeting

A first step in budgeting is to create expense function categories. Itemize these categories – be specific. You may end up with a minimal budget, but it is valuable to chart out (line item budgeting) what you might require and what you have to work with.

The main direct costs to consider for a workshop include:

• Event site rental (room hire)
• Catering (coffee/tea breaks, lunch)
• Closing reception
• Supplies/stationary (e.g., flip charts, markers, pads of paper, pens, folders, etc.)
• Participants' travel allowances (if applicable)
• Lodging
• Honoraria for keynote speaker(s), chairs and session speakers
• Professional photographer
• Production of background papers, information packs, and advance and ongoing publicity
• Production, printing and binding of handouts and other collateral materials
• Cost of translating program/proceedings into local language(s) (if appropriate)
• Distribution of handouts
• Website publication
• Program development and production
• Program printing and production costs
• Promotion
• Audio visual equipment rental
• Other equipment rental
• Contingency/last minute expenses
• Stipends (if any)

PR Play 15-13

The budget should reflect your best estimate of the actual cost of conducting the activities outlined in the workshop proposal. Budgets – like plans – may be adjusted.

- Other main budget elements for workshop expenses may include:
  - staff salaries/fees
  - telecommunications costs
  - photocopying costs
  - other facilities and administrative charges
  - postage, shipping and freight

More on Planning the Workshop
- Identify the focus of the workshop
- Plan the timing of the workshop
- Determine who should attend the workshop
- Select a venue
- Develop the workshop program
- Prepare information packs
- Make practical arrangements
- Publicize the workshop
- Run the workshop

Identifying the Focus of the Workshop
Breaking into groups
- Identify stages in the workshop during which breakout groups will meet.
- Identify and provide necessary resources for breakout sessions.
- Identify criteria for constituting breakout groups.
- Identify topics for each breakout group and decide beforehand methods for reporting back.

Using briefing notes and background materials
- Workshop organizers should prepare relevant briefing notes and background materials for all the different breakout groups or roundtable participants.
- Briefing notes should be short, clear and concise.
- Organizers should be on hand throughout the workshop to respond to questions from participants.

- Copies of workshop materials should be deposited where they can be publicly accessible, including the national archives, parliamentary library, a university library and on the Internet.

Making Practical Arrangements
- Room set-up
- Breakfast sessions
- Small and large group sessions
- Breaks and lunch
- Dinner sessions
- Use of visual aids

Publicizing the Workshop
- Organize an email exchange
- Develop a media plan
- Employ Web 2.0 (Chapter 10)
- Produce and distribute a news release
- Prepare for radio and television interviews

Monitoring and Evaluation
- Attitude survey
- Evaluation forms

Equipment needs
- SmartBoard® or Overhead projector
- Computer
- PowerPoint projector
- Microphone(s)
- Screen
- Tables
- Extra chairs
- Surfaces for demonstrations
- Equipment and supplies for specific learning activities

Benchmarking

What Is Benchmarking?

Benchmarking is described as "the continuous, systematic search for, and implementation of, best practices which lead to superior per-

---

PR Play 15-14

Nine Audience Involvement Techniques

1. Drama
2. Eye Communication
3. Movement
4. Visuals
5. Questions
6. Demonstrations
7. Samples/Gimmicks
8. Interest
9. Humor

PR Play 15-15
Key Questions for Strategic Communicators to Ask When Planning Any Program or Campaign

- What are our specific communication needs and goals?
- What are our most severe problems and their causes?
- Are our goals and expectations realistic and attainable?
- Are attitudes of key personnel consistent with the communication needs, goals and policies?
- How can the communication channels and organizational structure be revised to enhance communicating?
- What information needs to go to whom, when, why and how?
- How prevalent is rumor and why?
- How can the problems of specialized roles and differentiated status be overcome to facilitate improved communication?
- Is there undue reliance on certain communication media (for example the written word)?
- How can we assure better feedback and effectively evaluate the communication program?

---

formance." It is a disciplined, realistic approach to assessing and improving the performance to be expected in critical areas of business.

Benchmarking is learning from other companies' experience(s) – so it avoids "re-inventing the wheel." Practitioners who rely on benchmarking believe it to be:
- The most practical method of measuring and improving efficiency, performance and competitiveness.
- The most effective business improvement technique.
- Applicable to all businesses and nationalities.

Performance statistics help organizations determine where they stand in comparison to similar organizations. The benefits of benchmarking far outweigh any negatives.

Benchmarking answers three fundamental questions:
- Where are we now (baseline or stepping off point)?
- Where do we want to be?
- How do we get there?

Why Benchmark?

The pace of events is moving so fast that unless we can find some way to keep our sights on tomorrow, we cannot expect to be in touch today. According to Eileen Weisman of the W Group (Houston, Texas), benchmarking:

- Helps firms or organizations understand the "gap" between their firm and others.
- Helps create a need or urgency for change.
- Accelerates change.
- Leads to breakthrough and continuous improvement.
- Establishes a baseline.
- Moves the quality process to another level.

Benchmarking Is:

- An ongoing process for continuous improvement (measuring stick).
- Identifying areas where improvement would make the most significant difference to the bottom line, to key areas of the business or to customer relationships (relationship management).
- Setting standards for those areas according to the "best" practice that can be found.
- Finding out how the "best" companies meet those standards.
- Adapting and applying lessons learned from those approaches and ideas to meet and exceed those standards.
- Establishing what makes a difference in a customer's eyes between an ordinary supplier and an excellent one.

Benchmarking is Not:

- **Industrial tourism** – Just visiting other companies to find out what they are doing.
- **"Wow" visits** – Visits to companies so far "ahead" of you, you feel overwhelmed. It could deflate all enthusiasm for improvement.
- **"Feel good" trips** – Visits to companies renowned for excellence in some areas, but in reality are worse than your company in a number of others, should convince you that an overall comparison may not be needed after all.
- **Keeping up with the Jones'** – Benchmarking just because everyone else is doing it is a poor reason to use the technique. It would be a wasted resource, with no real business benefit.
- **Cloning** – Copying rather than adapting practices from elsewhere without regard to your culture, strategy, mission, etc.

PR Play 15-16
Benchmarking Can Be:

- Used for strategy setting.
- A catalyst for continuous improvement (measuring stick).
- A technique for planning and goal setting.
- A problem-solving tool.
- A method for market performance testing.
- Establishes a baseline setting (stepping off point).
- Educational and enriching.
- An opportunity for identifying breakthrough ideas.
- A mechanism to create "buy in" for change.

Eileen Weisman – The W Group – Houston, Texas

- **Measurement for measurement's sake** – Taking measurements randomly rather than analyzing what it is you need to measure in order to be able to effect and monitor improvement.
- **A guarantee** – Don't think that just because a technique or practice is successful for one company or organization, it will work for yours.

The Goal
- **Is** – Building on the success of others, rather than re-inventing wheels. By benchmarking on an on-going basis you are always addressing current best practice, not dated ideas. Benchmarking is always carried out with the intention of implementing improvements.
- **Is Not** – To get a warm feeling.

The Benchmarking Process
- **Organize and Plan**
  - Select subject area.
  - Define process to be benchmarked.
  - Identify potential benchmarking partners.
  - Identify data required, sources and appropriate methods of collection.
- **Data Analysis**
  - Collect the data and select benchmarking partners.
  - Determine the performance gap.
  - Establish the difference in the process.
  - Target future performance.

- **Action**
  - Communication and commitment.
  - Adjust targets and develop correctional improvement plan.
  - Implement and monitor.
- **Review**
  - Review progress and re-calibrate.

Ways to Collect Benchmarking Data

- **In-House Research**
  - Examine internal documents.
  - Conduct a direct exchange.
    - Written questionnaires, phone surveys, teleconferences and video links. May provide all the information required.
  - Make site visits to other facilities.
    - Should be last port of call to validate benchmarking information gathered.
- **Third Party Research**
  - Use of consultants and research firms (particularly for hard to get information about competitors).
- **Site Visits**
  - Should be last port of call to validate benchmarking information gathered.

More Benefits of Benchmarking

- Significantly reduces waste, rework and duplication.
- Increases awareness of what you do and how well you are doing it.
- Process understanding leads to more effective management.
- Helps set credible targets.
- Identifies what to change and why.
- Removes blinders and N-I-H ("Not Invented Here") attitudes.
- Provides external focus.
- Enables an organization to learn from outside.

Common Pitfalls

- **Insufficient commitment** – Not sufficiently "high level" or "sincere."
- **Insufficient planning** – An "easy, let's just do it" attitude.
- **Misunderstanding** – Of benchmarking and its purpose.
- **Not linking benchmarking to process** – Failure to "go behind" measures and understand the "how."

PR Play 15-17
Types of Benchmarking Partners

Internal
Own organization, any location

Advantages	Disadvantages
• Common language/ culture/systems	• Inhibit external focus
• Access to data	• Foster complacency
• Communication channels	• Only adequate returns
• Low threat	
• Good "test bed"	
• Relatively quick returns	

External
Other organizations measurably better in key areas

Advantages	Disadvantages
• Similar structure/ constraints	• Step-change less likely
• Relative ease of access to data	• Legal/ethical considerations
• Relatively low threat	• Industry paradigms may inhibit creativity

Best Practice
Organizations selected for "Best Practice" in key areas

Advantages	Disadvantages
• Potential improvement leaps	• Continuous/long term commitment
• Potential high returns	• Potentially difficult
• External focus	• Change always results
• Removes blinders/N-I-H ("Not Invented Here")	

- **Apples vs. Oranges** – Comparison with insufficient process analysis or partner "fit."
- **Not measuring the right factors** – Measuring "easy" issues, not those that will make a difference.

- **Not teaching people to "fish"** – Lack of education and awareness building in those responsible for, or involved in, benchmarking.
- **Lack of communication** – Or unclear communication. Benchmarking not linked to other corporate activity/goals so communication and relevance are blurred.
- **Failing to prioritize** – Trying to "change the world" at once and not identifying subjects, which are linked to key business processes.

Why Focus on Benchmarking Process?

Only when you know how your process performs and what its key enablers are can you understand, learn from and adapt the best practice or innovations from other companies which will then lead to competitive advantage.

Code of Conduct

Just as such other professional organizations as Public Relations Society of America (PRSA) have codes of ethics, so does The Benchmarking Centre. Here is a summary of its code:

Principles
- Legality
- Exchange
- Confidentiality
- Use
- First party contact
- Third party contact
- Preparation
- (Practice) Etiquette and Ethics
- (Be willing to participate in a) Benchmarking Exchange Protocol
  – "Never ask for something you would not be prepared to share in return."

For direct access to The Benchmarking Centre, go to:
www.aboutbenchmarking.com

Force Field or Conflict Analysis:
Understanding the Pressures For and Against Change

How to Use the Tool:

Force Field Analysis, also called Conflict Analysis, is a useful technique for looking at all the forces for and against a decision. In effect, it is a specialized method of weighing pros and cons.

By carrying out the analysis you can plan to strengthen the forces supporting a decision, and reduce the impact of opposition to it.

To carry out a Force Field Analysis, follow these steps:
- List all forces for change in one column, and all forces against change in another column.
- Assign a score to each force, from 1 (weak) to 5 (strong).

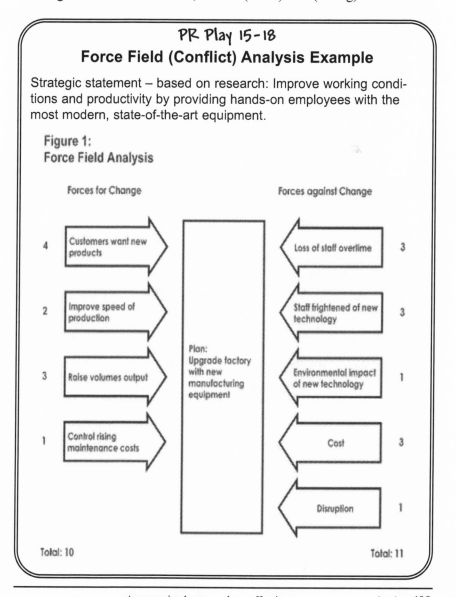

PR Play 15-18
Force Field (Conflict) Analysis Example

Strategic statement – based on research: Improve working conditions and productivity by providing hands-on employees with the most modern, state-of-the-art equipment.

Figure 1:
Force Field Analysis

Forces for Change | Forces against Change

4 Customers want new products | Loss of staff overtime 3

2 Improve speed of production | Staff frightened of new technology 3

Plan: Upgrade factory with new manufacturing equipment

3 Raise volumes output | Environmental impact of new technology 1

1 Control rising maintenance costs | Cost 3

Disruption 1

Total: 10 | Total: 11

- Draw a diagram showing the forces for and against change. Show the size of each force as a number next to it.

For example, imagine that you are a manager deciding whether to install new manufacturing equipment in your factory. You might draw up a force field analysis like the one in **PR Play 15-18**. (Also see page 501.)

Once you have carried out an analysis, you can decide whether your project is viable. In the example (PR Play 15-18), you might initially question whether it is worth going ahead with the plan.

When you have already decided to carry out a project, a Force Field Analysis can help you to work out how to improve its probability of success. Here you have two choices:
- To reduce the strength of the forces opposing a project, or
- To increase the forces pushing a project

Often the most desirable solution is the first: just trying to force change through may cause its own problems. People can be uncooperative if change is forced on them.

If you had to implement the project in the example (PR Play 15-18), the analysis might suggest a number of changes to the initial plan:
- By training staff (increase cost by 1) you could eliminate fear of technology (reduce fear by 2).
- It would be useful to show staff that change is necessary for business survival (new force in favor, +2).
- Staff could be shown that new machines would introduce variety and interest to their jobs (new force, +1).
- You could raise wages to reflect new productivity (cost +1, loss of overtime -2).
- Slightly different machines with filters to eliminate pollution could be installed (environmental impact -1).

These changes would swing the balance from 11:10 (against the plan), to 8:13 (in favor of the plan).

Key points:
Force Field Analysis is a useful technique for looking at all the forces for and against a plan. It helps you to weigh the importance of these factors and decide whether a plan is worth implementing. For more, go to: **http://www.mindtools.com/pages/article/newTED_06.htm**

PR Play 15-19

MIND TOOLS
Essential skills for an excellent career

The Internet's Most
Visited Career Skills Resource

Force Field Analysis Worksheet

- For instructions on Force Field Analysis, visit http://www.mindtools.com/rs/ForceField.
- For more business leadership skills visit http://www.mindtools.com/rpages/HowtoLead.htm.

Forces FOR change	Score		Forces AGAINST change	Score
		Change proposal		
TOTAL			**TOTAL**	

For new tools like this every two weeks, subscribe to the free Mind Tools newsletter:
http://www.mindtools.com/subscribe.htm

PRSA's "Seven C's of Communication"

PR Play 15-20

"Seven C's of Communication"

1. Credibility
2. Context
3. Content
4. Clarity
5. Continuity and Consistency
6. Channels
7. Capability of Audience

The Public Relations Society of America (PRSA) defines communication as – simply the "interchange of information – conveying thoughts from one party or group to another."

To achieve our goal of bringing about behavioral change, most, if not all, of the "Seven C's of Communication" must be achieved. (The main components of the "MAC Triad" are contained in the "Seven C's.")

1. **Credibility** – A climate of belief built on the institution's performance. Receiver must have confidence in the sender and high regard for the source's competence on the subject (source credibility).

2. **Context** – Communication programs must square with the realities of their environment. Context must provide for participation and playback, and must confirm, not contradict, the message. Effective communications require a supportive social environment – one largely set by the news media. The audience must have a frame of reference.

3. **Content** – The message must have meaning to the receiver – relevance. Audience determines content.

4. **Clarity** – The message must be put in simple terms to help assure it will be received exactly as intended. Communicate clearly, calculatingly, concisely, consistently, completely, specifically and simply.

5. **Continuity and Consistency** – Communication is an unending process, requiring repetition to achieve penetration. Messages must be consistent.

6. **Channels** – Established channels of communication that the receiver respects and uses should be employed. Creating new channels is difficult. Different channels have different effects and serve effectively in different stages of the diffusion process (pages 29-33). Different channels are called for in reaching target audiences. People associate varying values with the many channels of communication, and this, too, must be kept in mind.

7. **Capability of Audience** – Communication must take into account the capability of the audience. Communications are most effective when they require the least effort on the part of the recipient. This involves factors of availability, habits, reading ability and the receivers' knowledge. (See Effort-Benefit Ratio – *The ABCs of Strategic Communication* – AuthorHouse)

Some practitioners, including this book's author, separate continuity and consistency. Litwin defines continuity as establishing a firm or organization's identity by using the same distinct logo and design on all communication vehicles. Gannett's *USA Today* is an excellent example. *CBS Broadcasting's* all news radio stations have been using the same formats and similar jingles for nearly 50 years. Continuity provides "locking power" and quick recognition.

Andrea Fitting, CEO of Fitting Group, a marketing consulting firm, stresses the importance of *consistency*: "Standards must be applied to all communications with the outside world," she says. "If your literature – your brochures, product sheets and even your stationery, letterhead and business cards look as though they are from different companies, you obviously don't have someone coordinating your marketing efforts."

Litwin suggests public relations practitioners borrow a tactic used by retail store operators – at closing time many exit their stores backwards to see what customers see when they enter the store. Why not take periodic visual audits of your organization to check on its *continuity* and *consistency*?

Key Communicators
Also called – Opinion Leaders/Consumption Pioneers/Connectors/ Key Influencers
Town Council has authorized a reassessment of homes and other properties. Residents are under the impression real estate taxes will skyrocket. How do lawmakers end the rumor and disseminate the facts?

No matter what title you give them, Key Communicators are an important, but too many times neglected, message carrier. Many successful strategic communication programs use the Key Communicators (*KC*) concept as a major vehicle to help spread the word.

Who Should Be a Key Communicator?
*KC*s are influential residents and/or business people in a community.

They are members of internal publics at both large and small businesses or corporations. Whether part of an internal family or external public, Key Communicators are opinion makers, community leaders, or just the woman or man next door. *KC*s are vitally interested in the welfare of their municipality, schools or the company or organization for which they work. No community, company or organization is immune to rumors – and rumors continue to grow unless they are snuffed out in their earliest stages.

*KC*s talk to large numbers of other people. They are believed and trusted. They represent various segments of the community.

A school communication director starting a *KC* program might include PTA presidents and other officers, barbers, beauticians, bartenders, lawyers, doctors, dentists, bankers, real estate and insurance agents, the Welcome Wagon hostess, teachers, students, shopkeepers, secretaries and former school board members.

A local supermarket chain, wanting to stay in touch with its communities, might want to include many of the same when establishing its *KC* program.

Who needs *key communicators*? You do. We all do – particularly those of us who deal with the public and are supported by public funds. But even privately-run companies and retail stores should consider the concept. It is a terrific, albeit non-scientific, way to feel the pulse of the community. It is also a successful concept that helps build and maintain relationships and will quickly become an integral part of an organization's *relationship management program*.

The *KC* program should be one of maybe a half-dozen feedback techniques an organization has. It should be the hub of the face-to-face public relations program. It takes time to develop a successful *KC* program. But it's worth it. In the long run, *KC* programs save more time than you will spend creating one.

Getting Started

As strategic communication director for a local supermarket chain, you convince the new store manger to adopt your *key communicator* concept. Now that step one is accomplished, you go ahead and invite the presidents of the parent-teacher organizations of about 10 area schools to have lunch in the store with the manager. (This group, like all future groups, should be limited to 10 members, preferably fewer.)

During the luncheon, the manager and some staff discuss objectives of community involvement programs. He or she explains how those in attendance can help. Each is asked if he or she would like to be included as a *KC*. In most instances, nearly all accept the invitation to serve. Before leaving, everyone is asked to identify one or two people they depend on for news about their community – whether it be schools, local government, the recreation program, etc. From the list, invitations are extended for future meetings – some over lunch, others over mid-morning coffee.

Most *KC* meetings consist of people from a mixture of professions and vocations. These meetings with store management are the first and last time that *KC*s come together as a body.

How the Program Works

Following these initial meetings, *KC*s are kept in contact with the store and its involvement in town. Usually one management-type person is responsible for communicating with them regularly. Some organizations publish periodic newsletters for *KC*s – both on paper and as inline email attachments. One New Jersey school district calls it *Key Notes*. What follows is an example of how the *KC* program works in that (Washington Township) district.

When there is a crisis, the administrator in charge begins a cross platform/multiple platform rapid response dissemination of the facts. That would include blast emails, texting, website updates, releases to cable and broadcast television and radio, and other higher technology methods, which deliver news to any community.

No longer is a printed, hardcopy of a district news release or fact sheet the preferred information delivery vehicle, but rather an online version – perhaps even one which appears on the computer screen the moment an email is opened (known as an inline attachment). E-newsletters and blast emails have taken on a life of their own. The cross platforming might also include newsletter attachments (or home page links), podcasts, Vcasts, social media, blogs, tweets and blast voice mails.

*KC*s are encouraged to email or call the administrator in charge with questions, concerns or rumors that they, their friends, or their customers have. They must have access to the administrator with whom they are working. This kind of freedom, although technically available to all residents, must be clearly communicated. And if the administrator is not available – at that moment – to talk or respond, he must remember to respond to keep the communication channels open.

An Example

A scenario: One spring morning, a rumor spread throughout the community that all of the students in the high school were carrying chains and knives and "gang wars" were erupting in the school and at a nearby shopping center. Within minutes, *KC*s were competing with newspaper, radio and TV reporters to get the facts. The school's public information director went to the high school to talk with staff members and students to learn firsthand what was happening.

Yes, it was true that some students were carrying chains, knives and other potential weapons. No, it was *not* true that there were "gang wars" in the school. And no, it was *not* true that because one of the students was black these fights had "racial overtones."

The truth: two groups of students, each numbering fewer than a dozen, had challenged each other to fights and, in fact, did get into pushing and shoving matches. Each group did take on names. One group consisted of long-time residents. The other was composed of a number of students who recently had moved into the community. One group was rather "well dressed" when they went to school. The other wore jeans and T-shirts. And, yes, the board of education had authorized full-time plain-clothes police officers to walk the halls (because of concerns learned through the *KC* network). Eventually, the crisis was defused and even those involved admitted that while there may have been "bad feelings" between two cliques, it was far from "gang warfare."

That information was disseminated to the school district's 200 *KC*s, first via a blast email and text, 1-to-1 emergency notification, phone chain and then through *The Facts* newsletter on the school district's website as an online email attachment and and follow-up "snail" or regular mail. Social media played a key role as *KC*s used every available channel to reach smartphones, tablets and other devices.

Because friends and neighbors trust *KC*s, they are believed when they help the school district get its message into the community. Within a day, word had circulated throughout town that the situation at the high school was not nearly as bad as many had thought. Verification that plainclothes police officers would probably remain in the high school building until the end of the school year "just in case there were problems" was readily accepted.

The *KC* program enabled the school district to disseminate its message through a non-traditional, but nonetheless major, channel of communication other than the news media. This strategic tactic is professionally referred to as the *Three-step Flow* theory.

Originally called the *two-step flow*, it was a term used by Katz and Lazarsfeld to describe their observation that media messages flow from the media to opinion leaders (key communicators) to the rest of the audience. It is now accepted among many strategic communicators that the *two-step flow* skips the opinion leaders and goes directly from mass media (or cross platforming/multiple platforming) to the rest of the audience. The method that communicates to key communicators rather than an entire public is the *three-step flow* because the message emanates or encodes (step one) from a chief spokesperson (or CEO) of an organization, is sent (step two) to key communicators and KCs carry (step three) it to the rest of the public. Research is clear, KCs' messages are among the most trusted – highly credible and believable (trust and truth).

Two positive side effects were derived from this incident that was prevented from escalating. First, most of the 1,800 students stood up as proud members of their school. Several verbally attacked the news media for what they felt were unfair news reports. Because of the students' action, district administrators did not have to approach the local media to discuss the (lack of) objectivity in their reports, although they did hold a news briefing. The students, as responsible community members, took it upon themselves to contact the media and present their case. The residual effect were news stories about the student body and its leadership.

The other positive side effect was that many students and apparently many residents concluded that social problems in the high school, such as the one that caused these isolated fights, were due to overcrowding in a building filled far beyond capacity by a rapidly growing population.

Two weeks after the incident, voters were to decide whether they would permit the board of education to float bonds for a new middle school. (Middle school students were attending classes in the high school building on split sessions.) The bond issue won voter approval by more than two-to-one after it had been defeated no fewer than eight times in seven years.

An Authorized Grapevine

In essence, the *key communicator program* is an authorized grapevine that delivers facts to a community quickly and honestly. In a crisis situation, traditional communication – now known as legacy media (newspapers, magazines, TV and radio) – channels just cannot operate quickly enough to get the truth to those who need to know.

Professor Donald Bagin, Rowan (N.J.) University professor emeritus, conducted extensive research on the *KC* program. His results lead to these steps in forming and working with *KC*s.

1. Start by explaining the *KC* concept to a fairly small number of people who can serve as *KC* identifiers. Offer examples of where and how the concept has worked successfully.

As fully as possible, the *KC* database should include a representative membership of the community's churches, synagogues, clubs, civic associations and even coffee-drinking crowds or other social groups. Assure that all socioeconomic levels are represented.

2. Over a period of several weeks, the identifiers take advantage of social occasions to verbally survey other residents. They might ask such casual questions as, "Say, we're doing a survey on how well we're communicating our message. Could you tell me the names of a few people you have talked with recently about real estate taxes – or the mayor, or in the case of the supermarket about the new electronic checkout?" (They should be certain to assure the person they don't want to know what was discussed – just with whom they talked.)

These casual encounters will provide up to several hundred names for the *KC* organizer. Tabulations will show that a number of people will appear often. These are the community's *KC*s – upon whom this entire program will be built.

3. Analyze each *KC* in terms of impact throughout a community or area. That is, one *KC* may come into contact only with residents around one sub division. Another is the key person in an African American or Spanish-speaking community. This analysis will pinpoint whom to call depending on the situation. A community-wide problem will require

using the overall list. An incident in just one neighborhood will call for contacting *KC*s in that area only.

4. The management person (supermarket manager, schools' superintendent, mayor, etc.) should personally enlist the aid of each *KC*. Experience has shown that 95 percent of those asked will be pleased to cooperate. Among the reasons for the cooperation: "because we are not being asked to attend many meetings or to act as a formal advisory committee." Most *KC*s are busy people with many demands on their time. Adding the role of key communicator involves little more than providing community feedback and carrying messages from your company or organization to their friends and neighbors.

Send a letter to each prospective *KC* to explain the concept and describe how he or she can be of service. Arrange to have a brief meeting with each one soon.

Follow the letter with an email and a phone call. Letters alone will attract only about half of those invited to meetings, but a call will usually guarantee a larger turnout.

Meetings may be held on an individual basis with appropriate *KC* people invited. Keep the agenda and tone informal. Explain a few typical cases in which the *KC* concept would operate. Above all, keep meetings short – no more than an hour – or meet with people individually or in small groups over coffee in a local diner.

5. Emphasize, in meetings or conversations, the *KC* concept is based on a two-way exchange. You want to hear about rumblings or rumors running through the community. If facts are in error, you can call, text or email the *KC*s with the correct information and they in turn can pass it along. If hostile action is planned, *KC*s can alert municipal authorities so they can make counter plans.

Information must be shared with the *KC*s on a regular basis. If you are representing a municipal government, for example, send them background reports – on the proposed budget, on personnel turnover, on new construction, on senior citizen activities. Send them advance copies of council meeting agendas and an action follow-up. When you do whatever you can to make the *KC*s an informed group of people, they in turn will spread the word about the district and what it is trying to do.

PR Play 15-21
The Key to Communication

Many people still get their news about your school district through the grapevine. A key communicator program can help shape their perceptions.

By M. Larry Litwin, APR, Fellow PRSA

It has been nearly half a century since Rowan University Professor Emeritus Don Bagin coined the term "key communicator" to describe someone who, after being informed and updated by a school district, can serve as a sort of unofficial spokesperson – spreading accurate information about their district throughout the community.

Key communicators – sometimes referred to as influencers, connectors, consumption pioneers or opinion leaders – are "a collection of individuals who have influence over part of a community," says Tom Salter, senior communication officer, Montgomery (Ala.) County Schools. "A key communicator network is a loose-knit panel of opinion leaders who can shape community perceptions."

Since Bagin described the concept nearly 50 years ago, school district communications have changed. Websites, emails, cable and broadcast television and radio, and other higher technology methods now deliver news to all communities. No longer is a printed, hardcopy of district newsletters the preferred information delivery vehicle, but rather an online version – perhaps even one which appears on the computer screen the moment an email is opened (known as inline attachment). E-newsletters and blast emails have taken on a life of their own. The cross platforming might include newsletter attachments, text messaging, podcasts, Vcasts, social media, blogs and blast phone voice notifications.

But the key communicators, which function as an authorized grapevine that delivers facts to a community quickly and honestly, remain a school system's lifeline to the community – especially in time of crisis or when the district needs public support. KCs – properly "schooled" – can be strategic message "carriers." Key communicators are trusted local leaders who give a district's message extra credibility with the public.

Three South Jersey school districts established key communicator programs during the 1970s. Heather Simmons, Glassboro, Jan Giel,

cont.

PR Play 15-21 continued

Washington Township (Gloucester County) and Susan Bastnagle, Cherry Hill, inherited and have nurtured their programs to assure they would continue to be a lifeline to the community.

KC programs serve as the hub of the face-to-face public relations program because "they (key communicators) will gladly tell you what they – and their friends, neighbors and local businesspeople – think," Salter says.

"No matter how many times we've heard it," says Glassboro's Simmons, "as public relations professionals in education, we always have to be mindful that we are dealing with the two things that take priority in the life of all parents – their children and their wallets."

"Key communicator groups are helpful as we attempt to communicate to these families and other stakeholders with sensitivity, accuracy and efficiency," states Simmons, who serves as public relations consultant to the Glassboro Public Schools.

"Key communicators are valuable because they provide an opportunity to learn or confirm information, which helps us anticipate issues and make educated and researched decisions that relate to the public," says Katie Hardesty. Hardesty is in the process of establishing a key communicator network for the Cherry Hill Public Library where she serves as public relations and special events director. She is using what is often referred to as the "Rowan University KC model for schools."

"KCs will help us gauge the community, give easier access to focus groups and other informal research, and help us counter misinformation that might arise," Hardesty explains.

Like Cherry Hill, Washington Township has about 100 core key communicators who receive regular emails. Giel, community relations coordinator for the district, reflects that it takes time to develop and maintain a successful KC program. "But it's worth it," she says. "In the long run, KC programs save far more time than they take."

To make her point, Giel cites one recent example: "We used it (a KC) for rumor control when two of our middle schools were found to have mold."

cont.

PR Play 15-21 continued

These days New Jersey school systems – like most districts in the country – rarely bring their KCs together for large formal meetings. Two-way communication is accomplished through emails, interactive newsletters, telephone and informal small group get-togethers.

However, the Glassboro Public School district takes the time to bring its 130 KCs together three times a year to inform and discuss issues of importance and to seek input as the district develops its budget. The final meeting of the academic year – usually in April – is reserved for a post-mortem following the annual school election and to preview issues that may be coming up for the following year.

Public schools starting a KC program might consider including PTA presidents and other officers, local barbers, beauticians, lawyers, doctors, dentists, bankers, real estate and insurance agents, teachers, support staff, bus drivers, students, shopkeepers, and former school board members. A district's internal family – faculty and staff – must be included among those who play a vital role in the communication process. Parents and community members trust school employees to tell the truth about what's happening inside a school or at the district.

No rule, written or otherwise, states that all key communicators must be strong school district supporters – or supporters of public education in general. In fact, it might be best if some are detractors.

All, however, should be recognized as opinion shapers, community leaders, or just the woman or man next door willing to listen, talk and serve as a liaison (connector) between the schools and those with whom they come in contact. KCs are vitally interested in the welfare of their municipality, schools, or the company or organization for which they work.

No community, company or organization is immune to rumors – and rumors continue to grow unless they are snuffed out in their earliest stages.

"Research is clear," says Mark Marmur of Makovsky & Company Public Relations, in New York City. "Key communicators, effectively chosen, are the pulse of their community. It is an incredibly successful concept that helps build and maintain relationships and will quickly become an integral part of any organization's 'relationship marketing program.'"

cont.

PR Play 15-21 continued

Marmur notes that it is not only school systems that incorporate key communicator-type networks into their over-all public relations plan. Major corporations like Walt Disney World Resorts, Staples and smaller retailers like Hello, Sports Fans! (Cherry Hill) have relied on KCs for years to give them constant feedback and to relay positive and negative stories of their experience.

While Bastnagel, Cherry Hill's public information officer, courts key communicators, she believes, as does the Disney company, that electronic communications empowers everyone to be a key communicator. "Within minutes," she says, "we can have a video message from our superintendent or other administrator on our district website and I can email the link to thousands of subscribers on our email notification list."

"I'm obsessive about sending out my e-news every single week during the school year, so that anyone who sees it is equipped to be a key communicator. And even if they don't read it carefully each week, they know it's there as an information resource."

Online district newsletters can offer an additional advantage for a district: articles in the e-newsletters may contain links to "landing sites." Many times, those links contain a "casual" survey (convenience sample) asking for comments, reactions and other input to certain questions.

"When I need our key communicators for something and send an email to that effect, they are used to seeing my name and know they can trust me," says Simmons. "You can't put a value on that."

Like many others responsible for coordinating school system key communicator programs, Bastnagel faces the challenge of "rethinking the entire concept – how to meld the power and pervasiveness of electronic communications with the one-to-one, face-to-face feel of a key communicator program."

Says Bastnagel: "The key communicator program has changed as the power of electronic communications has evolved. Ten years ago, we reached out to our 100 or so key communicators with letters, phone calls and periodic face-to-face meetings. But, 10 years ago, I didn't have a smartphone and iPad®, lots of parents didn't have (or didn't use) email and

cont.

PR Play 15-21 continued

our district website was still under construction. Today, third graders have cell phones. It's a lot harder to stay ahead of the message."

However, the effort can pay off for your district. During the recent National School Public Relations Association (NSPRA) annual seminar, superintendents agreed: "Communication is a contact sport. If you are willing to mix it up in terms of communication and get close to people, and have face-to-face human contact, then you and your district will be successful."

Well thought out and effective key communicator networks should be an integral tactic in every school systems' strategic communication plan.

School Leader – New Jersey School Boards Association – September/October 2008

Etiquette

Etiquette – whether workplace, phone, email, dining, etc. – could be a deal breaker.

Defined, etiquette is the conventional requirements as to social behavior; proprieties of conduct as established in any class or community or for any occasion. Here are suggestions based on academic research:

Workplace Etiquette

Florida State University's Career Center offers these tips for *workplace etiquette*:

- Be timely. Arrive to work and meetings on time. Complete work assignments on time. (Some say, "If you are not early, you are late.")
- Be polite, pleasant and courteous.
- Learn office politics (one of Litwin's 9 P's of marketing – Chapter 11) – use effective listening skills to discover appropriate office behavior. Pay attention to the way things are done.
- Understand the unwritten rules of business.
  - The Boss is the Boss – right or wrong, the boss always has the last word.
  - Keep the boss informed. Good or bad, you don't want the boss to hear information mentioned from an inappropriate source.
  - Never go over the boss' head, without telling him/her first.
  - Make your boss look good. Promotion and opportunities will arise when you help to reach the organization's goals.

PR Play 15-22
Big 12 Dining Etiquette Rules
From Elon (N.C.) University PRSSA Chapter

1. Always wear your nametag on your right.
2. Allow the host to point out where the guests should sit.
3. Follow the host's lead. Once the host begins to eat – you eat.
4. Once seated, immediately place the napkin in your lap.
5. Utensils: eat from the outside in – NEVER pick up dropped silverware.
6. Your bread is to the left. Water is to the right.
7. Elbows should never rest on the table while eating.
8. Use the silverware to signal you're finished (the 4:00-10:00 position on a clock).
9. Take out food the same way it went in. (If you put a piece of food in your mouth with your fork and the food is unpleasant [tough or not tasty], you should remove the piece of food with your fork. Don't spit the food into a napkin or use your fingers to remove it.)
10. If you have to pick or clean your teeth – excuse yourself from the table.
11. Never order alcohol – even if the host does.
12. Whoever invited the guest will be paying unless discussed.

Professor Jessica Gisclair, Esq. – Adviser

- Appear as professional as possible. Being well groomed and clean is essential. Dress for your next job/promotion.
- Adopt a can-do attitude. Those who accept challenges and display creativity are valuable.
- Be flexible. By remaining flexible and implementing change you gain a reputation as a cooperative employee.
- Give credit to everyone who made a contribution to a project or event.
- Don't differentiate people by position or standing in a company.

Phone Etiquette

Azusa Pacific (Calif.) University (www.apu.edu/imt/telecom/etiquette.php) says part of doing business means doing business over the phone. Because the phone is such an important instrument in our daily business, below are some helpful hints, and proven phone techniques, that will help to make your phone conversations more effective.

Create a Good First Impression

- Try to answer the phone on the second ring. Answering a phone too fast can catch the caller off guard and waiting too long can make the caller angry.
- Answer with a friendly greeting. (Example – "Good Afternoon, IMC Customer Service, Nancy speaking. How may I help you?").
- Smile – it shows, even through the phone lines.
- Ask the caller for their name, even if their name is not necessary for the call. This shows you have taken an interest in them. Make sure that if you ask for their name, that you use it.
- Speak clearly and slowly. Never talk with anything in your mouth. This includes gum.
- Lower your voice if you normally speak loudly.
- Keep the phone two-finger widths away from your mouth

Putting Callers on Hold

When putting a caller on hold, always ask permission. If they ask why, provide them with the answer.
Examples:
"Would you mind holding while I get your file?"
" Can you hold briefly while I see if Mr. Adams is available?"

When taking a caller off of hold, always thank them for holding.

Transferring a Caller

1. If the caller needs to speak to another person or department, transfer the caller directly to the desired person's extension, not to the operator. This will save the caller having to explain his/her requests another time, and it will cut the number of times the caller needs to be transferred.
2. When transferring a caller, tell them who you are transferring them to, and announce the caller to the person you are transferring them to.

Taking Phone Messages

When taking a phone message for someone, always be sure to include the following information:
- Caller's name and company name if applicable.
- Time and date of call.
- What the call is regarding.
- If the caller wants a return phone call, and if so,
- Obtain a phone number that is best for the return.

Last Impressions

- Before hanging up, be sure that you have answered all the caller's questions.
- Always end with a pleasantry: "Have a nice day" or "It was nice speaking with you."
- Let the caller hang up first. This shows the caller that you weren't in a hurry to get off the phone with them.

Email Etiquette

Here are some pointers to remember when writing email, from *Gannett News Service*:
- **Be concise.** People don't like reading lengthy email messages. They want questions to be asked in the beginning so they are able to move on to other issues. Be aware of what you are writing and see if there are ways to shorten your response or question.
- **Make use of the subject line.** In the subject line, address the reason you are writing to the person. This will help the person receiving the message to determine the importance of when to respond.
- **Don't use capital letters unless necessary.** No one likes to read a message all in capital letters. It seems like they are getting yelled at.
- **Use templates for frequent responses.** If you have to reply to certain issues constantly, have a set message you can use to shorten the time it takes you to respond.
- **Don't discuss confidential information.** Most companies can monitor email content. So, make sure you are not writing things you don't want others to read.
- **Proofread.** Always read the email before you send it for grammatical errors and to make sure you are answering the question at hand.

PR Play 15-23
Thank-You Note Defined

Giving thanks? Do the *write* thing! At the most basic level, *Thank-You Notes* recognize the receipt of goods or services. A handwritten *Thank-You Note* is a symbolic way to invest in a friendship or business relationship.

Five basic *Thank-You Note* rules:
• Full sentences
• Proper spelling
• Grammar
• Punctuation
• Syntax

When is a *Thank-You Note* required?
• Whenever the *giver* of the gift is not present to see the recipient's reaction.
• Where gifts are collected but not opened.
• Where the recipient is not present.
• Whenever one receives flowers or a gift by mail or delivery.

What components should a *Thank-You Note* include?
• Date it.
• Personalize it with Dear Nancy – or – Nancy.
• When writing a *Thank-You Note* say "I want to thank you" rather than "wanted" because it is present tense.
• Mention the gift or present as acknowledgement of one's attendance at an event or function ("Thank you for sharing with me my induction into the PRSA College of Fellows. Your being there helped make the evening more special for my family and me.")
• Personal message including such attributes as "I will use the beautiful pen to sign all of my *Thank-You Notes*."
• Express possibly having lunch or dinner, soon.
• *Thank-You Notes* may also double as a receipt confirming the gift did reach its intended destination.
• Resist the urge to turn the *Thank-You Note* into a catch-up letter. Save that for a future email or letter.
• Keep the focus on the recipient.

cont.

PR Play 15-23 continued

How long do I have after receiving a gift (or service) to write a *Thank-You Note*?

- Within 24 hours of a job interview.
- Within one week of receiving a gift or service.
- Couples may have up to three months to send out *Thank-You Notes* for wedding presents.
- It is always better to send a late *Thank-You Note* than none at all.

May I email a *Thank-You Note* or send a Thank-You text message?

- It is preferable to no *Thank-You Note* at all, but it sends the wrong message – such as you are too busy or it is too much of a burden. Maintain sincerity.
- Email, texts, postcards, typed *Thank-You Notes* and mass-produced computer-generated cards are considered tacky.

If I am confident they will never compare them, can I send the same note to all guests?

- Although *Thank-You Notes* include many of the same elements they should never be identical.
- Your note should be customized (personal message – see above). Make specific references to your interactions – even their clothing or something said in a conversation.

At what age are *Thank-You Notes* required?

- They are required for all ages – even babies. Their parents should write them.
- It's a good way for children to practice their penmanship and social skills.
- You are never too young – or too old – to write a *Thank-You Note*.

Corinne Mucha – www.maidenhousefly.com

PR Play 15-24
Sample Thank-You Note

Larry,

Thank you for the kind note and enjoy the attached. Wear it proudly!

Good Luck,

D.

DOUGLAS R. CONANT
President and Chief Executive Officer
Campbell Soup Company
One Campbell Place
Camden, NJ 08103-1779

EXERCISES

PR Challenge 15-1

Prepare a tactical memo to your CEO recommending a *Key Communicator* program. List the specific steps you would take to build the program from the ground up.

PR Challenge 15-2

As special events planner, you have been asked by your CEO to help plan her daughter's wedding. She has given you a $49,000 budget with which to work. She tells you – half jokingly – "your job depends on this being successful." Referring back to Chapter 7 (as well as *this* chapter), list your plan's goal, three objectives and strategies, and the tactics that would accompany the objectives and strategies.

CHAPTER 16
Public Relations/Strategic Communication
Ethics and the Law

Effective public relations (strategic communication) is more than the art and science of building relationships that earn trust and motivate mutually supportive behaviors. It is more than outstanding communicators who think and plan strategically and systematically. It is more than publicity, press agentry and counseling upper management. The effective practitioner must be more than an outstanding writer who is proficient in verbal skills.

Above and beyond all else, the effective strategic communication counselor must be a public relations *ethicist* – one who practices the profession in an *open, honest, thorough* and *valid* (relevant) manner. Those four principles are the foundation for every ethics' code including PRSA's (Public Relations Society of America).

In fact, some might argue that for those of us who practice these four principles, no other ethics are needed in our profession. However, PRSA adopted a revised Member Code of Ethics in October 2000. The unabridged version is available on its Web site (www.prsa.org).

PRSA
PRSA requires its members to take an oath to practice ethically. Its members are socially responsible practitioners, acting in the public interest, who ensure their products and services meet both a client's and society's needs. They are moral practitioners.

Rowan University Professor Anthony Fulginiti, APR, and member of PRSA's College of Fellows, has conducted extensive research into public relations ethics. He warns, "Practitioners must not turn their backs to restrictions on their conduct. They do not hide in the dark corners of selfish ignorance. They face the light of moral practice – in facing the light of moral practice, they shine in its reflective brilliance."

Professor Fulginiti and others believe effective practitioners must scrutinize their activities, making certain they are "truthful storytellers." His advice – "We must know that as we bill clients for a dollar's worth of work, at the same time we pay a dollar of respect to society."

PR Play 16-1

In summary, PRSA lists the following 10 principles of behavior for the practice of public relations:

1. Conduct in accord with the *public interest*.
2. Exemplify high standards of *honesty and integrity*.
3. *Deal fairly* with the public.
4. Adhere to highest standards of *accuracy and truth*.
5. Do not knowingly disseminate *false or misleading information*.
6. Do not engage in any practice that *corrupts the channels of communication* or processes of government.
7. *Identify publicly* the name of the client or employer on whose behalf any public communication is made.
8. Do not make use of any individual or organization professing to be independent or unbiased but actually serving another or *undisclosed interest*.
9. Do not *guarantee the achievement* of specified results beyond member's control.
10. Do not represent *conflicting or competing interests*.

Ethics vs. Laws

Ethics are the expression of your morals – your beliefs. One's judgment is based on one's morals. Laws, on the other hand, are what you must do – rules established by authority.

When making moral decisions, the strategic communicator should ask:
- Do I have my own moral codes?
- Will my morals do harm?
- Do I share my morals with others?
- Do my morals have universal ring?

PR Play 16-2
PRSA Member Statement of Professional Values

This statement presents the core values of PRSA members and, more broadly, of the public relations profession. These values provide the foundation for the Member Code of Ethics and set the industry standard for the professional practice of public relations. These values are the fundamental beliefs that guide our behaviors and decision-making process. We believe our professional values are vital to the integrity of the profession as a whole.

ADVOCACY

We serve the public interest by acting as responsible advocates for those we represent. We provide a voice in the marketplace of ideas, facts, and viewpoints to aid informed public debate.

HONESTY

We adhere to the highest standards of accuracy and truth in advancing the interests of those we represent and in communicating with the public.

EXPERTISE

We acquire and responsibly use specialized knowledge and experience. We advance the profession through continued professional development, research and education. We build mutual understanding, credibility, and relationships among a wide array of institutions and audiences.

INDEPENDENCE

We provide objective counsel to those we represent. We are accountable for our actions.

LOYALTY

We are faithful to those we represent, while honoring our obligation to serve the public interest.

FAIRNESS

We deal fairly with clients, employers, competitors, peers, vendors, the media and the general public. We respect all opinions and support the right of free expression.

PR Play 16-3

Morals are to Ethics as Attitudes are to Opinions

Morals and Attitudes = Inner feelings (your personal beliefs)

Ethics and Opinions = Expression of your feelings (personal beliefs)

- Do my morals maintain loyalty to important relationships?
- Can I justify your morals?
- Are my morals based on sound philosophical or religious principles?
- Do my morals support society's important systems?
- Can my morals survive challenges and questions from colleagues?
- Can I comfortably rearrange my moral's ranking?

Areas of Understanding

Strategic communicators should have a general understanding of laws related to their profession, as well as government regulations and copyright and trademark laws.

A number of federal regulatory agencies directly or indirectly affect public relations:
- **Federal Trade Commission (FTC)** – The FTC enforces a variety of federal antitrust and consumer protection laws. It seeks to ensure that the nation's markets function competitively, free of undue restrictions. The commission works to eliminate unfair or deceptive advertising or public relations practices (through news releases). In general, the FTC's efforts are directed toward stopping actions that threaten consumers' opportunities to exercise informed choices.

Current FTC policy on deception contains three basic elements:
- Where there is representation, omission or practice, there must be a high probability that it will mislead the consumer.
- The perspective of the "reasonable consumer" is used to judge deception.
- The deception must lead to material injury. This policy makes deception difficult to prove.

If the FTC rules deception has occurred, it may issue one of three orders:

PR Play 16-4
Warren Buffett Warns Executives To Be Alert On Ethics

Don't be a lemming.

That is Warren Buffett's warning to top executives at his company, Berkshire Hathaway Inc. According to a story by The Associated Press, Buffett cautioned managers that many corporate scandals arise because questionable activity is accepted as normal behavior.

He said the rationale that "everyone else is doing it" is not acceptable. Rather, it should raise a red flag.

"Somewhere along the line they picked up the notion . . . that a number of well-respected managers were engaging in such practices and therefore it must be OK to do so," Buffett wrote. "It's a seductive argument."

Buffett said, "If you lose money for the company, I will be understanding. If you lose one shred of the company's reputation, I will be ruthless."

Courier-Post – "Work and Save" – Oct. 12, 2006

Consent Decree – The first step in the regulation process after the FTC determines that an ad is deceptive or unfair. Also called a consent order. The second step is a Cease- and-Desist Order requiring an advertiser to stop running a deceptive, misleading or unfair advertisement, campaign or claim. Corrective Advertising is the third step.

Cease-and-Desist Order – An FTC order requiring an advertiser to stop running a deceptive, misleading or unfair advertisement, campaign or claim. A cease-and-desist order is the second of three remedies for deceptive or unfair advertising.

Corrective Advertising – Ordered by the Federal Trade Commission for the purpose of correcting consumers' mistaken impressions created by prior advertising. Corrective advertising is ordered when consumer research determines that an ad is false and/or misleading. Under this remedy, the FTC orders the offending party to produce messages for consumers that correct the false impressions the ad made. The FTC may require a party to run corrective advertising even if the campaign in

> ## PR Play 16-5
> ## Material Event
> ## *TSC v. Northway, Inc.* (1976)
>
> - Established that a fact about a company is *material* if it would be significant to a reasonable investor in the total mix of information about the company.
> - Public Relations/Strategic Communication implications – sometimes, it is difficult to determine what is or is not *material*. If there is a question, contact the corporate attorney. Illegal insider trading refers generally to buying or selling a security, in breach of a fiduciary (trust and confidence) duty or other relationship of trust and confidence, while in possession of *material*, nonpublic information about the security. Insider trading violations may also include "tipping" such information, securities trading by the person "tipped," and securities trading by those who misappropriate such information.
> - It may best be explained by Federal Appeals Court Judge Debra Ann Livingston: "Insider trading rules restrict speech with the intended use of regulation being fairness for all stock traders."
> - The unequal disclosure of information violates federal regulations.

question has been discontinued. Corrective advertising is traditionally the third step in a three-step regulation process.

- **Securities and Exchange Commission (SEC)** – Monitors financial affairs. SEC guidelines call for full and timely disclosure of information that materially affects a company's stock – known as *a material event*. SEC regulations are clear – any information that could affect a stock's price must be disclosed through "broad dissemination" accessible to all publics, otherwise it might constitute (illegal) insider trading. News releases are one of the basic methods of satisfying required "broad dissemination" of material information. To assure "broad dissemination," the SEC recommends "standard disclosure" – releasing information through the listing exchange, all major wire services, such social media as Facebook and Twitter, and industry analysts.

- **Federal Communications Commission (FCC)** – Regulates the broadcast industry.
- **Food and Drug Administration (FDA)** – Covers product labeling, prescription drugs, cosmetics and over the counter medicines.

Legal Environment

Laurel O'Brien, former president of the Philadelphia chapter of PRSA, has compiled a "Legal Environment Summary." O'Brien's summary, presented during a series of workshops for her local chapter, includes areas that public relations practitioners must be familiar with to avoid ethical and legal problems:

Legal Environment – Privacy

Privacy is the right to be left alone – the right of an individual to be free from unwarranted publicity commonly known as "invasion of privacy," which falls under tort litigation. Torts are a wrongful act, damage or injury done willfully or negligently, but not involving breach of contract, for which a civil suit may be brought.

There are four torts of privacy:

1. Appropriation – A person can be liable for invasion of privacy if he or she appropriates for his or her own use, without permission, the name or likeness of another. *Strategic Communication Implications*:
   - Image advertising: the use of a photograph of an employee, customer, celebrity or other person in a corporate ad; the use of a tagline or catch phrase associated with a particular individual, implying that person's endorsement.
   - Employee publications: the use of an employee's photo or personal information in an internal company newsletter.
   - Promotional publications: the use of an employee's photo or personal information in an external newsletter or release.
2. Intrusion – A person is liable for invasion of privacy if he or she intrudes upon another's solitude, including through use of cameras or microphones. *Strategic Communication Implications*:
   - Participant monitoring of conversations: Federal law allows recording of phone calls and other electronic communications with the consent of at least one party to the call. A majority of the states and territories have adopted laws based on the federal standard. But 12 states require the consent of all parties to the call: California, Connecticut, Florida, Illinois, Maryland, Massachusetts, Michigan, Montana, Nevada, New Hampshire, Pennsylvania and Washington.
   - Using cameras or recording equipment (electronic intrusion) in places presumed to be private: an individual's home or office; doctors', accountants' or lawyers' offices.

3. Private Facts – The publication of private information that would be highly offensive to a reasonable person and is not of legitimate concern to the public. *Strategic Communication Implications*:
   - Revealing private information (such as state of health, finances, family concerns, sexual orientation) about an individual.
   - Information in the public domain does not violate private facts tort; neither does information that has been previously published nor information gleaned from an individual's actions (which make said actions obvious).

4. False Light – Dissemination of highly offensive false publicity with knowledge of or reckless disregard for the falsity; making someone look worse than they are. (Casting someone in false light could be positive, also – e.g., saying someone has a Ph.D. when, in fact, they do not.) Either could be embarrassing to the alleged victim. *Strategic Communication Implications*:
   - Omitting full information or context: Individual may be portrayed in a false light if a news story is heavily edited or context is lost or if a photograph taken on one occasion is used to illustrate something completely different.
   - Embellishment: Addition of characters or dialogue to an otherwise factual account.

Standard Defenses
- Newsworthiness: If event is particularly newsworthy; using employee's photo with news of a company breakthrough.
- Consent: Public relations practitioners should understand uses of release forms, including appropriate parties, scope duration, consideration, etc.

PR Play 16-6
Plaintiff's Burden of Proof

According to PRSA's O'Brien, the plaintiff must show all six of these elements are present to prove defamation:

• Defamation	• Fault
• Identification	• Falsity
• Publication	• Personal Harm

- Fault: *Time, Inc. (Life Magazine) v. Hill* (1967) held that even private individuals must prove *"New York Times* actual malice" – actual malice on the part of the media outlet if the story involves public interest.

Defamation

Defamation is:
- Any expression that tends to damage a person's standing in the community through an attack on an individual's character or professional abilities.
  - Libel – written, printed or pictorial defamation.
  - Slander – spoken or broadcast defamation.

- Every living individual has the right to sue to protect his or her own reputation.
  - Cannot sue for damage to another person.
  - Government units and corporations cannot sue for defamation.
  - Some people are considered "libel-proof" because their reputations are either so bad or so good that nothing anyone says can harm them (e.g., The President of the United States).
  - Plaintiff's Burden of Proof

Defamation
- Statements that tend to expose an individual to hatred, ridicule or contempt, including accusations of criminality, immorality or incompetence.
- Directly in story content, headlines, advertisements, photographs and cartoons.
- Or, when any of these is used out of context.

Identification
- Plaintiff must prove the defamation is about them personally.
- Must prove that a reader or viewer would link the statement to them by:
  - Name
  - Picture
  - Description
  - Nickname
  - Signature
  - Caricature
  - Circumstances

Publication

- Defamation requires at least three people:
  1. the defamer
  2. the defamed
  3. and at least one other person who overhears or reads the defamation.
- Even one copy of a news release, memo, letter or other written document can be libelous.

Fault

- Private individuals need only prove negligence.
- Public figures must prove reckless disregard for the truth.
- Malice must be intended and proven.
  - Also known as *"New York Times* actual malice" after the landmark 1964 case *New York Times v. Sullivan.*
- Who is a public figure?
  - Individuals whose influence is pervasive.
  - Private individuals who thrust themselves into a public debate.

Falsity

- Defamatory statement is probably false.

Personal Harm

- Proof of damage to an individual's reputation, mental anguish or actual monetary loss.

Defenses

O'Brien and others, expert in defamation, stress, *"Truth* is always a complete defense." Some other defenses are critical to the defense:

- Opinion – A pure statement of opinion or reasonable opinion based on facts.
- Absolute privilege – Government officials acting in their capacity, political candidates or consent of the person defamed.
- Qualified privilege – Reporters have qualified privilege to report on defamatory statements made during official meetings; some states also recognize "neutral reporting" standards.

PR Play 16-7
Copyrightable Works

- Writings
- Compilations
- Collections
- Photographs
- Works of music
- Works of art

- Graphic art
- Dramatic performances
- Lists
- Derivative works
- Sculpture

Legal Environment – Intellectual Property
Copyright
- Copyright protects creative individuals, allowing them to control the uses of their materials – known as "express work."
- To qualify for copyright, a work must be created independently with a modicum of intellectual effort and in some fixed form.
- Ideas, processes, methods of operation cannot be copyrighted.
- For individuals, copyright lasts for the life of the author plus 50 years.
- For companies, copyright lasts for 75 years from publication or 100 years from creation, whichever comes first.
- Copyright for commissioned works belongs to the author *until or unless he or she signs a work-for-hire agreement.* Absent such an agreement, the work may be used one time only.

To Protect Copyright
- Notice: Authors should place a copyright notice on their works with three elements – the word or symbol "copyright," the year of first publication and the name of the copyright owner.
- Registration: Although unregistered works are still protected, registration with the Registrar of Copyrights in Washington (Library of Congress) ensures that an author may sue for infringement.
- Deposit: Two copies of the copyrighted work should be deposited with the Library of Congress within three months of publication.

Work for Hire
- Work prepared by an employee within the scope of his or her employment.
- Work specially ordered or commissioned from a freelancer.

- Once the freelancer signs a *work-for-hire agreement*, copyright belongs to the employer.

Rights of Copyright
- Copyright Act of 1976 grants the author:
  - The power to copy or reproduce a work.
  - The power to authorize adaptations.
  - The right to distribute copies of a work.
  - The right to perform or display a work publicly.

Fair Use
- The privilege for individuals other than the owner to use copyrighted material in a reasonable manner without the owner's consent.
- Factors determining fair use:
  - Purpose and character of the use.
  - Nature of the copyrighted work.
  - Substantiality of the portion used.
  - Effect of the use upon the market for, or value of, the original.

Infringement of Copyright
- Owner/author must prove access and substantial similarity.
- Public relations implications:
  - Practitioners need to know who holds the rights to a work commissioned from a freelancer and keep adequate records.
  - Practitioners cannot reproduce and circulate news articles or journal papers (news clips) without obtaining permission.

Trade and Service Marks
- *Trademark* – A word, name or symbol, or device, or any combination, adopted and used by a manufacturer or merchant to identify its goods (products it manufactures) and distinguish them from those manufactured by others (e.g., Coca-Cola® carries the ®, but could carry the TM).
- *Service mark* – Like a trademark, however a service mark is used by companies or merchants who provide services rather than manufacture goods (e.g., Burwyn Associates Strategic Counselors/ Ethicists^{SM}).
- Both *trademarks* and *service marks* are protected under common law. Registration provides notice of a firm or organization's claim to ownership.
- *Trademarks* and *service marks* can be lost or abandoned if the owner does not rigorously guard its rights to sole ownership and pay strict attention to the Trademark and Patent Office Rules and Regulations.

PR Play 16-8
Key Decisions Affecting Public Relations

New York Times v. Sullivan (1964)

In 1960, the *New York Times* publishes "Heed Their Rising Voices" (picture, text), a fund-raising advertisement for the civil rights movement. The ad contained several minor errors of fact. Sullivan, one of three city Commissioners in Montgomery, Alabama, becomes aware of the ad. He sues the *New York Times* for libel, claiming that the ad refers to him in that he oversees the Montgomery Police Department, which was mentioned in it. The jury grants him damages of half a million dollars; the *New York Times* appeals to the Supreme Court.

Supreme Court Associate Justice William J. Brennan, writing for a unanimous Court, argued that that the "profound national commitment to the principle that debate on public issues should be uninhibited, robust, and wide-open" made the ad in question an instance of very valuable speech.

Was this value outweighed by the harm that falsities could cause, or the harm done to Sullivan's reputation? No, for the government should not be involved in judging truth; and government officials should be tough enough to take criticism.

Allowing libel lawsuits in cases like this one, further, would tend to "chill" future criticism of government officials, even legitimate criticism, for a "pall of fear and timidity" would fall over speakers, leading to "self-censorship."

Therefore, wrote Justice Brennan, a "public official" may not recover "damages for a defamatory falsehood relating to his official conduct unless he proves that the statement was made with 'actual malice' – that is, with knowledge that it was false or with reckless disregard" of the truth.

This is, after all, the rule governing defamation lawsuits brought by *citizens* against *officials*; it's only fair to apply it when *officials* sue citizens.

Strategic Communication Implications: Justice Hugo Black argued, in a concurring opinion, the First Amendment absolutely protects criticism of the government, even speech published with actual malice.

The judgment was reversed.

cont.

PR Play 16-8 continued

SEC v. Pig 'n Whistle Corp. (1972)

The Securities and Exchange Commission, which monitors and regulates financial affairs, ruled that a public relations firm may be held liable for securities fraud if the firm passes along misleading financial information about a client without conducting a reasonable investigation.

Strategic Communication Implications: Strategic counselors cannot simply do as the client orders. The value of strategic communication rests with the practitioner's ability to maintain objectivity and communicate only the truth. (*Conduit Theory* – In public relations and advertising, the agency or consultant may be held liable for fraud if it passes along misleading information provided by the client. The understanding is that the agency or counselor should have done ample research. For more, see *The ABCs of Strategic Communication* – AuthorHouse.)

Rely on Your Lawyer

Many times, the strategic counselor must persuade the firm or organization's attorneys that open, honest, thorough and valid communication is the only correct route to take. When it comes to ethics, the counselor must rely on his or her own beliefs. If in doubt about laws and regulations, consult the organization's attorneys. While we may not always agree, the lawyers are paid to interpret rules and regulations. They will help the strategic counselor keep current on those regulations and should be relied upon for their judgment.

The strategic counselor and organization's believability (truth) and credibility (trust) are much like a pitcher who is throwing a no-hitter. Once the first hit is given up, the no-hitter is gone forever.

Believability and credibility are much the same. Once they are gone, they are nearly impossible to regain. Know the ramifications of breaking your own ethics code and that of such organizations as PRSA. This might just be the time to conduct an audit of your personal *public relations and strategic communication ethics*.

PR Play 16-9
First Amendment

Congress shall make no law respecting an establishment of religion, or prohibiting the free exercise thereof; or abridging the freedom of speech, or of the press; or the right of the people peaceably to assemble, and to petition the government for a redress of grievances.

According to the Cornell University Law School Legal Information Institute, "*The First Amendment of the United States Constitution* protects the right to freedom of religion and freedom of expression from government interference. Freedom of expression consists of the rights to freedom of speech, press, assembly and to petition the government for a redress of grievances, and the implied rights of association and belief. The Supreme Court interprets the extent of the protection afforded to these rights. The First Amendment has been interpreted by the Court as applying to the entire federal government even though it is only expressly applicable to Congress. Furthermore, the Court has interpreted the due process clause of the 14th Amendment as protecting the rights in the First Amendment from interference by state governments.

"The most basic component of freedom of expression is the right of freedom of speech. The right to freedom of speech allows individuals to express themselves without interference or constraint by the government. The Supreme Court requires the government to provide substantial justification for the interference with the right of free speech where it attempts to regulate the content of the speech. A less stringent test is applied for content-neutral legislation. The Supreme Court has also recognized that the government may prohibit some speech that may cause a breach of the peace or cause violence. The right to free speech includes other mediums of expression that communicate a message.

"Despite popular misunderstanding, the right to freedom of the press guaranteed by the first amendment is not very different from the right to freedom of speech. It allows an individual to express themselves through publication and dissemination. It is part of the constitutional protection of freedom of expression. It does not afford members of the media any special rights or privileges not afforded to citizens in general."

EXERCISES

PR Challenge 16-1

Let's find out just how ethical you are (Part One):

True-False

1. It is not ethical to offer $100 to a reporter to assure coverage of an event.   T F

2. It is not ethical to let a reporter buy you lunch in exchange for proprietary information.   T F

3. It is not ethical to send a platter of sandwiches to a newsroom on Thanksgiving or Christmas Day.   T F

4. It is not ethical to accept an award-winning chocolate chip banana cake from an enterprising reporter who visits your house for an interview.   T F

5. Truth is always the ultimate defense in court cases against journalists.   T F

6. An ethics policy cannot be used against you in court unless you sign it.   T F

7. As an independent contractor or agency, it is ethical and justifiable to represent two or more competing clients – with full disclosure.   T F

8. Newspaper editorials and columns are held to the same standards of accuracy as news stories.   T F

9. If you give a journalist information in confidence and that confidence is broken, you may sue him/her for breaking that promise of confidentiality.   T F

10. It is ethical for an organization's spokesperson to be an unnamed source in a non-controversial story.   T F

11. Photographers and reporters always have the
    responsibility to fully depict a scene, rather than
    letting their personal judgment interfere.   T F

12. Public relations/media specialists can alter pictures
    for use with feature stories, but not pictures accompanying
    news or sports releases.   T F

13. It is not ethical to request that corrections/clarifications
    be published.   T F

14. An ethics code is all encompassing.   T F

15. Professor Steve Spear of MIT is correct when he says,
    the public remembers mistakes far longer than good deeds
    and, in fact, talk far more about mistakes than "good deeds."   T F

PR Challenge 16-2

Let's find out just how ethical you are (Part Two):

Questions

A) Each week, you, as media relations representative for a social-service agency, hand deliver a calendar of your agency's activities to a local newspaper. In appreciation for the editor's good work, you give two free tickets to the agency's benefit concert and dinner. Is this an ethical practice? (Please explain your answer.)

B) You represent a county commissioner who is facing serious allegations. Your client has ignored messages left for him on his home and cell phones. The reporter has warned that if a return call is not received by 10 p.m., the newspaper is running the story. Is this ethical on the newspaper's part and what advice would you give to your client?

C) You represent an amusement park which has just experienced a fatal fire inside its "haunted house." The fire marshal has invited a television news photographer to follow her inside the house as she looks for evidence. Do you, as the amusement park's strategic communication director, allow it and if so, do you accompany them? (Please explain your answer.)

PR Challenge 16-3

What have you done in the past month to improve your credibility and knowledge as a strategic counselor – current or future?

CHAPTER 17
Strategic Communication Skills Checklist

Preceding the *Skills Checklist* are the activities or strategic communication concentrations and disciplines listed in Chapter 3 – but worth repeating for reinforcement – plus major work assignments mastered by the profession's most successful practitioners.

According to PRSA (Public Relations Society of America) and others, public relations (strategic communication) may be involved in one or more of the following
concentrations:

- **Advertising** – Paid, (non) personal communication from an identified sponsor using (mass) media to persuade or influence an audience.
- **Communication** – Transfer of information to establish social interaction.
- **Community relations** – An aspect of strategic communication having responsibility for building relationships with constituent publics such as schools, charities, clubs and activist interests of the neighborhoods or metropolitan areas where an organization operates. Dealing with and communicating with the citizens and groups within an organization's home region.
- **Counseling** – Professional strategic public relations advice and/or services, and evaluation.
- **Development** – An aspect of the communication profession that incorporates public relations to assist with fund raising for the expansion or improvement of an organization.
- **Financial (public) relations** – Sometimes referred to as *investor relations*. An aspect of strategic communication responsible for building relations with the investor public including shareholders/stockholders; potential investors; financial analysts; the financial markets (stock exchanges); and the Securities and Exchange Commission.

- **Government relations** – An aspect of relationship-building between an organization and government at local, state and/or national levels especially involving the flow of information to and from legislative and regulatory bodies in an effort to influence public policy decisions compatible with the organization's interests (commonly called lobbying).
- **Industry relations** – Dealing and communicating with firms within the industry of which the organization is a part.
- **Issues management** – Systematic identification and action regarding public policies in their earliest stages, identifying these issues, measuring their development and planning and measuring organizational response.
- **Media relations** – Dealing with the communication media on a regular basis in seeking publicity for, or responding to media interest in, an individual, organization or event.
- **Member relations** – Dealing with internal and external communication aspects of member organizations.
- **Minority relations** – Mutually beneficial associations between social entities and the various minority publics in society especially Black, Hispanic, Asian and Native American groups at the local, regional or national levels.
- **Press agentry** – The promotion of an individual, product or service through the use of (free) publicity obtained from the mass media.
- **Promotion** – Methods and techniques designed to attract and retain listeners, viewers, readers, etc. to one of the mass media or to stimulate interest in a person, product, organization or cause.
- **Propaganda** – A one-sided message to influence or persuade a public. The use of ideas, information or opinion for the purpose of furthering or hindering a cause or promoting or denigrating an idea. Edward Bernays, known as the father of public relations (see Chapter 1), defined propaganda as: "The establishing of reciprocal understanding between an individual and a group."
- **Public affairs** – The "daily link between the private sector and government," which interprets business to government, and government to business, within the context of a larger social responsibility to preserve the openness and integrity of the democratic process. The task involves issues management – especially those issues of concern to special interest activities in the shaping of public policies and legislation.

- **Publicity** – Dissemination of planned and executed messages through selected media, without payment to the media, to further the particular interest of an organization or person.

Scott M. Cutlip, Allen H. Center and Glen M. Broom in *Effective Public Relations* (9th Edition) say that while some describe public relations work by listing the specialized parts of the function: media relations, investor relations, community relations, employee relations, government relations, etc., those labels do not describe the many activities and diverse assignments in the day-to-day practice. The following 10 categories summarize what strategic communication specialists do at work:

> **PR Play 17-1**
> ## Public Relations Work Assignments
>
> Writing and Editing
> Media Relations and
> Placement ("Pitching")
> Research
> Management and Administration
> Counseling
> Special Events
> Speaking
> Production
> Training
> Contact

- **Writing and Editing** –
  Composing print, broadcast and Web news releases, feature stories, newsletters to employees and external stakeholders, correspondence, Web site and other online media messages, shareholder and annual reports, speeches, brochures, film and PowerPoint® scripts, trade publication articles, institutional advertisements, and product and technical collateral materials.

- **Media Relations and Placement ("Pitching")** – Contacting news media, magazines, Sunday supplements, freelance writers and trade publications with the intent of getting them to publish or broadcast news and features about or originated by an organization. Responding to media requests for information, verification of stories, and access to authoritative sources.

- **Research** – Gathering information about public opinion, trends, emerging issues, political climate and legislation, media coverage, special-interest groups and other concerns related to an organization's stakeholders. Searching the Internet, online services, and electronic government databases. Designing program research, conducting surveys, and hiring research firms.

- **Management and Administration** – Programming and planning in collaboration with other managers – determining needs, establishing priorities, defining publics, setting goals and objectives, and developing strategies and tactics. Administering personnel, budget and program schedules.

- **Counseling** – Advising top management on the social, political and regulatory environments; consulting with the management team on how to avoid or respond to crises; and working with key decision makers to craft strategies for managing or responding to critical and sensitive issues.

- **Special Events** – Arranging and managing news conferences, 10K runs, conventions, open houses, ribbon cuttings and grand openings, anniversary celebrations, fund raising events, visiting dignitaries, contests, award programs, and other special observances or focused "happenings."

- **Speaking** – Appearing before groups, coaching others for speaking assignments and managing a speakers bureau to provide platforms for the organization before important audiences.

- **Production** – Creating communications using multimedia knowledge and skills, including art, typography, photography, layout and computer desktop publishing; audio and video recording and editing; and preparing such audiovisual presentations as PowerPoints®.

- **Training** – Preparing executives and other designated spokespeople to deal with media and to make other public appearances. Instructing others in the organization to improve writing and communication skills. Helping introduce changes in organizational culture, policy, structure and process.

- **Contact** – Serving as liaison with media, community, and other internal and external groups. Listening, negotiating, managing conflict, and reaching agreement as mediator between an organization and its important stakeholders. Meeting and entertaining as host to guests and visitors.

This is a checklist of strategic communication skills and abilities practitioners should possess. Rate your abilities and skills using a scale of 5 (much ability) to 1 (very little or no ability). Feel free to suggest other items that you do not see here and email them to the author – larry@larrylitwin.com.

A Public Relations Practitioner (Strategic Communicator/Counselor) Should Have the Ability to:

1. Prepare hard news stories for news releases.
2. Prepare feature stories for newspapers, magazines and trade journals.
3. Deal with media representatives.
4. Develop media kits.
5. Prepare and maintain media lists (ListServ/database – relationship marketing/management – 1-2-1 marketing).
6. Prepare Backgrounders.
7. Write effective business letters and memos to clients, customers, administrators, managers and staff managers.
8. Write a speech.
9. Deliver a speech or a task to a group.
10. Prepare newsletters from start to finish – electronic and print.
11. Be proficient in desktop publishing – *InDesign®, QuarkXPress®, PageMaker®.*
12. Prepare other publications (brochures, fliers, booklets, annual reports) – electronic and print.
13. Design online newsletters and inline attachments.
14. Fully understand one-to-one (1-1) marketing.

> ### PR Play 17-2
> ### Strategic Communication Concentrations
>
> Advertising
> Communication
> Community relations
> Counseling
> Development
> Financial (public) relations
> Government relations
> Industry relations
> Issues management
> Media relations
> Member relations
> Minority relations
> Press agentry
> Promotion
> Propaganda
> Public affairs
> Publicity

15. Write specifications for a printer.
16. Take pictures and transmit them electronically.
17. Write a communications policy for corporate administrators.
18. Research and write a media relations policy in collaboration with media representatives.
19. Apply management-by-objectives for strategic communication.
20. Conduct fund raising campaigns.
21. Design and place print and online advertisements or available space "ads."
22. Create, write and place radio, television and other electronic commercials and PSAs.
23. Gain public acceptance of new ideas or innovations.
24. Prepare and conduct public relations training programs.
25. Maintain confidences.
26. Prepare *PowerPoint*® presentations.
27. Prepare video presentations other than *PowerPoints*®.
28. Design company displays for public events.
29. Improve internal morale.
30. Determine community power structures.
31. Explain company ideas, philosophies and goals to community members.
32. Hold effective public meetings.
33. Set up advisory committees.
34. Conduct surveys.
35. Conduct focus panels.
36. Anticipate crises areas.
37. Deal with crisis situations.
38. Understand workforce diversity and get along with people.
39. Take lumps to protect superiors.
40. Keep ego under control.
41. Produce under pressure.
42. Handle critics.
43. Dictate correspondence.
44. Use a computer and other devices.
45. Access on-line databases for research.
46. Identify and use experts in the field.
47. Develop strategic communication plans.
48. Coordinate a news conference.
49. Read and digest information about the business field quickly.

50. Manage time efficiently and effectively – with effectancy.
51. Speak about your organization's products and or services from a prepared text or off-the-cuff – as if you know the subject as well as your own name.
52. Take orders and determine what the boss *really* wants you to do.
53. Create themes, slogans and symbols for ad campaigns, displays and strategic communication plans.
54. Develop and evaluate the company's communication plans and programs.
55. Develop and work within a budget.
56. Give orders and see that they are carried out. Delegate.
57. Know PR ethics and laws and their implications.
58. Apply ethical communication and business standards – be the conscience of the organization – chief integrity officer.
59. Deal with employee groups.
60. Level with top management people – tell them what they need to hear; not what they want to hear.
61. Act as liaison for top management and company personnel.
62. Deal with pressure groups.
63. Counsel company executives, managers, supervisors and staff members on their individual contributions to the PR program.
64. Understand and apply integrated communications ideas.
65. Understand and use computer communication, especially as it relates to pressure groups – so-called "social media" or Web 2.0 (Chapter 10).

A Strategic Communication Professional Should Also Know:

66. How to interview news sources effectively.
67. The principles of marketing and market research and the changing role of public relations and its impact on marketing and branding.
68. How to combine marketing and public relations activities.
69. How direct mail and telemarketing – using 1-to-1 – communication can help a public relations effort.
70. How to prove that strategic communication/public relations affects the bottom line.
71. How to "dress for success."
72. How to use the Internet and the latest PR technology.

73. How to design a PR program that shows positive impact on all three bottom lines – and be able to describe, in lay terms, the *"Triple Bottom Line Theory"* (see Chapter 2).
74. How to be aware of leaders, key publications, organizations and other respected sources in the profession.
75. How to interpret the PR function for management.
76. How to get from the strategic plan to the operational level.
77. How to evaluate and improve staff.
78. How to interview and work with consulting firms and other vendors or free lancers.
79. How to detect trends and implement them in an issues management program.
80. How to craft and write proposals and/or pitch letters.
81. How to write a position paper.
82. How to write and place op-ed "pieces" and other commentaries.
83. How to conduct a situation analysis.

PR Play 17-3
Eight Rules for Public Relations/Strategic Communication

- No matter what you do, it isn't enough.
- No matter what you do, it will be misinterpreted by someone.
- No matter how many copies you distribute, you will forget someone.
- No matter how many people proofread, something is misspelled.
- Media importance is awarded to an issue in direct opposition to the importance your boss gives the issue.
- Never fall prey to the thought that your organization's side of an issue is understood.
- Assume a total vacuum of comprehension on the part of all parties and you shall not be disappointed.
- No matter whom you know, somebody else knows somebody more important.

Originally featured in the April 1986 issue of *communications briefings*®, these "rules" were submitted by Ivan Kershner, administrative assistant, North Platte (Nebraska) Public Schools.

84. How to write effective reports.
85. How to take a report and boil it down to an executive summary.
86. How to conduct all forms of strategic research – formal and informal.
87. How to wind down at the end of the day.

Compiled by Rowan (N.J.) University Public Relations Graduate Students

EXERCISES
PR Challenge 17-1
Select the 10 professional skills that you most want to master. Explain why and what you will do with them.

PR Challenge 17-2
Now that you have completed *The Public Relations Practitioner's Playbook for (all) Strategic Communicators*, in your opinion, what are the five most important elements of the book? Compare your response to the response you gave to a similar question in Chapter 2.

INDEX

More Third-Party Endorsements

"Larry has always been the consummate professional. Do you know what makes a professional of this caliber? Talent, of course, but style – even more! With all his skill there's always a smile! Larry Litwin is certainly a role model for everyone – students, media moguls and public relations professionals. I'm honored to be his peer.

Sharla Feldscher
President – Sharla Feldscher Public Relations – Philadelphia, Pa.
Philadelphia Public Relations Association – Hall of Fame

"In a word, Larry Litwin's books are 'amazing.' I got hooked after hearing the buzz about *The PR Playbook.*"

Callie Pederson
University of North Dakota
Grand Forks, N.D.

"Reading *The PR Playbook* is like listening to Larry tell me the story of public relations. It's straight and to the point, in a conversational way!"

Kim Glovas
Reporter – KYW Newsradio
Philadelphia, Pa.

"I played a lot of sports in my life and had a lot of good 'coaches.' Professor Litwin is one of the best – right up there with my Mom and Dad."

Nicolas Morici
Mayor's Press Secretary
Atlantic City, N.J.

A veteran reporter, editor, public relations counselor and strategic adviser, Larry Litwin gives readers the anatomy of the public relations (strategic communication) profession. *The PR Practitioner's Playbook for (all) Strategic Communicators* is overflowing with how-to and hands-on techniques, tips, tactics, tools and strategies. From writing techniques, to planning campaigns to budgeting, Larry covers all topics play by play. (EMU's PRSSA calls it a "must have" and "most beloved" public relations book.)

Eastern Michigan University PRSSA
(Public Relations Student Society of America)
Ypsilanti, Mich.

Companion CD — Available

Students, practitioners and instructors are encouraged to use the companion CD (available from **www.larrylitwin.com**). It contains every "PR Play" which can be projected for use in group sessions. The CD also contains a Public Relations Plan plus audio and video PSAs (Public Service Announcements), student- and professionally-produced storyboards, electronic issue ads and commercials, a sample video news release and three PowerPoints® compatible with both *The Public Relations Practitioner's Playbook for (all) Strategic Communicators* and *The ABCs of Strategic Communication*.

Companion CD

X...Plays by Chapter

O...Audio Clips

    Cabrini College Public Service Announcement (PSA)

    New Jersey Education Association (NJEA) Issue Ad

    Washington Township Jaycees PSA #1

    Washington Township Jaycees PSA #2

X...Video Clips

    NJEA – Great Public Schools

    NJEA – It's All About TV

    NJEA – Welcome to New Jersey's Public Schools

    Producing PSAs and Video News Releases

O...Sample PSAs

    How to write PSAs

    Play 10-5 Washington Township Jaycees PSA

    Cabrini College PSA

    Play 10-12 Sample (TV) Storyboard

X...PowerPoint: "Anatomy of Public Relations"

O...PowerPoint: "Media Relations"

X...PowerPoint: "Public Relations Planning"

O...Crisis Communication Plan – Philadelphia Phillies

Made in the USA
Lexington, KY
02 February 2014